D1124227

MONEY AND POLITICS
IN AMERICA
1755-1775

The Institute of Early American History and Culture
is sponsored jointly by The College of William and Mary in Virginia
and The Colonial Williamsburg Foundation.

PUBLISHED FOR THE
Institute of Early American History and Culture
WILLIAMSBURG, VIRGINIA
by The University of North Carolina Press
CHAPEL HILL

MONEY AND POLITICS
IN AMERICA
1755-1775

FIVE SHILLINGS.

To Counterfeit is Death.

Printed by JAMES ADAMS, 1776.

A STUDY IN THE CURRENCY ACT OF 1764
AND THE POLITICAL ECONOMY OF REVOLUTION

by

Joseph Albert Ernst

Copyright © 1973 by
The University of North Carolina Press
All rights reserved

Manufactured in the United States of America
Printed by Heritage Printers, Inc., Charlotte, N. C.
ISBN 0–8078–1217–x
Library of Congress Catalog Card Number 73–6858

Library of Congress Cataloging in Publication Data

Ernst, Joseph Albert.
 Money and politics in America, 1755–1775: a study. . .   Ch. Hill

for the by the
 Bibliography: p. 379-393   Includes index
 1. United States—History—Revolution—Causes. 2. Currency question—United States. 3. Great Britain—Colonies—America—Financial questions. 4. United States—Politics and government—Colonial period. I. Institute of Early American History and Culture, Williamsburg, Va. II. Title.
 E210.E76   973.3'1   73–6858
 ISBN 0–8078–1217–x

973.31
E715m

193739

To Reneé

MILLS COLLEGE   WITHDRAWN
LIBRARY

Preface

This is a study in political economy. It is not intended to be read as a history of politics or economics alone. It is a work about both politics and economics and their interrelations. The subject is broadly the Currency Act of 1764. The political aspect of that subject appears in the intense interest it aroused in the colonial legislatures from New York to Georgia and in the continuous conflict it engendered between the Americans and the crown before 1775. In this field of colonial politics, I have tried to show how various interests and factions sought to control currency policies and practices for partisan ends. But this political history would be meaningless without reference to the colonial economy. Shifting economic conditions seriously affected political behavior, a point frequently overlooked by recent historians of the Revolution.

American reaction to the Currency Act was firmly rooted in the needs and demands of merchants, planters, and farmers. The demands of these groups reflected, in turn, the changes in the Atlantic economy during the eighteenth century as well as the conceptions the colonists held of the role of money in that economy. Merchants, planters, or farmers were seldom theorists. They probed the workings of the colonial economy as pragmatic businessmen interested in short-term considerations. On the rare occasions when they thought of long-term economic developments, they did so according to the accepted economic wisdom of the day. Their understanding of the role of money in the economy rested upon a few practical assumptions and the experience of daily business. In the light of present-day theory, the colonists appear at times to have been wrong about money and mistaken in judging its effects. All the same, their understanding (or misunderstanding) does help to explain the contemporary response to currency policies and practices.

In discussing colonial monetary behavior, the historian must invariably fall back on his own conceptual devices, and here he must tread carefully. While the Currency Act has not hitherto been the subject of a full-length study, colonial currency in general has a historiography nearly as rich as the Revolution itself. Writers have sought to "prove" from colonial practices such widely varying dogmas as the instability of any non-specie-backed currency, on one hand, and the restorative powers of paper money, on the other. These earlier studies, and more recent discussions of "currency finance," have in common the error of focusing solely on the *visible* money supply (e.g., paper currency, coin, and commodity notes) and projecting cause and effect from that. Such evaluations ignore the bulk of the money supply, which, like today, was in the form of book credit. And such writers have also ignored the *velocity* of money, a factor we can only guess at. But most important of all, these approaches have diverted the attention of historians from the truly significant question concerning the economics of money—the relationship of the currency system to the rest of the colonial economy. The ramifications of this relationship are explored at numerous points in the present work.

Another theme in the book concerns the activities of the colonial agents and the British merchants and their unsuccessful bid to effect a repeal of the Currency Act in 1766 and 1767. To the extent that the twists and turns of English politics in these same years serve as an appropriate backdrop to the repeal movement, English political history is sketched in. But the main consideration here lies in those London and Glasgow merchants and their colonial allies who had a vested interest in currency matters.

Finally, for that special reader, the historian of the American Revolution, there is the question of this study's implications for an understanding of that event. The principal point that emerges is the existence of a direct and fundamental conflict of interest between the British and American commercial classes. In an effort to protect their right to exploit or invest in the riches of the New World, the British political nation was fully prepared to ride roughshod over the colonials. The colonial ruling classes proved no less aggressive or less aware of their interest. They showed a remarkable determination to have a voice in the management of their own economic destinies. The proof and elaboration of such generalizations, however, would require a full "economic interpretation" of the Revolution. Perhaps it is time for that book to be written.

I have been especially fortunate in my critics and my friends over the years, and what is best about the present work is largely their doing. To Merrill Jensen, Roy Merrens, Marc Egnal, John Hemphill, Norman Fiering, Joy Dickinson Barnes, Gay Hayden, Rosemary Butera, Jack Granatstein, and William Abbot, I owe a special debt of thanks for their reading of the text at its various stages of development and, more important, for their criticisms and arguments. Dale Benson, John Bosher, Leslie Van Horn Brock, Lawrence Harper, Sheldon Harris, James Hutson, Paul Koistinen, James Lemon, T. J. A. Le Goff, Ronald Hoffman, Jacob Price, Edward Riley, Jonathan Rossie, Morton Rothstein, John Selby, Reba Soffer, and Thad Tate have also offered useful criticism and have read parts of the manuscript. For her patience in typing the seemingly endless drafts of the text I am indebted to Huguette Kulz, and for her invaluable help in proofreading, to Corry J. Kop.

In addition I wish to thank the American Council of Learned Societies, the Colonial Williamsburg Foundation, the Lilly Foundation and the William L. Clements Library, California State University at Northridge, the University of California, Los Angeles, the University of Wisconsin, and York University for their financial assistance and also to thank the editors of the *William and Mary Quarterly*, the *Virginia Magazine of History and Biography*, and *Explorations in Economic History* (formerly *Explorations in Entrepreneurial History*) for allowing me to reprint revised versions of material that first appeared in their publications.

I want to acknowledge as well the help given by historians and archivists throughout the United States and Canada. In the world of scholarship they are invaluable partners, and I remember fondly the days and weeks spent at the Alderman Library, University of Virginia; the Clements Library, University of Michigan; the Earl Gregg Swem Library, the College of William and Mary; the Huntington Library; the Library of Congress; the Maryland Hall of Records; the Maryland Historical Society; the New Jersey Historical Society; the New-York Historical Society; the New York Public Library; the Peabody Institute; the Perkins Library at Duke University; the South Carolina Historical Society; the University of California, Los Angeles, Graduate Library; the University of Michigan Graduate Library; The University of North Carolina Library; the University of Wisconsin Library; the Wisconsin State Historical Society; and the York University Library.

But I am particularly grateful in this connection for the aid and encouragement received from the staff of the Research Department at Colonial Williamsburg and from their director, Dr. Edward

Riley. I have imposed upon them time and time again over the past ten years, and yet they were unfailingly kind and generous in innumerable ways. This work could never have been written without their cooperation and without access to their magnificent collection of colonial records.

Finally my greatest debt is to Reneé, Sherri-Ann, Lauren, Elise, Joseph, and Roger, without whom this work would have been completed years earlier. Both the work and the author would have been the worse for it.

Contents

xi

PART FOUR
Coda

Tables and Graphs

A Glossary of Economic Terms for Political Historians

BALANCE OF PAYMENTS: The value of goods or merchandise exported plus the value of a number of so-called "invisible" exports—such as payments for shipping, insurance, and profits—versus the value of imports, "visible" and "invisible." In a given year, therefore, a decline in total exports, "visible" and "invisible," and a rise in total imports would produce an unfavorable balance of payments. Conversely, a rise in total exports and a fall in imports would produce a favorable balance of payments. *See also* BALANCE OF TRADE.

BALANCE OF TRADE: The value of goods or merchandise exported versus the value imported. Thus in a given year a fall in the value of goods imported and a rise in exports would lead to a favorable balance of trade; a rise in imports and a decline in exports, an unfavorable balance of trade. The essential difference between balance of trade and balance of payments is that the trade balance concerns only the so-called "visible" merchandise items. *See also* BALANCE OF PAYMENTS.

BILLS OF CREDIT: Another term for treasury notes. *See* TREASURY NOTES.

BILL OF EXCHANGE: A written order to pay that provided the chief means of transferring funds between the colonies and the mother country. In practice there were ordinarily three parties to a bill of exchange. Someone in America who had a sterling debt to pay, and had a claim on sterling money, would act as *drawer*. He would draft, or make, the bill and then send it to his creditor in Britain, the *drawee*, ordering the creditor to hand over a certain sum of money after a stated period of time to a third person, the *payee*. Thus the bill of exchange was used in colonial times to make transatlantic payments in much the same way as the modern bank check is used to make domestic payments. It should be noted that an exchange transaction might also involve other individuals. The drawer in America, for instance, was free to sell his sterling bill for local currency. In this case the buyer would be responsible for remitting the bill. Likewise, in Britain the payee had the right to make the bill negotiable by endorsing it. For a fuller discussion of the use of the bill of exchange in the colonial period, see James H. Soltow, *The Economic Role of Williamsburg* (Williamsburg, Va., 1965), 157–163.

BULLION: Gold and silver coinage.

COMMODITY EXPORTS: Those articles of commerce that are shipped to foreign markets. In the colonial context, such articles would normally be agricultural.

COMMODITY MONEY: An article, or articles, of commerce used as a local medium of exchange. Most colonies at one time or another employed specific commodities as money.

COMMODITY NOTES: Notes issued by the government on deposit of specified commodities at public warehouses or storage places. These notes typically passed as a local circulating medium and were received in payment for taxes. Sometimes, as in the case of tobacco notes in Virginia, they were also legal tender. *See also* WAREHOUSE RECEIPTS.

CURRENCY: As used in this study, another term for money in its function as the local circulating medium.

EXCHANGE RATE: The ratio of one currency to another. For example, to say that the exchange rate was 140 in Virginia would mean that £140 of the local currency was needed to purchase £100 British sterling. *See also* STERLING EXCHANGE RATE.

"FAVORABLE" BALANCE OF TRADE: *See* BALANCE OF TRADE.

FLEXIBLE, OR FREE, MARKET RATE OF EXCHANGE: *See* PEGGED RATE OF EXCHANGE.

GRESHAM'S LAW: The notion that "bad" money drives "good" money out of circulation. Thus with two kinds of money of the same denomination but of different "intrinsic" value in circulation, the money of greater "intrinsic" value will normally be withdrawn and hoarded.

HARD MONEY: Gold and silver coin.

IMBALANCE OF TRADE: When the value of goods or merchandise imported exceeds the value exported, trade is said to be imbalanced. *See also* BALANCE OF TRADE.

LAND BANK: A means used by several colonies to circulate paper money in the form of currency issued on loan and secured, or backed, by a mortgage. *See also* LOAN OFFICE.

LEGAL TENDER: Money that the law says a creditor must accept in payment of debts.

LIQUIDITY DEMAND: A shortened form of the term "liquidity demand for money," or the desire to turn a part of one's assets or wealth into cash.

LOAN OFFICE: As used in this study, another term for land bank. *See* LAND BANK.

MEANS OF PAYMENT: *See* MEDIUM OF EXCHANGE.

MEDIUM OF EXCHANGE: Another term for money in its function as a medium or means of local payment.

NEGOTIABLE INSTRUMENT: A piece of paper, or "credit instrument," serving as evidence of the existence of a debt, and of an obligation to pay that debt, that is transferable to a third person.

PAPER CURRENCY: Money in the form of paper, or paper money.

PAR: As used in this study, par, or "par of exchange," is the established value of a local colonial currency, generally with respect to pounds sterling.

PEGGED RATE OF EXCHANGE: The rate of exchange may be said to be flexible or fixed. If flexible, it may fluctuate freely from day to day as determined by the interplay of the supply and demand for one currency as against the supply and demand for another. If fixed, or pegged, by law, the rate of exchange is not permitted to vary beyond defined limits. *See also* EXCHANGE RATE.

POUNDS CURRENCY: As used in this study, the value of anything stated in the local currency of a colony. Pounds sterling would be the value of anything stated in terms of English sterling.

POUNDS STERLING: *See* POUNDS CURRENCY.

QUANTITY THEORY OF MONEY: At its simplest, the notion that the level of prices is directly related to the quantity of money in circulation.

RATE OF EXCHANGE: *See* EXCHANGE RATE.

SINKING FUND: As used in this study, a sum of money set aside to meet, redeem, or sink an issue of paper money.

SPECIE: Gold and silver in the form of either coin or bullion.

SPECIE STANDARD: A specie or metallic standard wherein all money is gold or silver (or both) or is readily redeemable in gold or silver.

STERLING EXCHANGE RATE: The ratio between the value of a given currency and the value of sterling.

TAX CERTIFICATES: One of several forms of paper money issued by the colonial governments in anticipation of future tax receipts.

TERMS OF TRADE: Import prices relative to export prices.

TREASURY NOTES: One of several forms of paper money issued by the various colonial governments in anticipation of future tax receipts. *See* TAX CERTIFICATES.

"UNFAVORABLE" BALANCE OF TRADE: *See* BALANCE OF TRADE.

VALUE ADDED: The amount of value added onto a product as it goes through each successive stage of production.

VELOCITY OF MONEY: The speed or rapidity with which money changes hands in any given period of time.

WAREHOUSE RECEIPTS: A chit or receipt given for goods received at a public warehouse. In the colonial period warehouse receipts, as in the case of tobacco notes, readily passed as a circulating medium. *See* COMMODITY NOTES.

Part One
Introduction to the Problem

Chapter 1

Some Forbidding Issues

A discussion of economic theory and practice is likely to antagonize the student of political history. To begin a political study in this manner may therefore be courting disaster. But like it or not, certain political events are unintelligible without reference to some kind of economic framework. It is impossible to write about paper money and politics without saying something about issues as specific and forbidding as the determination of the rate of exchange and the quantity theory of money. If these issues are to be faced, it is arguable that they are best handled at the outset with a minimum of fuss and without undue resort to models, mathematics, or a specialized vocabulary. Such at any rate is my plan in the present chapter. It has the advantage of allowing the story that follows to unfold without interruption and of gathering the economic explanations in one place for quick, if not easy, reference along the way.[1]

THE LIMITATIONS OF THE QUANTITY THEORY

Eighteen years ago E. James Ferguson, in an influential interpretation of colonial paper money practices, surveyed the institutional

1. The present chapter is a much revised and extended version of my article, "Colonial Currency: A Modest Inquiry into the Uses of the Easy Chair and the Meaning of the Colonial System of Freely Floating International Exchange," *Explorations in Entrepreneurial History*, 2d Ser., VI (1969), 187–197. My concern at that time was in part with the apparent unwillingness of the practitioners of the so-called "new" economic history, who have promised us a restructuring of the past, to get out of the "easy chair" and into the archives, where they might test their formulations against the evidence. It appears that there still is cause to be concerned. For the latest example of the "easy chair" approach, see Roger W. Weiss, "The Issue of Paper Money in the American Colonies, 1720–1774," *Journal of Economic History*, XXX (1970), 770–784. On this same subject, see also the comments of J. R. T. Hughes, "Fact and Theory in Economic History," *Explorations in Entrepreneurial History*, 2d Ser., II (1966), 75–100.

3

studies of paper currency as well as the debate over sound money.[2] In presenting his views, Ferguson tended to adopt both the categories and concerns of earlier writers. Issues such as the debtor-creditor explanation of currency practices and the origin of British monetary policies, for instance, received a great deal of his attention. On the other hand Ferguson's interest in financial history led him to stress the treasury method of creating debt money. This was the method of paying government creditors in legal tender notes issued in anticipation of taxes; he dubbed it "currency finance" and later used the term as a descriptive device in his study of public finance after 1776. Nevertheless Ferguson's interpretation turned largely on the question of sound money, and he contended that on balance colonial paper money practices proved successful. He found that the use of paper notes to provide a medium of exchange, furnish agricultural credit, and meet government and wartime obligations worked without unduly disturbing the general stability of sterling exchange rates, much less any other prices.

Such a view reflects, even while it corrects, the traditional approach to colonial monetary history. Furthermore it conveys a misleading impression of the complicated issues sheltered under the wide umbrella of "general stability of exchange rates," issues that lay at the heart of the Currency Act controversy. A direct outgrowth of the debate over sound money, the question of sterling exchange rates has generated more learned discussion and more misunderstanding than any other monetary question. The problem does not lie in the operation of international payments, the mechanisms of exchange, or the uses of bills of exchange in colonial times. In outline at least these are clear enough.[3] The dispute concerns the determination of sterling rates and the relationship between the price of sterling and changes in the levels of currency, of commerce, and of British investments.

2. "Currency Finance: An Interpretation of Colonial Monetary Practices," *William and Mary Quarterly*, 3d Ser., X (1953), 153–180. Ferguson's account is heavily dependent upon Leslie Van Horn Brock, "The Currency of the American Colonies, 1700–1764: A Study in Colonial Finance and Imperial Relations" (Ph.D. diss., University of Michigan, 1941), which provides the best description and analysis of American paper money practices for the period it covers. My own debt to Professor Brock's work is equally large, as is the debt of anyone who ventures into this little-understood field. Nonetheless it should be noted that the approach taken in the present study differs radically from that in "The Currency of the American Colonies." Interested readers are invited to compare the two. For additional references to the subject see the extensive bibliography in the Ferguson article.

3. See, for example, James H. Soltow, "The Role of Williamsburg in the Virginia Economy, 1750–1775," *WMQ*, 3d Ser., XV (1958), 474–477.

Standard explanations of the fluctuations of sterling rates in early America range widely. The older, though not altogether discredited, nineteenth-century view was that large-scale emissions of cheap paper money drove exchange rates "out of bounds." More recent thinking holds that the rates were "largely the results of conditions of international trade" and tended towards stability.[4] To begin with, it must be said that the nineteenth-century historians, despite a well-known bias against the fiat money of their own age, generally understood the relationship between the competitive interplay of supply and demand for sterling in colonial America and the overall determination of sterling exchange rates. They wrote as if the determinants of supply and demand, apart from paper currency, could be taken as more or less constant over the long run. Within the framework of the mechanics of exchange, they focused instead upon the problem of what they took to be the exceptionally high levels of sterling rates for colonial currency and their erratic fluctuations, especially in New England. And they found the cause in paper currency practices. Paper money simply depreciated. Such an interpretation assumed monetary conditions approaching pure price inflation. It also postulated, of course, conditions of equilibrium, or the self-regulating effect of exchange rates on colonial imports and exports and on short-term British investments in the colonial economy.[5]

Any discussion of simple price inflation, or an overall increase in prices, including sterling exchange rates, bears on the quantity theory of money and the purchasing-power concept of the rate of exchange. At its simplest the quantity theory asserts that more money leads to higher prices, or, more formally, that the general level of prices tends to vary with the amount of money in circulation. The more complex version adds that prices also vary directly with the velocity of circulation of money and inversely with the volume of trade. When at different times the printing presses of South Carolina and Rhode Island, for instance, flooded everyone and everything in a wave of "cheap money," even the oversimplified quantity theory offered a compelling answer to the question of colonial currency practices as a causative factor in the exchange market.[6] But

4. Ferguson, "Currency Finance," *ibid.*, 3d Ser., X (1953), 157–158, and Robert East, "The Business Entrepreneur in a Changing Colonial Economy, 1763–1795," *Jour. Econ. Hist.*, Supplement, VI (1946), 24.

5. See the discussion in Ferguson, "Currency Finance," *WMQ*, 3d Ser., X (1953). The point about pure price inflation is often overlooked.

6. In recent years Milton Friedman has done much to revive the quantity theory

has the quantity theory proven useful in analyzing currency practices, prices, and sterling exchange rates where runaway inflation was not the issue? It has not.

For one thing, painstaking observers of the colonial currency system are inevitably left with the feeling that the data on monetary conditions are either incomplete or irrelevant, or both. At best the statistical record is fragmentary and impressionistic. Business letters say little about the volume of gold and silver coin, bullion, book credit, and negotiable instruments that served the colonies as a means of payment. They say even less about velocity, or the speed at which money passed from hand to hand. Treasury and loan office records offer some information about the amount of paper currency outstanding, but again next to nothing is known about velocity. Despite these yawning gaps in our knowledge some historians continue to attempt to correlate paper money, prices, and exchange rates; and this is testimony to the fatal attraction of general principles. To avoid a quagmire of unfounded generalities, the student of colonial currency must remain true to the facts and prudent where there are none.

Reliance on the quantity-theory approach to prices and exchange rates raises other problems as well. In holding rigidly to the quantity

---

as a valid tool of economic analysis. See, for instance, his *Studies in the Quantity Theory of Money* (Chicago, 1956). For a discussion of paper money practices in South Carolina see Richard M. Jellison, "Paper Currency in Colonial South Carolina, 1703–1764" (Ph.D. diss., Indiana University, 1952). For Rhode Island see John Blanchard MacInnes, "Rhode Island Bills of Public Credit, 1710–1755" (Ph.D. diss., Brown University, 1952). In instances such as South Carolina and Rhode Island, runaway prices seem to have driven coin out of circulation, so that in theory, at least, sterling exchange rates would more or less reflect the purchasing power of paper currency as measured by the domestic price level. Even this statement is deceptive, however. Is the purchasing power of money relative to the price of all other goods and services, so that if the price of everything else other than money rises rapidly in the same proportion, there is inflation, especially runaway inflation? This rarely happens in the real world. In every period some prices rise and others fall, or at least they move at different rates, and economists necessarily use an index of some particular prices to indicate inflation. But which index will do for the 18th-century colonial experience? A consumer price index? Certainly not as defined today: a measure of changes in the prices of goods and services purchased by the families of clerical workers and of wage earners in the cities. In addition the statement about runaway prices driving coin out of circulation assumes the operation of Gresham's Law. To be more precise, that law assumes that within limits the colonial attempt to maintain an homogenous currency supply, and thus a parity in the value of paper money and coin, proved unsuccessful. On this point see Andrew Burnaby, *Travels Through the Middle Settlements in North-America. In the Years 1759 and 1760. With Observations upon the State of the Colonies* (Ithaca, N.Y., 1960 [orig. publ. London, 1775]), 29.

theory and trying to show how monetary policy influenced overall price levels, historians have tended to ignore the other forces at work at the time and to overlook the seasonal, short-run, and cyclical nature of colonial prices. On the other hand they have also generally failed to take into account the effect on exchange rates of swings in the volume of British loans to America, shifts in British wartime expenditures in the colonies, and changes in the colonies' terms of trade and volume of trade.[7] All these omissions make any of their statements about the connections—causal or coincidental—between paper money, prices, and sterling exchange, gratuitous. Such connections did exist, of course, but in a number of important ways they were related to the structure of colonial trade and not simply, or even essentially, to the quantity of money in the marketplace.

Let us take, for example, the prices of British manufactures in America. Such prices normally reflected significant changes in sterling rates. Thus, as sterling rates crept upwards, so did the cost of making remittances to British suppliers. And the colonial merchants adjusted their prices accordingly—either that or they bravely accepted falling profit margins. There was nothing automatic about the process, however. While these same merchants increased or decreased their prices with an eye to exchange movements whenever possible, other marketplace considerations, such as gluts, credit shifts, demand factors, and so on, also affected prices. Similarly, there was an important connection between sterling exchange rates and the colonial prices for certain commodity exports, such as tobacco, wheat, flour, and rice. Colonial merchants normally made their purchases for British houses by drawing sterling bills payable just after delivery of the commodities. But the bills were converted immediately into local purchasing power. In consequence, other things being equal, as the foreign demand for commodities, and hence prices, increased, so did the volume of bills available. And as the volume of sterling bills increased and their price, or the sterling exchange rate, decreased, the cost of the commodities to the local merchants rose accordingly. Again, whenever possible, these merchants took whatever measures they could to force commodity prices down and to bring them into line with their costs.[8]

7. The most important example is Brock, "Currency of the American Colonies."
8. A detailed and sophisticated treatment of all colonial prices, including sterling exchange rates, is to be found in the much neglected but invaluable study of William S. Sachs, "The Business Outlook in the Northern Colonies, 1750–1775" (Ph.D. diss.,

For the most part, then, available evidence suggests a complex rather than a simple answer to the question of fluctuations in the money supply, in sterling exchange rates, and in local price levels, and an answer having far more to do with the structure of colonial trade and short-run economic changes than with the amount of paper currency in circulation and the quantity theory of money.

Fortunately for our purposes, there are several studies of money and prices in Pennsylvania that exemplify the misapplied use of the quantity theory. At the turn of the century, C. W. MacFarlane in an essay on "Pennsylvania Paper Currency" came to the conclusion that despite the great increase in paper money before 1750 local prices did not rise to any appreciable extent.[9] He found that after 1750, on the other hand, the price of exports soared while that of imports changed only slightly. The disparity, he suggested, might have had more to do with the changes in Pennsylvania's terms of trade than with the stock of paper currency. Nearly forty years later, in their classic study of *Prices in Colonial Pennsylvania*, Bezanson, Gray, and Hussey offered evidence in support of MacFarlane's contention and showed prices ordinarily responding to seasonal and cyclical influences governed by the effects of war and the interplay of shifts in external market demands and local commodity supplies. In reviewing the work, however, Curtis Nettels singled out the lack of any discussion of monetary factors and their possible influence on prices and called for a "companion study" of Pennsylvania paper currency. Only this, as he put it, would clearly demonstrate the relation between paper money and local prices.[10]

Just three years later the "New Deal" economist Richard Lester gathered together a number of fugitive essays in economic journalism under the heading *Monetary Experiments, Early American and Recent Scandinavian*, and included among them a short piece on Pennsylvania of the sort Nettels desired.[11] Chiefly concerned with

---

Columbia University, 1957). Less important but still useful is the older study of Anne Bezanson, Robert D. Gray, and Miriam Hussey, *Prices in Colonial Pennsylvania* (Philadelphia, 1935), 314–336. It should be noted that the statements in this paragraph omit the important problem of elasticity of demand and therefore oversimplify the issues involved.

9. *Annals of the American Academy of Political and Social Sciences*, VIII (1896), 50–126.

10. Bezanson *et al.*, *Prices in Colonial Pennsylvania*, 314–336. The review by Nettels appeared in the *American Historical Review*, XLI (1935–1936), 549–550.

11. (Princeton, N.J., 1939), chap. 3. This material had appeared earlier in Lester's article "Currency Issues to Overcome Depressions in Pennsylvania, 1732 and 1729," *Journal of Political Economy*, XLVI (1938), 324–375.

efforts to overcome business depressions, Lester's analysis largely turned on the supposed impact of paper currency on the price level. In his calculations Lester, like MacFarlane, glossed over both the problem of the size of the *total* money supply and all the other reasons discussed in the Bezanson study for changes in the price level.

Lester's hapless attempt to relate paper money to prices excluded other monetary factors (and many nonmonetary factors) and resulted in a garbling of fact and theory. When the two came into conflict, Lester seemed convinced that theory alone sufficed to prove his point. As for the gross contradictions in the evidence, they could be dismissed by pleading extenuating circumstances. An instance is the account of the years during and after the French and Indian War. On one page Lester explained that when the war was over "Pennsylvania began to reduce the amount of paper money in circulation. A net sum of £25,000 was retired from 1760 to 1769, which helped to bring about a 13 percent decline in the price level from 1762 to 1769."[12] On the page before, he had asserted with equal authority that between 1755 and 1760 wartime issues totaled some £485,000. This represented an "increase of almost 599 percent in the paper money of the colony within six years," but "prices in Pennsylvania did not rise in proportion to the increase," because of a number of incidental reasons.[13] In short a mere 5 percent reduction in the stock of paper is immediately and causally related to a 13 percent drop in prices, while a 600 percent increase bears almost no relationship to the price level!

Another few years passed before Paton Yoder in a lengthy unpublished dissertation produced the "full companion study of Pennsylvania currency" of the kind Nettels had called for.[14] Yoder's general approach was the by-now traditional one. But he came to a remarkable conclusion. He affirmed that there was clear-cut evidence of a relationship between prices and the quantity of paper money in circulation. In fact the response of prices to changes in the paper currency supply seemed "fairly evident." The only difficulty, Yoder noted, was that the "amount of response usually defies measurement and is subject to no determinable rules."[15]

Apart from an overriding concern with the quantity theory, the

12. Lester, *Monetary Experiments*, 108.
13. *Ibid.*, 107.
14. "Paper Currency in Colonial Pennsylvania" (Ph.D. diss., Indiana University, 1941).
15. *Ibid.*, 344–345.

several investigations into Pennsylvania's paper money system brought forth some extreme claims. The most important is that the province's paper issues provided the means of overcoming depression by stimulating business expansion through the increase of imports, local trade, exports, and even, incredibly enough, population. Lester, of course, had convinced himself that the evidence for the effectiveness of paper emissions in reviving a flagging economy in the case of Pennsylvania and the other middle colonies was unmistakable.[16] Yoder showed more caution. The effect of changes in the supply of paper on British imports, he declared, "is that in some cases increases in paper money tended temporarily to increase imports, while in other cases the result was not so manifest. We cannot, by any conceivable device, measure the general encouragement given to trade throughout the period by the emission of a currency." The fact remains that neither Lester nor Yoder presented any evidence or argument strong enough to establish causality. Here as before a preoccupation with the matter of paper currency led both men to neglect the effect of the total money supply and of economic factors other than monetary.[17]

Another View of Exchange Movements

All this shows some of the more important limitations of the quantity-theory approach to paper money and the price of sterling exchange. More recently, however, writers have tended to concentrate less on the quantity theory of money and more on the relationships between trade and the overall determination of sterling exchange rates. They have argued that, when the balance of trade ran against the colonies, the demand for sterling bills to pay debts abroad outstripped the supply of bills. Under such conditions exchange rates inevitably climbed. Yet over prolonged periods and in most colonies, these same writers have found stability of exchange rates.[18]

16. *Ibid.*, 329–330; Lester, *Monetary Experiments*, chaps. 3–4.

17. The quote is from "Paper Currency in Colonial Pennsylvania," 329. The latest discussion of this problem is Weiss, "Paper Money in the American Colonies," *Jour. Econ. Hist.*, XXX (1970), esp. 775–777. Weiss's work shows only the sketchiest knowledge of the primary and secondary literature.

18. The question has always interested economic writers from the mercantilists through the Keynesians, but it has taken on added significance since the Great Depression and the modern debate over autarky. Ferguson is chiefly responsible for bringing the problem to the attention of the present generation of colonial scholars.

This view has three important consequences. In the first place, it resurrects the centuries-old balance-of-trade explanation of exchange movements. That account omitted all components of supply and demand for sterling other than visible trade; it omitted, that is, such components as the costs or returns from shipping, insurance, and other services. What is more important, it ignored the movement of foreign short-term loans. These additional factors, included on any modern balance-of-payments sheet, exerted an important influence on exchange rates. When in the eighteenth century, for instance, Britain borrowed capital in the Amsterdam market, the ebb and flow of Dutch and other European investments pressed heavily on Britain's foreign exchange rates. However, statistical evidence on such capital movements in the period is tenuous.[19] In the case of the colonies, it is equally thin. But measurable or not, the flow of capital funds arising out of "investment" in the colonies, or more simply British credit sales to America and nonpayment of debts due British merchants, was real and is not to be ignored.[20] In the second place, like the quantity theory the modern balance-of-trade view avoids discussion of the difficulties concerning underlying short-run forces operating in the economy at any given time. Such forces largely governed both the supply and demand functions for sterling exchange, their interrelationship, and their connection with the broader economic currents of the period.

A full examination of sterling exchange rates awaits a thorough investigation of the character of the colonial economy—or more precisely, economies, since they were largely regional in nature. It also requires a study in the dynamics of economic change at a time when commercial and agricultural activity was geared to the short run. Little is known about this subject. Furthermore the few studies that are available have been inclined to view the several sectors of the economy as static and separate entities. They decidedly were not. And finally, so vaguely have any interrelationships been perceived that it is difficult to identify or relate the variables affecting exchange rates. Nonetheless enough of the scholarship of the past twenty years or so has at least touched on dynamic behavior in

19. See Charles Wilson, *England's Apprenticeship, 1603–1763* (Oxford, 1965), 324. More extensive discussion is to be found in Phyllis Deane and W. A. Cole, *British Economic Growth 1688–1959: Trends and Structure* (Cambridge, 1962). For a modern analysis of the problem in colonial areas, see Gunnar Myrdal, *Asian Drama: An Inquiry into the Poverty of Nations*, II (New York, 1968), chap. 13.
20. See, for instance, John M. Hemphill II, ed., "John Wayles Rates His Neighbours," *Virginia Magazine of History and Biography*, LXVI (1958), 305.

places like Virginia to allow some reconstruction of exchange movements and their causes.

In its bare essentials an exchange rate is a price, a price or value of a sterling bill of exchange measured in provincial currency. An ordinary supply and demand analysis of events in Virginia at the beginning of the Revolutionary era, therefore, points up the manner in which short-run market forces regulated sterling exchange in the middle and southern colonies.[21] To some extent the argument holds for New England as well, but it should be remembered that by 1763, following the lead of Massachusetts, the New England colonies had drastically curtailed their circulation of paper currency and returned, more or less, to a modified specie standard.[22] Before going deeper into the difficulties of colonial exchange rates, two features of the following explanation require brief comment. What follows is an overview. It is necessarily somewhat abstract and perhaps not the sort of fare historians are accustomed to or, for that matter, interested in. Consequently those who want a more concrete discussion of the various theoretical points raised here may wish to turn first to chapter three.

STERLING EXCHANGE RATES IN VIRGINIA—AN EXAMPLE

Ultimately sterling exchange rates in Virginia—and elsewhere in America—turned on the state of the balance of payments. But they were affected as well by the meaning and operation of par, or more precisely par of exchange, and of the mixed monetary standard in the colony. Primarily the balance of payments reflected the fluctuating trade *and* credit relations between a rapidly developing, capital-short, staple economy and a more advanced mercantile and industrial nation. It also reflected Virginia's balance of trade (in items visible and invisible) with the other colonial areas and especially with the West Indies.

In general then, three broad economic conditions acted upon the

21. See especially Calvin B. Coulter, Jr., "The Virginia Merchant" (Ph.D. diss., Princeton University, 1944), app. 2; John M. Hemphill II, "Virginia and the English Commercial System, 1689–1733: Studies in the Development of a Colonial Economy under Imperial Control" (Ph.D. diss., Princeton University, 1964); James H. Soltow, *The Economic Role of Williamsburg* (Charlottesville, Va., 1965), 164–176; Robert Polk Thomson, "The Merchant in Virginia, 1700–1775" (Ph.D. diss., University of Wisconsin, 1955).

22. On New England's currency system before 1764 see Brock, "Currency of the American Colonies." There is no study for the period after 1764. Much material on the subject, however, is to be found in Sachs, "Business Outlook."

movement of exchange rates. First was the tobacco trade. Prosperity in this trade normally produced a ready supply of bills of exchange in Virginia as well as a small inflow of coin, so that, other things being equal, exchange rates would tend to fall. In addition high tobacco prices prompted British merchants to extend credit freely to their Virginia customers, credit drawn in part in the form of sterling bills. In consequence sterling exchange rates could be expected to fall even further. Changes in British credit flows, however, also depended on financial and economic conditions in the mother country independent of the tobacco market. Thus the state of credit acted as a second variable in the exchange market. This is especially the case after mid-century. By that time broad and wrenching changes were transforming the Atlantic economy. Before 1775, for instance, available statistics suggest that the balance of visible trade with the metropolis favored Virginia by a substantial margin. Thereafter imports from Britain dramatically increased in response to a marked expansion of the metropolitan economy, which now found it possible to inject significant new purchasing power into the colonial marketplace. By contrast Virginia's exports to Britain, despite annual fluctuations, did not greatly exceed an average reached some twenty years earlier. In the end a qualitative change in creditor-debtor relations seems to have taken place as the debt to British mercantile houses began to pile up. In this situation exchange rates could still be expected to remain stable as long as British suppliers continued to expand credit. But the supply of credit ebbed as well as flowed. And when British merchants happened to restrict credit and repatriate their colonial assets, as they did for instance at the end of the French and Indian War, exchange rates inevitably rose. A slump in the tobacco trade of course had a similar effect, while a combination of scarce credit and a depression of tobacco prices generated substantial upward pressures on sterling rates.

The last of the three broad economic conditions influencing sterling exchange movements was the state of the West Indian markets. Disturbances in this area also tended to reduce the supply of sterling bills, and especially of coin, that Virginia obtained in exchange for shipments of farm and forest products. Once again the effect was to boost sterling rates. In sum, the major factor in determining the relative movements of sterling exchange rates in Virginia was the balance of payments and not simply the balance of trade.

The one remaining question to be settled is the matter of par. To begin with, outside New England the colonial paper money system rested upon an irredeemable monetary standard, a standard that did not make paper convertible to specie. But while paper could not be redeemed for hard cash, colonies like Virginia, on turning to the printing press for their currency, still supported a limited bimetallic standard. Thus after 1755 what little gold and silver coin normally circulated in Virginia as a domestic exchange medium and lawful tender did so at somewhat inflated sterling values, values fixed by local laws in conformity with the Proclamation of 1704 and the parliamentary act of 1708. This practice of overvaluing hard money was commonplace. It grew out of a natural desire to prevent a valuable commodity from taking flight in periods of a heavy imbalance of payments when sterling bills were in short supply. As one historian has recently written:

It is usually stated that the colonial legislatures undertook overvaluation of colonial currency in order to attract a greater circulation of specie, but, in fact, overvaluation was ordinarily undertaken as a desperate remedy for the external drain of coin which resulted because of the chronically adverse balance of payments in the trade between the colonies and the mother country whenever the prices of colonial exports were depressed or English credits for colonial economic development fell short of the expanding needs in America. In almost every instance, the fact of overvaluation preceded the law which is alleged to have created it. Therefore the motivation for such legislation and the interpretation placed upon the laws themselves have been founded generally upon faulty analysis, and their passage has usually been misconstrued as the triumph of an inflationary party in the colonial legislatures.[23]

23. The Virginia laws referred to are in William Waller Hening, ed., *The Statutes at Large; Being a Collection of All the Laws of Virginia, from the First Session of the Legislature, in the Year 1619* (Richmond, Va., 1819–1823), IV, 218–220. The quote is from Hemphill, "Virginia and the English Commercial System," 147. The discussion in these previous three paragraphs owes as much to my reading of the works cited in n. 21 above as it does to my own research. The way in which the discussion is organized, however, depends to a large extent on my reading of Hemphill, *ibid.*, chap. 3, and I am indebted to him for calling the chapter to my attention. The point about the sustained high levels of American imports after the Seven Years' War is a subject that is presently being explored by Marc Egnal, who is completing a dissertation at the University of Wisconsin on the political economy of Pennsylvania in the mid-eighteenth century. The more inclusive question of the colonial balance of payments requires a detailed investigation. Only Sachs, "Business Outlook," appears to have grasped the difficulties involved in the subject. Recent quantitative approaches are: James Shepherd, "A Balance of Payments for the Thirteen Colonies, 1768–1772: A Summary," *Jour. Econ. Hist.*, XXV (1965), 691–695, and Robert P. Thomas, "A Quantitative Approach to the Study of the Effect of British Imperial Policy upon Colonial Welfare: Some Preliminary Findings,"

In other words, whenever the supply of bills of exchange in Virginia was inadequate to the demand for sterling remittances—either because of a depression in the tobacco market or of a reversal in credit flows—coin was shipped away to England as an alternative, albeit expensive, form of payment. Or to put it more formally, competition among Virginians for available bills of exchange occasionally drove the cost of these bills beyond the local or domestic value of coin relative both to paper money and to the cost and risk of shipping gold and silver out of the province. At such times hard money would be swept off to the metropolitan centers of empire to settle accounts.

This practice of, indeed necessity for, substituting coin as a foreign remittance in periods of heavy external drains pressed heavily on free exchange rates operating through market adjustments to the legal and domestic value of coin. At such times the pegged rate for coin suggested broad limits for exchange rates on both hard money and paper currency. The upper limits of fluctuation depended on the *willingness* and *ability* of Virginians to remit coin instead of sterling bills. But the normal dearth of coin in Virginia meant that any extended external drain quickly reduced specie stocks to the vanishing point. In consequence, because the rate of exchange is a price determined by the play of market forces, in the absence of coin any short-run disequilibrium in the supply and demand for sterling bills could boost sterling exchange rates in terms of paper money to new and extraordinary heights. This seems to be what happened in Virginia in 1762. Rates fell again only after a period of retrenchment and after the panic in London's financial circles had subsided. What little specie did remain in Virginia commanded a premium—despite the laws rating paper and coin as equal and lawful for all obligations in an obvious effort to preserve a homogeneous money supply and to bolster paper currency values. In brief, at a time of panic and depression, the limited metallic standard broke down, leaving fiat money to do the work as best it could.[24]

ibid., 615–638. These works are at best suggestive, though they seem to have been uncritically accepted as valid and refined analyses of the problem.

24. The shipping of specie instead of a sterling bill was of course common practice in all the colonies and was based on advice to be found in printed handbooks that contained tables showing the relationship between varying exchange rates, specie values, insurance costs for shipping coin, etc. See, for instance, John Austin Stevens, Jr., ed., *Colonial Records of the New York Chamber of Commerce, 1768–1784* (New York, 1867), 308, under the heading "Arbitration of a Remittance in Dollars"; see also the table in Philip L. White, *The Beekmans of New York in*

The final point to be made concerning the matter of par of exchange is that a reversal of the preceding conditions would clearly help to define the lower limits of the fluctuations of sterling exchange rates. When favorable trade and credit conditions drove sterling rates far below the pegged value of coin in Virginia, the same British merchants found it profitable to export coin in lieu of sterling bills. But there was nothing automatic about the process. Classical equilibrium theory does not apply. Implicit in that notion "and preserved even in its most relativistic forms is the idea that, when a change calls forth other changes as reaction, these secondary changes are counterdirected to the primary change." That is, there was no automatic, or semiautomatic, in-and-out flow of "metal" whenever the market, or free, rate for bills of exchange got out of hand in Virginia. As an underdeveloped economy caught in a "colonial" relation to a dominant metropolitan economy, the colony suffered from a chronic scarcity of specie. And it is only within a general framework of economic fluctuation and "informal imperialism" that exchange rates in Virginia, and elsewhere in colonial America, are to be understood.[25]

In any consideration of colonial currency two conclusions seem inescapable: hitherto there have been too few studies of the structure and functioning of the colonial economy adequate to explain events; and the sources available for an analysis of the colonial monetary system are generally either incomplete or unreliable, or both. Taken together these facts go a long way towards explaining why earlier historians have failed to understand the operation of the currency system and its connections with the wider economy. There will have to be a large number of detailed monographic studies of the various aspects of the colonial economy before there can be any

---

Politics and Commerce, 1647–1877 (New York, 1956), 641, which shows James Beekman's imports and remittances for the years 1752 to 1775, and White's discussion of the subject on 285–287. There was of course nothing mechanical in the decision to remit specie instead of a sterling bill. On the matter of arbitrage see Soltow, *Economic Role of Williamsburg*, 170–171. For another view of what was happening to the local stock of hard money in Virginia and the effect on sterling exchange rates, a view that I reject, see Burnaby, *Travels*, 29. In addition see chap. 3 below for an exemplification of the various points made in this and the preceding few paragraphs.

25. The quote is from Gunnar Myrdal, *Rich Lands and Poor: The Road to World Prosperity* (New York, 1958), 9; see also *ibid.*, 144–146. For a detailed analysis of the conditions affecting the flow of "metal" see Hemphill, "Virginia and the English Commercial System," chap. 3.

final reckoning of the currency question. In the meantime this account of the Currency Act of 1764, its causes and consequences, may—I hope—light a shadowy corner of history and reveal the many possibilities for further investigation.

Chapter 2

A Summary View
of British Paper Money Policies

In writing about monetary problems, seventeenth- and eighteenth-century publicists tended to focus on the utility of money.[1] As treasure, money provided the "sinews of war"; as capital, the dynamic element in the growth of a mercantile economy. "He that hath the longest purse will certainly have the longest sword," Simon Clement asserted in 1695.[2] "Plenty of Money never fails to make trade flourish," Jacob Vanderlint added a few decades later. And where trade flourishes, there "the people always increase greatly and become generally happy; whence such nations ever grow more potent and formidable. This hath always been found true in fact, and is almost self evident."[3] There was no idolatry of money for its own sake then, but rather for its energy, which was to be used to protect and enrich both the people and the sovereign.[4]

The money question was clearly but a part of the larger question of how to achieve national power and plenty, a subject known at the time as a "branch of the science of a statesman or legislator"

1. The best studies of monetary theory for the period under discussion are Douglas Vickers, *Studies in the Theory of Money, 1690–1776* (Philadelphia, 1959), and J. Keith Horsefield, *British Monetary Experiments, 1650–1710* (Cambridge, Mass., 1960). See also Horsefield, "The Duties of a Banker. I: The Eighteenth-Century View," and "The Duties of a Banker. II: The Effects of Inconvertibility," in T. S. Ashton and R. S. Sayers, eds., *Papers in English Monetary History* (Oxford, 1953), 1–36.

2. *A Discourse of the General Notions of Money, Trade, and Exchange . . .* (London, 1695), 31.

3. *Money Answers All Things: Or an Essay to Make Money Sufficiently Plentiful Amongst all Ranks of People . . .* (London, 1734), 16.

4. Jacob Viner, "Power versus Plenty as Objectives of Foreign Policy in the Seventeenth and Eighteenth Centuries," *World Politics*, I (1948), 1–29. See also Viner, *Studies in the Theory of International Trade* (New York, 1937).

18

called "political economy."[5] The means best suited to these ends was generally held to be the "mercantile system." This term was invented in the later eighteenth century to describe the system of commercial empire based on economic self-sufficiency and a growing overseas trade that the emerging nation-states of Europe developed after 1500. Believing in a world that could support "but a certain proportion of trade" and in "a limit to the vent and consumption of all sorts of commodities," nations took what they could get.[6] Each tried to create a commercial monopoly of its own and, where possible, to cut into the markets of others. Coupled to this theory of a finite international marketplace was a primitive concept of capital investment. In Daniel Defoe's words: "Money begets money, trade circulates and the tide of money flows with it; one hand washes the other and both hands wash the face."[7]

Broadly conceived, Britain's mercantile system sought to increase the flow of public revenues and to foster the industrial growth of the mother country—with special attention to the protection and encouragement of the maritime industries in the seventeenth century and to the manufacturing industries during the first half of the eighteenth century. As set down in the Acts of Trade and Navigation and subsequent legislation, the system promised control of colonial markets and a dependable supply of raw materials and needed commodities. As one historian has recently noted, the official view of the colonies was that "they were property yielding returns much like a gentleman's estate"; the ultimate goal was to draw to the mother country all the profits of the produce and manufactures of America by creating a favorable trade balance with every province.[8] In

5. Adam Smith, *An Inquiry into the Nature and Causes of the Wealth of Nations*, ed. C. J. Bullock, The Harvard Classics, X (New York, 1937), 310ff.

6. Joseph Harris, *An Essay Upon Money and Coins* (London, 1757), 101. The term "mercantile system," of course, was taken by Adam Smith from the works of the physiocrats.

7. Daniel Defoe, *The Compleat English Tradesman*, II (London, 1732), Pt. ii, 118.

8. D. A. Farnie, "The Commercial Empire of the Atlantic, 1607–1783," *Economic History Review*, 2d Ser., XV (1962), 205. On the question of trade balances compare the views of Charles Wilson, "Treasure and Trade Balances: The Mercantilist Problem," *ibid.*, II (1949), 152–161, with those of E. F. Heckscher, "Multi-Lateralism, Baltic Trade, and the Mercantilists," *ibid.*, III (1950), 219–228. The best study of the Acts of Trade remains Lawrence A. Harper, *The English Navigation Laws: A Seventeenth-Century Experiment in Social Engineering* (New York, 1939). The revenue question is explored in George L. Beer, *The Commercial Policy of England toward the American Colonies* (New York, 1948), 14–18. In this regard see the review by Herbert Heaton, "Heckscher on Mercantilism," *Journal of Political Economy*, XLV (1937), 370–393.

brief the wealth of America was to be drained away for the benefit of a metropolis that had the duty to "nourish and cultivate, to protect and govern."[9]

The question of how colonial accounts were to be adjusted was not yet settled. Unlike Spanish America, which remitted the products of its mines, the British provinces had no native gold and silver for export. In theory they could have remitted instead the produce of their soil. And indeed a limited kind of barter exchange did exist between the metropolis and the southern colonies.[10] However, efforts to develop similar trade with the provinces to the north failed, and northern agriculture generally competed with British farming. As a result New England and the middle colonies early established large export markets of their own outside the British Isles, while the southern colonies adopted the same practice at a later date. But as soon as any of the colonies in trade with British and foreign markets built up either sterling credits (to be drawn in bills of exchange) or stocks of coin, they were drained away to settle commercial imbalances with the mother country, leaving little money behind to serve as a medium of local exchange. And the miscellaneous foreign coin that did remain in domestic circulation was often debased and counterfeited and always difficult to convert into sterling values.[11]

Imperial authorities did little to ease conditions. Laws in England banned exports of sterling coin, or of bullion smelted from such coin, and the government rejected the idea of creating a strictly colonial coinage.[12] In order to provide for local exchange and to facilitate domestic trade, the colonists thus had to look to their own solutions.

9. It is interesting to speculate in this connection about the kind of work Lewis Namier might have accomplished if he attended to the problems outlined in his introduction to *England in the Age of the American Revolution* (London, 1930), 29–35.

10. For a general discussion of this point and of the various issues related to it, see Curtis P. Nettels, *The Money Supply of the American Colonies before 1720* (Madison, Wis., 1934).

11. See Bernard Bailyn, *The New England Merchants in the Seventeenth Century* (Cambridge, Mass., 1955); Virginia D. Harrington, *The New York Merchant on the Eve of Revolution* (New York, 1935); and Arthur L. Jensen, *The Maritime Commerce of Colonial Philadelphia* (Madison, Wis., 1963). It is well known that silver service was in wide use in the colonies, and in theory it might have provided a store of treasure that could be melted down in a period when the local coin supply was under heavy pressure for use as a sterling remittance. In practice, however, this does not generally seem to have been the case, as Jacob Viner points out in *Studies in the Theory of International Trade*, a work that is required reading for anyone interested in the colonial currency question.

12. See Nettels, *Money Supply*, chap. 6. Small amounts of British coin did reach the colonies.

Merchants early developed an extensive and efficient system of book credit and barter to make up for the deficiency of coin.[13] In addition private credit instruments such as promissory notes or notes of hand, while they did not generally circulate except within the mercantile community, also enjoyed wide use from the beginning.[14] But all classes felt the need for some kind of public currency. Commodity money served for a time.[15] Produce such as tobacco, sugar, and wheat passed everywhere in the first stages of settlement as an exchange medium; and the colonial assemblies often made it legal tender at fixed values for the discharge of public and private debts. Later, after the enactment of quality inspection and storage laws, an advanced kind of commodity money called warehouse receipts circulated in places such as Virginia, North Carolina, and Maryland. Although commodity money of one kind or another continued to be used throughout the colonial period, it had obvious defects. For one thing it was expensive. It also raised difficulties for both the merchants and the crown, because it allowed debtors to insist on paying their debts in inferior goods at inflated values. More important, commodity money failed to satisfy the monetary demands of a rapidly growing population and of increasingly complex market economies and social organizations. By the beginning of the eighteenth century, then, the problem of providing a domestic circulating medium had become acute in several of the provinces. Fifty years later the condition had spread to all of them.

Money was needed locally not only to provide means of exchange but also to meet the costs of local government and especially the heavy requirements for military support. During the opening years of the eighteenth century, England and her colonies spent much of their time, energy, and wealth in making war on their neighbors. The returns on this investment proved unusually good. Overseas trade made substantial gains, and the general economic position of the empire greatly improved. Nevertheless demands for wartime funds placed an impossible burden on the system of taxation, and

13. See, for example, W. T. Baxter, *The House of Hancock: Business in Boston, 1724–1775* (Cambridge, Mass., 1945), chap. 3.
14. On the use of these instruments see T. S. Ashton, *Economic Fluctuations in England, 1700–1800* (Oxford, 1959), 106–108; Ashton, *An Economic History of England: The Eighteenth Century* (New York, 1955), 185–186; William S. Sachs and Ari Hoogenboom, *The Enterprising Colonials: Society on the Eve of the Revolution* (Chicago, 1965), 96, 118.
15. See Donald B. Scheick, "The Regulation of Commodity Currency in Colonial Virginia" (Ph.D. diss., Indiana University, 1954).

government was soon forced to find other expedients to finance the military. In England, as P. G. M. Dickson has recently shown, the result was a "financial revolution" and the development of a system of public borrowing that in its essential outlines was completed in time for the great war with France in 1756.[16] In the colonies, by contrast, constant requests for military aid led to a very different kind of financial revolution. There the relative poverty, the underdeveloped state of the economy, the impact of British imperial policy, the lack of moneyed capital, and the controlling influence of British merchant-creditors prevented any such government borrowing over the long or short run. To support the heavy burden of military expenses and other public demands, the colonies developed instead a system of forced short-term lending by issuing notes in anticipation of future tax returns. Usually referred to as "currency finance," this technique seems to have been modeled after the practices of the Bank of England and the chancellor of the Exchequer, which were already issuing notes charged against the public revenue in the late 1690s.[17] "Currency finance" therefore appears to be the product both of economic conditions in America and of the general climate of contemporary economic thought and practice.

Another urgent monetary need in America was for a source of long-term public credit to assist in capital formation and to provide some kind of liquidity for farmers, planters, land speculators, merchants, and others with their assets locked up in real estate. Land banks, or loan offices, that would issue paper in the form of loans against realty offered a ready solution. A late seventeenth-century English innovation, land banks were one of the more exotic, if unsuccessful, schemes for fiscal and monetary reform during a revolutionary period in the development of English public credit.[18] In the colonies prospects for radical monetary experiments proved more favorable; the idea of the loan office quickly caught on. And the system established deep roots before the War for Independence.[19]

---

16. *The Financial Revolution in England: A Study in the Development of Public Credit, 1688–1756* (New York, 1967).

17. This is essentially an abbreviated version of a review of Dickson's study, *ibid.*, which appeared in the *WMQ*, 3d Ser., XXVI (1969), 156–158. For a discussion of "currency finance," see Ferguson, "Currency Finance," *WMQ*, 3d Ser., X (1953), 153–180.

18. See Horsefield, *British Monetary Experiments*.

19. For a general discussion see Theodore Thayer, "The Land-Bank System in the American Colonies," *Jour. Econ. Hist.*, XIII (1953), 145.

BRITISH MONETARY POLICY BEFORE PAPER MONEY

Before paper money came into general use in America, imperial authorities had established several monetary policies applicable to the colonies. In the first place, the metropolis prohibited the Americans from minting their own coin, and thereby debasing the sterling standard, and insisted on a free flow of gold and silver, apart from English coin, within the empire. Second, and more to the point, it demanded that the royal revenues and sterling investments made by English merchants be protected against American legal tender laws and overvalued foreign coin. For nearly a half century after the Restoration, while the colonies struggled to attract and support a local circulation of ready money by means of an inflationary and competitive boosting of specie values, imperial authorities had sought to reduce the various American currencies to a single standard. The culmination of these efforts came in 1704. In that year the crown, through the use of the royal proclamation, had attempted a general regulation of American currencies by limiting the value of the standard piece of eight to six shillings, or a maximum overvaluation of 33 ⅓ percent.[20] The proclamation, however, and the parliamentary enactment that quickly followed it in 1708, proved disappointing. It was questionable whether such policies were appropriate to a system of paper money. Common opinion in the eighteenth century held that specie had an intrinsic value; merchants and the writers of the time had some understanding of the ebbs and flows of gold and silver. But precisely what paper money values comprised, how they were to be measured and how controlled, were secrets hidden from the light of reason.

One of the major questions facing British policy makers was how to set safe limits to the creation of paper money. On this the economic theorists of the eighteenth century found themselves in general agreement with the businessmen of the age: experience alone would determine the quantity of money to be kept in circulation. Educated opinion in general held that the volume of money outstanding, whether paper or coin, would vary from country to country according to the state of trade and to commercial habits and manners. Overstepping these bounds invited monetary inflation and a drain of gold. Furthermore, in the case of paper money alone, it

20. See Hemphill, "Virginia and the English Commercial System," chap. 3.

was thought that the best protection was to have the currency fully secured by gold and silver reserves.[21] More controversial was a dissenting view that tangible assets like land and securities would also provide paper with an adequate backing. Shared by only a few writers at any time, that view proved even less popular after the shattering collapse in 1720 of the South Sea scheme and John Law's Mississippi Company.[22]

In the colonies the problem remained that the volume of paper money in circulation bore at best only a remote relationship to the stated needs of trade. Not economic thinking but the logic of events—the costs of war and of running a government—chiefly determined the amount of paper currency created, the level of taxes, and the amount of paper destroyed. And it seems that politicians then as now could not always be relied upon to tax as heavily as economic orthodoxy required. Consequently British policy makers soon ran up against several obstacles to the application of contemporary monetary theory. If, therefore, after half a century of fumbling experiments with American paper money, the mother country fell back upon first principles—that money, as the measure of other things, should be fixed in its own value and that only gold and silver enjoyed this quality—it was because the few who had some understanding of the behavior of paper money could not reconcile the conflicting demands of trade, war, and public finance, on the one hand, or satisfy demands for a stable currency and for the security of sterling investments and of royal revenues, on the other.

ORIGINS OF PAPER MONEY POLICY, 1707–1720

Late in the year 1706 imperial authorities registered their first official response to colonial paper money.[23] That September a complaint of the merchants trading to Barbados against the depreciation

21. See Vickers, *Studies in the Theory of Money*.
22. See Horsefield, *British Monetary Experiments*, and Dickson, *Financial Revolution*, chaps. 5–6.
23. Anyone who undertakes to survey the literature in his field necessarily cuts his own swath through the tangle of secondary works. In the field of colonial monetary history, however, there is only one work of any substance to attend to —exceptions to the contrary notwithstanding—and this is the Brock study, "Currency of the American Colonies." At this point I should like to acknowledge my debt to Professor Brock for the discussion that follows. The differences in our interpretations should be apparent to anyone who bothers to compare my statement of the problem with his.

of a recent legal tender land-bank issue prompted an investigation by the Board of Trade, which, shortly after taking petitions and testimony from the Royal African Company and other interested parties, recommended a royal veto of the act in question. Like the merchants, the Board opposed the use of any lawful currency not redeemable in gold and silver in the belief that fiat money would only cheat the island's chief creditors: the local businessmen, the London merchants and suppliers, and the slave traders. There were two aspects to the problem. Domestic legal tender laws required local inhabitants or anyone operating a business on Barbados to accept payment in paper money, whatever its value, for all obligations —including debts formerly payable in hard cash. However, since legal tender laws carried no force outside the boundaries of the colony, "outlanders" presumably enjoyed immunity from the disruptions of the local currency. Thus debts payable elsewhere than in Barbados, such as sterling accounts with London merchants, for instance, could be discharged either in sterling money and good bills of exchange or their equivalent in foreign coin or specie. But even so, English merchants stood to lose heavily under certain conditions. If, for example, a legal agent, factor, or business partner on the island had power of attorney from a London firm to settle an overdue account originally payable in England, the debt, whatever its value, could be legally discharged in paper.[24]

In this instance, as later, the Board of Trade showed a marked concern to protect the value of English debts from the eroding effects of a depreciated currency. In addition the Board feared that a fiat money threatened to disrupt commerce, raise prices, and curtail royal revenues. Finally, the feeling was that the Barbados land bank would weaken the determination to procure coin through normal trade channels and make it the local exchange medium. The Privy Council fully supported the Board's position, and the crown ultimately disallowed the act. Furthermore, in an effort to prevent similar occurrences elsewhere, the queen instructed her American governors to reject any future paper money measures that lacked prior approval of the crown or that failed to include a clause suspending their operation until they came under royal review. As a point of comparison, however, it must be noted that no one as yet had bothered to complain about the earlier currency issues of Massachusetts

24. These points about the relationship between the payments of debts, foreign and domestic, and fiat money laws are discussed at length in chap. 3.

and South Carolina, where paper money had not noticeably disturbed existing exchange rates and was not a legal tender.[25]
Following the Barbados decision, the Board of Trade apparently
felt it had a rule of thumb whereby it might gauge the merits of
further paper emissions. In 1709, in language reminiscent of their
earlier recommendation, the commissioners condemned a recent
New York fiat money issue redeemable in taxes. The law in question was found to work an intolerable hardship upon those creditors
who had lent hard money or sold goods under contracts payable
within the province in coin. Nonetheless, by this time the Privy
Council was ready to reject the Board's recommendations and allow
the measure to stand; the money, it seems, had helped cover the
costs of mounting an attack against French Canada.[26]
  Money as the "sinews of war" was a familiar metaphor that served
as a principle. Because of the shortage of specie developing in America during Queen Anne's War and because of the inability of the
colonies in general to finance expensive military operations out of
existing tax revenues, imperial authorities generally acquiesced in
the wartime emission of paper notes charged against future taxes.
They did not even object when, near the end of that conflict,
Massachusetts declared its recent paper currency issues, which
passed at a par with coin, to be a full legal tender. On the other
hand, a £50,000 appropriation of *unsecured* paper to outfit an expedition against Quebec drew quick fire from the Board of Trade.
Anticipating reimbursement by the Royal Exchequer, which in the
past had shared provincial military expenses, Massachusetts had
made no effort to back its £50,000. But the commissioners of trade

  25. July 1, Sept. 26, Oct. 10, 15, 17, 21, 1706, in W. Noel Sainsbury *et al.*,
eds., *Calendar of State Papers, Colonial Series, America and West Indies* . . . (London, 1860–1953), XXIII, 166, 229, 261, 268–270, 271–274, 276, hereafter cited as *Cal.
State Papers, Col.* See also Sept. 17, 24, Oct. 3, 8, 10, 15, Nov. 1, 7, 1706, in *Journal
of the Commissioners for Trade and Plantations . . . Preserved in the Public Record
Office* . . . (London, 1920–1938), *April 1704 to December 1708–09*, 280–282, 285–286,
hereafter this volume cited as *Jour. of Comm. Trade, 1704–1708–09*; Oct. 21, 1706,
in W. L. Grant and James Munro, eds., *Acts of the Privy Council of England,
Colonial Series* (London, 1908–1912), III, 5–10, hereafter cited as *Acts of Privy
Council, Col.*; Leonard W. Labaree, ed., *Royal Instructions to British Colonial
Governors, 1670–1776* (New York, 1935), I, 141–142, 200. For a discussion of the
early paper currency issues of Massachusetts and South Carolina, see Nettels,
Money Supply, and Jellison, "Paper Currency in South Carolina."
  26. Nov. 29, Dec. 15, 1709, *Cal. State Papers, Col.*, XXIV, 537, 552; Oct. 31, Dec.
22, 1709, Jan. 12, 1710, *Jour. of Comm. Trade, 1708-9–1714-5*, 82, 108, 113; *The
Colonial Laws of New York from the Year 1664 to the Revolution* (New York,
1894–1896), I, 654–658, 666–668, 669–674, hereafter cited as *Col. Laws N.Y.*; Nettels,
Money Supply, 274–275.

did not think mere anticipation a sufficient security. The Massachusetts governor received directions to withhold consent from future paper currency issues unless backed by adequate redemption funds.[27]

Imperial authorities had come a long way since the Barbados decision. At that time all fiat money had been judged fraudulent and unacceptable. Subsequently official feeling had come around to the view that, when properly secured, such money might well prove to be a tolerable wartime expedient.

As a consequence of Queen Anne's War, the British Empire expanded in all ways, especially in commerce. The American colonies and Massachusetts in particular prospered, thereby aggravating the normal tendency for the demands of the local economy to outrun the money supply,[28] a situation that became even more critical after the Bay Colony began rapidly to redeem currency issues struck during the war. The timing was unfortunate, however, because the end of the wartime trade with the West Indies had temporarily reduced the heavy flow of specie and bills of exchange to the mainland. Likewise termination of British military expenditures in America and the withdrawal of the queen's soldiers also dried up the supply of specie. But the abrupt contraction of money did not affect all economic groups in the same way. The old merchant class had built up its own small reserves of capital and could count on British suppliers for further credits and loans. Consequently it favored only limited increases in paper money. On the other hand rising merchants, debtors, small farmers, land speculators, and others with no ready access to British capital demanded a large volume of paper currency and facilities for the creation of short-run loans.[29] The Massachusetts land-bank struggle of 1714 developed out of just such a situation. The merchant aristocrats, who dominated the "prerogative party," controlled the Council, and enjoyed the support of the governor, backed a public land-bank plan giving them substantial

27. Governor Dudley to Board of Trade (hereafter cited as B.T.), Nov. 15, 1710, Dudley to Mr. Popple, Nov. 15, 1710, Postmasters General to the Lord High Treasurer, May 16, 1713, B.T. to the Lord High Treasurer, June 26, 1713, all in *Cal. State Papers, Col.*, XXV, 266–267, 271, XXVII, 179–180, 193. See also William D. Metz, "Politics and Finance in Massachusetts, 1713–1741" (Ph.D. diss., University of Wisconsin, 1945), 64–66.

28. For a general discussion see Ralph Davis, *The Rise of the English Shipping Industry in the Seventeenth and Eighteenth Centuries* (London, 1962). For a detailed discussion of the Massachusetts economy in the period see Metz, "Politics and Finance."

29. Metz, "Politics and Finance," chaps. 1, 2, and esp. 45–56.

control over the amount of paper in circulation. Opposing interests attached themselves to the "popular party" and endorsed a rival scheme for creating a private and more liberal land bank.

In time both Massachusetts factions turned for approval to the Board of Trade. Not unexpectedly, the Board upheld the prerogative party and its proposal for a restrictive public bank. Nonetheless, in 1715, while considering conflicting opinions on the rival bank schemes, the commissioners of trade retreated one more step from the position taken at the time of the Barbados incident. They recognized in effect that a stringency of coin made some form of lawful paper useful for carrying on local trade and for "other necessary occasions." This new principle readily served as a precedent in a New York decision.[30]

Late in 1717 a revenue and currency bill to pay provincial debts drew fire from the Grand Jury of the City and County of New York. No sooner did the measure pass the General Assembly than the jurors, who included several of the province's leading merchants, called upon the governor, Robert Hunter, to veto it. Among other things, the jurors found that the proposed fiat money issue lacked adequate security and thus posed a threat to public credit and to trade. Hunter was unimpressed. Professing to believe that the charges were politically inspired, he turned the address over to the assembly, and for their trouble the jurors found themselves hauled before the bar of the house, where they were severely reprimanded. When the controversial act subsequently became law, the opposition shifted its efforts to the other side of the Atlantic. Led by a group of prominent New York City merchants, the opponents mounted a campaign to obtain royal intercession. As a result the following spring a number of London merchants acting on behalf of themselves and their "friends" in New York petitioned the crown and the Board of Trade to put a stop to the debt act until the king had an opportunity to consider the possibility that the law was both "unwarranted" and an actual danger to credit and trade in New York, to the continued circulation of hard cash there, to the value of the existing paper money supply, and to the security of English debts.[31]

30. *Ibid.*, chaps. 3, 4; May 10, June 15, July 7, B.T. to Secretary Stanhope, Aug. 26, 1715, in *Cal. State Papers, Col.*, XXVIII, 170–172, 203–204, 222–225, 273.

31. For a more detailed analysis, compare Jerome R. Reich, *Leisler's Rebellion: A Study of Democracy in New York, 1664–1720* (Chicago, 1953), chaps. 7, 8, and esp. 167–172; Irving Mark, *Agrarian Conflicts in Colonial New York, 1711–1775* (New York, 1940), chap. 3; and Lawrence H. Leder, *Robert Livingston, 1654–1728,*

When informed of the merchants' charges, Governor Hunter vigorously denied them, and with the backing of his Council and of the House of Representatives, which was dominated at the time by a pro-Hunter faction, countered with some charges of his own. Current trade data, he explained to the Board, showed that New York's currency issues—including the issue of 1717, which had already been struck and placed in general circulation—had considerably advanced both commerce and the commonweal, had not depreciated, and had ample security. Under the circumstances, Hunter stated, any attempt to recall this latest issue amounted to an invitation to economic chaos. As to the true cause of the opposition, "whatsoever the pretended one be," it was that wealthy New York merchants, men of "private views piques and interests," were protesting that the present currency emission, like the former one, encouraged and enabled "the many to venture their stocks in trade to the prejudice of the few who had so long monopoliz'd it."[32]

Already disposed to support the governor for political reasons, the Board of Trade was persuaded that the merchant petitioners were either "misinformed or imposed on." The act was allowed to stand. The principle announced four years earlier in the Massachusetts land-bank case applied equally well to New York. The money after all was necessary not only to the proper conduct of trade but also to the support of government and the payment of the public debt. The Board, however, did enter a caveat against the lack of a suspending clause. Though judging the existing redemption funds to be adequate, the commissioners felt a need to have some control over the amount as well as the security of future currency emissions. An excess of bills, the Board believed, would inevitably lead to depreciation.[33]

To achieve such goals the Board undertook to set out a more definite policy. The commissioners obtained instructions from the

---

and the Politics of Colonial New York (Chapel Hill, N.C., 1961), chap. 5. Leder's emphasis on the domestic politics distorts the issues underlying the debt act of 1717. Nonetheless it serves as an important corrective to the accounts of Reich and Mark. For a somewhat briefer though more balanced account see Patricia U. Bonomi, *A Factious People: Politics and Society in Colonial New York* (New York, 1971), 82–86.

32. Gov. Robert Hunter to Popple, Dec. 3, 1717, *Cal. State Papers, Col.*, XXX, 118.

33. The analysis in the preceeding three paragraphs is based on the following entries in *Cal. State Papers, Col.*: XXX, xxxviii–xl, 102, 104, 118, 142, 159, 161, 192–193, 232, 237–238, 243–245, 249–250, 324, 328–329, 338, 342–343, 359–360, 365, 381–384, XXXI, xix–xx, 112–113.

king requiring all royal governors to ensure that existing paper be redeemed on time and that future currency measures include a suspending clause. Only active intervention by the Privy Council forced the abandonment of the requirement for a suspending clause concerning any measure specifically designed to meet the limited expenses of colonial governments. The resulting loophole was plugged a few years later in connection with a New Jersey law. And despite some variations depending on local needs, the instructions had achieved the essential form they retained throughout the remainder of the colonial period.[34]

By 1720, then, the Board of Trade had come around to accepting as necessary those legal tender bills of credit issued by colonial treasuries and loan offices to meet either current military and government expenses or market demands for an instrument of local trade. For their part the colonies were to set aside sufficient tax and mortgage funds to redeem their paper money at the times stipulated in the various acts of emission. In addition, except for small appropriations covering government expenses, they were to attach a clause suspending operation of the law until the crown had a chance to review it. The currency problem appeared to have been partly solved.

PROBLEMS OF ENFORCEMENT, 1720–1744

Imperial authorities now seemed to be equipped with a yardstick with which to judge the merits of future paper money laws. Over the next twenty years, however, they condemned only three paper currency acts, one in Barbados and two in South Carolina. In the process they often ignored strong protests from British merchant creditors who understandably had grown more wary of any paper issue after the ignominious collapse of the South Sea Company and of John Law's "system" in 1720. The storm in South Carolina's currency affairs was to merge with the larger monetary crisis developing in New England, a crisis that ultimately prompted Parliament to intervene and pass the Currency Act of 1751.

South Carolina was the bête noire of the early critics of American

34. Apr. 22, 28, May 13, 27, June 18, 19, 1719, *Jour. of Comm. Trade, 1718–1722*, 60, 63, 68, 69; Labaree, ed., *Royal Instructions*, I, 218. A similar policy resulted from the Barbados experience in 1706, but was regularly enforced only after the New York decision. See Nettels, *Money Supply*, 271. For an excellent discussion of New Jersey currency, and of British monetary policies in the period, see Annis J. Keyes, "New Jersey Paper Currency" (M.A. thesis, Yale University, 1927).

paper money.[35] Bills pouring from its presses choked the local channels of circulation and flooded the province in a wave of cheap
money. Carolina struck its first legal tender treasury issue in 1703
to finance an expedition against Saint Augustine. But instead of
gradually taxing the money away again as planned, the province
spent the tax returns on improving local defenses. Within a decade
another £30,000 of treasury notes, plus £50,000 in loan office bills,
entered the monetary stream. Any slack in the money supply was
quickly taken up, and currency values soon collapsed. Under the
circumstances local merchants petitioned the Board of Trade to halt
the flow of paper and obtained a royal order directing the proprietary government to restore monetary stability. But there was
little the proprietors could do. Over the next few years the assembly
pumped additional currency issues into circulation. By 1721, on
the eve of South Carolina's conversion into a royal colony, the
sterling exchange rate had jumped to five to one.[36]

When the planter-controlled Commons House proposed still another paper money measure in 1722, Charleston's mercantile community applied to the legislature for an end to inflation and to the
injustices suffered by the creditor class because of the use of fiat
money. The house replied by passing the contested measure and
arresting the petitioners for insolence. Release came only after the
merchants confessed to the falsity of their charges and agreed to
pay heavy fines. Some members of the group turned next to the
Board of Trade for redress. Joined by their British suppliers, they
warned the commissioners that "the contagion is great and will
spread to all the other colonies, and no opportunities will be wanting
to oppress and defraud the British subjects of their just debts." Subsequently the king exercised the royal veto, censured the Commons
House for high-handed conduct, and called for the speedy redemption of existing currency and for an end to future emissions.[37]

Crown instructions notwithstanding, the lower house continued
to vote additional paper issues as well as to extend the life of bills
already in circulation. By 1729 the periodic disruption of monetary

35. See the Jellison study, "Paper Currency in South Carolina," and M. Eugene
Sirmans, *Colonial South Carolina: A Political History, 1663–1763* (Chapel Hill,
N.C., 1966).
36. See Sirmans, *Colonial South Carolina*, chaps. 6–7, and Jellison, "Paper Currency in South Carolina," chaps. 1–3.
37. May 24, July 10, 25, 26, 1723, *Jour. of Comm. Trade, 1722-23–1728*, 24, 37–
38, 39; Aug. 27, 1723, *Cal. State Papers, Col.*, XXXIII, 334; Sirmans, *Colonial South
Carolina*, 148–149.

and trade conditions in the province led a small group of British
merchants to petition for an end to paper money not only in South
Carolina but everywhere in America and for the restoration of the
use of foreign coin in line with the parliamentary act of 1708. The
Board of Trade shelved the request, however. Like the majority of
merchants in the Carolina trade, the Board felt some paper money
"under proper regulation" provided a necessary means of local exchange and of paying the current expenses of government.[38]

Eight years later majority opinion had changed. After South
Carolina's irrepressible legislature had voted yet another paper
money issue, the London merchants trading to the province petitioned the crown to intervene on behalf of themselves, their Bristol
colleagues, and all other British traders. This matter no sooner came
under consideration at the Board of Trade, however, than several of
the same merchants submitted a more general scheme to the commissioners for the remedy of the mischief to "commerce from the
practice of issuing paper money, and the raising the value of the
coin."[39] Coincidentally, a few weeks later, the Board received from
an entirely different source a proposal for "a new sort of British
coin" in America.[40] And over the next couple of years still other
plans came before the Board for resolving the paper currency question. But while the Board sedulously reviewed both these "final"
solutions and the more immediate problem of the growing monetary
chaos in New England, colonial paper money practices unexpectedly came under parliamentary scrutiny.[41]

On petition from a group of British merchants trading to America,
the House of Commons in the summer of 1739 called upon the commissioners of trade for a report on the state of all bills of credit struck
in the colonies since 1700 and on existing monetary policy. As the
mass of information began coming in from America, the Board initiated a formal study of the matter, although it also passed copies of

---

38. Aug. 14, 1729, *Cal. State Papers, Col.*, XXXVI, 466; Feb. 4, Mar. 12, 1730,
Jour. of Comm. Trade, 1728-29-1734, 91, 181–182. For an analysis of the response
to paper money by the major economic and political interests, see Sirmans, *Colonial
South Carolina*, 145–148. See also Keyes, "New Jersey Paper Currency," 69.

39. June 7, 15, 22, 23, Oct. 8, Nov. 2, 1738, *Jour. of Comm. Trade, 1734-35-1741*,
242, 244, 246, 247, 255, 257; Sirmans, *Colonial South Carolina*, 185–186, 205–206;
George Chalmers, *Opinions of Eminent Lawyers* . . . (Burlington, Eng., 1858), 425–
428.

40. Oct. 18, Nov. 2, 1738, *Jour. of Comm. Trade, 1734-35-1741*, 255, 257.

41. May 30, June 6, 1739, *ibid.*, 281, 283; see also Jan. 15, Oct. 29, 1740, *ibid.*, 314,
356.

this material along to Parliament without official comment.[42] Consequently in April, near the end of the session and after only a brief consideration of the data, the House of Commons—apparently acting on its own—resolved that the issue of paper money as lawful tender in private transactions discouraged commerce by "occasioning a confusion in dealings and lessening of credit."[43] The House then gave its sanction to present policies by asking that all governors be obliged to enforce the act of 1708 and to reject any currency measure lacking a suspending clause. More ominous was its request for an opinion from the Board of Trade "on the most easy and effectual manner of sinking and discharging" all colonial paper, a request the Board honored by promptly polling governors in America for their opinion on how best to achieve such objectives with the least prejudice to the local inhabitants.[44]

Notwithstanding the growing criticism of colonial paper money practices, and despite an obvious economic motivation, the parliamentary moves may well have had political inspiration. At any rate, leaders of an opposition faction in the House of Commons had reportedly begun the investigation of American currency in an effort to "puzle and perplex" the ministers and "Spirit up the Plantations against them."[45] If so, the ministry refused to be confounded.

Well over a year passed while the Board of Trade, attended by the American agents and the British merchants, conducted lengthy hearings on colonial paper currency. In January 1741 the commissioners finally sent their findings to Parliament. Like the majority of merchants, the Board favored a continuance of the paper money system and offered no recommendations on how to redeem existing currency supplies. The commissioners argued that the currency practices of the several colonies required separate consideration, but that, generally speaking, governors should follow existing policies

---

42. June 13, 1739, Apr. 15, 1740, *Journals of the House of Commons* (London, 1742–), XXIII, 379, 520; Jan. 17, 23, 31, Feb. 6, 12, 13, 19, 27, Mar. 6, 7, 11, 12, 27, 1740, *Jour. of Comm. Trade, 1734-5–1741*, 314-322, 326; Richard Partridge to Governor Wanton, Apr. 4, 1740, in Gertrude Selwyn Kimball, ed., *The Correspondence of the Colonial Governors of Rhode Island, 1723-1775* (Cambridge, Mass., 1902), I, 142.

43. Apr. 24, 25, 1740, *Jours. of Commons*, XXIII, 526, 527, 528; May 14, 16, 21, 1740, *Jour. of Comm. Trade, 1734-5–1741*, 332-333.

44. Apr. 25, 1740, *Jours. of Commons*, XXIII, 528. See Keyes, "New Jersey Currency," chap. 6.

45. Richard Partridge to Governor Wanton, Mar. 2, 1740, Kimball, ed., *Corr. of Col. Governors of R.I.*, I, 152-153; Apr. 25, 1740, *Jours. of Commons*, XXIII, 528.

and insist upon a suspending clause for all new currency measures as well as the prompt retirement of outstanding bills of credit. As they saw it, the greatest difficulty was with the charter colonies, which could and did ignore royal instructions. Satisfied that there was no overriding reason to enact general regulatory legislation and thus "spirit up the plantations," the House of Commons at the behest of the Board turned its attention instead to Massachusetts, where the land-bank question had flared up again.[46]

The currency stringency that in 1714 had compelled a class of rising merchants, small farmers, debtors, and land speculators to support a private land bank vanished in subsequent years. Then in 1735 the Bay Colony's currency supply faced the threat of further restrictions. Royal instructions fixed £30,000 as the maximum amount of new paper that the government could issue against any contingency expenses. Moreover, changing business practices had made those merchants heavily engaged in the import trade increasingly susceptible to monetary inflation and rising sterling exchange rates. As Thomas Hutchinson noted, before 1710 or thereabouts English manufacturers had ordinarily shipped their goods to the colonies in care of English commission merchants. Though never abandoned, this commission system became less attractive as the colonial merchants increasingly traded on their own account, a practice that effectively shifted the risks of the marketplace from the backs of the English manufacturers and merchants to the colonial firms. The American merchants, who also sold on credit, now had to repay their English correspondents fixed sums in sterling within periods of from six to nine months from the date of invoice. Henceforth a depreciating currency or a sudden jump in sterling exchange rates could jeopardize an entire year's profit.

Thus the structure of trade had undergone some serious changes when two different groups of private bankers moved to circumvent the restriction on public currency issues. The first group included the land bankers and their allies, who in the face of a growing depression revived their earlier efforts to loosen credit. The second

46. June 12, 18, Oct. 7, 14, Nov. 29, 1740, Jan. 2, 3, 5, 22, 29, 1741, *Jour. of Comm. Trade, 1734-5–1741*, 336, 337, 346, 349, 359, 360, 368, 369; Report of the Lords of Trade to the House of Commons relative to Bills of Credit in the Plantations, Jan. 21, 1741, in William A. Whitehead *et al.*, eds., *Documents Relating to the Colonial History of the State of New Jersey (Archives of the State of New Jersey*, 1st Ser., I–XXXIII [Newark, Paterson, Trenton, etc., 1880–1928]), VI, 122–125, hereafter cited as *N.J. Archives*; Jan. 22, 1741, *Jours. of Commons*, XXIII, 609, 610. See also Metz, "Politics and Finance," chap. 9, and Brock, "Currency of the American Colonies," 182–184, 204.

consisted of silver bankers. Led by a number of large Eastern Seaboard merchants, they supported the creation of a so-called silver
bank to issue notes backed at full face value. More conservative in
their monetary views than the land bankers, the silverites wished
to maintain an adequate supply of a local currency and a relatively
stable exchange rate on sterling. But both groups proved anathema
to the old merchants. Supported by their London suppliers, they
applied directly to imperial authorities for an extension to America
of the South Sea Bubble Act of 1720. Parliament agreed and passed
an ex post facto law eliminating private banks of issue in the colonies.
In addition it rendered Massachusetts's year-old land bank illegal,
voided its notes, and left its sponsors with an obligation to pay the
bank's debts at full value.[47]

Boston's great merchants remained dissatisfied. Currency practices in the neighboring colonies continued to threaten their interests in much the same way as did the land bank of 1740. Their
dissatisfaction stemmed basically from the regional character of the
circulation of paper money in America. To be sure, paper currency
was a legal tender only within the colony of issue. But money of
any kind flowed freely into and through the local channels of trade
that cut across the various political boundaries. Because trade was
regional in character, so was the flow of money.[48] Within the controlling urban centers of any given trade area, the business community typically accepted the paper money of neighboring colonies
at the value these colonies placed on foreign coin. Outside the great
commercial centers, the currency of another colony was likely to
pass at a large discount. As a consequence, early in 1743 Massachusetts's new governor, William Shirley, following up a letter by

47. Brock, "Currency of the American Colonies," 123–127; Labaree, ed., *Royal
Instructions*, I, 220, 221; Metz, "Politics and Finance," chap. 10. The best published
study of the land bank is George A. Billias, *The Massachusetts Land Bankers of
1740*, University of Maine Studies, 2d Ser., No. 74 (Orono, Me., 1959). Billias is
anxious to disprove the debtor-creditor thesis associated with the land-bank question. But his failure to analyze the economic changes in the period raises serious
doubts as to the validity of his argument. A companion study of the silver bank
is not available, but I am indebted to Peter Barry of the University of Wisconsin
for the analysis presented here. I am also in his debt for the Thomas Hutchinson
reference to be found in Hutchinson's *History of the Colony and Province of
Massachusetts-Bay*, ed. Lawrence S. Mayo (Cambridge, Mass., 1936), II, 340–341.
For additional comments and references to the events taking place in Massachusetts
see my article "Colonial Currency," *Explorations in Entrepreneurial History*, 2d
Ser., VI (1969), 187–188.
48. See the suggestive article by William S. Sachs, "Interurban Correspondents
and the Development of a National Economy before the Revolution: New York
as a Case Study," *New York History*, XXXVI (1955), 320–335.

MILLS COLLEGE
LIBRARY

his predecessor, Jonathan Belcher, complained to the Board of Trade against the monetary imperialism of Rhode Island and to a lesser extent of Connecticut. Shirley contended that the charter colonies' easy money policies posed an immediate threat to Boston's commanding position in New England trade and would eventually bury the area in a flood of paper. But he was equally concerned over a conspiracy he saw at work. It seemed that the same merchants who had backed the Bay Colony's private bank now willingly and illegally took Rhode Island and Connecticut notes in payment of private debts and introduced them into the local stream of circulation. Informed that a currency bill might come before Parliament, Shirley asked for strict restraints on Rhode Island but cautioned against any "immediate total suppression" of New England currency in general. Properly safeguarded, paper still served as a local exchange medium and a means of paying government expenses. The governor might have saved himself the trouble. The bill in question failed to materialize.[49]

A year later, in the spring of 1744, a group of London merchants who had been critical of colonial paper currency practices for some time appears to have submitted to the commissioners of trade a monetary control scheme of one sort or another and to have received encouragement. In any event, shortly thereafter several of the same merchants petitioned for parliamentary "interposition" in colonial currency, reminding the House of Commons of the stand it had taken back in April 1740. The House responded by ordering a committee, which included the legal adviser to the Board of Trade and one commissioner, to draw up and present a suitable regulatory bill. The ideas in the bill originated therefore with the Board and not Parliament.[50]

In sum, before 1744 the Board of Trade generally believed that paper money performed a number of important functions when cor-

49. Mar. 19, 1743, in Charles H. Lincoln, ed., *Correspondence of William Shirley, Governor of Massachusetts and Military Commander in America, 1731–1760* (New York, 1912), I, 103–107; Dec. 23, 1743, in J. G. Palfrey, *History of New England* (Boston, 1858–1890), V, 105–106, where Shirley's letter is quoted in full; Brock, "Currency of the American Colonies," 202–203. The Board of Trade had for a short period in 1742 taken up the question of prohibiting American paper money in connection with its investigation into a Massachusetts currency act of 1740. In this case Governor Shirley and the merchants of both Boston and London had been the instigators. See Feb. 3, 5, 17, 19, 24, Mar. 2, 11, 17, Apr. 30, 1742, *Jour. of Comm. Trade, 1741-2–1749*, 7, 8, 9, 11, 17.

50. Mar. 22, Apr. 3, 1744, *ibid.*, 104–105; Apr. 18, 1744, *Jours. of Commons*, XXIV, 658.

rectly handled: it provided the "sinews of war," paid the current costs of government, and served as the "handmaiden of trade." The Board was increasingly concerned, however, with the ever-growing cry of creditors on both sides of the Atlantic for the protection of local debts and of sterling investments against the corrosive effects of cheap money.[51] Also weighing heavily on their deliberations was the expressed hostility of Parliament and the demand of the established merchants in America for a limit to the amount of paper money falling into the hands of a rising merchant class.

Beset by contradictions, the Board aimed in general at balancing the various factors and interests. In particular it made stability of sterling exchange rates a major goal of monetary policy. To promote this stability, the Board at first had insisted that paper money be backed by sufficient redemption funds and be withdrawn from circulation after a reasonable time, ordinarily a maximum of five years; ostensibly the value of public notes, like private notes, depended upon their security and their prompt redemption. Later the commissioners had moved to adjust the supply of paper currency to commercial demands in accord with the prevailing quantity theory of money. In the case of Massachusetts, however, and at least one other New England colony, the Board members had been far more demanding and had tried to restrict the volume of paper to the small amount needed to pay the contingent expenses of government.[52] The means of enforcing the several policies remained the royal instruction, the suspending clause, and the king's veto power. But such controls had proven relatively ineffective. By the 1740s governor after governor had violated his instructions. Nor was the royal veto any real check. It remained impossible to exercise the veto without inflicting serious losses on those local inhabitants who had already accepted the new paper money in good faith and at face value. Consequently the crown had used its power only twice in the period; once in the case of Barbados, and once in the case of South Carolina. In general the colonies were left to make their own monetary arrangements.

THE CURRENCY ACT OF 1751

In the late spring of 1744 the measure prepared by the Board of Trade finally came out of parliamentary committee. Theoretically

---

51. See the discussion in chaps. 1 and 3 of the present study.
52. See Keyes, "New Jersey Paper Currency," chap. 6.

the bill aimed at reaffirming existing policies. Actually it was a highly restrictive piece of legislation fundamentally opposed to any new paper emissions—with certain exceptions. In effect the measure sought to remedy the problem of fluctuating exchange rates and to protect American and British creditors by narrowly limiting both the volume of paper outstanding and the use of the legal tender clause. In the future the crown was to permit only those currency issues necessary to meet the costs of local government and the threats of war and invasion. Any new paper would pass as lawful tender in public transactions alone; policies designed to meet conditions in New England would be applied to the colonies in general.

More significant, the means of enforcing the new measure transcended any monetary considerations and seemed to have been intended as a way of tightening imperial control over every aspect of colonial life. In the past the crown had had little power to enforce its monetary policies in the charter colonies and at best only uneven success at implementing them elsewhere in America. Under the proposed bill *all* colonial acts contrary to royal instructions would be nullified; positive law was to confer upon the crown a final and absolute veto over every American assembly. So blatant an attack on colonial self-government in the guise of currency control produced a wave of protesting letters and petitions from America. Ultimately, however, the issue was shunted aside as Parliament buried itself in a debate over the loss of a major sea battle with the Spanish and French navies. As in the past the question of impending war claimed priority over all considerations; statecraft dictated that under the circumstances the mother country placate the Americans.[53]

For the moment the critics of colonial currency had lost the initiative. But King George's War was no sooner at an end than the regulatory bill was revived. Again the colonies united in opposing any indiscriminate curb on paper money or any attempt to give the royal instructions the force of law. This time their lobbying efforts among friends in trade and in Parliament were crowned with success. The clause affecting instructions was deleted, and the currency question postponed to a later date.[54]

53. An abstract of the proposed bill may be found in *N.J. Archives*, XV, 427–428. See also Brock, "Currency of the American Colonies," 206–217. The New York response to the threatened measure is touched upon in Bonomi, *A Factious People*, 137–138.

54. *Ibid.*, 219–228; Feb. 16, Mar. 3, 1749, *Jours. of Commons*, XXV, 746, 766. See also Charles A. Barker, *The Background of the Revolution in Maryland* (New Haven, Conn., 1940), 190–191.

A year passed before further action was taken. During this time a hard money faction in Massachusetts under the leadership of Thomas Hutchinson, then Speaker of the House of Representatives, had pushed through a measure for using the parliamentary reimbursement covering the Cape Breton expedition to fund the province's paper currency. But as Hutchinson himself recognized, the move was pointless unless it proved possible to get the other New England governments "to conform their currency to Massachusetts." Despite various efforts to prevent a loss, much of the coin from the parliamentary grant rapidly drained away to neighboring colonies, or went into hiding, while the paper bills of the other governments and especially Rhode Island flowed back in, in an ever-rising tide. By 1749 the hard money forces were driven to petition the General Court for intercolonial regulations; nothing could be done to "prevent the measures we have taken" from being ineffectual, they asserted, until all outside paper could be banned from local circulation.[55]

Currency reform in New England obviously required some form of parliamentary intervention. Accordingly, when in 1750 the old merchant aristocrats of Rhode Island, feeling the threat of rising sterling exchange rates and of growing competition from local traders, renewed the attack on the colonial currency system, Parliament quickly responded. What had prompted the merchants' move was the vote in 1750 by the Rhode Island assembly of a £50,000 loan office issue in answer to insistent local demands for an ample money supply and easy credit. At this point the great merchants enlisted the support of their British suppliers in petitioning the crown and the Board of Trade for relief.[56] As a consequence the proposals of 1744 were exhumed and introduced anew into the House of Commons. The outcome, the Currency Act of 1751, reflected at best an uneasy compromise between the supporters and the critics of colonial paper money practices.

The Currency Act of 1751 made no mention of the attempt to strengthen the royal instructions. Injected into the House debate, the provision to that effect was amended to death. Nor did the 1751 Currency Act apply to all the colonies or to all kinds of paper

---

55. For a detailed discussion of these events see MacInnes, "Rhode Island Bills of Credit," II, 509–526, and Malcolm Freiberg, "Thomas Hutchinson and the Province Currency," *New England Quarterly*, XXX (1957), 197–204. See also n. 47 above.

56. See MacInnes, "Rhode Island Bills of Credit," II, 509–526.

money. It covered only the regional trade area affected by Rhode Island's paper bills and only public issues. In 1741 Parliament had already, in effect, banned private emissions with the extension of the South Sea Bubble Act. With that extension and the new law, it was now fully expected that all the New England colonies would follow the example set by Massachusetts and eventually return to the system of specie currency envisaged in the parliamentary act of 1708. In the meantime, in line with the proposals of 1744, the Currency Act of 1751 declared that future public issues could be struck only when necessary in order to provide either military aids in time of war and invasion or funds for the "current service" of government. Even then the new bills were restricted in their volume and were not to be legal tender in the payment of any private obligations. As for existing paper bills, they could not be extended beyond their original redemption periods. Finally, any governor found acting contrary to the act would suffer immediate dismissal from the king's service, a provision far less severe than that which would have given the royal instructions the force of law in America.[57]

In establishing its monetary policies the Board of Trade had tried from the beginning to strike a balance between conflicting interests and attitudes. On the one side were arrayed those British merchants trading to places like South Carolina and New England. As creditors they demanded full protection for sterling debts payable in America in local currency. They tended to believe in the intrinsic value of gold and silver and to view all fiat money as fraudulent and bound in time to depreciate in terms of sterling. Before 1730 or so their aim was to eliminate all paper from the stream of circulation and to return to the system of specie payments spelled out in the parliamentary act of 1708. Nonetheless the logic of events ultimately led many of them to accept the usefulness of some paper currency, provided that it was issued for limited purposes, was properly secured, and was not lawful for sterling or other private obligations. Their colonial counterparts, the established merchants and traders, were of a similar mind. They also wished to restrict the volume and tender of paper money, both as a barrier to inflation—which only increased their costs of doing business and cut into profits—and to the ambitions of a rising and competing merchant class. Few Americans advocated outright rejection of paper money and a simple return to specie.

57. 24 Geo. II, c. 53, Danby Pickering, ed., *Statutes at Large . . . of Great Britain. Anno 1761, continued to 1806* (Cambridge, 1762–1807), XX, 277–290.

On the other side stood those British merchant-creditors who traded to places like the middle colonies where sterling exchange rates held relatively steady. More willing to accept fiat money in the settlement of their American accounts, they supported the need for a supply of paper money adequate to fill the local stream of circulation and buoy up commerce. Ranged alongside them were the colonial businessmen, land speculators, and other interested men, who looked to local facilities as a source of liquidity and of money and credit adequate to finance their expansion, as well as the farmers, who hoped for parity, and the debtors, who wished to ease their burden of payments.

In this welter of conflicting interests the Board of Trade at first favored separate consideration of the currency needs of the various colonies. For the most part the commissioners favored those paper issues that had proper security and did not exceed an amount sufficient to support American participation in imperial wars, the cost of local government, and the growth of British trade. Later, and especially after royal controls over paper currency proved relatively ineffective, the Board swung over to a program of general parliamentary regulation aimed at the protection of all creditor interests and a strict limit to the issue and use of any paper money. The commissioners then attempted to tighten control over every aspect of the colonial economy by giving the royal instruction the force of law in America. Frustrated in this move by the advent of King George's War and the concerted opposition of the Americans and their British suppliers, the Board of Trade and its allies took what they could get —the Currency Act of 1751.

To sum up, the failure of crown regulation of paper money ultimately led to intervention by Parliament. The result was that during this period of so-called "salutary neglect" in American colonial history there occurred in fact and in theory a vast increase in metropolitan control over a major area of the colonial economy. At the time the centralization of control went largely unnoticed. Attacks on the new law were forthcoming, but they were made on the grounds of expediency, not principle.[58] To the Board of Trade, however, passage of the Currency Act of 1751 meant that the "sense" of Parliament was clear at last. Armed with the royal instruction and the king's veto power—weapons that had proven relatively inef-

58. For an account of the response of the New England colonies to the Currency Act of 1751 see Brock, "Currency of the American Colonies," chaps. 6–8.

fectual in the past—the Board slowly moved to extend the provisions of the Currency Act to the remaining colonies. But the French and Indian War forced a temporary abandonment of any such plans, and the commissioners generally had to assess the monetary needs of colonies according to the more realistic guidelines established back before 1740.[59] Nonetheless the prejudice that only gold and silver could serve as money grew apace. The act of 1751 proved to be but a prelude to the Currency Act of 1764.

59. See, for example, the instructions sent to Francis Bernard as governor of New Jersey in 1758 that are printed in Evarts Boutell Greene, *The Provincial Governor in the English Colonies of North America* (New York, 1898), 240; Labaree, ed., *Royal Instructions*, I, 223–227. See also Keyes, "New Jersey Paper Currency," chap. 9.

Chapter 3

The Currency Act of 1764

Virginia Monetary Practices
and the Protection of British Debts

Royal controls had proven inadequate to the task of extending the principles expressed in the Currency Act of 1751 to the colonies outside New England. Consequently, at the end of the French and Indian War and with the apparent support of the recently installed Grenville ministry, the Board of Trade called for new parliamentary legislation. As a result the regulation and reform of the colonial currency system became part of the larger postwar effort by the British government to rationalize the administration of the empire: that is, to increase the American revenue, bring colonial commercial practices into line with mercantile doctrines and the Acts of Trade, and assert authority over a wide range of economic activities in America. The upshot was the adoption of the Currency Act of 1764, which in some ways exceeded the restrictions imposed by the earlier law.

In a narrower and more immediate sense the Currency Act of 1764 was called into being by British merchant-creditors trading to Virginia and North Carolina, who were anxious to protect the value of their colonial debts and investments. Most important were the London merchants. Heavily engaged in the direct purchase of tobacco in exchange for British goods, they found that many of their transactions in America were in sterling. As early as 1757 they had raised a cry against the use of paper currency as legal tender in the payment of domestic debts contracted in sterling. The merchants of Glasgow, on the other hand, who were also deeply involved in the tobacco trade, cared little about a possible threat to sterling debts. Their investments were tied up in the Virginia store trade and in book credit specifically payable in local currency, coin as well as paper. They therefore took a dim view of any plan that tended to discredit paper money when offered in settlement of any obligations, sterling or otherwise. From their standpoint it was the responsibility of the British government to maintain the stability of paper money, to bolster its value when necessary, and to uphold its full legal tender quality in all payments.

Nevertheless the Currency Act of 1764 was not simply the outcome of a struggle to give legislative sanction to intensely held if contradictory attitudes of British creditors. More important, the Currency Act was also a response to the "hard money" bias of the Board of Trade and to the dynamic economic conditions in the period: the worsening of the terms of trade in Virginia after 1759, a financial crisis in Britain at the end of the French and Indian War, and the resulting sharp rise in sterling exchange rates in the expanding but underdeveloped Virginia economy.[1]

ORIGINS OF VIRGINIA'S PAPER MONEY SYSTEM, 1750–1757

The immediate reason for the creation of Virginia's paper money system was the insolvency of the public treasury and the colony's militant claim to the upper Ohio Valley. Evidence suggests that the treasury was in default as early as 1753, despite a reported balance of some £8,000 in specie. An audit taken in 1754 showed a balance of £4,000, but the treasury that year plainly failed to make good all its debts. It seems that the treasurer and Speaker of the House of Burgesses, John Robinson, had embezzled public funds in order to make private, usurious loans.[2] When therefore the General As-

1. The following chapter is a modified version of an article that originally appeared as "Genesis of the Currency Act of 1764: Virginia Paper Money and the Protection of British Investments," *WMQ*, 3d Ser., XXIII (1965), 33–74. For a contrasting interpretation of the background of the Currency Act of 1764, see Lawrence H. Gipson, "Virginia Planter Debts before the American Revolution," *VMHB*, LXIX (1961), 259–277, and Jack M. Sosin, "Imperial Regulation of Colonial Paper Money, 1764–1773," *Pennsylvania Magazine of History and Biography*, LXXXVIII (1964), 174–186.
2. Oct. 25, 29, 1754, H. R. McIlwaine and John Pendleton Kennedy, eds., *Journals of the House of Burgesses of Virginia, 1619–1776* (Richmond, 1905–1915), *1752–1755, 1756–1758*, 219, 222, hereafter cited as *Jours. of Burgesses*. See also the accusation of "A Freeholder" that the treasury was in default in 1753 despite a specie balance of some £8,000 currency. Purdie and Dixon's *Virginia Gazette* (Williamsburg), Oct. 17, 1766, reprinted in *Jours. of Burgesses, 1766–1769*, xvii. For evidence

sembly in the spring of the same year tried to raise money in support of the claim to the Ohio, it was forced to float a public loan at 6 to 8 percent interest to be repaid through additional tax levies. But money was scarce and subscribers few. The coin current only a few years before had "chiefly vanished" into the trough of a deepening depression.[3]

More basic reasons for issuing paper money in Virginia were the expansion of population, the conversion of a barter economy into a rapidly growing market economy, the changing structure of the imperial economy, and the short-run depression in the tobacco trade after 1752. The first half of the eighteenth century in Virginia was marked by steady economic growth punctuated by financial crisis and the periodic curtailment of tobacco markets. It was also characterized by a kind of direct barter exchange with the metropolis whereby tobacco shipments financed much of the heavy capital outlays for slaves and a wide variety of British imports. In addition to tobacco, relatively small amounts of coin and sterling bills of exchange earned in the sale of provisions and forest products to the West Indies were also remitted home to cover sterling accounts.[4] Likewise, short-term British credit was a significant item in Virginia's balance of payments at the time; inflows of credit not only relieved the external drains on specie but freed some cash for use in local transactions.[5] In this connection an ancillary means of easing pressures for a domestic currency supply was Virginia's system of commodity notes.[6] Tied directly to the production of exportable tobacco, the volume of tobacco notes outstanding bore a close relationship to local economic activity and the need for a means of payment. But towards the end of the period the use of tobacco notes proved increasingly less satisfactory because of the relative increase in the production of market commodities other than tobacco.

tending to support the charge, see Hening, ed., *Statutes of Va.*, VI, 373. See also James Mercer to Daniel P. Custis, May 31, 1754, in Custis Papers, 1683–1759, Box I, folder 1754–1755, Virginia Historical Society, Richmond; account with Robinson, Carter Burwell Account Book, 1738–1755, Colonial Williamsburg Foundation Rerearch Department Library, Williamsburg, Va. I am indebted to Harold Gill for the last reference. Robinson's embezzlement of some £100,000 in paper currency is a familiar story. See David J. Mays, *Edmund Pendleton, 1721–1803: A Biography* (Cambridge, Mass., 1952), I, chap. 2.

3. Hening, ed., *Statutes of Va.*, VI, 417–420; Richard Bland to Thomas Adams, Aug. 1, 1771, "Letters," *WMQ*, 1st Ser., V (1896–1897), 151. Levies were generally made in coin or tobacco, the tobacco to be converted into money through sales.

4. See Hemphill, "Virginia and the English Commercial System."

5. See discussion of this and related issues in chap. 1 above.

6. Scheick, "Commodity Currency in Colonial Virginia."

Around mid-century a further complication in the existing currency system arose as a result of developments in the Atlantic economy. Beginning in the 1750s there was a dramatic jump in Virginia's imports, as the planters began to purchase increasing amounts of those goods that their English heritage taught them to prize as comforts of life. At the same time the Virginians rapidly increased their holdings in land and slaves. The buying spree and agricultural expansion were largely financed by the heavy influx of Scottish and also English credit that became available in the period in response to the marked growth of the metropolitan economy.[7] Therefore the local demand for a circulating medium became far more sensitive to shifts in British financial conditions than ever before. In the event of a financial crisis abroad, and a move by sterling creditors to collect their outstanding American debts, the local demand for money of any kind would rapidly increase as debtors rushed to convert their assets into cash. A call for the creation of a local source of public credit and currency was a normal by-product of such a situation.

In brief, long-run conditions urged the cause of a paper currency along. And if there were lingering doubts about the wisdom of that proposal, the short-run situation soon dispelled them. After nearly five years of prosperity and expansion, Virginia in 1752 had begun to feel the full effects of overproduction of tobacco, rapidly declining prices, and heavy external drains on sterling bills and specie. Tobacco, "the only medium of raising money," was in a slump. British suppliers were withholding credit and demanding remittances. "It is a rare thing to see a dollar," planter George Hume of Culpeper County wrote in the summer of 1754, "and at publick places where great monied men will bet on cock fights, horse races, etc., the noise is not now as it used to be—one pistol to 2 or 3 pistoles to one—it is now common cry 2 cows and calves to one or 3 to one or sometimes 4 hogsheads tobacco to one . . . so I do not know how we shall maintain a war, the French[have]very much the advantage of us."[8] Francis Jerdone, one of Virginia's largest merchants

---

7. See Coulter, "Virginia Merchant," chaps. 4–5.
8. Mercer to Custis, May 31, 1754, Custis Papers, I, 1754–1755. For a survey of economic conditions from 1736 to 1754, see Coulter, "Virginia Merchant," chap. 4. Coulter's work on business cycles has been helpful throughout this chapter. See also Ashton, *Economic Fluctuations in England*, 20–21, 60, 123, 148; Robert Dinwiddie to Col. Joshua Fry, Mar. 18, [1754], R. A. Brock, ed., *The Official Records of Robert Dinwiddie, Lieutenant-Governor of the Colony of Virginia, 1751–1758* . . . (Virginia Historical Society, *Collections*, N.S., III–IV [Richmond, 1883–1884]),

and tobacco buyers, summed up the situation with the remark that these were "ticklish times."[9] The House of Burgesses briefly considered a scheme in August 1754 to issue £20,000 in treasury notes for a period of one year. But so intense was the aversion to paper money among the legislators that no action was taken. A few months later General Edward Braddock arrived on the scene creating expectations of a western victory and a demand for a new source of military funds. "Money, the acknowledged Sinews of War, was necessary, immediately necessary."[10] Unable to float a loan or to draw money from an insolvent treasury, the Burgesses reluctantly revived its paper currency scheme and in May 1755 appropriated for Braddock's use £20,000 of legal tender treasury notes. The defeat of Braddock made necessary an issue of £40,000 more, and had the surviving troops agreed to a counterattack, the house would have voted another £100,000.[11]

I, 110; George Hume to Capt. John Hume, Aug. 22, 1754, "Letters of Hume Family," *WMQ*, 1st Ser., VIII (1899-1900), 89.

9. Jerdone to Samuel Rickards, Dec. 14, 1754, and to Capt. Hugh Crawford, Sept. 12, 1754, "Letter Book of Francis Jerdone," *WMQ*, 1st Ser., XIV (1905-1906), 141-145.

10. Robert Carter Nicholas to Purdie and Dixon's *Va. Gaz.*, Sept. 22, 1773, in "Paper Money in Colonial Virginia," *WMQ*, 1st Ser., XX (1911-1912), 247. See also Jack P. Greene, ed., *The Diary of Colonel Landon Carter of Sabine Hall, 1752-1778* (Charlottesville, Va., 1965), I, 112, 123-124.

11. Hening, ed., *Statutes of Va.*, VI, 461-468. See table 5 in Appendix I and Mays, *Pendleton*, I, 94. Before the issue of treasury notes, the Burgesses first tried raising money by means of a lottery. See Hening, ed., *Statutes of Va.*, VI, 453-461. Before 1755 and the issuance of a paper currency there was of course a Virginia "money of account" expressed in pounds, shillings, and pence. Such "money" had both a value in pounds different from that of sterling and a sterling exchange rate on London. Thus it happened that the various foreign silver coins that circulated freely throughout the province came to have a higher value in "money of account" than they had in sterling. More specifically, foreign coins of all kinds passed "current" at inflated sterling values as settled by local statutes of 1710, 1714, and 1728, and within limits fixed by the Proclamation of 1704 and the parliamentary act of 1708, the last of which defined maximum values at which specie could pass in America as 33⅓% above point exchange between foreign silver and sterling money. Money passing at the maximum rate came to be called "proclamation money." For an excellent discussion of Virginia's monetary system before 1755, see Hemphill, "Virginia and the English Commercial System." For the different methods used to finance the war against the French and Indians, see Richard L. Morton, *Colonial Virginia* (Chapel Hill, N.C., 1960), II, 657, 659, 675-677, 685-686, 694-695, 703-706, 712, 725-727, 728-733, 735-736, 745-749, 789. Taxes to supply redemption funds for this and subsequent currency issues were levied on such items as white and Negro tithables, imported slaves, land, tobacco, wheel carriages, licenses, and writs. For a detailed discussion of redemption taxes, see esp. C.O. 323/19, Public Record Office. (All P.R.O. material cited is from the microfilm

Before the end of 1755 the Burgesses passed a loan office bill for
a £200,000 issue of eight-year notes. The avowed purpose was to
protect the colony against *"the Encroachments and Depredations
of the* French *and* Indians." More important, however, was the need
to relieve the scarcity of money and of agricultural and business
credit and to buttress falling realty values. Tobacco and grain crops
that year were short. So were British loans. In addition British army
paymasters were starting to drain what remained of the small stock
of hard money north to New York by selling Virginians sterling
bills drawn on London at a lower exchange than that offered by
private houses. By the beginning of 1756 there was reportedly less
than " £20,000 Cash in the Whole Country." [12]

Sensing that there would be trouble, Virginia's lieutenant governor, Robert Dinwiddie, refused to take any action on the loan
office measure before dissolving the assembly in November 1755 in
order to consult with the Board of Trade.[13] A leading foe of paper
money, Dinwiddie suggested to the Board that in the future all
colonial civil and military officers be paid in a special coin after the
manner of the French. He admitted that for the present the lack

---

available at the Colonial Williamsburg Foundation Research Department, Williamsburg, Va., with the exception of some transcriptions of the Correspondence of the
Board of Trade cited in n. 102 below.) Although the paper money act specifically
restricted the currency to wartime purposes, Treasurer John Robinson used a part
of the money to pay off disgruntled creditors who had outstanding specie claims
against the colony. See, for example, June 7, 1757, *Jours. of Burgesses, 1752–1755,
1756–1758,* 489.

12. Nov. 8, 1755, *ibid.,* 330–332; Charles Steuart to William Bowden, between
Oct. 15 and Nov. 20, 1755, Letterbooks of Charles Steuart, II, 1754–1763, Historical
Society of Pennsylvania, Philadelphia (microfilm available at Col. Williamsburg
Research Lib.); James Maury to John Fontaine, Aug. 9, 1755, Ann Maury, *Memoirs
of a Huguenot Family* (New York, 1853), 380; Dinwiddie to Halifax, May 24,
1756, in Brock, ed., *Records of Dinwiddie,* II, 418; Coulter, "Virginia Merchant,"
app. 2, n. 15. Late in 1754 the British government sent some £10,000 sterling in
specie to aid General Braddock and to buy presents for the Indians; in the process
it restored a bit of Virginia's dwindling stock of hard money. See Dinwiddie to
B.T., Nov. 16, 1754, Brock, ed., *Records of Dinwiddie,* I, 401, and Dinwiddie to
Loudoun, Dec. 24, 1757, Louis K. Koontz, ed., *Robert Dinwiddie Correspondence
. . .* (Berkeley and Los Angeles, 1951), 1443, which is a microfilm publication. On
the other hand, the amount of the bullion sent to Braddock ever got to Virginia; see the
testimony of James Balfour in B. R. Smith, "The Committee of the Whole House
to Consider the American Papers (January and February 1766)" (M.A. thesis,
University of Sheffield, 1956), 164.

13. Dinwiddie to B.T., Nov. 15, 1755, C.O. 5/1328, P.R.O. That same day the
Council rejected the loan office bill. See Nov. 8, 1755, H. R. McIlwaine, ed., *Legislative Journals of the Council of Colonial Virginia* (Richmond, 1918–1919), III,
1156.

of specie in Virginia made wartime paper currency issues expedient. But he felt that the proposed loan office would only "encourage extravagance and idleness" and in general prove to be pernicious to credit. The Board of Trade agreed and found the Burgesses' attempt at establishing a loan office in "time of danger and distress" to be a just cause of dissolution.[14] The loan office question made brief appearances in 1756 and again the following year; in both cases it failed to get out of committee.[15] In addition, early in 1757 Speaker Robinson, with the support of leading members of the Burgesses, considered the creation of a private bank and loan office— a plan that seems to have gotten nowhere.[16] Not until 1765, when another depression occurred, was there a repetition of the demand for a public or private source of agricultural and business capital. Meanwhile heavy emissions of treasury notes provided Virginia's only circulating medium and helped ease the credit and tax situation.[17]

The legal tender quality of the early currency emissions drew some protests from anxious British merchants.[18] Nevertheless it was an £180,000 treasury issue in April 1757 that set in motion a train of events terminating in the Currency Act of 1764. Acting on a hint from John Campbell, Lord Loudoun, Virginia's titular governor, the Burgesses voted to cut wartime costs by exchanging some £100,000 of interest-bearing treasury notes redeemable in 1761 for a like amount of interest-free notes redeemable in 1765. To sweeten the deal an extra £80,000 was voted for military support. An additional reason for the move was to help smooth out the currency system, since speculators and others were beginning to withdraw the old notes from circulation for the sake of their interest. As a result there

14. Dinwiddie to James Abercromby, Nov. 15, [1755], Dinwiddie to B.T., Feb. 23, 1756, Dinwiddie to Halifax, Feb. 24, 1756, all in Brock, ed., *Records of Dinwiddie*, II, 277–278, 341–342, 346–347; B.T. to Dinwiddie, Feb. 17, 1756, Koontz, ed., *Dinwiddie Correspondence*, 863.

15. Mar. 26, Apr. 6, 20, 24, 1756, Apr. 21, 1757, *Jours. of Burgesses, 1752–1755, 1756–1758*, 339–340, 357, 372, 383, 427, 428.

16. "A Plan for a Bank and Loan Office," [1757], British Colonial Records Project, S. R., Gays House, Holyport, Berkshire, Fairfax of Cameron Manuscripts, George William Fairfax, 1724, 1787, Letters and Documents, I, 1742–1761, item 5 (copy available at Col. Williamsburg Research Lib.).

17. See n. 12 above and chap. 6. See also table 5 in Appendix 1; Steuart to Bowden, between Oct. 15 and Nov. 20, 1755, Steuart Letterbooks.

18. See Abercromby to Dinwiddie, Aug. 9, 1757, Letterbook of James Abercromby, Virginia State Library, Richmond (microfilm available at Col. Williamsburg Research Lib.).

was already a noticeable difference in the value of the various issues. In time this would mean a complete "stagnation of payments."[19]

Reluctant to approve the package, Dinwiddie seized on the fact that the £180,000 was redeemable in seven years instead of five, as the Currency Act of 1751 and previous Virginia law required.[20] A bare majority of the Council, led by Richard Corbin, who served as collection agent for some of the largest British mercantile houses, shared Dinwiddie's concern and added that replacing the old interest-bearing notes with interest-free ones constituted a "Prostitution of the public Faith." The bill failed by a narrow margin. However, its supporters in the House of Burgesses and the Council rallied quickly and replied that the act of 1751 did not affect Virginia. It was no "prostitution" to pay off the interest that had already accrued while eliminating future charges to prevent "avaricious and designing Men, from making private Gain of the public Distress." The house then resurrected the supply bill and managed to get it through the Council when an opposition member found it necessary to step outside for a moment. Despite "great Heat" and Dinwiddie's stated intention of abiding by the spirit of the Currency Act of 1751, the bill was signed into law. The pressure of military demand could not be ignored.[21]

When Dinwiddie reported the measure to the Board of Trade, he said nothing about the legal tender quality of the new money. For that matter he had neglected to mention that earlier paper currency issues were also a full legal tender.[22] Either wartime anxiety or ill health (in September 1756 he reported a paralytic stroke that "reaches my head") may explain Dinwiddie's negligence, although

19. See table 1 in Appendix 1; Hening, ed., *Statutes of Va.*, VII, 69–86; Jerman Baker to Duncan Rose, Feb. 15, 1764, *WMQ*, 1st Ser., XII (1903–1904), 240; Jerdone to Alexander Speirs and Hugh Brown, May 15, 1756, June 25, 1757, Letterbook of Francis Jerdone, College of William and Mary, Williamsburg, Va.; and Apr. 21, 1757, *Jours. of Burgesses, 1752–1755, 1756–1758*, 427.

20. See table 5 in Appendix 1 and Pickering, ed., *Statutes of Great Britain*, XX, 306–309.

21. Dinwiddie to B.T., Sept. 12, 1757, C.O. 5/1339, P.R.O.; May 31, June 3, 1757, McIlwaine, ed., *Leg. Jours. of Va. Council*, III, 1172–1173, 1174; Edmund Jenings to Richard Corbin, Nov. 24, 1757, Feb. 10, 1758, Letterbook of Edmund Jenings, II, III, 1753, Jenings Family Mementoes and Papers, 2 boxes, Va. Hist. Soc., Richmond.

22. The Board learned of the legal tender quality of the first currency issues late in Nov. 1757. See Matthew Lamb's report on 21 acts passed in Virginia in 1755, C.O. 5/1329/48–50, P.R.O. On June 21, 1758, the Board found out that the issue of Apr. 1757 was also legal tender and noted Dinwiddie's failure to communicate that fact. See the marginal notation in the petition of the London merchants, n.d., C.O. 5/1329/45.

as we shall see he had a convenient memory. In any event, in reviewing the legislation the Board of Trade seemed unmindful of any legal tender clause or its implications and approved the latest wartime appropriation on the familiar grounds of necessity.[23]

BRITISH MERCHANT PROTEST, 1757–1760

In November 1757 Virginia's colonial agent, James Abercromby, wrote that a group of English merchants, fearing depreciation of their sterling debts, might ask for repeal of the recent currency measure. A short time later Abercromby reported that he had managed to win over the merchants in talks that winter, a view shared by Francis Fauquier, who was scheduled to replace the ailing Dinwiddie as lieutenant governor.[24] But Abercromby and Fauquier had not counted on the determined opposition of Councillor Corbin. Having lost the fight to block the £180,000 issue in the Council, Corbin worked to have the measure disapproved in England.[25] As a result of his prompting, in June 1758 some merchants of London and Bristol independently petitioned the crown against the act of 1757 and a related Virginia act of 1749 governing the payment of all sterling obligations settled in court.

The gist of the petitions is clear. The merchants complained that under the terms of the 1749 law any executions for sterling debts could be satisfied by a payment in current money; paper as well as coin was acceptable at an advance of 25 percent on sterling, which represented the legal exchange rate between Virginia currency and English money. Since the actual or free exchange rate hovered around 45 percent, the merchants claimed that they would lose

23. Dinwiddie to Abercromby, Sept. 24, 1756, Brock, ed., *Dinwiddie Correspondence*, II, 522.

24. Abercromby to Dinwiddie, Nov. 3, 1757, Abercromby to Corbin, Mar. 5, 1758, Abercromby to John Blair, Mar. 31, 1758, July 6, 1759, and Expense Account, Jan. 1753–Jan. 1758, all in Abercromby Letterbook; Francis Fauquier to B.T., Apr. 10, 1759, C.O. 5/1329, P.R.O.

25. See Corbin to James Buchanan, Apr. 28, 1758, Letterbook of Richard Corbin, 1758–1768, Col. Williamsburg Research Lib.; Edmund Jenings to Corbin, Nov. 24, 1757, Feb. 10, June 27, 1758, Jenings Letterbook. Corbin was probably not the only Virginian to protest against the recent currency emissions. See, for example, Jerdone to Speirs and Brown, June 25, 1757, Jerdone Letterbook. Abercromby was still busy as late as Mar. 31 trying to win the merchants over, but by this time he was less hopeful. Abercromby to Blair, Mar. 31, 1758, Abercromby Letterbook. George Chalmers claimed that the merchants also asked for redress because of the high taxes at home: *An Introduction to the History of the Revolt of the American Colonies*..., II (Boston, 1845), 354.

heavily on remitting any sterling debts settled through court action. The grievance against the act of 1757 was similar in nature: the law was an ex post facto measure affecting all domestic sterling debts, that is, debts payable in Virginia that were contracted before as well as after 1757. Such debts could now be discharged in legal tender paper "of a local, uncertain, and fluctuating value" according to the nominal or mandatory, and not the actual, rate of exchange.

The petitions did not call for repeal. With the laws of 1749 and 1757 already in effect, any such action would produce "great Inconveniencies." Instead the merchants wished "to remove the hardships arising" from both acts and to have sterling debts due before 1757 paid only in "Sterling Money only." Debts contracted since then "between Your Majesty's Subjects in Great Britain and Virginia" were also to be considered sterling obligations payable in like manner, unless otherwise stated. There was no exception. Given the option the merchants might consent to accept paper money in amounts that they deemed necessary for the purchase of sterling bills of exchange to the original and full value of sterling debts.[26]

In short the cautious British merchants demanded absolute protection against any fluctuations in the rate of exchange. Such risks were to be borne by the Virginians alone. The Board of Trade agreed. After brief consultation with colonial agent Abercromby and ex-Lieutenant Governor Dinwiddie during July, it prepared to lay the question before Parliament. But Abercromby somehow succeeded in getting permission for the colony to respond to the merchants' charges before any such drastic action was taken. In the meantime the Board recommended that the Privy Council draw up a royal instruction to meet the petitioners' demands. Six months would pass before the Council acted.[27]

26. Feb. 2, 1759, _Acts of Privy Council, Col._, IV, 392. Two similar memorials were presented, one by the merchants of London on behalf of the merchants of London, Bristol, Liverpool, and Glasgow, and the other by the merchants of Bristol alone: C.O. 5/1329/56–57, P.R.O. See June 21, 1758, _Jour. of Comm. Trade, 1754–1758_, 410. The London merchants' petition appearing Oct. 7, 1758, _Jours. of Burgesses, 1758–1761_, 40–41, as a copy sent by Abercromby, differs slightly from the copy in the Colonial Office Papers. The Burgesses' copy, for example, contains nothing on the subject of a rising exchange rate. Surviving records indicate that the expected memorial from the Liverpool merchants never arrived. See Abercromby to Fauquier, June 23, 1758, Abercromby Letterbook.

27. Abercromby to Fauquier, Feb. 7, 1763, Abercromby Letterbook; July 5, 6, 12, 1758, _Jour. of Comm. Trade, 1754–1758_, 411–413, 414; Feb. 2, 1759, _Acts of Privy Council, Col._, IV, 390–392; Board of Trade to king in Council, July 12, 1758, in C.O. 5/1367, P.R.O. Both the merchants' memorials and the representation of the Board refer to £80,000 actually emitted. See table 5 in Appendix 1.

Many of the same merchants had petitioned as far back as December 1751 against Virginia's currency issues. The grievance at that time was that the act of 1749 made executions for sterling debts payable in current money at the legal exchange rate of 125 while the actual rate fluctuated around 135.[28] Before the year 1749 Virginia law, in harmony with the parliamentary act of 1708 that regulated the maximum value and tender of foreign coin in America, forbade the use of local currency as a lawful tender for debts contracted in Great Britain or expressly made in sterling money and for protested sterling bills of exchange.[29] In practice, however, all sterling debts settled in court were paid in local currency at the legal rate of exchange. Debtors and creditors alike accepted the situation until 1745, when actual exchange rates climbed above the legal rate. Thereafter sheriffs executing court judgments faced debtors' demands for payment at 25 percent advance on sterling debts and creditor demands for settlement at the free market rate of exchange. In 1749, in an effort to resolve the conflict of interest, the General Assembly made current money lawful tender for all sterling executions at the legal rate, assuming that, except in wartime when exchange rates at times exceed 125, sterling creditors would "rarely be sufferers." Everyone, except the merchant-creditors, seemed satisfied with the arrangement.[30]

Before the merchants' petitions arrived at the Board of Trade late in 1751, the king had already confirmed the act of 1749. Consequently, when the petitioners appeared before the Board they were sent to the Privy Council for relief, although the Board did take time to write Dinwiddie suggesting amelioratory action. The following March, therefore, the House of Burgesses actually began work on amending the controversial act. But on learning of the royal confirmation, the house immediately dropped the amendment, claiming it could not repeal a law already approved by the crown. Meanwhile the Privy Council had returned the merchants' case to the Board of Trade, which did not receive it until some two and one-half years later, due to an oversight by the merchants' solicitor. In 1755 Dinwiddie finally received a royal instruction to press

28. C.O. 5/1328/61–64, P.R.O. See also Nov. 19, 1751, *Jour. of Comm. Trade, 1749–1753*, 240.

29. See Hening, ed., *Statutes of Va.*, IV, 218–220.

30. William Gooch to B.T., [Nov. 1749?], C.O. 5/1327, P.R.O.; Hening, ed., *Statutes of Va.*, V, 526–540. The law was to become effective in June 1751. The date of the act is given as Oct. 1748 by Hening, but in fact it was signed into law on May 10, 1749. See *Jours. of Burgesses, 1742–1747, 1748–1749*, 400.

for a law governing exchange without a clause prejudicial to merchant interests.[31] Accordingly, that summer, at the time of Virginia's first paper money issue, the Burgesses amended the act of 1749 to allow courts of record to settle all executions for sterling debts in local currency—paper as well as coin—at a "just" rate of exchange. A just rate was taken to be the actual rate at the time of court judgment, which would guarantee against the merchants ever being out of pocket.[32]

But the merchant-petitioners of 1758 said nothing of the amendment for a number of reasons. Four points were at issue in 1758. First, advisers told the merchants that the act of 1749 was still in force because it had already received royal confirmation. Until the act was repealed, the amendment of 1755 could not take effect; unscrupulous Virginians could still pay sterling debts settled in court at the legal and not the actual exchange rate.[33] Further, though the merchants privately admitted to the Board that in practice most Virginia courts did act to have sterling debts in default paid at prevailing exchange rates, not all courts of record, then or later, strictly enforced the 1755 amendment. Courts that did provide enforcement were the General Court, the court of hustings at Williamsburg, and the York county court, all of which were already popular with merchants because of their swift and just settlements of debt cases. Some county courts, however, under the sway of indebted planters, seem to have settled below the actual rate. Probably such instances were rare, except in times of depression.[34] Third, the amendment of

31. Nov. 26, 1751, Apr. 2, June 26, 27, Aug. 6, 1754, *Jour. of Comm. Trade, 1750–1753,* 233, *1754–1759,* 26, 53–54, 63; Oct. 31, Nov. 26, Dec. 12, 1751, Aug. 6, 1754, *Acts of Privy Council, Col.,* IV, 135, 143–144, 145; Mar. 21, Apr. 11, 1752, *Jours. of Burgesses, 1752–1755, 1756–1758,* 49–84; Labaree, ed., *Royal Instructions,* I, 236.

32. Hening, ed., *Statutes of Va.,* VI, 478–483. On the progress of the bill through the legislature see May 1–July 9, 1755, *Jours. of Burgesses, 1752–1755, 1756–1758,* 232–233, 248, 249, 253, 260, 268, 269, 274, 280, 293; also May 27–28, June 24, 1755, McIlwaine, ed., *Leg. Jours. of Va. Council,* III, 1137–1139, 1140. Fauquier to B.T., Jan. 5, 1759, C.O. 5/1329, P.R.O.

33. Memorial of the London Merchants to B.T., n.d., C.O. 5/1330/129–130. The Board read the memorial Dec. 22, 1762. Corbin to Buchanan, May 29, 1762, Corbin Letterbook.

34. Feb. 2, 1759, *Acts of Privy Council, Col.,* IV, 390; Corbin to Robert Cary, Aug. 22, 1762, Corbin Letterbook; Jerdone to Alexander MacKintosh, June 25, 1757, and to Capt. Archibald Crawford, Sept. 10, 1762, both in Jerdone Letterbook. In the Crawford letter Jerdone remarked, "At last King Williams Court [judges] in their great wisdom thought fit to settle the Exchange at 52-½ per cent, whereas I am informed the present current exchange is 60 per cent." See also Soltow, *Economic Role of Williamsburg,* 104–105.

1755 did not protect holders of protested sterling bills against fluctuations in rates of exchange. Under the Virginia act of 1749, as noted earlier, protested sterling bills were payable in currency at 25 percent advance on sterling, a provision that drew a petition from the British merchants when the actual rate of exchange rose above 125. The amendment of 1755 changed the law governing sterling bills to read: after October 1, 1756, "it shall be mentioned and expressed in such bills, the sum in current money that was paid or allowed for the same." If the bill was protested, the stated sum, plus 10 percent damages, was collectable in currency. In other words the actual market exchange rate that prevailed when the bill was drawn established the rate that governed the payment of the bill when it was protested. Between the time a bill was drawn and was presented for payment after being protested, exchange rates could, and at times did, rise even higher. The consequence in such cases, as Richard Corbin once pointed out to Dinwiddie, was that the holder of protested bills "even with the ten percent for Damages [could] not purchase bills of equal Value."[35] Finally, the amendment of 1755 did not legally regulate the payment of domestic sterling debts, that is, debts payable in Virginia. By law such debts could be paid in paper as if they were current money obligations. In practice they were generally paid at the actual rate of exchange between paper and sterling.[36]

Whatever their grievances, the British merchants wanted what both the amendment of 1755 and Virginia's currency laws denied them—the right to take paper money on their own terms or to leave it. In their quest they were more interested in securing the certain protection of English sterling than in relying upon what they considered to be the uncertain operation of a legal tender system and the Virginia law courts.

The Board of Trade also knew of the 1755 amendment to the act of 1749. A copy arrived in October 1755 and without a reading was sent to the attorney general's office for study, where it lay gathering dust for three years.[37] Everyone who handled the amendment was

35. Hening, ed., *Statutes of Va.*, VI, 478–483; Jerdone to MacKintosh, June 25, 1757, Jerdone Letterbook; Corbin to Dinwiddie, Apr. 20, 1758, Corbin Letterbook.
36. See, for example, Jerdone to Speirs and Brown, Oct. 29, 1758, and Jerdone to Francis Willis, Jr., and Col. Samuel Buckner, Feb. 2, 1759, both in Jerdone Letterbook. See also, however, Pleadings to the Right Honorable Earl of Dunmore, *Lionel Lyde* v. *Munroe's Administrators*, U.S. Circuit Court, Virginia District (1797)—Ended Cases, Restored, Va. State Lib.
37. Oct. 29, 1755, *Jour. of Comm. Trade, 1754–1758*, 181; Abercromby's comments on a letter from Blair to Dinwiddie, May 29, 1759, C.O. 5/1329/168, P.R.O.

guilty of neglect or irresponsibility. The Burgesses had overlooked that the amendment's title only hinted at its importance; Dinwiddie after signing the act failed to press the colonial agent to urge its approval; Abercromby, skimming only the first few paragraphs of the measure, did not see its significance; and Dinwiddie, in testimony before the Board in the summer of 1758, apparently forgot the act even existed.[38]

In January 1759, as a matter of routine, the Board of Trade took up all Virginia laws passed in 1755, including the amendment. At almost the same moment the Board drafted a set of additional instructions based on its earlier recommendations to the Privy Council. These instructions, as has been noted, were designed to meet the merchants' demands for changes in the very acts covered by the amendment of 1755; namely the statute of 1749 governing executions for sterling debts and the statute of 1757 issuing £180,000 of legal tender currency. The instructions directed the legislature to amend the acts of 1749 and 1757 so that all debts "contracted in sterling money" that became due before the commencement of the laws in question would be payable in sterling money. On the other hand debts since contracted between British subjects and any Virginian would be payable in bills of credit—providing the creditor would be willing to receive them and then, not according to the nominal value of such money, but according to "the real difference of exchange between such paper bills and sterling money at the time of discharging such debts." A copy went off to Virginia on February 9.[39]

One day earlier, on February 8, the Board, which had shelved the amendment three years before, retrieved and read it. After brief consultation with former Lieutenant Governor Dinwiddie, the Board turned the amendment over to the London merchants for an opinion as to "how far the evil complained of from the paper money acts is thereby removed." But the question so divided the merchants that after two months of study they found "their way of reasoning . . . by no means unanimous" and could make no reply. Another three

---

38. Dinwiddie to Abercromby, Sept. 6, 1755, Brock, ed., *Dinwiddie Correspondence*, II, 197–198; July 5, 1758, *Jour. of Comm. Trade, 1754–1758*, 411–412; Abercromby's comments in C.O. 5/1329/168, P.R.O.; Abercromby to Dinwiddie, Nov. 3, 1757, Abercromby Letterbook.
39. Jan. 24, Feb. 8, 1759, *Jour. of Comm. Trade, 1759–1763*, 9–10, 14; Labaree, ed., *Royal Instructions*, I, 237–238.

years would elapse before the amendment would come again before the Board.[40]

No precise reason for the division among the merchants appears in the record. Certainly the merchants did not have the option of taking either paper or coin in the payment of sterling obligations. The security that they believed only gold and silver provided continued to elude them. But as Fauquier later noted, they "set down quiet under the present laws of the Colony by which their Sterling Debts are actually secured to them." And it is reasonable to argue that they also "set down quiet" early in 1759 because Virginia had just begun to emerge from the bottom of a depression. After years of retrenchment and debt liquidation, storekeepers in Virginia and their British suppliers were anxious to let the good times roll.[41] It is no coincidence that the "quiet" would end after another decline in economic fortunes in Virginia and Britain.

Virginia's General Assembly rejected, in spirit at least, the Board's additional instructions of February 1759, almost a year before they arrived. On October 7, 1758, Fauquier, who had arrived in the colony a few months earlier, received a copy of the London merchants' petition of the summer. All in all Fauquier was more concerned for the moment with getting a new currency supply bill through the Burgesses in the face of growing anxiety over the heavy burden of wartime taxes. In fact, in that connection he had already decided to ignore recent instructions from the Board of Trade to separate the offices of Speaker of the House of Burgesses and public treasurer held by political boss John Robinson because of Robinson's promise to support the supply bill; and on October 7 that measure was still three days away from a final vote. Without comment Fauquier passed the petition along to the Burgesses, which tabled it. A few days later the house passed the currency bill and then adjourned.[42] In the Council, however, there was an amendment to the new bill to the effect that all sterling debts were to be "excepted in the same Manner as the King's Quitrents" from payment in local currency. The amendment failed, and Fauquier later re-

40. Abercromby to Blair, May 30, 1759, Abercromby Letterbook; Jan. 24, 31, Feb. 8, 13, 21, 27, May 23, 1759, *Jour. of Comm. Trade, 1759–1763*, 9–10, 14–15, 20, 39.
41. Fauquier to B.T., Apr. 10, 1759, Nov. 3, 1762, C.O. 5/1329, 5/1330, P.R.O.
42. Fauquier to B.T., June 28, Sept. 23, 1758, Apr. 10, 1759, *ibid.*; Oct. 7, 10, 1758, *Jours. of Burgesses, 1758–1761*, 41, 43, 45; Abercromby to Fauquier, June 23, 1758, Abercromby Letterbook.

ported that the merchants' memorial carried no weight with a majority of either house.[43]

On reconvening, the Burgesses continued to ignore the petition. But on November 11, the last day of the session, the document received indirect recognition when the Council, led by John Blair and William Nelson, with an assist from the local merchants and with Burgesses support, drafted a public letter censuring Abercromby for his generally inadequate defense of Virginia currency practices and his particular failure to report the amendment of 1755 to the Board of Trade.[44] The reprimand and a detailed explanation of how the amendment protected British creditors arrived in London in May 1759, three months after the dispatch of the additional instructions. Also included was a letter from Fauquier covering the same ground.[45]

Before the Board's additional instructions reached Virginia in July 1759, the General Assembly voted two more currency issues in response to wartime demands and the general lack of coin. "If all the Specie . . . were to be brought together and thrown in one Heap, it would not amount to £100 Sterling so much is the Colony drained at present by Money sent to New York," Fauquier wrote in January of the following year. In subsequent letters he explained to the Board of Trade that his continued reliance on Robinson was necessary to push new currency supply bills through a house "which seems to groan under the expense they have been at," and he reported the conviction of "both the Legislative Bodies here" that the merchants were protected as well as could be from suffering any damage. Nevertheless, after receiving the instructions, Fauquier held out hope that the Burgesses would comply. The "chief people here," he thought, would pass a bill in whatever manner desired, "it being their Intentions that all Sterling Debts . . . should be fully satisfied and paid." If, however, the "Merchants had paid due Attention to their present Situation," they would know their sterling debts were already secure. But judging by a recent letter from a British mercantile house, the lieutenant governor could only con-

43. Fauquier to B.T., Oct. 21, 1758, Apr. 10, 1759, C.O. 5/1329, P.R.O.
44. Fauquier to B.T., Jan. 5, 1759, *ibid.*; Abercromby to Blair, May 19, 30, 1759, Abercromby Letterbook. As acting governor of Virginia from Jan. 12 to June 5, 1758, Blair was responsible for the issue of some £32,000 currency in support of the war. See table 5 in Appendix 1; Blair to B.T., June 20, 1758, C.O. 5/1329, P.R.O.; and Abercromby to Blair, Mar. 31, 1758, Abercromby Letterbook.
45. Abercromby to Blair, May 30, 1759, Abercromby Letterbook; May 23, 1759, *Jour. of Comm. Trade, 1759–1763,* 39; Fauquier to B.T., Jan. 5, 1759, C.O. 5/1329, P.R.O.

clude that the merchants were ignorant of the laws then in force.[46] On receiving the Board's instructions, Fauquier's first move was to consult with his Council. The councillors suggested that the instructions had been complied with but that the legislature should be informed of them when it met next.[47] That November during a special session called to aid North and South Carolina in their renewed war against the Cherokee, the Burgesses received the unwelcome news. Despite Fauquier's hopes of compliance, the house promptly resolved that the amendment of 1755 secured British property in *"the fullest and amplest Manner"* and then, with great reluctance, appropriated an additional £10,000 currency to field a regiment against the Indians. Nevertheless a concession was made to merchant fears. If it proved possible, in lieu of a new currency issue, the treasury was to take the appropriation out of Virginia's parliamentary grant. As it turned out, however, the grant arrived too late to put a stop to the printing presses.[48]

In the Council the new appropriation met with a protest from Philip Ludwell and Philip Ludwell Lee. They found it insufficient for the protection of the Virginia frontier and in violation of the instructions forbidding paper to be a legal tender for sterling debts. The two men also deprecated the lack of any provision for the immediate destruction of the new notes after their return to the treasury.[49] With an eye to military conditions, a majority of the Council approved the paper money issue despite the Board's instructions. Fauquier, too, seemed more concerned with meeting wartime requirements than with following the instructions; he signed the bill into law and warned the Board of Trade that the currency question had stirred the Burgesses to the point where it might mean the loss of the regiment when the present appropriation ran out the next spring. Only on the question of the need for the prompt destruction of paper money did Ludwell and Lee receive support. The Council quickly introduced a suitable bill for that purpose and called upon the lower house for approval.[50]

The Council's new measure raised a complex problem. Virginia's

46. See table 5 in Appendix 1; Fauquier to B.T., Jan. 5, Apr. 10, June 9, July 14, Oct. 13, 1759, C.O. 5/1329, P.R.O.; and Dinwiddie to B.T., Dec. 1759, *ibid.*

47. Sept. 3, 1759, Benjamin Hillman, ed., *Executive Journals of the Council of Colonial Virginia*, VI (Richmond, Va., 1966), 145–146.

48. Hening, ed., *Statutes of Va.*, VII, 331–337. See table 5 in Appendix 1 and Nov. 1, 8, 1759, *Jours. of Burgesses, 1758–1761*, 134–141.

49. Nov. 19, 1759, in McIlwaine, ed., *Leg. Jours. of Va. Council*, III, 1227.

50. Nov. 19–20, 1759, *ibid.*, 1227–1228; Fauquier to B.T., Dec. 17, 1759, C.O. 5/1329, P.R.O.

paper money was issued in anticipation of taxes, and at first any one tax was to be paid with the notes of a specified issue. Right from the start, however, Treasurer Robinson took in any and all paper that was tendered. Either he could burn the various notes paid in on taxes and credit them to the redemption of a designated currency emission or he could place them in a sinking fund to be destroyed all at once on the day of redemption. But when in 1757 the assembly emitted some £180,000 redeemable in March 1765, with the stipulation that all paper notes were now acceptable for all taxes, a potentially serious problem arose. By 1765 paper issued after 1757 would clearly come into the treasurer's hands for the taxes laid against the £180,000 emission; consequently many of the 1757 notes due to be redeemed would still be circulating. One obvious remedy was to have enough money in the treasury in 1765 bearing later redemption dates to replace the notes due to be retired by that time. Thus the legislature passed a law prohibiting the destruction before March 1765 of any treasury notes issued after 1757.[51] In effect what the new Council bill offered was another solution to the problem and a way to burn all the various notes paid into the treasury. While designed to protect currency values and to prevent retired paper from circulating through loss or fraud, the measure got nowhere. The Burgesses had already repudiated the Board's additional instructions, and it lost no time in rejecting the Council plan as an infringement of the control of the purse by the popular house.[52]

Just after the adjourning of the legislature in December 1759, a committee of correspondence, created by and responsible to the General Assembly, wrote a lengthy defense of both Virginia's currency practices and of the assembly's rejection of the Board's instructions. The defense focused on the origin and meaning of the act of 1749 and the amendment of 1755. The points stressed were two: that the courts settled judgments for sterling debts paid in paper at the "very highest" free market exchange rates and that the legal tender provision allowed Virginians, who had no coin and had taken paper in good faith, to discharge their debts with the money at hand.

In the agent's instructions accompanying the defense, the committee went further and argued that sterling debts were safer under Virginia laws than if "nothing but sterling or lawful Money of Great

51. Hening, ed., *Statutes of Va.*, VII, 69–87. See, for example, Apr. 29, 1756, Apr. 4, 1759, *Jours. of Burgesses, 1752–1755, 1756–1758*, 388, *1758–1761*, 116.
52. Nov. 20, 1759, *Jours. of Burgesses, 1758–1761*, 151.

Britain were held a Tender." A creditor paid £1000 sterling still had to buy a bill of exchange. And if bills sold over par, as they did by 10 percent in December 1759, a creditor suffered a £10 loss. Under the amendment of 1755, on the other hand, the creditor who was owed a £100 sterling debt when the rate of exchange was 135 "hath his whole £135 decreed to him, with which a Bill is bought and the full Debt remitted." Moreover exchange was 10 percent lower "than it was last War" when nothing but gold and silver coin was current, "a Circumstance very favourable to the Credit of our paper." In his concluding remarks the committee chairman and guiding hand in drafting the letter, William Nelson, added an angry censure at James Abercromby, the colonial agent for the governor and Council. "If our notable Agent at the other End of the town had known and stated these things to the Merchants," Nelson declared, "they would hardly have thought it necessary to present any Memorial about it."[53] At this point Abercromby was relieved of all responsibility in any future negotiations over fiat money. The agent's handling of the paper money and "Pistol fee" questions had so antagonized the Burgesses that it refused either to recognize or to pay him. Anxious to have cooperation, especially on matters affecting currency and military aids, Fauquier proved willing to settle the matter and signed into law a bill providing for a second colonial agent who would better represent the interests of the lower house.[54]

Abercromby was to have the last word, however. About "Mr. Nelson's Belief," he later wrote to his confidant Richard Corbin, "No Man ever took more Pains to bring the Merchants to adopt [it] than I did." But he explained: "I cannot alter the nature of things, find laws where they are not, thereby turn paper into gold and silver, nor can I make others be convinced of the possibility of so doing.

53. Committee of Correspondence to Edward Montague, Dec. 12, 1759, in "Proceedings of the Virginia Committee of Correspondence, 1759–1767," *VMHB*, X (1902–1903), 345–347; "Instructions to the Agent in Defence of the paper Currency," in "Proc. of Va. Comm. of Corres., 1759–1767," *ibid.*, XI (1903–1904), 1–5; Abercromby's comments, C.O. 5/1329/168, P.R.O.

54. See Abercromby to Blair, July 6, 1759, Abercromby Letterbook; Corbin to Abercromby, Apr. 26, 1758, Corbin Letterbook; Corbin to Abercromby, Mar. 22, 1759, in C.O. 5/1329, P.R.O.; Abercromby's comments, *ibid.*, fol. 168; Fauquier to B.T., Oct. 21, 1758, *ibid.*; Fauquier to B.T., Sept. 1, 1760, *Jours. of Burgesses, 1758–1761*, 288. See also Jack P. Greene, *The Quest for Power: The Lower Houses of Assembly in the Southern Royal Colonies, 1689–1776* (Chapel Hill, N.C., 1963), 280–284. Greene ignores the close connection between the agency and currency questions.

... My friend, Mr. Dinwiddie's arguments have no better success. What we cannot do then by conviction, may be done by persuasion to acquiesce under the necessary expedient of paper money at least while the war continues."[55]

Concerning the new agent, Edward Montague, he could not be found before the end of January 1761 even to receive the committee's instructions or his credentials. Nonetheless, as Abercromby had expected, the British government did approve future currency issues on grounds of wartime necessity. As for the merchant-creditors, they also "set down quiet." In the first place the London merchants were divided in their opinion concerning the amendment of 1755. More important, the brief return of prosperity to Virginia had soothed the pocketbook nerves of everyone concerned.

THE "QUIET YEARS," 1760–1761

Freed from all but military demands, the Board of Trade eased up on its objections to Virginia's currency practices and approved two further wartime issues, which were voted in the spring of 1760 and amounted to some £52,000 currency.[56] The second of these, an appropriation of £32,000, did cause some trouble, but it was strictly a domestic affair. The appropriation passed "but by a single voice," a slim margin that had nothing to do with the growing burden of wartime taxes. At issue was the contest "between the old Settlers who have bred great quantity of Slaves, and would make a Monopoly of them by a duty which they hoped would amount to a prohibition; and the rising Generation who wants Slaves, and don't care to pay the Monopolists for them at the price they have lately bore, which was exceedingly high." Such reasons, according to Fauquier, were "not urged in the arguments on either side," but were the "true foundation of the Squabble." The "rising Generation" had successfully tacked onto the supply bill a rider that cut in half the existing prohibitive 20 percent duty on slaves and then had "jockeyed" the measure through the House of Burgesses. Although the lieutenant governor feared a "Battle in the next Session," the slavery and currency questions never again interfered with each other.[57]

55. Jan. 1, 1760, Abercromby Letterbook.
56. See table 5 in Appendix 1.
57. Abercromby to Fauquier, Mar. 9, 1761, Abercromby Letterbook; Fauquier to B.T., Dec. 17, 1759, Nov. 3, 1762, C.O. 5/1329, 5/1330, P.R.O. For the full story

During the quiet years the Burgesses, too, seemed to be in a conciliatory mood and took steps to support the credit of paper money. In March 1759 it set up a committee to examine semiannually all notes coming into the treasurer's hands and to burn those redeemable on or before March 1765, a move vigorously opposed by Robinson and his friends as a reflection on the treasurer's character. The man behind this move appears to have been Richard Henry Lee. Lee became a burgess in 1758 and immediately began to oppose Robinson on the question of his holding down the office of both Speaker and provincial treasurer. Lee's opposition may well have grown out of rumors of Robinson's laxity in treasury affairs; but at least as important was an old feud between Robinson, supported by the James River planters, and Lee's father, Thomas Lee, backed by the Northern Neck interests, over control of the Speakership and of western lands. In any event Lee was clearly responsible for a decision made by the House of Burgesses late in 1761 to burn *all* paper money paid in for taxes, a move that made an even greater "Bussle and was a Bone of great Contention in both branches of the Legislature."[58] In addition the Lee measure extended the life of all circulating paper to 1769 as a means of getting around the problem connected with the former practice of staggering redemption dates and with the need to have enough money on hand in the treasury to retire some £210,000 by 1765.

Fauquier signed the controversial bill into law in December 1761, but because it contained a clause suspending its operation until reviewed by the king, it did not take immediate effect. It was not until the spring of 1762 that the act reached the Board of Trade, where it lay unread until early the following year. The timing was bad for Virginia; the Board had just acted on another merchants' complaint against Virginia's currency practices by making a strong representation in favor of the petitioners. Nevertheless Montague, who was

---

of the connection between the currency and slave questions, see Fauquier to B.T., June 2, 1760, Sept. 15, 1761, *Jours. of Burgesses, 1758–1761*, 284–285, 296–297. See also Hening, ed., *Statutes of Va.*, VI, 217–221, 353–354, 419, 466, 468, VII, 81, 237–239, 281, 282–283, 338–340, 363, 383, 640, VIII, 190–191, 336–338, 343–344, 530–532.

58. Hening, ed., *Statutes of Va.*, VII, 353, 465–466; "A Freeholder," Oct. 17, 1766, and Nicholas to the Printer, Purdie and Dixon's *Va. Gaz.*, Sept. 5, 1766. Alexander White to Lee, n.d., David Boyd to Lee, Nov. 17, 1766, "Speech of Richard Henry Lee in Committee of Whole House," May [24], 1763, all in "Selections and Excerpts from the Lee Papers," *Southern Literary Messenger*, XXVII (1858), 117–118, XXX (1860), 133–135. See also Oct. 18, 25, 29, 1754, Mar. 6, 1760, *Jours. of Burgesses, 1752–1755, 1756–1758*, 211, 219, 222, *1758–1761*, 160; Fauquier to B.T., Feb. 24, 1762, C.O. 5/1330, P.R.O. See also n. 3 above.

present at the Board hearings, argued forcefully for the Lee measure. But without bothering to understand the problem involved or the solution intended, the Board permanently shelved the act on grounds established back in the 1720s: namely, that the failure to redeem currency on time and its extension to longer periods was a major cause of depreciation.[59]

Now at war with Spain, Britain by 1762 was busy requisitioning troops in Virginia and elsewhere. Fauquier had barely managed to keep a regiment in the field against the Indians the previous year, and he was not optimistic about the future. However, on the advice of his Council and Virginia's absentee governor, Sir Jeffrey Amherst, he called the legislature into special session in March.[60] By a surprisingly large and favorable vote of sixty-six to three the Burgesses issued an immediate call for a thousand soldiers and £30,000 of legal tender to support them. Those members of the Council who were present in Williamsburg at the time divided on the bill, and Fauquier, fearful of losing the measure if it were brought to a vote, had Speaker Robinson—an old supporter by now—hold the bill in the house until some known supporters of paper money could be brought into town. Even then, and despite pressure from Fauquier, the measure squeaked through the Council by only a five-to-four vote.[61] The minority voices of William and Thomas Nelson, Richard Corbin, and Philip Ludwell Lee considered the act a poor excuse to issue more treasury notes. "To check the growth of those bitter herbs," they publicly protested the excess of currency already in circulation, the deficiency of taxes to redeem the projected issue, the disregard of the Board's additional instructions, and the failure of Virginia law to protect British creditors.[62] Of crucial importance was the fact that the former leader in the fight for paper currency, William Nelson, was now numbered among the opponents.

At first Fauquier claimed the hostility to paper was a pose; the councillors who opposed the bill, he believed, really objected to the cost of the militia. A few months later he came up with another ex-

59. Feb. 4, 1763, *Jour. of Comm. Trade, 1759–1763*, 333–334.
60. Mar. 11, 1762, Hillman, ed., *Exec. Jours. of Va. Council*, 208; Mar. 30, 1762, *Jours. of Burgesses, 1761–1765*, 47–58; Fauquier to Jeffrey Amherst, Mar. 12, 1762, Amherst Papers, 1760–1763, W.O. 34/37, Public Record Office; Fauquier to earl of Egremont, Apr. 8, 1762, C.O. 5/1345, P.R.O.
61. See table 5 in Appendix 1. In addition see Fauquier to B.T., Apr. 8, 1762, C.O. 5/1330, P.R.O; Apr. 3, 1762, Hillman, ed., *Exec. Jours. of Va. Council*, 211–212; Mar. 31, Apr. 6, 1762, McIlwaine, ed., *Leg. Jours. of Va. Council*, III, 1278, 1280–1281.
62. Apr. 6, 1762, *ibid.*, 1281.

planation. He wrote to Amherst that "some gentlemen in the House of Burgesses who have always been zealous promoters of all supply bills may be deterred from persevering by some insinuations which have been thrown out as if they were gainers by emissions of paper money." Fauquier hinted darkly that there was an "intrigue in relation to the emission of more paper money." By the end of the year he had come around to the true reason for the growing opposition: a sharply rising rate of exchange. He notified the commissioners of trade that several local merchants had already sent them a secret petition against future issues of paper. Many more were privately making the same complaints in letters to their British suppliers. Here was the reason for William Nelson's shift on the currency question.[63] The quiet years were over.

THE DEBATE OVER RISING EXCHANGE RATES, 1762

As Fauquier admitted late in 1762, the troop question hinged on the supposed relation between currency and rising exchange rates. In fact, although the volume of Virginia paper currency was certainly one of several factors operating in the exchange market at the time, the sharp upward trend in the rate of exchange had less to do with the amount of paper outstanding than with other matters.

Available statistics suggest that before the mid-eighteenth century the tobacco colonies enjoyed a substantially favorable trade balance with the mother country. But in the late 1740s the value of total exports began to level off while the value of imports dramatically increased in response to the expansion of British credit in the period. Thus, writing in 1766, John Wayles, Thomas Jefferson's father-in-law and the agent and chief debt collector for Farrell and Jones, the tobacco merchants of Bristol, noted that "within these 25 years £1000 due to a Merchant was looked upon as a Sum imense and never to be got over. Ten times that sum is now spoke of with Indifference and thought no great burthen on some Estates. Indeed in that Series of time Property is become more Valuable and many Estates have increased more than tenfold. But then Luxury and expensive living have gone hand in hand with the increase of wealth. . . . All this is in great measure owing to the Credit which

63. Fauquier to B.T., Apr. 8, July 10, Nov. 3, 1762, C.O. 5/1330, P.R.O.; Fauquier to Amherst, Sept. 25, 1762, W.O. 34/37, P.R.O.; Letters of John Syme to Farrell and Jones, May 10, 21, 1763, in *Jones' Exor.* v. *John Syme,* U.S. Circuit Court, Va. District (1797)—Ended Cases, Restored; Abercromby to Fauquier, Nov. 10, 1762, Abercromby Letterbook.

the Planters have had from England and which has enabled them
to Improve their Estates to the pitch they are Arrivd at, tho many
are ignorant of the true Cause."[64] As noted earlier, such credit became available in the normal course of business. By running in arrears
as much as their British correspondents, who supplied them with
goods from Europe, would allow, the colonists effectively obtained
for their own use a revolving and growing fund of British capital
that freed much of the cash earned in Virginia's export trade for
the purchase of land and slaves. In consequence, when trade with the
mother country turned unfavorable, as it did near the end of the
Seven Years' War at a time when Virginia's overall trade balance
also seems to have taken a turn for the worse, the availability of
that revolving fund of British credit became the key to the movement of sterling exchange rates. In effect, as credit expanded exchange rates fell to par or under. As it contracted and British suppliers repatriated their investment, the rates rose above par.[65]

Sharply rising exchange rates in 1762 reflected not only a worsening financial crisis and poor tobacco markets in Britain, but a dearth
of specie in Virginia. Toward the end of 1761 tobacco houses in
England and Scotland, finding their own credit sources drying up,
started cutting back on short-term loans to Virginia, which ordinarily took the form of sterling bills. But credit got progressively

64. The trade statistics are taken from *Historical Statistics of the United States,*
757, 221–234. On the expansion of credit see Coulter, "Virginia Merchant." The
quote is from Hemphill, ed., "John Wayles," *VMHB,* LXVI (1958), 305.

65. On the trade balance with the mother country see United States Bureau of
the Census, *Historical Statistics of the United States, Colonial Times to 1957* (Washington, D.C., 1960), 757, 221–234. On the broader question of Virginia's overall
trade balance, almost nothing is known. The generalizations here are based largely
on a careful reading of Sachs, "Business Enterprise" and Coulter, "Virginia Merchant." For another view of exchange rate fluctuations, see Emory G. Evans,
"Planter Indebtedness and the Coming Revolution in Virginia," *WMQ,* 3d Ser.,
XIX (1962), 511–533. Evans rejects Gipson's assumption, in "Virginia Planter
Debts," *VMHB,* LXIX (1961), 259–277, that increased emissions of paper money
drove up the rates of sterling exchange and that the emissions were a "cheap money"
device employed by American debtors to write off a part of their indebtedness to
British creditors. He explains a rising exchange by saying that the gentry through
extravagant purchases of British goods brought about an imbalance of trade and
a hike in the rate of sterling exchange. My discussion of short-run fluctuations is
based upon merchant letterbooks; Coulter, "Virginia Merchant"; Henry Hamilton,
An Economic History of Scotland in the Eighteenth Century (Oxford, 1963),
308–311; and an exchange of ideas with Marc Egnal, John Hemphill, and Jacob
M. Price. For the aggravating effect of widespread counterfeiting of Virginia's
paper currency that began about this time, see Nellie Norkus, "Francis Fauquier,
Lieutenant Governor of Virginia, 1758–1768: A Study in Colonial Problems" (Ph.D.
diss., University of Pittsburgh, 1954), 265.

tighter, and in their anxiety to remain solvent the British merchants began also to dun the Virginians for past debts. Meanwhile the low price for tobacco in Britain and the prospects for peace (which was expected to lower prices even further) prompted a temporary abatement of tobacco imports. In sum the overall effect was to reduce the amount of sterling exchange available in Virginia at a time when the possibility of remitting tobacco was greatly impaired.

Nor was it possible to substitute coin as a means of easing the pressure on sterling rates. An adequate supply of hard money was simply not available for the purpose, while the abrupt rise in exchange rates quickly led to speculation in exchange among those who did have the hard cash to spare. In the latter case either there were illegal advances in the price of coin or coin was shipped out of the province for the purchase of sterling bills elsewhere. In short the makeweight of balance, the metallic standard, that had previously kept exchange rates hovering around par had broken down. Paper money was left to do the job as best it could. It was only a matter of time before the joint pressure of the heavy demand for sterling bills and their short supply rapidly drove the rate of exchange "beyond all bounds."[66]

At this point the local merchants and the resident Scottish factors became acutely aware of the critical difference between their sterling debts and their other accounts outstanding. Their sterling debts were payable in sterling bills of exchange: other indebtedness, in the form either of an open line of store credit or of small currency loans, was payable in paper. As has been shown the amendment of 1755 did offer some protection to the sterling creditor from the vagaries of exchange. Nothing protected local merchants collecting book debts and currency loans. They lost money whenever exchange rates rose beyond expectations between the time a debt was entered and the time it was paid. Thus a trader who allowed for an exchange rate of around 140 when setting his retail prices on imported goods payable in sterling lost heavily on sterling remittances when exchange jumped to 160, as it did late in 1762. In that year William Allason, merchant of Falmouth, Virginia, declared he and others had been "amazingly infatuated for some years past by giving too extensive Credits to our Customers in consequences of the Credit we ourselves had with our friends at home . . . and now in

66. William Allason to Capt. Robert Douglas, n.d., but preceding a letter of Aug. 9, 1762, Letterbook of William Allason, 1757–1770, Va. State Lib., Richmond (microfilm available at Col. Williamsburg Research Lib.).

Order to Assist our friends which we before neglected are obliged to remit at a very high Exchange Such as no trade can afford."[67]

Virginia traders generally understood the combined effects on the exchange rate of the collapse of credit, the reduced exports of low-priced tobacco, and the heavy imports of British goods. But many blamed the frequent and large emissions of paper money as well. They also knew that, in the absence of coin, paper currency provided the only medium of local payment, and they thus wished only to restrict the quantity of outstanding paper in hopes of lowering exchange rates. Charles Steuart, merchant of Norfolk, wrote: "I hope as the quantity of our paper money will be considerably lessened soon and no more emitted, that our exchange will fall considerably soon and in a few months return to nearly its usual course." It was for just such reasons, according to Fauquier, that at the close of 1762 local merchants helped persuade the Burgesses to reject another currency supply bill. By that time they had already turned to the Board of Trade and their British suppliers for help. In the summer of 1762 Fauquier had reported to the Board that several merchants had petitioned against "future emissions of paper money"; but he added with a note of pique, "I am ignorant of [the] content." Several months later Fauquier warned that the Board would soon hear from the merchants of London who were "acted upon by gentlemen of this country."[68]

Council member Richard Corbin, who began inveighing against paper money back in 1755, added his voice to the chorus of complaints in July 1762. At the end of the month, after taking oaths as deputy receiver general of Virginia and collector of the king's quitrents, Corbin immediately took measures to increase the profits of his office. The quitrent fee of two shillings per hundred acres payable in sterling had in the absence of specie come to be levied in paper at the legal exchange rate of 125. With the actual rate edging 160, Corbin faced the same losses on his sterling remittances as

67. Allason to James Dunlop, Sept. 12, 1762, Feb. 24, 1763, Allason Letterbook. An abrupt rise in exchange generally led to speculation in exchange and illegal advances in the price of coin. See, for example, Jerdone to Speirs and Brown, Apr. 28, 1759, Jerdone Letterbook; Allason to his brother, Feb. 24, 1763, Allason Letterbook; and Burnaby, *Travels*, 29.

68. Allason to Capt. Robert Douglas, Aug. 9, 1762, to Dunlop, Feb. 24, 1763, Allason Letterbook; Steuart to Scott and Pringle, Nov. 5, 1762, Steuart Letterbook; Jerman Baker to Duncan Rose, Feb. 15, 1764, *WMQ*, 1st Ser., XII (1903–1904), 241; Fauquier to B.T., July 10, Nov. 3, 1762, Jan. 10, 1763, C.O. 5/1330, P.R.O.; B.T. to Fauquier, Mar. 11, 1763, C.O. 5/1368, P.R.O.; Abercromby to Fauquier, Nov. 10, 1762, Abercromby Letterbook.

the local merchants did. At first he appealed to the Virginia Council to have the quitrents made payable in paper at the market exchange rate. The Council proved sympathetic and willingly stated for the record that quitrents should be paid at the actual rate of exchange. Nonetheless Corbin was referred to the Lords of the Treasury in London for official action.

In his petition to the Treasury Corbin claimed that Virginia's paper currency supply, based on an insufficient redemption fund and exceeding the demands of trade, had driven exchange rates out of bounds and specie out of the country, to the detriment of the king's revenue and, he neglected to add, his own profits as well, since he drew a commission on his collections. Corbin wanted a parliamentary regulation to establish currency on an equitable basis as well as the personal right to pay all Virginia officials in paper at the quitrent rate, or 25 percent advance on sterling. Thus bills of exchange used to pay civil officers could be remitted on the quitrent account. In other words Corbin was anxious to shift his losses—and the king's—to the members of the Virginia Council and other civic officers, a fact he had failed to mention to the councillors in July. To the British merchants for whom he acted as influence peddler and debt collector, Corbin proposed still another solution: prevent future currency issues except in emergencies, provide adequate redemption funds, make the money lawful for public debts only, keep the paper in circulation for short periods, and destroy it as soon as it returned to the Virginia treasury. These measures, which echoed the Currency Act of 1751, would reestablish credit, and specie would flow back into Virginia to facilitate quitrent and debt collections.[69]

Corbin engaged in one other dispute over paper. In the spring of 1762 he challenged Fauquier to debate publicly the question of the relation between currency and exchange rates. Fearful that "discontent about the large emissions of paper money [might] one day or other be the loss of the regiment," Fauquier accepted and published a signed article in the *Virginia Gazette* defending existing currency practices. Corbin wrote an unsigned rebuttal. Unfortun-

---

69. July 30, 1762, Hillman, ed., *Exec. Jours. of Va. Council*, 228–230; Corbin's Memorial to the Lords Commissioners of the Treasury, n.d., C.O. 5/1330/126–127; Corbin to Athawes, May 21, Corbin to Buchanan, May 29, Corbin to Edward Jenings, July 5, Corbin to Messrs. Hanbury, July 22, Corbin to Cary, Aug. 22, Corbin to John Roberts, Sept. 6, all in Corbin Letterbook for 1762. See the review of Corbin's complaints by Auditor General Robert Cholmondeley, July 11, 1764, T. 1/430, Public Record Office.

ately these issues of the *Gazette* do not seem to have survived, but the lieutenant governor had already made his position clear to both the House of Burgesses and the Board of Trade.

According to Fauquier a more fundamental cause of the rise of exchange than the emissions of paper money was the increase of imports "to such a Height that the Crops of Tobacco will not pay for them, so that the Colony is so far from having Money to draw for in England." This fact, Fauquier continued, "most thinking Gentlemen of the Colony see and acknowledge" but close their eyes to. At the same time Fauquier admitted that "meddling with the Mediums of Trade and Commerce, whether it be Bullion or Paper, is of a most delicate Nature, and is often attended with a long Train of very distant Consequences, not always obvious to a Man of the greatest Sagacity."[70] On the other side Corbin continued to blame the "exorbitant rise of exchange" on the large emissions of inadequately secured paper money that, following Gresham's Law, drove out gold and silver. His aim was to revive credit and thus restore for the use of the next generation "that Precious Jewel, which their degenerate ancestors considered only as a Rough Pebble."[71]

THREATS OF PARLIAMENTARY INTERVENTION, 1762–1763

After a late summer recess, the Board of Trade resumed business early in November 1762 and found a memorial of the London merchants waiting for them. Appeals to the merchants by agents Abercromby and Montague to withhold the petition until the colony had a chance to consider it had failed. Though some merchants privately admitted the "utility and necessity of paper currency," the majority led by Edward Athawes, a "warm advocate" against paper, decided that Virginia had paid so little attention to the Board's additional instructions they could pay none to Virginia's agents.[72] The latest memorial sounded a cry heard in the prior

70. Fauquier to B.T., Nov. 3, 1762, Jan. 10, 1763, C.O. 5/1330, P.R.O.; Nov. 3, 1762, *Jours. of Burgesses, 1761–1765*, 65.

71. Corbin to Philip Ludwell, Aug. 13, 1764, Corbin Letterbook.

72. Abercromby to Fauquier, Nov. 10, 1762, Abercromby Letterbook; Nov. 17, Dec. 16, 1762, *Jour. of Comm. Trade, 1759–1763*, 294–295, 316; Edward Montague to General Assembly Committee of Correspondence, Feb. 5, 1763, Landon Carter Papers, Alderman Library, University of Virginia, Charlottesville (improperly cataloged as Montague to Arthur Lee, July 5, 1763, in Walter Ray Wineman, *The Landon Carter Papers in the University of Virginia Library, A Calendar and Biographical Sketch* [Charlottesville, Va., 1962], 15, no. 76).

petitions of the British merchants. And its echoes went back as far as the sixteenth century and beyond. Gold and silver alone had an intrinsic value that gave absolute protection to sterling debts. The merchants asked therefore that paper money be excluded as legal tender for sterling obligations. In addition they found Virginia's redemption funds to be insufficient. And they renewed their claim that the act of 1749 was legally still in force, since it had received royal assent, while the amendment of 1755 had not. In sum the original law was still on the books, and thus 125 remained the legal rate of exchange for sterling debts settled in the provincial courts.

Even if the act of 1749 had been repealed, according to the merchants, sterling debts would not be secure, because the amendment of 1755 permitted the Virginia judges to "settle the Exchange upon a sterling Judgment in such a manner as they shall think just." "However uprightly and impartially hitherto exercised," this practice introduced a "Mode and form of Justice unheard of" in Britain; it was also "insufficient inasmuch as the Exchange hath arisen between the time of such Orders of Court and a possibility of the Creditors obtaining a Remittance." Finally, the merchants noted that the House of Burgesses had rejected their earlier petition of 1758 and the Board's additional instructions of 1759 covering the same grievances. They now demanded belated justice.[73]

The Lords of the Treasury sent the Corbin memorial to the Board of Trade a month later. The Board reviewed that complaint along with those of the merchants and of the Virginia councillors who opposed the currency appropriation of the past spring. On December 22, having read the various documents in the case, the Board laid aside the entire matter until the merchants and the Virginia agents could be heard from.

The protagonists arrived at the beginning of February, and as its first order of business the Board read memorials from the aggrieved merchants of Liverpool, Bristol, and Glasgow. They were similar in substance and often in wording to the London merchants' petition.[74] Then the Board heard the two sides argue for and against legal tender currency. One merchant reportedly "entered upon a

73. Memorial of London merchants to B.T., n.d., in C.O. 5/1330/129–130. See also the comments of Abercromby to Fauquier, Nov. 10, 1762, Abercromby Letterbook.

74. Dec. 16, 22, 1762, Jan. 17, 25, 31, Feb. 1, 1763, in *Jour. of Comm. Trade, 1759–1763*, 316, 323, 328, 330–331; Fauquier to B.T., Apr. 8, July 10, 1762, in C.O. 5/1330, P.R.O.; Memorials of merchants of London, Glasgow, and Liverpool, n.d., in C.O. 5/1330/129–130, 137–138, P.R.O.

topick foreign to his subject and of a too delicate nature to be treated by a Merchant: He remarked the growing independency of the Colony: the Little deference paid to his Majesty's orders and even the contempt shewn them." Another observed that if the merchants spent money on the colonies they should have the benefit. Describing the proceedings to his father, Charles Carroll thought he saw the members of the Board smile. "No doubt," Carroll sneered, they were amused "by the solidity of those remarks." Finally Montague "artfully put the following question: Gentlemen is there any one here who is not as ready to transact business and receive Commissions since the emission of Paper money as before? He was answered by an eminent Merchant in the negative: that he could not nor would not give further credit while the present grievance remained unredressed."[75]

In the end the merchants' "torrent of clamor and variety of suffering" carried the day. The Board prepared to place the question before Parliament without delay. The agents, however, won time for the colony to attempt to remedy the situation without outside interference, a concession for which the Board and the merchants tried to get Montague to sign a declaration that the House of Burgesses would at last obey the late additional instructions. The agent refused, claiming that if the currency "must receive such a stab, it should come from other hands than this."[76]

At this point the Board adopted a series of resolutions that expressed the sense of the merchants' memorials and of Corbin's as well. First it stated that issuing fiat money was contrary to the "spirit" of the Currency Act of 1751 and destructive to colonial credit, British commerce, and crown revenues. The Board considered this to be the case in Virginia because of the emission of "large quantitys of such paper bills ... upon insufficient and uncertain funds ... and the declaring them by law to be a legal tender"; these were the "principal causes of the great rise, and uncertain and fluctuating state of the exchange." Furthermore the Board made clear that the amendment of 1759 did "not give security ... in the recovery of sterling debts," nor was British property "amply or fully secured thereby." In addition the Burgesses had failed to comply with the Board's instructions of 1759, instructions "founded in reason, jus-

---

75. Charles Carroll, Jr., to his father, Jan. 31, 1763, "Extracts from the Carroll Papers," *Maryland Historical Magazine*, XI (1916), 325.
76. Montague to Comm. of Corres., Feb. 5, 1763, Landon Carter Papers; Abercromby to Fauquier, Feb. 7, 1763, Abercromby Letterbook.

tice and equity." Finally, if the house continued to ignore the royal instructions and the need for increased taxes to redeem existing bills on time, the Board resolved to turn the currency question over to Parliament for solution.[77]

What the Board threatened was that Parliament would abolish *all* outstanding Virginia paper and compel the colony to redeem it at face value. The threat so worried the Virginians that they later received the Currency Act of 1764 with a feeling of relief; the law was a compromise and a far less Draconian measure than the one hinted at in February 1763.[78] The Board also threatened some kind of extension of the Currency Act of 1751 or the establishment of such controls "adviseable, for the support of the publick credit of the colony, and the relief of the merchants." Copies of the resolutions went to the agents, the merchants, the lieutenant governor, and the Lords of the Treasury.[79]

Enclosed with Fauquier's copy was a reprimand for his public expressions on the subject of exchange and on the need for wartime currency emissions. Fauquier, as noted, had ascribed the rise of exchange to an imbalance of trade with Britain. Now as before the Board of Trade blamed it on an excess of paper money and a deficiency of redemption funds. As for the plea of wartime expediency, the Board countered that it was not paper as such but paper as a legal tender that the British merchants found objectionable. Properly secured currency needed no legislative sanctions. More important was the Board's censure of Fauquier for treating the late additional instructions of 1759 as a subject to be discussed rather than as a command to be followed. For this reason, the Board claimed, the Burgesses had responded to the instructions with an unreasonable defense of the existing currency system. Come "to a Sense of the Duty you owe to His Majesty," the Board concluded, "leave no means untryed to procure for the Merchants that relief and Satisfaction which their Case appears to require." Letters from the two agents only underscored dangers of the situation that had developed. "You may be assured," Abercromby wrote, "they will go to Parliament against the legislature of Virginia," a Parliament,

---

77. Feb. 2, 1763, *Jour. of Comm. Trade, 1759–1763,* 331–332; Charles Steuart to James Parker, Jan. 29, 1764, "1763–1782, Letters between Capt. Parker and his Friend Charles Steuart," Parker Family Papers, Liverpool Record Office, Liverpool (microfilm available at Col. Williamsburg Research Lib.).

78. Comm. of Corres. to Montague, June 15, 1764, "Proc. of Va. Comm. of Corres., 1759–1767," *VMHB,* XII (1904–1905), 6.

79. Feb. 2, 4, 5, 7, 1763, *Jour. of Comm. Trade, 1759–1763,* 331–332, 333–334.

he added, that has "no extraordinary regard for the interests of America when put in competition with that of England."[80]

Fauquier submitted to his Council for consideration both the Board's resolutions and Abercromby's letter in late April 1763. The Council members urged him to convene the legislature at once and later declared "their readiness to concur in any measures that shall be judged further expedient to strengthen the credit of the Paper currency, and satisfy all concerned therein." They added that the wartime currency issues were necessary and that existing redemption funds probably sufficed to sink the various issues at the periods prescribed by law.[81] The governor delivered the resolutions to the General Assembly on May 19 along with a plea to eliminate legal tender clauses, redeem existing currency on time, and satisfy the British merchants in regard to sterling debts. A refusal, he threatened, meant only that the matter would be taken to a higher power. The house was unmoved. It noted that Virginia had struck paper to meet the crown's wartime demands when specie or any other kind of money was unavailable. To pay the militia and local traders in notes without a legal tender provision would be unjust. As for the redemption funds, the colony's tax laws were adequate, and with the courts executing sterling debts at the actual rates of exchange the merchants' investments were secure. One circumstance the law could not guard against was the fluctuation in exchange rates between the time of court judgment and the purchase of a bill of exchange. In such cases, although losing some money on a rising exchange, creditors as often gained on a falling one. It was therefore a mark of "weakness or caprice" to insist on changes in the law governing sterling debts. Nevertheless the Burgesses promised to reconsider the entire subject. Fauquier thought the answer showed "some warmth," but he was otherwise hopeful.[82]

A few days later Richard Henry Lee made the accusation he had been working up to since he first raised the issue of the mandatory burning of treasury notes. As a member of an ad hoc committee to audit the treasury books in accordance with the provisions of the

---

80. B.T. to Fauquier, Feb. 7, 1763, C.O. 5/1368, P.R.O.; Abercromby to Fauquier, Feb. 7, 1763, Abercromby Letterbook; Montague to Comm. of Corres., Feb. 5, 1763, Landon Carter Papers.

81. Apr. 28, 1763, Hillman, ed., *Exec. Jours. of Va. Council*, 252–253; May 19, 1763, McIlwaine, ed., *Leg. Jours. of Va. Council*, III, 1305 (quoted); Fauquier to B.T., May 24, 1763, C.O. 5/1330, P.R.O.

82. May 19, 20, 1763, *Jours. of Burgesses, 1761–1765*, 173–174; Fauquier to B.T., May 24, 1763, C.O. 5/1330, P.R.O.

law of 1760, Lee reported to the Burgesses an enormous deficiency "sufficient to alarm not the merchants of Britain only, but every thinking person." As much as £65,000 could not be accounted for. Some £35,000 was only reported to be in the treasury. Lee demanded a strict investigation, an action that would hound his political career for years to come. Robinson coolly met the challenge by creating a committee to make the treasury probe with Lee as a member. He also placed Lee on the committee to reply to Lieutenant Governor Fauquier and the British merchants.[83]

For the moment Robinson succeeded in bridling Lee by daring him to take the charges made in the privacy of the House of Burgesses into the open. If he reported his suspicions publicly, Lee risked bankrupting the credit of the colony and of many leading politicos and planters. He would also vindicate the charges of the London merchants.

The committee investigating the treasury did indeed report on May 24 a sizable deficiency, nearly £40,000, but attributed it to the large arrears of several sheriffs against whom judgments were pending. Moreover, on paper at least, uncollected taxes exceeded the value of the outstanding treasury notes by some £11,500.[84] Four days later in the reply to the merchants, which Lee himself drafted, the house specifically exonerated Robinson and local currency practices by reporting existing taxes sufficient to redeem all the paper still in circulation. The suspicion of a delinquency in tax collections was confirmed, but the Burgesses insisted that it could easily be remedied by prosecuting the sheriffs responsible. The remainder of the address was a justification of Virginia's currency system, the gist of which was that legal tender paper was a defense against exploitation. If the British merchants had the legal right to refuse paper currency, the more avaricious among them would demand as much paper as they could get.[85]

Responsibility for the Council's reply to the address fell upon Richard Corbin, who declared that the councillors would "chear-

83. "Speech of Richard Henry Lee in Committee of Whole House," May [23], 1763, "Selections and Excerpts from the Lee Papers," *So. Lit. Messenger,* XXX (1860), 133–135; May 23, 1763, *Jours. of Burgesses, 1761–1765,* 176, xi–xviii. See also Charles Francis Adams, ed., *The Works of John Adams,* III (Boston, 1865), 31–35; Arthur Lee to Carter Braxton, May 22, 1779, *The Deane Papers,* III (New-York Historical Society, *Collections,* XXI [New York, 1889]), 465, 468.

84. May 24, 1763, *Jours. of Burgesses, 1761–1765,* 177–178, 179–181.

85. May 28, 1763, *ibid.,* 188–192; draft of house reply in Lee's hand, Revolutionary Lee Papers, 1750–1809, Alderman Lib., Univ. of Va., Charlottesville (microfilm available at Col. Williamsburg Research Lib.).

fully have given our concurrence in every Measure for the better support" of credit. However, as the lower house initiated all money bills, the members could only pledge their "unshaken resolution of adhering to his late Majesty's Instructions." Fauquier dryly remarked that he wished the councillors had been able to show "that fidelity and that Resolution by Acts, which you can only do by Professions."[86]

The issue was clear; the positions defined. British merchant creditors tended to see legal tender paper as the principal danger to their sterling debts in a time of depression. Virginia debtors saw it as a protection against the threat of insolvency and confiscation. Both feared for their property but had little chance to compromise. Not even an alchemist could transmute paper into gold.

Fauquier accepted that no deficiency in redemption taxes existed and that the delinquent collections could be taken care of, but expressed disappointment at the failure to satisfy the merchants by removing the legal tender clause. He privately approached leading legislators to convince them that, if currency were secure, it needed no legal tender sanctions. Only four men followed the governor's lead; the rest ignored him. Stung by his personal defeat, Fauquier prorogued the legislature until August.[87] During the adjournment the committee of correspondence of the General Assembly sent Montague a copy of the legislature's reply to the Board's resolutions and also evidence concerning the tax situation and court judgments affecting sterling debts. In a short commentary the committee discussed the disadvantages of eliminating legal tender and Corbin's personal responsibility for his losses on quitrent collections. If, it was argued, Corbin persisted in accepting paper in lieu of specie even though Virginia law specifically exempted quitrents from such

---

86. May 31, 1763, McIlwaine, ed., *Leg. Jours. of Va. Council*, III, 1310–1311.

87. Fauquier to B.T., May 24, June 1, 1763, C.O. 5/1330, P.R.O.; May 31, 1763, *Jours. of Burgesses, 1761–1765*, 197. Although the Burgesses did not fully satisfy critics of paper currency either in Virginia or in Britain, it did move to enhance public credit by creating an additional tax-redemption fund, by tightening controls over tax collectors, by ordering the treasurer to give public notice from time to time of the amount of treasury notes in his hands that would pass current after Mar. 1765 and to exchange them for notes redeemable in Mar. 1765, and by repealing a "bankruptcy" law unacceptable to British creditors. See Fauquier to B.T., June 1, 1763, C.O. 5/1330, P.R.O., and May 24, 1763, *Jours. of Burgesses, 1761–1765*, 181, and Gipson, "Virginia Planter Debts," *VMHB*, LXIX (1961), 268–272. See also George Washington to Robert Stewart, Aug. 13, 1763, John C. Fitzpatrick, ed., *The Writings of George Washington* . . . , II (Washington, D.C., 1931), 403–404.

payment, then he was only testifying to the desirability of paper.[88]

The Board of Trade received copies of the May session of the Virginia legislature on October 14 along with covering letters from Fauquier. That same day the Board turned the reply of the House of Burgesses over to the London merchants for an opinion. Two months later, at the insistence of the merchants, the Board brought Montague and the petitioners together for another hearing. Apparently satisfied that Virginia's redemption funds were indeed adequate, the merchants turned instead to the question of the protection of sterling debts. After a reportedly confused discussion they submitted to the Board a single proposition to which the several interests could agree: judgments for sterling obligations "should not be discharged, but in sterling money in Virginia or Great Britain." If payment was in sterling bills of exchange, court judgments were not to be discharged until such bills were finally and fully paid. Only thus could the merchants guard themselves against losses from the fluctuations of the exchange rate. The Board approved the proposal and, as in the past, recommended parliamentary action. But at the agents' request, the merchants drew back and agreed to place their trust once more in the "equity of the legislature of Virginia"— with the understanding that this time any delay would invite immediate intervention by Parliament.[89]

THE CURRENCY ACT OF 1764

Despite the promise to give Virginia time to mend its ways, there were clear signs that the British government had already determined to reform the colonial currency system as part of the larger postwar effort to rationalize the empire. Thus a scant day after Virginia got its final chance to appease the London merchants, the chief justice of Pennsylvania, William Allen, who was in London at the time, reported that the Grenville ministry would seek parliamentary regulations of the currency practices of all the colonies outside New England and not just of Virginia alone. According to the chief justice, the ministry would sponsor a bill to the effect "that no paper money made hereafter is to be a tender," which Allen added "is in other words to say that we shall have no more." Furthermore the

---

88. June 16, 1763, "Proc. of Va. Comm. of Corres.," *VMHB*, XI (1903–1904), 345–349.
89. Oct. 14, Dec. 8, 1763, in *Jour. of Comm. Trade, 1759–1763*, 395, 418, *1764–1767*, 3, 4; B.T. to Fauquier, Dec. 9, 1763, C.O. 5/1368, P.R.O.

proposed measure was part of a package deal that included a duty on American trade with the West Indies and a stamp tax.[90] The source of the chief justice's information remains unknown. And though the evidence is spotty, the ministry apparently did have under consideration by the late fall of 1763 at least two different currency schemes.

Certainly by the middle of October 1763, Grenville, some of his aides, and the commissioners of the Treasury had given serious thought to a recommendation from Henry McCulloh, the London merchant and North Carolina land speculator, favoring the creation of a colonial paper currency system under the control of the mother country and secured by a fund arising out of an American stamp tax. Recently McCulloh has been the subject of a number of articles bearing on the formulation of imperial policy at the end of the French and Indian War. His role in the preparation of the Stamp Act and in the drafting of proposals later incorporated in the Revenue Act of 1764 is well documented. Familiar, too, is McCulloh's abiding interest in the currency question; over the years he had suggested to the British government several different solutions. There is no evidence, however, that his suggestions had any effect on imperial monetary policies until the summer of 1763. By then the Grenville ministry had made up its mind to increase the American revenue, and towards the middle of the year research began on the problem. It was at this point that McCulloh sent a timely if unsolicited outline of a plan for a Stamp Act to one of Grenville's secretaries at the Treasury. The scheme that seems to have been a new draft of a proposal first submitted to the earl of Halifax in 1755 met with some enthusiasm, and McCulloh suddenly found himself cast in the unexpected role of expert and ministerial adviser upon American affairs. Accordingly in September he received an order to collaborate "on a plan for a general Stamp Law throughout America and the West Indies."[91] On October 10 McCulloh had

90. To Benjamin Chew, Dec. 9, 1763, Donald A. Kimball and Miriam Quinn, eds., "William Allen-Benjamin Chew Correspondence, 1763–1764," *PMHB*, XC (1966), 217.
91. On McCulloh see John High, "Henry McCulloh, Progenitor of the Stamp Act," *North Carolina Historical Review*, XLIX (1952), 24–38; Allen S. Johnson, "The Political Career of George Grenville, 1712–1770" (Ph.D. diss., Duke University, 1955), 262, 277; Charles R. Ritcheson, "The Preparation of the Stamp Act," *WMQ*, 3d Ser., X (1953), 547–552; Charles G. Sellers, Jr., "Private Profits and British Colonial Policy: The Speculations of Henry McCulloh," *ibid.*, VIII (1951), 535–551; John Cannon, "Henry McCulloch and Henry McCulloh," *ibid.*, XV (1958), 71–73; Jack P. Greene, ed., " 'A Dress of Horror': Henry McCulloh's

completed a working draft and two days later discussed the plan
with Treasury officials.

McCulloh's Stamp Act proposal has been discussed at length elsewhere. But it is not generally known that the scheme was closely
tied to a plan for a continental currency. Specifically McCulloh
recommended "issuing Exchequer Bills of Union upon the Credit
of the fund [from the stamp tax] as a General relief to the Mother
Country and preserving one Uniform Course as a Medium in Trade."
Thus he never intended that any of the new tax money "should be
transmitted to England but only meant to raise a Fund from the
Colonies to obtain a Credit for Securing the Issuing of Exchequer
Bills . . . in order to preserve One Uniform Course of Trade and
the Colonies bearing the Expence of preserving the Crown's ac-
quisitions in keeping up the Militias and providing Cash to purchase
presents for the Indians . . . and for Raising Bounties to encourage
people to Settle in the said Colonies."[92] In proposing an American
revenue, McCulloh seems to have had at least as great an interest in
solving the currency problem as in covering the costs of an expanded
empire.

The conference with the Treasury officials seems to have gone
well enough, and shortly afterwards Grenville gave the plan his
approval. Exactly what Grenville had in mind, however, remains
unclear, for on November 19 the plan again came under the scrutiny
of the minister and his chief aides. And this time they rejected it in
favor of a stamp tax alone. In short, as Chief Justice Allen's letter
and other evidence suggests, the Grenville ministry put aside the
idea of a continental currency possibly for further study. Instead
the ministry opted for a simple and immediate ban of all legal tender
paper money in the colonies outside New England. Currency reform would still be part of the government's plan to fashion a new
imperial system, but for the moment at least there was no place for
any "Exchequer Bills of Union."[93]

Barely three months after the confrontation between the London
merchants and the Virginia agent and the decision to lay aside the

Objections to the Stamp Act," *Huntington Library Quarterly*, XXVI (1963), 253–
262.

92. "State of Articles proposed by Mr. M., Oct. 10, 1763," Additional Manuscript
35910, fols. 357–360, British Museum (copy available in Perkins Library, Duke University, Durham, N.C.).

93. The first conference was held on Oct. 12; see note attached to document,
ibid. For a brief discussion of these events see Ritcheson, "Stamp Act," WMQ, 3d
Ser., X (1953), 552.

McCulloh recommendations, the Board of Trade initiated a study of colonial currency practices in the colonies south of New England. Most probably the investigation was undertaken at the behest of the ministry, but there were other and equally important reasons behind the move, including the conclusion of the French and Indian War, the "hard money" bias of the commissioners of trade, and the antagonism to paper money of the newly appointed president of the Board of Trade, Wills Hill, Lord Hillsborough. Whatever the precise relationship among the several factors involved, Virginia continued to be the focus of attention. When a few weeks later the Board recommended new parliamentary currency controls, the supporting evidence was drawn primarily from the Virginia file.

At the beginning of 1764 the Board invited the merchants trading with the colonies south of New England, along with the colonial agents, to appear on January 19. At that time there would be a debate on the merits of extending the Currency Act of 1751. Though several of the merchants did show up to give their testimony, little else happened. A few days later the question of Virginia currency came up again in connection with the reading of two petitions from Glasgow.

Two years earlier the merchants of Glasgow had had every intention of presenting a detailed response to the Burgesses' latest defense of Virginia currency. But after learning that the Board had already ordered Virginia to eliminate the clause of legal tender in the payment of sterling debts, they had paused to discuss the matter further. Any such act, they had decided, would only injure their interest, which was tied up in the Virginia store trade and in book credit. For that reason they had tacked another petition onto the original and presented both to the Board of Trade, where they were read on January 21. The original petition focussed on Virginia's tax arrears, the small quantity of notes already burned, the nearly £50,000 reportedly lying unburned in the treasury, and the ease of counterfeiting Virginia paper. In sum the Glasgow merchants were not yet convinced that Virginia's credit was on a firm footing. The second petition examined the high price of exchange. It began by pointing out that the debts on the Glasgow merchants' books were in local currency. The problem therefore was to lower the sterling exchange rate in Virginia in order to reduce the cost of making remittances. Any law that distinguished between sterling and currency debts, however, threatened to increase the price of exchange. The remedy was to stop further currency emissions, prosecute delinquent tax collectors, punctually burn redemption-fund money, make additional levies in case of tax deficiencies, and attach a 5 percent interest to all circulating bills.[94] The merchants of London and Glasgow seemed to be pursuing the same ends by disparate means. Both wished to protect their property. But the one wanted to eliminate legal tender paper as far as possible, and the other to preserve it but enhance its value.

The Board's position was hardening. It returned to the question of the Currency Act of 1751 late in January when it ordered the governor of New York, the proprietors, chief justice, and agent of Pennsylvania, and former governors of Massachusetts Bay, New Jersey, Virginia, South Carolina, and Georgia to appear for a hearing on February 2. At that time, after some discussion, it was generally agreed that there was a need for eliminating further fiat money emissions and for redeeming circulating paper at the times prescribed by law. Only the agent and proprietors of Pennsylvania demurred and asked for time to canvass the views of the colony.

The hearings resumed a day later in the presence of the agents of New York, New Jersey, Virginia, North Carolina, South Carolina, and Georgia, all of whom asked for some time to consult with their colonies. The Board, however, found any further delay inconvenient. It wanted to know immediately whether the agents would oppose a move in Parliament "to prohibit all future emissions from being legal tenders, and also to compel the calling in and sinking of all paper money now current at such times as are fixed by the several acts of assembly emitting such paper money and that the legal tender shall continue no longer than till such periods." The agents countered with a plan of their own. They declared that a "certain quantity of paper currency ought to be allowed of in each colony, to be a legal tender in all contracts and dealings within the colonies, and that time should be allowed for each colony to consider and report what the sum should be." The scheme fell on deaf ears. The Board sought consent, not advice, and the agents would be no more successful over the next half dozen years than they were that day in persuading the British authorities to adopt their views.

The Board sent the king in Council on February 9 a representa-

94. Jan. 10, 19, 21, 23, 1764, in *Jour. of Comm. Trade, 1764–1767*, 3, 4; Jan. 10, 1764, C.O. 5/1330, P.R.O.; John McCall to Robinson Dangerfield, Feb. 6, 1764, *Broadus v. McCall and Co.*, Carolina County Appeals and Land Cases, 1771–1807, Pt. I, LVI, 69–70, Va. State Lib., Richmond. I am indebted to Emory Evans for this last reference.

tion written by Hillsborough favoring a parliamentary ban on all
future legal tender paper issued in the provinces to the south of
New England. To point up the theoretical defects of paper currency, Hillsborough returned to "first principles." "A Medium of
Trade," he assumed, "must in it's nature not only be a measure of
the Value; but an equivalent, and that in a Country which has any
Foreign Trade, the Equivalent must be of a material, which is universally of intrinsic Value. . . . That different Countries must agree
upon the material for this measure and Equivalent, which they have
tacitly done in favour of Gold or Silver; but never will or did, or
can do so with regard to Paper. That Gold or Silver are the Materials fittest for this measure and equivalent . . . and that Paper is
perhaps as unfit as anything can possibly be. . . ."

Hillsborough declined to enter into any lengthy theoretical discussion of paper currency and mentioned only a few of its supposed
effects. The larger the quantity of bills of credit "the less the value
with regard to other Commodities," and when there was no power
to stop the flood of paper, depreciation was inevitable. Most important, paper banished coin. To point up the practical defects of
paper currency, Hillsborough attached to his recommendation the
recent petitions against Virginia paper money—and one memorial
against North Carolina dated 1759.[95]

Hillsborough added the Carolina petition at the behest of Anthony
Bacon, a London merchant trading with both North Carolina and
Virginia and member of Parliament for Aylesbury who had succeeded John Wilkes in that post on January 25, 1764.[96] The grievance against North Carolina grew out of the colony's emission of
some £60,000 of legal tender currency between 1748 and 1755 and
a spiraling rate of sterling exchange.[97] Actual exchange rates rose
far above the legal rate of 133 ⅓. In 1756 exchange fluctuated

95. Jan. 26, Feb. 2, 3, 7, 9, 1764, *Jour. of Comm. Trade, 1764–1767*, 9, 15, 18, 19;
Feb. 10, Mar. 9, 1764, *Acts of Privy Council, Col.*, IV, 623–631, 641–646; Joseph
Sherwood to Samuel Smith, Treasurer of New Jersey, Feb. 4, 1764, in Letters of
Joseph Sherwood, New Jersey Historical Society, Newark.

96. See L. B. Namier, "Charles Garth, Agent for South Carolina, Part II," *English Historical Review*, LIV (1939), 640–646; Ninetta S. Jucker, ed., *The Jenkinson
Papers, 1760–1766* (London, 1949), 194n, 259n.

97. See table 6 in Appendix 1 and "The Petition of Merchants in London who
Trade to North Carolina and of Gentlemen and Merchants in and from that
Colony," 1759, William L. Saunders, ed., *The Colonial Records of North Carolina*
(Raleigh, N.C., 1886–1890), VI, 16–17, hereafter cited as *Col. Recs. N.C.* For a dis-
cussion of the currency practices of North Carolina see Brock, "Currency of the
American Colonies," 428–445; Charles J. Bullock, *Essays on the Monetary History
of the United States* (New York, 1900), 125–204.

around 180; a year later it had moved to 190. In March 1759 the London merchants trading to the colony petitioned for a law making all debts owing to them payable in paper at the going market exchange rate. The Board of Trade quickly approved the demand and shot off an additional instruction to North Carolina's governor, Arthur Dobbs, identical in aim with that sent in the recent and similar case of Virginia. Dobbs was to obtain an amendment to the currency acts of 1748 and 1754, so that all sterling debts due before 1748 would be payable in sterling money only. Debts contracted since then were to be payable at the creditor's choosing either in paper at the actual exchange rate or again in sterling money. The governor submitted the directive and the merchants' memorial to the legislature in November. The house rejected both, however, and pointed to the dearth of specie and the acute need for fiat money.[98]

Like the Virginians, the Carolinians feared for their property. Without a legal tender currency, declared the house, the few persons who "had hoarded up a little Bullion" could buy up all property in distress at a monopolist's price. No amendment to existing laws was necessary, it argued, since the courts as a matter of practice had always made judgments for protested sterling bills of exchange at the actual and not the legal sterling exchange rates. A major concession was made, however. In the future, currency appropriations would drop specific references to paper being legal tender for sterling debts. Nothing more was heard from the Board of Trade until Lord Hillsborough chose to resurrect the North Carolina petition as additional evidence of the practical defects of all legal tender paper currencies.[99]

Hillsborough's recommendations of February 9, 1764, called for a blanket prohibition of future legal tender currency issues in those colonies unaffected by the Currency Act of 1751. Paper money already in circulation was not to be reissued or extended. Governors assenting to acts contrary to such regulations were to be forced out of the king's service and fined £1,000 sterling. There was a belated attempt by colonial agents Charles Garth of South Carolina and William Knox of Georgia to forestall action by proposing an alternate plan that met the essential demands of the London merchants. But this failed. Within a month the Privy Council ordered

98. *Col. Recs. N.C.*, VI, 16–17, 22–24, 43–44, 54–56, 70–73, 116, 134, 138–139, 218–219.

99. Dobbs to B.T., Jan. 19, 1760, *Col. Recs. N.C.*, VI, 218–219; Nov. 26, 1760, *Jour. of Comm. Trade, 1759–1763*, 143.

the Board's recommendations laid before Parliament whenever the crown advised, and Hillsborough, who seems to have been working closely with Grenville, was anxious to get on with the business. "I wait your Commands," he wrote Grenville. Although he expected a currency measure to pass without opposition, there was no time to lose.[100]

For reasons unknown, at this point the Board of Trade with the apparent support of the ministry planned to drop the currency question for the remainder of the year. It is possible that the arguments of the American agents and their supporters had finally made their mark and that Grenville had decided that the problem required more research. Certainly the Board launched just such an investigation into the state of colonial paper money shortly after the Currency Act of 1764 became law and then neglected to follow it up. In any event, on March 29, acting on his own initiative, Anthony Bacon, in the House of Commons, "started the question" of the need for a measure to restrain colonial currency. Bacon's motives are not clear. He had of course shown a keen interest in the recent Board hearings and had requested the addition of the North Carolina petition to the Privy Council report. Also it was known that he was a friend of Hillsborough's and that the continuing crisis in the Virginia economy and the growing number of bankruptcies in the tobacco trade had in at least one case immediately affected his interests.[101]

Between March 29 and April 4, when Bacon "moved for permission to bring in" a currency control bill, Charles Garth, who was in the House gallery, hurriedly provided several members with arguments against the regulatory measure. Bacon was also busy drumming up support. By April 4 he had won over at least one member of the Board of Trade, George Rice, who also sat in the House and who seconded the motion for leave to bring in a paper money bill. But no sooner was the motion made and seconded than "Peregrine Cust, a London merchant, . . . and Sir William Meredith opposed the motion." Straddling these two positions was Charles

100. Feb. 13, 1764, *Jour. of Comm. Trade, 1764–1767,* 21; Feb. 10, Mar. 9, 1764, *Acts of Privy Council, Col.,* IV, 623; the earl of Hillsborough to George Grenville, Mar. [?], 1764, as quoted in Sosin, "Imperial Regulation of Paper Money," *PMHB,* LXXXVIII (1964), 184. See also Secretary Calvert to Gov. Horatio Sharpe, Feb. 29, 1764, William Hand Browne *et al.,* eds., *Archives of Maryland* (Baltimore, 1883–1952), XIV, 140, hereafter cited as *Md. Archives.*

101. See n. 96 above and Jucker, ed., *Jenkinson Papers,* 277–278. See also *Pennsylvania Journal; and the Weekly Advertiser* (Philadelphia), Dec. 16, 1772.

Townshend. He reportedly " 'thought the Colonies ought to have some currency that should be legal tender under proper regulations,' but considered that the evils complained of required the immediate interposition of Parliament." According to Garth a lengthy debate then ensued, after which the two commissioners of trade sitting in the Commons at the time, Rice and Soame Jenyns, who seemingly took an active part in the affair, "proposed to Sir William Meredith and our friends that the present Bill should be confined to the single point of preventing the Colonies for the future from passing Acts issuing paper bills with the clause of legal tender, but not affect or set a period to any at present subsisting. Sir William Meredith came to me in the gallery to acquaint me with the proposition made and as the sense of the House was strong in favour of restraining the provinces of this power, [a feeling given impetus perhaps by an equally strong desire at the time to regulate the paper emissions of private banks of issue in Scotland], we [Garth and some other agents] thought it best to close with the proposition."

The matter then went to a committee made up of the various representatives in the debate—Bacon, Townshend, Rice, Soame Jenyns, Sir William Meredith, and Sir William Baker (a longtime foe of colonial currency)—who were charged with the drafting of a bill. When presented, however, the bill reportedly did not survive the first reading without important changes bearing on "the Situation of the Paper Currency" of Maryland and "the Tax for Payment thereof." The exact nature of these textual changes remains a mystery, but they conceivably had something to do with striking out a clause requiring the redemption of existing currency at face value, thus interfering with plans to sink the Maryland loan office issue of 1733 in sterling bills at a discount of one-third of nominal value. What is clear is that William Hunt and Osgood and Capel Hanbury, the trustees of the sinking fund for the Maryland loan office, failed in a related move to exempt that province from any new regulations. On April 12 the bills as amended passed the House of Commons. A week later the House of Lords and the crown gave the final stamp of approval.[102]

102. See Namier, "Charles Garth," *Eng. Hist. Rev.*, LIV (1939), 640ff; Apr. 4, 5, 6, 10, 11, 12, 18, 19, 1764, *Jours. of Commons*, XXIX, 1027, 1032, 1039, 1044, 1046, 1049, 1053, 1956; William Hunt, Osgood and Capel Hanbury [Trustees for the Paper Currency] to Charles Hammond, George Steuart, John Bullen, Commissioners of the Paper Currency, in Proprietary Papers, 1705–1767, Black Book, V, Archives of Maryland, Annapolis; Joseph Sherwood to Samuel Smith, Apr. 19,

The Currency Act of 1764 applied only to the colonies south of New England and in no way affected the act of 1751. On the other hand the act of 1764 did have the effect of extending policies imposed by the earlier law, although there were three principal differences between the two. On two counts the 1764 act was less severe: unlike the 1751 measure it placed no limits on the amount of paper in circulation or on the period of redemption, and it did not restrict the issuance of paper to government and wartime expenditures, as the 1751 law did. On one count the act of 1764 was more stringent. The act of 1751 banned paper as legal tender in private—but not public—debt payments. Here the wording of the Currency Act of 1764 was ambiguous, but before 1774 the Board of Trade generally interpreted the act as prohibiting all paper money issued after September 1764 as legal tender in any transactions, private or public.[103] The colonies thought the prohibition applied to private obligations only and by using various dodges often had their way in the matter. Nevertheless the Currency Act of 1764 remained an important issue to a people anxious to gain control over their economic as well as their political destinies.

The initial reaction in Virginia to the Currency Act of 1764 was one of relief. The Burgesses, fearing the destruction of *all existing* legal tender paper, consciously avoided any move that would further antagonize the British merchants and the Board. As it was, a part of the treasury notes in circulation would continue to be full legal tender until 1769, when the last wartime issues would be sunk. Thus in July 1764 the committee of correspondence wrote Montague: "We, as has been repeatedly observed, were never Fond of a Paper Currency, and had our only Solicitude proceeded from an Apprehension, that the over bearing Dispositions of the Merchants might

---

1764, Sherwood Letters. The account given here differs from that to be found in an earlier published version. A number of errors have been corrected following advice received from Professors Leslie Van Horn Brock and Jacob Price. On Apr. 5, 1764, the house also resolved to have all American colonies give an accounting of the bills of credit issued since 1749, the year the last such request was made. The earlier accounts served as raw material in the debate that led to the passage of the Currency Act of 1751. But in 1764 the House of Commons did not wait until all the facts were in before passing a new currency law. See Halifax to B.T., May 8, 1764, enclosing resolution of the House of Commons of Apr. 5, 1764, in the transcriptions of the Correspondence of the Board of Trade, 286, P.R.O., in the Hist. Soc. Pa., Philadelphia.

103. 24 Geo. II, c. 53, and 4 Geo. III, c. 34, Pickering, ed., *Statutes of Great Britain*, XX, 306–309, XXVI, 103–105. See chap. 1 above.

have had weight enough to effect their purpose, which would inevitably have involved the Country in the greatest Difficulties and Distresses."[104]

In any explanation of the Currency Act of 1764, there are a number of major factors to be considered. Of primary importance is the complete failure of the Board of Trade and Privy Council to impose their will on Virginia. Had they been able to effect the restrictions they wanted, the Currency Act would have been largely unnecessary. But royal controls had broken down, leaving a void into which Parliament rushed as soon as the war was over. Equally important were the general postwar moves to tighten imperial controls and the specific desire of the Grenville ministry to reform the colonial currency system, the long-standing "hard money" bias of the Board of Trade, Virginia's paper money practice, and the response of British merchants concerned with the security of their Virginia debts during periods of depression. That response gave rise to a four-sided debate over legal tender paper involving the Virginia planters, the London merchants, the Board of Trade, and the Glasgow mercantile houses that did business in Virginia through their factors. Economic interests and opinions about the nature of money largely determined who took what side.

The planters who dominated the House of Burgesses were defenders of legal tender currency. Most of them viewed paper as a wartime expedient forced on Virginia by the dearth of specie. A favored few who benefited from the peculations of John Robinson also saw it as a source of credit in a time of economic distress—their distress, not the country's. Nearly all of them defended the legal tender quality of that money as their one safeguard against supposedly avaricious merchant-creditors. The second side in the debate was taken by the London merchants, who demanded absolute security for their sterling obligations. They wanted sterling debts paid in sterling money or, at their option, in specie and non-legal tender paper at a rate of exchange that suited them. The Board of Trade generally sympathized with the economic interests and monetary demands of the Londoners but went further with its "hard money"

104. July 28, 1764, "Proc. of Va. Comm. of Corres.," *VMHB*, XII (1904-1905), 11. See also Steuart to Parker, May 4, 1764, Parker Family Papers; John Tayloe to Carter, Apr. 26, 1764, Landon Carter Papers; B.T. to Fauquier, July 13, 1764, C.O. 5/1368, P.R.O.; Oct. 30, Nov. 8, 1764, *Jours. of Burgesses, 1761-1765*, 227-229, 241.

views. The Board repudiated legal tender paper altogether in theory and would have liked to have done so in practice as well.

Taking a stand in the middle were the Glasgow merchants, whose investments in Virginia were tied up in book credit payable in local currency. They needed paper money as a local exchange medium and, on the question of legal tender, approached the position held by the planters. Any distinction between the lawful tender qualities of paper currency when used in sterling transactions as opposed to other payments would only depreciate currency values. On the other hand the Glaswegians lost money on their sterling remittances whenever a jump in exchange rates could not readily be covered by an advance in the prices of imports. They therefore favored a regulated legal tender currency that would maintain its value in relation to sterling, and as believers in the quantity theory of money, they wanted a limited emission of new paper, a short period of circulation, and prompt redemption through adequate taxation. As a final prop to currency values, the Glasgow merchants asked that all paper notes pay 5 percent interest.

The debate ended in a compromise, the Currency Act of 1764, which at first pleased everyone and a year later no one.

Chapter 4

The Repeal Movement

Imperial Politics and Revolutionary Crisis

Within a year of the passage of the Currency Act of 1764, the rapid contraction of wartime paper money issues and a growing shortage of specie led New York, Pennsylvania, and South Carolina to instruct their colonial agents to lobby for the law's repeal. Backing the agents were many of the same London merchants who, anxious to secure their sterling debts in Virginia and North Carolina, had been instrumental in obtaining the Currency Act in the first place. Without changing their demand for some kind of adequate safeguard for sterling investments, by 1766 they had come around to favoring an expansion of lawful currency in a move calculated to boost flagging American sales and remittances.

During these same years the lobby of merchants and agents proved its political effectiveness in helping to repeal the Stamp Act and amend the Revenue Act of 1764. But the alliance failed to either repeal or revise the Currency Act, for reasons arising from the growing antagonism between Britain and the colonies rather than from any problems of paper money. Most important, the attack on the Currency Act became enmeshed in the struggle over parliamentary taxation and the continuing search by a succession of postwar ministries for an American revenue. As a result the repeal movement emerged as one of the more tangled strands in the fabric of imperial politics during the opening years of the Revolutionary crisis.[1]

1. The following chapter is a modified version of an article that originally appeared as "The Currency Act Repeal Movement: A Study of Imperial Politics and Revolutionary Crisis, 1764–1767," *WMQ*, 3d Ser., XXV (1968), 177–211. Two recently published articles that bear directly on the question of currency and the

THE INITIAL RESPONSE TO THE CURRENCY ACT, 1764

Three years before the Treaty of Paris of 1763 the middle colonies began the drift from war prosperity to postwar depression. Trade with the Caribbean and the supply of specie sharply declined following the naval blockade of the foreign West Indies and the cutback in army contracts after the fall of Canada. Adverse trade balances with the mother country and a sudden contraction of British credit only aggravated the situation. Having pursued a generally liberal credit policy during the early war years, thus boosting their American exports, English and Scottish mercantile houses had started to retrench in 1761 in the face of an impending financial crisis at home. A few years later, as bankruptcies reached a thirty-five-year high, the same houses began to call in their American loans. By this time American terms of trade with the Caribbean had taken an unfavorable turn, further reducing the income of the middle colonies and the ability to pay British creditors. In the spring of 1764 newspapers widely reported that the price of flour, the chief export to the islands, was very low and "all the Produce of the West Indies extravagantly high."[2] At this inauspicious moment Parliament chose to pass the Revenue Act of 1764, adding still another obstacle to the Caribbean trade and to that flow of specie that helped bridge the widening trade gap between the mainland colonies and Britain.

In New York local developments intensified the general commercial and financial distress. As headquarters for the British army, the province fattened on the military trade until 1761, when the troops left for the war in the Caribbean and took with them a treasure in coin and supply contracts. Then just before the war's end, local merchants, anticipating the stimulating effects of peace, placed heavy orders in Britain. But prospects seemed bleak. British prices rose, while in New York crops fell short, farm income was down, business dull, inventories swollen, profits low, credit and cash scarce, and payments slow. "Every thing is tumbling down, even the traders themselves," observed merchant and Council member John

Revolution and offer short and contrasting accounts of the Currency Act repeal movement are Jack P. Greene and Richard J. Jellison, "The Currency Act of 1764 in Imperial-Colonial Relations, 1764–1766," *ibid.*, XVIII (1961), 485–518, and Sosin, "Imperial Regulation of Colonial Paper Money," *PMHB*, LXXXVIII (1964), 185–192.

2. Advertisement for a provincial lottery in *New-York Mercury*, Apr. 9, 1764.

Watts. Sterling exchange on London hovered around a high of 90 percent, and "all the Gold and Silver" had drained away to Britain "so that we have nothing remaining but Paper Currancy."[3]

Business conditions had shown little improvement, and agriculture had just begun to revive when sometime in March 1764 word reached New York that, on complaint of "diverse Merchants trading to *Virginia*," the Board of Trade would shortly recommend that Parliment extend the Currency Act of 1751 to all the colonies.[4] While New Yorkers in and out of government denounced the possibility of "such a mighty disturbance" in the interest of a "few peddlers" in the Virginia trade, the General Assembly's committee of correspondence withheld official comment until the opening of the spring legislative session in April.[5] As an old friend to paper money, the New York assembly resolved shortly after reconvening that any loss of legal tender paper would bankrupt the province and on April 19 directed that colonial agent Robert Charles be advised of the proper state of local currency in order to oppose, alone or with counsel, any legislation to restrict the use of paper money.[6] That very day Parliament passed the Currency Act, just two weeks after the Revenue Act of 1764. As one early British commentator put it, if the Revenue Act removed the "substance of money," the Currency Act removed its "shadow."[7]

A copy of the new currency law, accompanied by the news of the Revenue Act and the proposed stamp tax, arrived in New York during the legislature's summer recess. Private individuals once more voiced loud complaints against the threat to trade and government finance, but official reaction was again delayed until the General

3. To Scott, Pringle, Cheap, and Co., Feb. 5, 1764, and to Gedney Clarke, Dec. 2, 1763, in *Letter Book of John Watts, Merchant and Councillor of New York* ... (N.-Y. Hist. Soc., *Colls.*, LXI [New York, 1928]), 228, 204, 205, hereafter cited as *Letter Book of John Watts*. The foregoing discussion is based largely on the skillful and detailed analysis of economic conditions in the middle colonies and New England at the time by Sachs, "Business Outlook," chaps. 1–3. For an earlier and still useful discussion see Harrington, *New York Merchant*, chaps. 8–9.

4. Abraham Lott, ed., *Journal of the Votes and Proceedings of the General Assembly of the Colony of New York* ... (New York, 1764–1766), II, 739.

5. Watts to Gen. Robert Monckton, Apr. 14, 1764, in *Letter Book of John Watts*, 243.

6. Apr. 19, 1764, Lott, ed., *Jour. of N.Y. Assembly*, II, 739. For a discussion of New York's currency practices prior to 1764 see Brock, "Currency of the American Colonies."

7. David Macpherson, *Annals of Commerce, Manufactures, Fisheries and Navigation* ... (London, 1805), III, 398.

Assembly met in September and voted to petition Parliament for redress of all the recent grievances. The principal objection was to the proposed stamp tax, although the Currency Act received some attention. The lower house stressed that treasury notes had long served as the "sinews of war" and as the ordinary means of paying the current expenses of government. In addition treasury notes provided the chief medium of local exchange, and according to the house, when properly secured and keyed to commercial demands, the notes advanced the prosperity of Americans and Britons alike by supporting the flow of imports, exports, and remittances. Perhaps the feeling in New York at the time was best expressed by merchant John Watts. Writing to Moses Franks, Watts noted that "the Evils these Exertions (of Paper Money) have brought upon us, we are blamd for, when they are in themselves inevitable. We have no resources upon an Emergency but in Paper Money and if it be duely sunk we dont see the great Mischief of it to the Publick."[8]

Before adjourning in early November the house took one further action in connection with the Currency Act by pointedly refusing to renew the Loan Office Act of 1737. Initially scheduled to expire in 1743, the measure was extended from time to time, the last extension coming in 1763. Of the original £40,000 loan, one-quarter would be redeemed in 1765; then equal amounts would be sunk yearly until 1768, when the entire issue would be paid up. Meanwhile the loan office provided a means of local payment and a major source of public credit. In addition the legislature regularly appropriated the interest from the loan, a sum amounting to some £2,000 annually, for the use of the government. The last such appropriation covered the period ending April 1765. Though marginal, the income was significant, a fact that had not been lost on the house. Said John Watts: "The Colony is so chagrined at the Treatment of their Paper Money, considering how dutifully they have obeyed the requisitions of the Crown, that brought it all upon them, that they would not hear of so much as offering the Forty Thousand Pounds

8. Watts to Moses Franks, June 9, 1764, Watts to General Monckton, June 30, 1764, *Letter Book of John Watts*, 263–264, 269–270; Oct. 18, 1764, Lott, ed., *Jour. of N.Y. Assembly*, II, 769–780; Cadwallader Colden to Robert Charles, June 8, 1764, *The Colden Letter Books, 1760–1775* (N.-Y. Hist. Soc., *Colls.*, IX–X [New York, 1877–1878]), I, 300–301. For a detailed account of the legislative events involving the protest against the stamp tax and leading up to the petition, see Roger J. Champagne, "The Sons of Liberty and the Aristocracy in New York Politics, 1765–1790" (Ph.D. diss., University of Wisconsin, 1960), 28–31.

Act to the Lieut. Governor, of course it goes on sinking and the Government looses the Fund."[9]

The importance of the "fund" depended on the lack of any "settled Revenue" in New York. Quitrents, for instance, were entirely at the king's disposal. On the other hand a duty of some three shillings per ton on most incoming shipping, like the several local property taxes, was used to redeem specified currency issues. Doubtless fines and license fees generated some revenue, but the only dependable source of existing government funds besides the loan office proved to be the "Duty Act." Passed for the first time in 1753 and annually renewed, it taxed a wide range of imports and before the war produced revenues upwards of £5,000 yearly. The postwar depression cut that sum by half, and thereafter the levy barely covered the current costs of government; the ebbing tide of business presaged even further reductions. In short the loss of the loan office fund constituted a major financial loss, and there is little reason to doubt Watt's claim that the house had angrily lashed out at the Currency Act. Still it seems likely that the assembly recognized that the same act forbade any extension of paper currency issues past September 1, 1764, and that therefore any renewal of the loan would only raise the question of a possible violation of parliamentary law.[10]

A related fiscal action taken immediately following the vote on the loan office was the enactment of a piece of apparent class legislation in response to merchant demands for tax relief and for a ready supply of sterling remittances in a moment of financial distress. In 1756 the house had resolved to use the promised parliamentary reimbursements for New York's contributions to the Seven Years' War to cancel the colony's wartime paper emissions. Instead most of the grants, made in specie and sterling bills, were spent di-

9. Watts to Gen. Robert Monckton, Nov. 10, 1764, *Letter Book of John Watts*, 309–310; *Col. Laws. N.Y.*, II, 1015–1047, III, 294–295, 381–382, 784–787, IV, 156–159, 199–202, 301–304, 385–387, 491–494, 554–556, 649–652, 708–710. For a discussion of the original act of 1737 see Berthold Fernow, "Coins and Currency of New York," in James G. Wilson, ed., *The Memorial History of the City of New York*, IV (New York, 1893), 321–322. The 1737 law was the prototype for all subsequent loan office acts.

10. Gov. William Hardy to B.T., Dec. 2, 1756, Gov. Sir Henry Moore to Secretary of State Shelburne, Feb. 21, 1767, E. B. O'Callaghan and B. Fernow, eds., *Documents Relative to the Colonial History of the State of New-York* (Albany, N.Y., 1853–1887), 906–908, hereafter cited as *N.Y. Col. Docs.*; *Col. Laws N.Y.*, II, 843–847ff, 963–981ff; Watts to Monckton, June 30, 1764, *Letter Book of John Watts*, 269–270.

rectly on military aids for bringing the struggle against France to a successful conclusion. Finally in 1764 the legislators decided to abide by the spirit of their original resolution. In New York City complaints about taxes had increased alarmingly. But in the country, though higher than before the war, taxes proved less burdensome, and complaints were fewer. Urban-mercantile pressures, therefore, apparently prompted the house to cut tax levies by voting to redeem half the currency due in taxes during 1766 and 1767 with whatever sums remained from the various parliamentary grants. This interpretation is strengthened by the experience in Philadelphia a few years earlier, when under virtually identical circumstances most of the grant money, whether in coin or in sterling bills, simply fell into the hands of merchants when the currency was redeemed. Hard pressed to make remittances, they promptly shipped it off to Britain to clear their accounts.[11]

Economic conditions in Pennsylvania after 1760 closely paralleled those in New York. At the end of the war, trade appeared to be in a "melancholy" state. Although some voices had expressed fear that the wartime currency issues might create an oversupply of bills of credit, cash of any kind was reported as "Monstrous scarce." Business failures were on the rise, real estate values on the decline. Local merchants tended to view the downturn as a response to the heavy wartime credit purchases from Britain, the high price of manufactures, overcompetition among sellers, and the growing scarcity of money.[12] Whether or not the complaints about "hard

11. *Col. Laws N.Y.*, IV, 801–804. For a contemporary view of the tax problem see Watts to Sir William Baker, Apr. 22, 1763, *Letter Book of John Watts*, 138. A general discussion of the matter of the parliamentary reimbursements is to be found in Lawrence H. Gipson, *The Triumphant Empire: Thunder-Clouds Gather in the West, 1763–1766* (New York, 1961), chap. 3; see also *ibid.*, 76–81, for a very different view of New York currency than the one presented here. The Philadelphia experience is briefly discussed by James H. Hutson in "Benjamin Franklin and the Parliamentary Grant for 1758," *WMQ*, 3d Ser., XXIII (1966), 589.

12. The most recent study of business conditions in Pennsylvania is Arthur L. Jensen, *The Maritime Commerce of Colonial Philadelphia* (Madison, Wis., 1963). Sachs, "Business Outlook," though covering much of the same material in less detail, is more convincing. Anne Bezanson *et al.*, *Prices in Colonial Pennsylvania* (Philadelphia, 1935), gives a general picture of economic conditions as well as an extended discussion of prices. More merchant correspondence for Pennsylvania has been published than for any other colony, so that statements about the state of the economy are easily documented. See, for instance, Edward Shippen to Colonel Shippen, Dec. 25, 1765, Thomas Balch, ed., *Letters and Papers Relating Chiefly to the Provincial History of Pennsylvania* ... (Philadelphia, 1855), 213–214; Samuel Rhoads, Jr., to Neate, Pigou, and Booth, May 4, June 22, Oct. 20, 1764, Henry D. Biddle, ed., "Extracts from the Letter-Book of Samuel Rhoads, Jr., of

times" were exaggerated, the arrival of news of the Revenue and
Currency Acts elicited from the merchants a solemn prediction that
the new restrictions would "prove extremely detrimental." They
explained in well-worn phrases that the ban on currency alone
would cut into imports, slow remittances, impede local debt collections, reduce commodity exports, and in general force the province back to a barter economy.[13]

At the very least, interest rates were expected to rise as the gap
between the demand and supply of credit and money widened.
William Allen, one of the more prosperous Philadelphia merchants,
wrote David Barclay and Sons of London that, unless there was some
expectation of an advance in his Bank of England stock, the sooner
it was sold the better. "I can make a better Interest of my money
here," Allen said, "and as our Money is yearly sinking, it will, as it
grows less, improve its values."[14] In October the House of Representatives took up the cry about a monetary shortage and instructed
colonial agent Richard Jackson to pay strict attention to future currency developments. Under the present restraints, the representatives
declared, "we shall, in a few Years, be without a necessary Medium
of Trade."[15]

Philadelphia," *PMHB*, XIV (1890), 422–424; Benjamin Marshall to Dr. James
Tapscott, June 22, Oct. 22, 1764, Thomas Stewardson, ed., "Extracts from the
Letter-Book of Benjamin Marshall, 1763–1766," *ibid.*, XX (1896), 206–208. See also
"To the Printer," *Pa. Jour.*, Sept. 5, 1765, for a good summary view of economic
conditions. Harry D. Berg, "Economic Consequences of the French and Indian
War for the Philadelphia Merchants," *Pennsylvania History*, XIII (1946), 185–193,
and Wilbur C. Plummer, "Consumer Credit in Colonial Philadelphia," *PMHB*,
LXVI (1942), 385–409, also contain much useful information.

13. See, for example, May 4, June 22, Oct. 20, 1764, Biddle, ed., "Letter-Book
of Samuel Rhoads, Jr.," *PMHB*, XIV (1890), 422–424; see esp. the views of John
Dickinson in *The Late Regulations Respecting the British Colonies on the Continent
of America Considered*... (Philadelphia, 1765), reprinted in Paul L. Ford, ed.,
The Writings of John Dickinson... (Historical Society of Pennsylvania, *Memoirs*,
XIV [Philadelphia, 1895]), 217–221.

14. Dec. 19, 1764, Lewis B. Walker, ed., *Extracts from Chief Justice William
Allen's Letter Book* (Pottsville, Pa., 1897), 66. Compare this remark with Watts
to Edward Antille, Esq., July 29, 1763, *Letter Book of John Watts*, 163. While interest rates in New York in the period are almost double that in England, Watts
feels that it is still best to keep money invested abroad because locally the paper
currency is liable to depreciate: see also *ibid.*, 176–177. The remark is important
because Watts strongly advocates the use of a domestic paper currency—when
properly regulated. The question of the relationship between paper money and
the rate of interest in America is an important one and needs to be explored.

15. "Votes and Proceedings of the House of Representatives," in Charles F.
Hoban, ed., *Pennsylvania Archives*, 8th Ser., VII (Harrisburg, Pa., 1935), 5680,
hereafter cited as *Pa. Archives*. The house had considered proposing a general
currency plan for America but gave up the idea, feeling that the separate interests

To meet these initial demands from America, the ministry did little except to encourage the importation of copper coin "for the benefit of small change in the retail trade" of cities like New York and Philadelphia and for the supply of the Indians, who were said to be "exceedingly fond of our copper money, which they string round their necks."[16] And in the late summer of 1764 the British government reportedly toyed with a scheme for pumping a large number of English bank notes of "inferior value" into the commercial provinces.[17] The next year rumor after rumor appeared in colonial newspapers promising some sort of relief from the dearth of money and the ban on legal tender paper. Thus in September, to cite one of the more bizarre examples, the *Virginia Gazette* quoted a dispatch from London to the effect that the home government had proposed granting the colonies liberty to open silver and gold mines, "which it is well-known that fertile country abounds with." One action was taken at the time. In response to a petition from Bristol written on behalf of many other commercial centers, the Treasury ordered all British naval commanders not to molest or intercept foreign ships carrying bullion to the colonies.[18] If imperial authorities deferred action on the currency question in 1765, so too did the colonies. There was a growing preoccupation on both sides of the Atlantic with the Stamp Act and the question of parliamentary taxation and, to a lesser extent, with the Revenue Act and the reform of the West Indies trade.

---

of the colonies would prevent any joint action. See John J. Zimmerman, "Benjamin Franklin: A Study of Pennsylvania Politics and the Colonial Agency, 1755–1775" (Ph.D. diss., University of Michigan, 1956), 208–209.

16. News item from London dated Oct. 30, 1764, in *Pennsylvania Gazette* (Philadelphia), Jan. 24, 1765; news item from London dated Mar. 30, 1764, *N.-Y. Mercury*, May 28, 1764.

17. News item from London dated Aug. 13, 1764, *Pa. Gaz.*, Oct. 18, 1764. See also Maurice Morgann to Shelburne, [undated, 1763?], "On American commerce and government, especially in the newly acquired territories," Shelburne Papers, LXXXV, 26–28, William L. Clements Library, Ann Arbor, Mich.

18. See news items from London dated Feb. 8, May 13, 1765, *Pa. Gaz.*, Apr. 18, July 25, 1765; Purdie and Dixon's *Va. Gaz.*, Sept. 15, 1765. Various plans for supplying the colonies with a circulating medium, apart from paper currency, kept coming up for consideration every year in England but were never acted upon; see, for instance, news items from London, *N.-Y. Mercury*, Apr. 28, 1766, Jan. 16, 1767, June 21, 1768; *Pennsylvania Chronicle, and Universal Advertiser* (Philadelphia), Apr. 20, 1767, Aug. 31, 1768. For a brief note on the trade in foreign bullion, see the testimony by the Bristol merchant William Reeve in B. Smith, "Committee to Consider the American Papers," 237. Smith provides a typescript copy of all the evidence, which is not otherwise available, that was given to the parliamentary committee.

FRANKLIN'S "PAPER MONEY SCHEME," 1765–1766

But the Currency Act was by no means a dead issue. Early in 1765 Benjamin Franklin intruded it into the postwar debate over ways to help service Britain's wartime debt and defend an expanded empire. In February, at one of many meetings with the American agents over his proposed stamp tax, George Grenville challenged anyone present to come up with a "Mode of Raising Money for Public Service that the People would have less Objection to." Franklin, who had arrived two months before with a master plan to secure a royal government for Pennsylvania and a larger voice in imperial affairs for all the colonies, promptly offered a "Paper Money Scheme." It called for a general loan office to be established by Parliament with the interest payments to be appropriated for the American service. This, Franklin confided to his friend and political lieutenant, Joseph Galloway, would make for a "lighter and more bearable Tax than the Stamps, because those that pay it have an Equivalent in the Use of the Money." It would also furnish "a Currency which we much wanted, and could not obtain under the restrictions lately laid on us."[19]

This was, of course, not the first time Grenville had heard of a continental currency plan to be paid for by the colonists. A year and a half earlier Henry McCulloh had suggested one.[20] But of the two Franklin's currency scheme proved to be the more significant.

Franklin's proposal for a continental currency grew out of an early correspondence with Richard Jackson. In 1754 Jackson had drafted a "Plan of a Provincial Bank" upon which Franklin had over the years grafted his own views. Ten years later, now agent for Pennsylvania as well as secretary and advisor to Grenville, Jackson wrote Franklin of the chancellor's tax plans and of "a Bill in Embryo for restraining your Paper currency and of all N[orth] America."[21]

---

19. Franklin to Galloway, Oct. 11, 1766, in Benjamin Franklin: Original Letters to Joseph Galloway, 1766–1775, Clements Lib., Ann Arbor, Mich. Verner W. Crane has published two brief accounts of Franklin's connection with the Currency Act repeal movement in "Benjamin Franklin and the Stamp Act," Colonial Society of Massachusetts, *Transactions*, XXXII (1937), 57–59, 60, and *Benjamin Franklin's Letters to the Press, 1758–1775* (Chapel Hill, N.C., 1950), 25–28, 78–80, 99–100. On Franklin's plans as Pennsylvania agent see William S. Hanna, *Benjamin Franklin and Pennsylvania Politics* (Stanford, Calif., 1964), 173–175.

20. See "State of Articles proposed by Mr. M., Oct. 10, 1763," Additional MSS 35910, fols. 137–360, British Museum (copy available in Perkins Library, Duke Univ.). For a discussion of the "McCulloh controversy," see chap. 3.

21. See Franklin to Jackson, Dec. 6, 1753, Jackson to Franklin, Mar. 17, 1754

Franklin's first move was to get a paper money measure through the Pennsylvania General Assembly before Parliament banned paper currency altogether. Only then did he direct his full attention to the Currency Act and Grenville's tax program. In late June 1764 he wrote Jackson, "I note what you say of the Colonies applying for a Stamp Act. In my Opinion there is not only no Likelihood that they will generally agree in such an Application, but even that one Colony will propose it to the others." Still, if Britain made the traditional request for a gross sum and left the colonies to raise it at a general congress, Franklin felt they might "fall on some such general Tax, as a Stamp Act" rather than set a quota for each colony. The idea amounted to little more than a variation of his old Albany Plan. In any event Franklin claimed to know of a "better Mode by far, both for us and for you . . . but a Letter will not suit the Discussion of it." That better way was none other than the paper money scheme offered to Grenville as a substitute for the stamp tax.[22]

Franklin's proposal called for taxing his countrymen while providing them with a common circulating medium and a source of agricultural and commercial credit. It combined the familiar principles of the colonial loan office and the specific features of a Pennsylvania act of 1739. In effect Parliament would repeal the Currency Act of 1764, the act of 1708 regulating the maximum values at which foreign coin would pass in America, and the act of 1741 banning certain forms of wildcat banking throughout the empire. Paper money already in circulation was to be called in and destroyed. After eliminating existing currency controls and supplies, Parliament would authorize the erection of a colonial loan office system to issue some millions of pounds of legal tender notes printed in England for ten-year periods. Loans were to require "double Security by a mortgage of real clear Estate"; counterfeiting was to be punishable by death. According to Franklin the plan's chief advantages were that it would help free coin to serve as a "Means of remittance to Britain" and provide the colonies with a lawful tender "sufficient for all Purposes." In addition the suggested annual interest charge

(which includes Jackson's 1754 plan), Jan. 26, 1764, Carl Van Doren, ed., *Letters and Papers of Benjamin Franklin and Richard Jackson, 1753–1785* (Philadelphia, 1947), 1–2, 41–54, 139. Franklin's 1764 proposal is printed in Crane, ed., *Franklin's Letters to the Press*, 28–30.

22. See Franklin to Jackson, June 25, 1764, Van Doren, ed., *Letters and Papers of Franklin and Jackson*, 168 (quoted), and an undated memorandum quoted and considered in Carl Van Doren, *Benjamin Franklin* (New York, 1938), 334.

of 6 percent would operate as a general tax but not "an unpleasing one."[23]

At the moment Grenville, "being besotted with his Stamp Scheme," paid paper money little heed.[24] Without investigating whether Franklin's plan was feasible, or even preferable to a stamp tax from the American point of view, he initiated on February 6, 1765, a series of parliamentary debates that culminated in the passage of the Stamp Act in March. Three months later the king rid himself of Grenville, who had succeeded in alienating both the colonies and crown, and brought in the Old Whigs.

Franklin was delighted. He met with Lords Rockingham and Dartmouth, respectively the head of the new government and the new president of the Board of Trade, in November and pleaded for the suspension of the Stamp Act on some decent pretext without bringing the "Question of Right to a Decision." Instead Franklin proposed "either a thorough Union with America, or that Government here would proceed in the old Method of Requisition."[25] Apparently his paper money scheme also came up for discussion. Early the next month Thomas Pownall, former governor of Massachusetts and New Jersey, wrote Thomas Hutchinson from London that "Ben Franklin and I are going this morning to Lord Rockingham's on the subject of a Paper we have jointly given in relative to the procuring a general Paper Currency for the Colonies, by authority of Government here and connected with the Bank of England—you will find it referr'd to in p. 111—of The Administration of the Colonies—as there suspended from publication."[26]

By this time the possibility of creating a continental currency had already come to the attention of the new Rockingham ministry. Henry McCulloh had revived, with some slight changes, the paper money scheme first presented to Grenville. But McCulloh's propo-

---

23. Crane, ed., *Franklin's Letters to the Press*, 28–30. For a critical discussion of the feasibility of Franklin's plan, see Yoder, "Paper Currency in Colonial Pennsylvania," 380–401.

24. Franklin to Galloway, Nov. 8, 1766, Original Letters to Joseph Galloway.

25. In connection with the lengthy controversy concerning whether or not Grenville was actually willing to consider an option to the Stamp Act, see Gipson, *Triumphant Empire*, 270, n. 73. The quote is from Crane, "Franklin and the Stamp Act," Col. Soc. Mass., *Trans.*, XXXII (1937), 66.

26. Quoted in Crane, ed., *Franklin's Letters to the Press*, 27. Crane discusses in detail the textual differences between the Franklin draft and Pownall's published version. See also Thomas Pownall, *The Administration of the Colonies*, 2d ed. (London, 1765), 111, and *ibid.*, 4th ed. (London, 1768), 240–253.

sal again proved unacceptable, this time because it was tied to the idea of maintaining the Stamp Act. Specifically McCulloh argued that there was not coin enough in most colonies to enable the people to heed the law and "Pay in Specie." The only thing that could be done "in Relief of the Colonies" was to issue "Exchequer Orders" in all payments to America and thus provide the basis for a new colonial "Coinage" and for obedience to the law. By contrast the plan Franklin and Hutchinson had in mind offered a substitute for a stamp tax. And according to Franklin the Rockinghamites "really strengthened one another and their Friends in the Resolution of repealing the Stamp Act, on a Supposition that by this Plan of a Loan Office they could raise a greater Sum with more satisfaction to the People." The December meeting with Rockingham was only the first of frequent conferences over the possibility of creating a continental currency.[27]

Far more important than the paper money scheme to the repeal of the Stamp Act was the lobby of "the Merchants of London trading to North America." Formally organized on December 4, 1765, the merchants aimed at rendering all possible service to the colonies. Their efforts in 1765 and 1766 in connection with the tax and trade questions have been discussed elsewhere.[28] Less familiar is their alliance with the colonial agents in a concerted drive to secure repeal of the Currency Act of 1764 during the years 1766, 1767, and 1768. While the Rockinghamites weighed Franklin's loan office plan, many of the same London merchants who had been instrumental in securing the Currency Act now moved into action against the Stamp Act. They quickly initiated a drive for repeal as a part of a general reform of colonial trade designed to spur Britain's flagging postwar commerce. The merchants persisted, however, in demanding the right to refuse any future paper money issues as lawful for *sterling* debts, a condition they had laid down in 1757 during the struggle over Virginia currency practices. The point caused no great trouble. For

27. Franklin to Galloway, Oct. 11, 1766, Original Letters to Joseph Galloway. The information about McCulloh is from D. H. Watson, "Barlow Trecothick and Other Associates of Lord Rockingham during the Stamp Act Crisis, 1765–1766" (M.A. thesis, University of Sheffield, 1957), 155–157. See also n. 20 above.

28. Lucy S. Sutherland, "Edmund Burke and the First Rockingham Ministry," *Eng. Hist. Rev.*, XLVII (1932), 46–70. For further information on the merchants, see Watson, "Barlow Trecothick," and Lucy S. Sutherland, "The City of London in Eighteenth-Century Politics," in Richard Pares and A. J. P. Taylor, eds., *Essays Presented to Sir Lewis Namier* (New York, 1956), 49–75. The members of the London merchants' committee were actually elected representatives of merchant groups trading to the individual colonies. See Watson, "Barlow Trecothick," 38, 218.

their part the agents' chief concern was to maintain the legal tender
quality of paper currency in all *domestic* payments—in order both
to safeguard debtors against the caprice of creditors and to facilitate
the circulation of paper by enforcing its acceptability. In addition a
legal tender paper currency was a familiar and ancient system in the
colonies.[29]

The London merchants had barely organized when in February
1766 the House of Commons undertook a major inquiry into the
state of the colonies. Focused largely on American demands for the
repeal of the Stamp Act and the revision of the Revenue Act, the
investigation also included questions concerning the "Vast debt
owing" from America, "the Impracticality of Payment in Specie,
the Scarcity thereof" and the "want of a proper medium in Paper."[30]
The carefully staged testimony of Franklin on the Stamp and Revenue Acts, together with the prepared statements of the London
merchants, added great weight to the claim of a monetary pinch in
the colonies. And in his testimony, at least, Franklin made a point
of listing the Currency Act, together with the Stamp Act and the
restrictions on trade, as a principal reason for America's growing dissatisfaction with Parliament.[31]

From the start of the inquiry newspapers on both sides of the At-

29. See the discussion in "British Merchant Protest, 1757–1760," in chap. 3 above.
For a contrasting interpretation of the need for the legal tender quality of currency
see Sosin, "Imperial Regulation of Colonial Paper Money," *PMHB*, LXXXVIII
(1964), 185–192, esp. 188. A comparison of the London merchants' memorial of
Dec. 1762 with the letters of the London merchants' committee of Feb. 28, Mar.
18, and June 13, 1766, shows that at least 10 out of the original 18 petitioners of
1762 favored repeal of the Currency Act. See *Acts of Privy Council, Col.,* IV,
643; and Massachusetts Historical Society, *Proceedings,* LV (1923), 217, 219–220,
222–223.

30. Joseph W. Barnwell, ed., "Hon. Charles Garth, M.P., The Last Colonial
Agent of South Carolina in England, and Some of his Work," *South Carolina
Historical and Genealogical Magazine,* XXVI (1925), 89. An excellent discussion
of the inquiry is B. Smith, "Committee to Consider the American Papers." See also
the related work by Watson, "Barlow Trecothick." The actual evidence presented
concerning the currency question was less than useful; see B. Smith, "Committee
to Consider the American Papers," 139.

31. The *Examination* is printed in Albert H. Smyth, ed., *Writings of Benjamin
Franklin* (New York, 1905–1907), IV, 412–448. Questions 14, 15, 16, 23–25, 30, 40,
41, 42, and 74–78 refer to colonial money problems. See also the discussion of
Franklin's marginal notes and his *Examination* in Crane, "Franklin and the Stamp
Act," Col. Soc. Mass., *Trans.,* XXXII (1937), 68, 70–72, and Franklin's unpublished
"Fragments of the Stamp-Act Pamphlet," Crane, ed., *Franklin's Letters to the
Press,* 63–73; the British merchants' memorials and statements in *Jours. of Com-
mons,* XXX, 462–463, 465, 501, 503; and Merrill Jensen, ed., *English Historical
Documents: American Colonial Documents to 1776,* IX (New York, 1962), 687.

lantic confidently predicted the elimination of the Stamp Act, reasonable relief from the Revenue Act, and repeal of the Currency Act. Some papers even hinted at an emission of exchequer notes for America and the minting of a colonial coinage at New York.[32] As expected, on March 11, 1766, the House of Commons repealed the Stamp Act. But shortly after, the victorious coalition of North American and West Indian merchants split over the proposed liberalization of the foreign West Indian trade. Consequently the London merchants gave the amendment of the Revenue Act priority over any changes in the currency law. So did Rockingham's followers. They agreed to push the reform of the Caribbean trade, against the wishes of the West Indians, and to let the money question slide until the next session. The effect of this decision was to scotch a recent petition for repeal of the Currency Act coming out of Pennsylvania, the first colony officially and specifically to call for such a move.[33]

The Pennsylvania economy had touched bottom in 1765 and then leveled off again as local merchants began to take advantage of nonimportation and the debt moratorium associated with the closing of the courts to reduce inventories and straighten out finances. However, demand for British goods continued dull, as did sales in the West Indies. If the Caribbean seemed beyond their control, the Pennsylvanians nevertheless believed that they could promote local sales by judiciously increasing the paper money supply. Money did appear to be scarce. By the beginning of 1766 the amount of paper in circulation ran close to £290,000 out of the total of £330,000 outstanding at the end of the war. Coin supplies apparently diminished far more rapidly. Short-term British credit, on the other hand, eased slightly. But if, generally speaking, the volume of money was down, so was the velocity, for merchants tended to hold on to cash as a hedge against a protracted depression. Moreover, starting in the

32. See, for example, news items from London dated Feb. 10, 1766, printed in various newspapers: *Newport Mercury*, Apr. 28, 1766; *Pa. Gaz.*, May 1, 1766; Rind's *Va. Gaz.*, May 16, 1766. See also news item from London dated Mar. 1, 1766, *Pa. Gaz.*, May 1, 1766; another news item from London dated Mar. 1, 1766, *ibid.*, May 8, 1766; Fred J. Hinkhouse, *The Preliminaries of the American Revolution as seen in the English Press, 1763–1775* (New York, 1926), 45–48.

33. Sutherland, "Burke and the First Rockingham Ministry," *Eng. Hist. Rev.*, XLVII (1932), 68–70; Garth to South Carolina Committee of Correspondence, June 6, 1766, Barnwell, ed., "Garth Correspondence," *S.C. Hist. Gen. Mag.*, XXVIII (1927), 232. The need possibly to alter the Currency Act seems to have come up as early as Dec. 31, 1765, at a dinner at Rockingham's attended by some of the leading members of the merchants' committee; see Watson, "Barlow Trecothick," 7–8.

late fall of 1765 European demands for American wheat and flour suddenly boosted the cash price for such items in the colonial market and thereby increased the demand for a local medium of exchange.[34] Convinced of the ill effects of the monetary stringency on sales of British goods and of the need to facilitate the grain and flour trade, the Pennsylvania General Assembly early in January petitioned the House of Commons for repeal of the Currency Act. Prohibiting the emission of moderate sums of paper money was throttling the economy, the petition declared. Paper money had lifted the province from the stage of barter and commutation to a money economy in which contracts multiplied, personal and real estates rose to their proper values, numbers increased, "Trade became extended, and the Settlement of the Country proceeded with more Rapidity than the most sanguine Expectations could suggest." The petitioners went on to claim that the same happy effects had ever flowed from the use of paper bills of credit "in Proportion to the Sums emitted, without the least Inconveniency or Prejudice to the Merchants of *Great-Britain*, or the People of this Province." Most important, according to the petition, commerce could not be carried on "to any beneficial Extent, without a proper Medium of circulating Cash." And since a trade imbalance with Britain made it impossible to keep a permanent stock of gold and silver in circulation, Pennsylvania had to have the liberty of issuing reasonable quantities of paper. Furthermore the money had to be legal tender, because under British law the person of every debtor was "a Security to his Creditor for the Performance of the Contract, and Discharge of the Debt." Otherwise the debtor would be subject to the whims of his creditor. The petition anticipated that in 1773, when the existing supply of bills of credit would all be sunk, "Commerce with our Mother Country will languish and expire with them." It was in the interest of both parties, therefore, that the Currency Act be repealed.[35]

Pennsylvania's petition arrived in London sometime in March. With the help of Richard Jackson, who was a member of Parliament, Franklin had the document presented to the House of Commons early in April. Then apparently at Jackson's request, Franklin, aided by John Huske—a member of Parliament, former New England merchant, and close associate of Charles Townshend's—drew

34. Sachs, "Business Outlook," 193–203.
35. "House of Representatives," *Pa. Archives*, VII, 5818, 5824–5827. In addition the petition noted that part of the outstanding currency circulated in the neighboring colonies of New Jersey and Maryland. See also Israel Pemberton to Benjamin Franklin, May 15, 1766, William Smith Letterbook, Hist. Soc. Pa., Philadelphia.

up a Currency Act repeal bill to be brought into the Commons "with
the seeming approbation of the Ministers." As Franklin later noted,
nothing was done. The session was nearly at an end, and two Board
members sitting in the House, Robert Nugent and Jeremiah Dyson,
vigorously opposed the measure. Then, too, the administration and
the merchants had already withdrawn their support of repeal because of the rift over the reform of the West Indies trade.[36]

Pennsylvania's was not the only call for repeal that session. Possibly in an effort to clear the way for Franklin's continental currency
and tax scheme, just before the House of Commons adjourned for
the summer, a member moved for leave to bring in a bill repealing
not only the act of 1708 governing the value of foreign coin in
America but also the Currency Acts of 1751 and 1764. The ministry
promptly killed the motion—an action, according to Franklin, designed to give the ministers time to settle the plan "to their own
Minds" and to canvass American views so that the loan office, whenever carried into execution, would be as perfect as possible. Whatever truth there was in his assertion, Franklin claimed that he hoped
the plan would meet with "general Consent as it was a Matter of
great Importance." He was careful, however, not to press the issue.
In the meantime the agents learned that the entire subject would
come up for reconsideration during the adjournment of Parliament
so that some beneficial plan for all America might be offered at the
next session.[37]

Franklin was playing a double game. Before the Stamp Act crisis
he had accepted the need for an American revenue and the right of
parliamentary taxation. He had questioned only the expediency of
the Stamp Act. His substitute plan, for example, clearly acknowledged the principle and necessity of a tax. By the fall of 1766, however, Franklin had come to recognize the depth of the crisis in imperial relations and of American feelings, and his own views of the
empire and parliamentary authority were undergoing rapid changes.
In October he wrote Galloway that he believed his loan office plan

36. Franklin to the Committee of Correspondence of the Assembly of Pennsylvania, Apr. 12, June 10, 1766, "Original Letters and Documents," *PMHB*, V (1881),
353–354; Franklin to Galloway, Oct. 11, 1766, Original Letters to Joseph Galloway.
See also John Huske to Charles Townshend, Apr. 9, 1767, Sir Lewis Namier and
John Brooke, *Charles Townshend* (London, 1964), 187–188, and the descriptions of
Nugent and Dyson in Sir Lewis Namier and John Brook, *The House of Commons,
1754–1790* (New York, 1964), II, 371–373, III, 218–222.

37. Franklin to Galloway, Oct. 11, 1766, Original Letters to Joseph Galloway;
Garth to S.C. Comm. of Corres., June 6, 1766, Barnwell, ed., "Garth Correspondence," *S.C. Hist. Gen. Mag.*, XXVIII (1927), 232.

had helped pave the way for the repeal of the Stamp Act. But he no longer viewed that plan as a solution to either the currency or tax problem. Instead Franklin wanted a simple repeal of the Currency Act of 1764 and a return to former currency practices and royal controls. He was, he declared, coming to see the colonies as "so many separate states, only subject to the same king, as England and Scotland were before the union."[38] It followed that the Americans should regulate their own economic destinies, including their currency supply, independent of Parliament.

Fortunately for the sake of Franklin's reputation in America, the Rockingham ministry fell on July 5, 1766—before it could take any action on its expressed intention of implementing his idea for a continental loan office. When the succeeding Pitt-Grafton ministry showed no immediate interest in the plan, Franklin successfully contrived to conceal his authorship, as well he might. By the fall of 1766 news of the scheme had already reached the colonies and began showing up in the provincial newspapers. The response was not favorable. As Galloway explained to Franklin's son, Governor William Franklin of New Jersey, "I have heard from many very warm objections against such a Plan, and in the present Temper of Americans, I think it would occasion great Clamours. I have been full in my Sentiments to him [B. Franklin] on the Subject."[39]

38. Franklin to Galloway, Oct. 11, 1766, Original Letters to Joseph Galloway; Franklin to William Franklin, Mar. 13, 1768, Smyth, ed., *Writings of Franklin*, V, 114–115. For a full discussion of Franklin's views of empire see Crane, "Franklin and the Stamp Act," Col. Soc. Mass., *Trans.*, XXXII (1937), 56–57; Crane, ed., *Franklin's Letters to the Press*, xxvii–xlvi.

39. Dec. 21, 1766, quoted in Crane, "Franklin and the Stamp Act," Col. Soc. Mass., *Trans.*, XXXII (1937), 59. On what was known about the plan in America see, for example, the news item from Charleston dated Nov. 17, 1766, in *South-Carolina Gazette* (Charleston), Nov. 10–17, 1766, and "The News Boy's Verses," New Year's Day Supplement, 1767, in *New-York Journal, or General Advertiser*, Jan. 1, 1767:

> We have often been told they have form'd a Design,
> To levy a *Tax* on the *Money we coin*;
> And that this is the Reason *no Bills* must be pass'd—
> —That compell'd by our Wants, we may yield at the last.
> An Office is plann'd, wherein Money on Loan
> May be had—*on a Tax, for the Use of our own.*
> *Security ample*, at first must be made,
> And the *Int'rest* must all to *Great-Britain* be paid;
> —Take heed oh my Friends! if you swallow the Bait;
> You'll surely be brought to Repentence too late;
> You'll find it another *Stamp-Act* in Disguise,
> So I warn you to shun it, if Freedom you prize.

PETITIONS FOR REPEAL, 1766–1767

During the next six months the Currency Act repeal movement was temporarily rid of the Franklin scheme. Meanwhile South Carolina joined Pennsylvania in petitioning for repeal and a return to former practices and policies. In August 1764, shortly after receiving news of the Currency Act, the South Carolina Commons House of Assembly instructed its agent, Charles Garth, to obtain royal consent to a treasury issue of £280,000 in legal tender bills.[40] The desire for paper money in South Carolina, as opposed to New York and Pennsylvania, was a reflection of both good and bad times. The South Carolinians feared that the rapidly expanding economy and population would soon outstrip the £100,000 of lawful currency struck back in 1731, nearly a quarter of which already circulated in neighboring Georgia and North Carolina.

Garth appears to have had little success in carrying out his instructions, and the following spring he declined "any further Application concerning the Augmentation" of legal tender paper, probably because of the chance for a general repeal of the Currency Act and the growing preoccupation in England with the question of a Stamp Act and the right of parliamentary taxation. In any event the Commons House approved Garth's request and deferred further action until June 1766; by then it had learned of the joint attack on the Currency Act by the London merchants and colonial agents, and it ordered Garth to work for repeal.[41] Prominent in the attempt to head off the passage of the Currency Act in the first place, Garth had kept close watch on subsequent developments and had already taken the initiative. In July he informed the Commons House that repeal could now possibly be obtained through petition, "it having lately, since the Prorogation [of Parliament] been thrown out, that this was no part of the Complaints taken up at the [Stamp Act] Congress, and that no Colony Petition'd but Pennsylvania, and that the

40. Apr. 6, 1765, Journals of the Commons House of Assembly of South Carolina, William Sumner Jenkins, ed., *Records of the States of the United States of America: A Microfilm Compilation* (Washington, D.C., 1949), hereafter cited as Jours. of S.C. Commons House. Because pagination is not consecutive, page citations are omitted. See also Committee of Correspondence of the S.C. Commons House of Assembly to Charles Garth, Sept. 4, 1764, Robert W. Gibbes, ed., *Documentary History of the American Revolution Consisting of Letters and Papers . . .* (New York, 1853–1857), I, 2.
41. June 24, 1766, Jours. of S.C. Commons House.

four [New England] Colonies who were some years since prohibited to give the Sanction of legal Tender to their Emissions have never complained." According to the agent the ministry believed this would be the case with the colonies outside New England regardless of whether they liked the restraint at first; the colonies therefore had no choice but to ask for repeal. Garth concluded: "If we do not succeed we are but where we were, at least we shall check unfair, and I believe untrue Constructions."[42]

That September, after receiving his instructions, Garth repeated his plea. He added, however, that a reshuffling of the ministry in August had returned Lord Hillsborough—the man chiefly responsible for the framing of the Currency Act—to the Board of Trade to replace Dartmouth as president. Hillsborough would be a powerful adversary, but the agent believed that if all the aggrieved colonies applied for repeal there was little reason to be doubtful of success.[43]

In late November 1766 the South Carolina assembly met Garth's request by petitioning the crown for repeal of the Currency Act and permission to strike an additional £350,000 in fiat money. The petition essentially spelled out the arguments of August 1764. It noted that not only did the province lack specie enough to answer its demand for money but also foreign coin was not legal tender. The only lawful money was the £106,500 currency issued in 1731 and reissued in 1746. Although no provision existed for the redemption of this money, only some £70,000 or so actually circulated; the remainder was presumably lost or destroyed. Since 1731, the petition continued, trade and population had increased enormously. Annual exports averaged £350,000, while taxes were double the value of the entire stock of lawful currency. The petition claimed that the result was a monetary stringency that adversely affected both British and local interests. The inadequate currency supply had supposedly dragged down realty values, and colonial debtors, lacking an adequate medium of local exchange, were said to be in danger of losing their estates by default. In self-defense the province would have to cut back British imports to relieve the drain on specie. Perhaps it would even be driven to manufacture for itself. The petition concluded that, as it was an absolute necessity to establish a legal tender paper currency as a medium of trade, repeal was in the in-

42. Garth to S.C. Comm. of Corres., July 9, 1766, Barnwell, ed., "Garth Correspondence," *S.C. Hist. Gen. Mag.*, XXIX (1928), 41.
43. Garth to S.C. Comm. of Corres., Sept. 3, Sept. 26, 1766, *ibid.*, 43–45.

terest of all. South Carolina's petition reached London early in January just ahead of a similar document from New York.[44]

Economic prospects in New York at the beginning of 1766 were characterized by the same conditions affecting Pennsylvania. The economic slump appears to have bottomed out in late 1765, as local merchants and traders began to sell off their inventories and untangle their finances following the closing of the courts and the stoppage of British trade in connection with the Stamp Act and nonimportation. In the meantime, although local demand for English goods remained slack, the export trade in wheat and flour was beginning to assume the proportions of a boom. Under the circumstances there was a growing complaint of the scarcity of cash and of credit sufficient to stimulate the purchase of imported goods and to facilitate exports.[45]

It was in response to such conditions and in anticipation of an early repeal of the Currency Act that Speaker Philip Livingston requested that the New York General Assembly be summoned in order to pass a currency measure replacing the existing stock of bills of credit scheduled to be fully redeemed two years hence. Failing word of the Currency Act, New York's governor, Sir Henry Moore, postponed any action before finally calling the legislature into session in the middle of June. By that time news of the Stamp Act repeal had arrived creating widespread optimism among the merchants and eliciting predictions of the imminent revival of prosperity. Demand for an added supply of money and credit suddenly assumed a note of urgency. As soon as the assembly convened, Speaker Livingston moved to draft and present a measure for issuing the familiar bills of credit on loan, a move that the house had indignantly rejected just two years earlier. Times had changed, and the representatives could no longer afford to stand on principle.[46]

44. S.C. Commons House Petition to the crown, Nov. 28, 1766, Original Correspondence of the Board of Trade—South Carolina, 1760–1775, C.O. 5/378–380, P.R.O.; Nov. 28, 1766, Jours. of S.C. Commons House; Garth to S.C. Comm. of Corres., Jan. 31, 1767, Barnwell, ed., "Garth Correspondence," *S.C. Hist. Gen. Mag.*, XXIX (1928), 129. See also the extract of a letter from Charleston, Purdie and Dixon's *Va. Gaz.*, Oct. 29, 1767.

45. Moore to Lords of Trade, Mar. 28, 1766, *N.Y. Col. Docs.*, VII, 821; June 17, 1766, Jour. of N.Y. Assembly (after 1764 references are to the microfilm version in Jenkins, ed., *Microfilm Records of the States*). On the question of the growing scarcity of cash see John Van Cortlandt to Robert Tucker, Mar. 20, 1766, Van Cortlandt to John William Hoffman, July 25, 1766, John Van Cortlandt Letterbook, (A), 1762–1769, New York Public Library, New York City. See also n. 34 above.

46. Moore to Lords of Trade, Mar. 28, 1766, "Representation of the Lords of

Moore still had no word of the Currency Act, and two weeks later he prorogued the assembly, thus preventing any final vote on the loan office. Three months passed before the legislature reconvened. By then, in response to his recent request to the Board of Trade for an "indulgence" because of the postwar depression and the early redemption date of New York's remaining currency, Sir Henry had obtained a release from his instructions against signing paper money measures except during war and invasion. On the other hand there was no relaxation of the provisions of the Currency Act of 1764; that required parliamentary action. To put New York "upon a foot of equal advantage with neighbouring Colonies where the . . . paper credit is extended to more distant periods," the governor could allow the issuance of just over a quarter million pounds of *non-legal tender* bills. The assembly had only to agree to create an adequate redemption fund, redeem the money within five years, and attach a suspending clause to the act of emission, conditions that the Board of Trade had tried to impose on all colonies with mixed success ever since 1720.[47]

Sir Henry was delighted with the concession. The assembly was not. It disputed the crown's right to insist upon a suspending clause —a long-standing grievance—or to veto a money bill. Moreover the indulgence seemed to offer nothing that the Currency Act did not already permit; for example, as the house stressed, the 1764 act in no way prohibited or limited non-legal tender currency issues.[48] Consequently the assembly urged the governor to assent instead to an emergency emission of only £130,000. The redemption period was to be extended to eight years, and the suspending clause dropped. However, Sir Henry would agree only to submit the suggested measure to the Board of Trade for review. Under the circumstances the house temporarily gave up the scheme in the hope of

Trade on the Circulation of Bills of Credit," May 16, 1766, Lords of Trade to Moore, July 11, 1766, *N.Y. Col. Docs.,* VII, 820–821, 827–828, 843–845.

47. "Representation of the Lords of Trade on the Circulation of Bills of Credit," May 16, 1766, Lords of Trade to Moore, July 11, 1766, *ibid.,* 827–828, 843–845. For a different interpretation of this action see Greene and Jellison, "Currency Act of 1764," *WMQ,* 3d Ser., XVIII (1961), 494–495. See also the discussion in chap. 2 above.

48. Nov. 13, 1766, *Jour of N.Y. Assembly.* See also James Duane to Robert R. Livingston, Nov. 15, 1766, Livingston-Redmond Papers, Roll 6, Franklin D. Roosevelt Library, Hyde Park, New York; Moore to Lords of Trade, Nov. 15, 1766, *N.Y. Col. Docs.,* VII, 878. On the past history of the question of the suspending clause and currency bills, see Bernhard Knollenberg, *Origin of the American Revolution: 1759–1766* (New York, 1960), 63–66, 69.

an outright repeal of the Currency Act, a law seen by a growing number of New Yorkers as "an unreasonable restriction on our own property."[49] Auspices were good. The assembly had already received a copy of a repeal bill from Robert Charles, who reported that it would come before the present session of Parliament.[50] Moore was optimistic and felt that the suspending clause matter was simply a way of preventing New York from doing anything until repeal was accomplished and paper money again became lawful for everything except British debts.[51] His interpretation of events was strengthened somewhat by the arrival of a dispatch from the Board of Trade setting forth the various arguments for and against legal tender paper and requesting the governor to canvass the reactions of leading merchants.[52]

In London meanwhile Garth presented the South Carolina petition sometime in mid-January 1767 to the earl of Shelburne, the newly appointed secretary of state for the Southern Department, which included American affairs. Shelburne promised to advise the Privy Council about the petition at the earliest moment and to promote repeal "to the utmost of his power." A similar pledge of support from the new chancellor of the Exchequer, Charles Townshend, gave Garth some encouragement, although he noted "a great Diversity of Opinions subsisting about the propriety of a Paper Currency to be at all a legal Tender, and even among the Servants of the Crown in Administration."[53] Franklin also allowed himself a show of optimism, especially after Lord Clare replaced Hillsborough as president of the Board of Trade in February. In fact, since the ministerial changes in the fall of 1766, Franklin and Jackson had been "making all the Impressions possible whenever we can be heard."[54] In addition there were fresh rumors of the possibility of the creation of a mint in New York and of the issuance of quantities of English bank notes.[55] Another favorable sign was the reactivation of the North Ameri-

49. Moore to Lords of Trade, Nov. 15, 1766, *N.Y. Col. Docs.*, VII, 878; *N.-Y. Jour.*, Nov. 27, 1766.
50. Moore to Lords of Trade, Dec. 19, 1766, *N.Y. Col. Docs.*, 884.
51. Peter R. Livingston to his father, Nov. 24, 1766, Livingston-Redmond Papers, Roll 6. See also Moore to B.T., Dec. 19, 1766, *N.Y. Col. Docs.*, VII, 884.
52. B.T. to Moore, July 11, 1766, *N.Y. Col. Docs.*, VII, 844.
53. Garth to S.C. Comm. of Corres., Jan. 31, 1767, Barnwell, ed., "Garth Correspondence," *S.C. Hist. Gen. Mag.*, XXIX (1928), 129.
54. Franklin to Galloway, Dec. 13, 1766, Original Letters to Joseph Galloway.
55. News item from London dated Mar. 6, 1766, *N.-Y. Mercury*, Apr. 28, 1766.

can merchants earlier in January and the election by them of a select body to consider a plan for the circulation of paper currency in the colonies. The merchants, who persisted in the belief that an expanded currency supply would increase American sales and remittances, were thoroughly sanguine about the chances for success and agreed to work directly with the agents in preparing a number of plans for final consideration.[56] At its first session on January 12, 1767, the select committee dropped all other plans in favor of a simple repeal of the Currency Act and a return to earlier practices—with the understanding that future paper money issues would not extend to sterling debts contracted by or in behalf of merchants residing in Great Britain.[57] On January 28 a general meeting of the merchants, with both Garth and Franklin present, adopted the committee resolutions and named "six respectable Merchants to attend the Kings Ministers, and desire their Concurrence and Aid" at the upcoming session of Parliament.[58] In the meantime Franklin was to outline a repeal bill to be filled in by Jackson, who was delegated to bring the measure into the House of Commons after it reconvened. Franklin was also to draft some "Hints or Arguments" for use in the House of Lords by the duke of Grafton, head of the new ministry.[59]

As it turned out, the "six respectable Merchants" got nowhere with the ministry.[60] Despite Garth and Franklin's growing optimism, the merchants' proposals, the New York General Assembly resolutions, and the South Carolina petition were lost in the rising tide of antagonism between the mother country and her colonies. Thus Shelburne, notwithstanding earlier promises of all-out support, sent the proposals and the petition to the Board of Trade with only perfunctory comments. The Board simply shelved the matter for the time being, although at Garth's insistence the South Carolina address, at least, received a cursory reading before being dismissed.[61]

56. Extract of a letter from London dated Jan. 10, 1767, *Pa. Chron.*, Apr. 6, 1767.
57. Extract of a letter from London dated Jan. 12, 1767, *ibid.*, Apr. 6, 1767; extract of a letter from London dated Feb. 12, 1767, *Pa. Gaz.*, Apr. 23, 1767.
58. Garth to S.C. Comm. of Corres., Jan. 31, 1767, Barnwell, ed., "Garth Correspondence," *S.C. Hist. Gen. Mag.*, XXIX (1928), 130.
59. Franklin to Jackson, Feb. 13, 1767, Van Doren, ed., *Letters and Papers of Franklin and Jackson*, 196–197. Franklin, it should be noted, wanted a statutory limit placed on the volume of legal tender currency to be issued in each colony. *Ibid.*, 197.
60. Extract of letter from London dated Feb. 12, 1767, *Pa. Gaz.*, Apr. 23, 1767.
61. Shelburne to B.T., Feb. 13, 1767, Shelburne Papers, LIII, 41–42; Feb. 17, 1767, *Jour. of Comm. Trade, 1764–1767*, 367; Garth to S.C. Comm. of Corres., Jan. 31,

Shelburne's volte-face stemmed from the growing reluctance of New York, and the colonies generally, to submit to British policy despite repeal of the Stamp Act and revision of the Revenue Act.[62] The refusal of the New York General Assembly in the summer of 1766 to adhere to the letter of the Quartering Act in supplying the king's troops had precipitated a special cabinet meeting and a call for strict obedience in the future. In December the assembly repeated its performance. The news reached Shelburne early in February 1767, just before he submitted the South Carolina petition for repeal of the Currency Act to the Board of Trade.[63]

Shelburne was also affected by a move taken by the New York merchants late in 1766. On hearing that the newly appointed chancellor of the Exchequer, Charles Townshend, viewed the Revenue Act of 1766 as a useless reform, the New Yorkers had petitioned the House of Commons for changes in the law. They specifically cited its ill effects on local trade, profits, and specie reserves.[64] There was

---

1767, Barnwell, ed., "Garth Correspondence," *S.C. Hist. Gen. Mag.,* XXIX (1928), 129.

62. Garth to S.C. Comm. of Corres., May 17, 1767, *ibid.,* 223.

63. *Ibid.,* 223–224; Shelburne to Chatham, Feb. 6, 1767, W. S. Taylor and J. H. Pringle, eds., *Correspondence of William Pitt, Earl of Chatham* (London, 1838–1840), III, 191–194. See the discussion by Elmer Olm, "The Chatham Ministry and the American Colonies, 1766–1768" (Ph.D. diss., University of Michigan, 1960), 58–61; Nicholas Varga, "The New York Restraining Act: Its Passage and Some Effects, 1766–1768," *N.Y. Hist.,* XXXVII (1956), 233–258; John Shy, *Toward Lexington: The Role of the British Army in the Coming of the American Revolution* (Princeton, N.J., 1965), chap. 6. Despite the excellence of Shy's analysis of the Quartering Act controversy in England, his discussion of the problem as it affected New York misses altogether the connections among such variables as the provisioning of troops, the emission of paper money, and the political struggle between the two factions of New York politics, the Livingstons and the De Lanceys.

64. The petition is printed in *Jours. of Commons,* XXXI, 158–160. See also Moore to Shelburne, Apr. 20, 1767, *N.Y. Col. Docs.,* VII, 920–921; Feb. 16, 1767, *Jour. of Comm. Trade, 1764–1767,* 366; James Duane to Robert R. Livingston, Nov. 15, 1766, Livingston-Redmond Papers, Roll 6; Garth to S.C. Comm. of Corres., Mar. 12, 1767, Barnwell, ed., "Garth Correspondence," *S.C. Hist. Gen. Mag.,* XXIX (1928), 216–217. On the news of Townshend's opposition see the New York merchants to Charles Townshend, Dec. 16, 1766, Charles Townshend Papers, VII, 31 (microfilm available at Col. Williamsburg Research Lib., Williamsburg, Va. See also Varga, "New York Restraining Act," *N.Y. Hist.,* XXXVII (1956), 239. The instigator of the merchants' petition was the retired New York merchant William Kelly. Early in 1764 Kelly and a few others had been asked by the merchants of New York to draw up a statement of trade to be sent on to Parliament in an effort to stave off the threatened passage of the Revenue Act. In Feb. 1765 Kelly went off to London to petition the Board of Trade for a 20,000-acre grant in western New York and to check his estimates of New York's balance of trade against official British records. Despite Kelly's ministerial connections, no grant

much truth in such claims, and the petitioners won the support of the Boston merchants, who prepared a similar petition but withheld it at the last moment because of the angry response to the New York complaint. The ministry, it seems, had proven less sympathetic. The earl of Chatham found the New York petition absurd, and so did Shelburne, who had taken a leading part in writing and passing the act of 1766. The secretary's judgment might also have been affected by his having received the New York merchants' protest at the same time as the news of the New York assembly's failure to obey the Quartering Act.[65] Even the committee of North American merchants was alienated by the New York action. Largely responsible for lobbying the 1766 law through Parliament, the Londoners fumed at the New Yorkers for seeking further redress. The committee damned America and especially New York for not recognizing that it had "labored indefatigably and with the best Intentions" of serving the colonies.[66] The merchants wasted no time in telling the ministry that the memorial was unjust in its charge and most unfortunate in its timing. It could only impede the Currency Act repeal movement, which the New York assembly favored and which the merchants believed stood a fair chance of success.[67]

Also at issue early in 1767 was the hesitation of both New York and Massachusetts to heed ministerial entreaties and fully indemnify the victims of the Stamp Act riots. All in all, as Chatham noted, the government could find little reason to bestow any favors on Ameri-

---

of land was forthcoming. On the other hand he was able to inform the ministry of the large discrepancies between his own and British estimates of the value of New York's trade with the mother country; as is now known, customs records expressed values based on prices common at the time of William III. In Jan. and Feb. 1766, at the time of the parliamentary investigation into American trade, Kelly appeared as one of the ministerial witnesses to give evidence on conditions in New York. See B. Smith, "Committee to Consider the American Papers," 174–178, and Varga, "New York Restraining Act," *N.Y. Hist.*, XXXVII (1956), 239.

65. Chatham to Shelburne, Feb. 3, 1767, Taylor and Pringle, eds., *Correspondence of Pitt*, III, 188–189; Merrill Jensen, *The Founding of a Nation: A History of the American Revolution, 1763–1776* (Oxford, 1968), 208–209. See also the account in Jack M. Sosin, *Agents and Merchants: British Colonial Policy, 1760–1775* (Lincoln, Neb., 1961), 82–85, 98–100. On Shelburne's role in liberalizing the West Indian trade see John M. Norris, *Shelburne and Reform* (London, 1963), 36–38.

66. Extract of letter from London dated Feb. 12, 1767, *Pa. Gaz.*, Apr. 23, 1767. See also Shelburne to Chatham, Feb. 6, 1767, Chatham to Shelburne, Feb. 7, 1767, Taylor and Pringle, eds., *Correspondence of Pitt*, III, 191–194.

67. "Anonymous concerning New York Petition," London, Feb. 21, 1767, in Townshend Papers, VIII, 31. See also D. Barclay and Sons to Israel Pemberton, Mar. 3, 1767, William Smith Letterbook.

ca.[68] The legislature and merchants of New York had helped injure their own cause.

FRANKLIN, THE MERCHANTS, AND THE MINISTRY, 1767

At the beginning of February 1767 the committee of North American merchants finally received an answer to its plea for repeal of the Currency Act. The Board of Trade sent the committee an extract of its recommendations of February 1764, which had paved the way for the passage of the Currency Act and which a number of the present commissioners had signed. The object was to demonstrate once and for all the evils of paper money. When read before a general meeting of the merchants, the extract did make "some Impression," but before taking action the committee referred the document to agents Franklin, Charles, Garth, and Edward Montague of Virginia for an opinion. Garth and Franklin met at once, settled a "Representation," and submitted it to the merchants on March 10.[69]

The Franklin "Representation" was a polemical piece based on the premise that "on the whole, no Method has hitherto been found to establish a Medium of Trade in lieu of Money, equal in all its Advantages to Bills of Credit, funded on sufficient Taxes for discharging it, or on Land Security, of double the Value for repaying it, at the End of the Term; and in the mean Time made a GENERAL LEGAL TENDER." The object was to disprove both the validity of the recommendation that had been drafted by Hillsborough when president of the Board of Trade and the feasibility of any currency scheme short of a full legal tender. Hillsborough's report had argued that paper money drove hard money out of America; British merchants suffered losses on their American debts because of the depreciation of paper; the Currency Act of 1751 had a good effect in New England; a medium of commerce should have an intrinsic value, which gold and silver alone had; colonial assemblies in the

68. To Shelburne, Feb. 7, 1767, Taylor and Pringle, eds., *Correspondence of Pitt*, III, 193–194. On Massachusetts and indemnification see Harold W. Currie, "Massachusetts Politics and the Colonial Agency, 1762–1770" (Ph.D. diss., University of Michigan, 1960), 155–164; on New York, Olm, "Chatham Ministry," 153–154.

69. "Extract of a letter from a Merchant in London, dated March 14, 1767," in Crane, ed., *Franklin's Letters to the Press*, 80. Crane identifies the author as Franklin. See also Garth to S.C. Comm. of Corres., Mar. 12, 1767, Barnwell, ed., "Garth Correspondence," *S.C. Hist. Gen. Mag.*, XXIX (1928), 220.

control of debtors issued paper money with fraud in mind; and, finally, that in the middle colonies, where paper was best supported, it never kept its nominal value but "constantly depreciated to a certain Degree" whenever the quantity exceeded the needs of trade.

Franklin replied to each of the arguments in turn. He pointed out that the colonies' adverse trade balance, not paper money, drove gold and silver out of circulation, that the dwindling supply of specie forced Americans to turn to paper, and that sterling debts paid in paper generally were discharged at commercial exchange at the "full sterling Sum." Further he insisted that the New England situation was unique and that, while specie was indeed a superior medium of exchange because of its universal acceptance, a regulated paper currency was the next best thing. Some colonial paper money practices had in fact been fraudulent, but it was foolish to punish all for the sins of a few. Lastly he explained that the depreciation of paper was a complex question not simply to be explained away as a reflection of the quantity of money around. Franklin paid only brief attention to the feasibility of a currency without the device of legal tender. Like most Americans he felt the device to be absolutely necessary to protect debtors and to enforce the acceptability of paper. He dismissed out of hand any continental currency scheme because, he said, it would sweep all gold and silver off to England. Instead Franklin concentrated on an analysis of a currency system then in use in Maryland. Briefly he noted that the colonies could conceivably raise a fund by "some yearly Tax, securely lodged in the Bank of England as it arises." During the period in which money issued under such a scheme would circulate, the fund would theoretically accumulate to an amount sufficient to discharge all paper at its original value. Franklin was partial to the idea, but he claimed that unless such paper was made a legal tender its value would fluctuate wildly before finally achieving a par with sterling at the time of redemption; and wide swings in currency values hurt both debtors and creditors. Another possibility that Franklin considered was issuing a paper currency carrying interest. This was, he conceded, a way of supporting currency values. However, the New England colonies had tried just such a scheme and found it wanting for a number of other reasons. It was useless for smaller denominations, where it was too difficult to calculate interest. On the other hand, as redemption neared, merchants and others were likely to withhold the currency from circulation to keep as a kind of bond, thus de-

feating its purpose as money. Franklin's conclusions were predictable: the colonies outside New England had evolved for themselves
the best of all possible paper money systems. He also argued that
since a well-regulated legal tender currency could only increase
British trade to America, the alternative to repeal of the Currency
Act was retrenchment.[70]

Franklin's ability to convince the London merchants of the desirability of a legal tender paper money system was a critical factor
in keeping the Currency Act repeal movement alive. After the fracas
over New York, the ministry decided not to favor the colonies with
a repeal unless strongly urged to do so by the merchants trading
to America. Franklin's "Representation" did not, however, immediately stir the merchants into action. At a meeting on March 11
several merchants "expressed their Satisfaction" and deemed the
reply a "full Answer" to the Hillsborough report, but the majority
divided in its views. A final decision was postponed until March 17,
when a move to achieve a consensus failed. In fact it took another
month and many more sessions with the agents before the merchants
could agree on a reply to the Board of Trade.[71] Still another month
passed before the report was actually delivered, accompanied by a
copy of Franklin's answer to Hillsborough. The gist of the reply was
that the merchants were of the opinion that "the most speedy and
effectual Relief to the Colonies, in respect to the present distressed
State of their Commerce, for Want of a Medium of Trade, will be
the Repeal" of the Currency Act of 1764. They offered the by-now
well-worn argument that repeal could not hurt mercantile interests,

70. The full text is in Smyth, ed., *Writings of Franklin*, V, 1–14. Compare the
"Representation" with analysis of paper currency in Francis Bernard, *Select Letters on the Trade and Government of America* ... (London, 1774), 46–63; and
Dickinson, *Late Regulations*, 217–221. On the authorship of the Board recommendations of 1764, see Garth to S.C. Comm. of Corres., Sept. 26, 1766, Barnwell, ed.,
"Garth Correspondence," *S.C. Hist. Gen. Mag.*, XXIX (1928), 45. On the re-
ception in America of Franklin's "Representation," see William Franklin to Benjamin Franklin, June 10, 1767, William Duane, ed., *Letters to Benjamin Franklin,
from His Family and Friends, 1751–1790* (New York, 1859), 32–34. The question of
the depreciation of paper money or the connection between the price of currency
and other things is a subject that has been largely unexplored with the important
exception of Bezanson *et al.*, *Prices in Colonial Pennsylvania*. That study by itself
establishes the validity of Franklin's contention that a simple quantity theory of
money was an inadequate analytical tool. See also in this regard chap. 1 above.

71. "Extract of a letter from a Merchant in London, dated March 14, 1767,"
in Crane, ed., *Franklin's Letters to the Press*, 80–81. Crane identifies the author as
Franklin. See also letter from London dated Feb. 12, 1767, in *Pa. Chron.*, Apr. 27,
1767; "Extract of a letter from a Merchant in London, April 11, [1767]," Crane,
ed., *Franklin's Letters to the Press*, 92. Crane identifies the author as Franklin.

provided that legal tender devices did not extend to sterling debts contracted with or on behalf of British residents.[72]

Neither the merchants' report nor Franklin's "Representation" effectively countered the hard-money bias of the Board of Trade. In general the commissioners persisted in opposing all attempts to repeal the act of 1764 or to relax existing controls. The one exception seems to have been the Board president, Lord Clare, who had opposed such a move back in 1766 but had begun "to come over a little towards favouring the legal tender" for limited issues of loan office but not treasury notes.[73] Overall, however, gains and losses counterbalanced each other. Thus, for instance, on the agents' side the representative of Virginia, Edward Montague, joined the opposition to repeal. After waging an unsuccessful fight against many of the same merchants on the paper money question *before* the passage of the Currency Act, Montague clearly enjoyed "great satisfaction in observing the merchants suffering by their own Rod which they were fully forwarned would be first applied to themselves." The agent wrote Shelburne at the beginning of May: "I observe they feel it very strongly now and call out on the Agents to become Petitioners for their Relief. For one, I enter my Protest against any Interposition in the Affair otherwise than for the Protection of what paper still exists in Virginia."[74] Whatever pleasure Montague took at the discomfiture of the merchants, his remarks about Virginia currency were gratuitous. In the Old Dominion, Treasurer John Robinson had illegally pumped over £100,000 of legal tender treasury notes, more than half of the local currency supply, back into circulation.[75]

Despite the opposition of the Board of Trade and of others, it was only a short time before the ministry felt the cumulative effects of the merchants' reply, Franklin's arguments, and the obvious need

72. "Extract of a Letter from London, dated May 22, 1767," Crane, ed., *Franklin's Letters to the Press*, 100. Crane identifies the author as Franklin. See also news item from London dated May 16, 1767, *Pa. Gaz.*, July 23, 1767, and "Extract of a letter from a Merchant in London, April 11, [1767]," Crane, ed., *Franklin's Letters to the Press*, 92. What appears to be the London merchants' full report is to be found in "A Plea of the London Merchants in Favour of Paper Currency in North America," [no date except 1767], Shelburne Papers, XLVIII, 633–635. The "Plea" may also have been the work of Franklin; see Franklin to Galloway, Apr. 14, 1767, Original Letters to Joseph Galloway.

73. Franklin to Galloway, Apr. 14, May 20, June 13, 1767, Original Letters to Joseph Galloway; John Huske to Charles Townshend, Apr. 9, 1767, Namier and Brooke, *Charles Townshend*, 187–188.

74. Montague to Shelburne, May 6, 1767, Shelburne Papers, XLVIII, 629–630.

75. See chap. 3 above.

for a colonial currency to meet crown requisitions and support trade. Continuing complaints of a dearth of money and a need for a paper currency from places as far apart as Nova Scotia and New Jersey also helped.[76] Though the Board was reportedly still averse to repeal, the agents and merchants alike entertained some hope of convincing the government of the rightness of their cause. Putting aside misgivings about the "Strength of the Opposition, the daily Expectations of new Changes in the Ministry, and the present Resentment against America," the merchants went ahead with the preparation of a petition to Parliament "on which the Repeal was to be founded."[77] The petition simply called for speedy elimination of the Currency Act—with the proviso, of course, that future paper issues would not be lawful for any sterling debts contracted by or for British merchants. Finally on May 11 at a meeting with the agents, some members of the ministry cautiously committed themselves to an agreement to sponsor a repeal bill affirming the crown's former right to allow or withhold its assent to any currency acts passed in America.[78]

Two days later the incubus of Franklin's former scheme for a British land bank in the colonies arose to plague the negotiations and to wreck the chance of any immediate repeal. Like the Rockinghamites before them, certain members of the Pitt-Grafton ministry held out hope that they might raise a revenue in America on the interest drawn from an issue of loan office bills. Early in May, Thomas Whatley, one of Townshend's secretaries, reported that "a Paper Currency under Government Security is amongst other Things now under Consideration."[79] Aware of what was going on, Franklin quickly moved to wreck the revival of a plan that threatened his American reputation. If it became known that the good doctor was the author of a scheme for parliamentary taxation of the colonies, he would be politically dead in America. With the support of Garth and others, Franklin assured the ministry that no colony would accept a currency system coupled to a revenue measure. He

76. Franklin to Galloway, Apr. 14, May 20, 1767, Original Letters to Joseph Galloway; Lt. Gov. William Franklin to Shelburne, Nov. 22, 1766, Shelburne Papers, LI, 400; Feb. 17, 1767, *Jour. of Comm. Trade, 1764–1767*, 367; Greene and Jellison, "Currency Act of 1764," *WMQ*, 3d Ser., XVIII (1961), 498.

77. Extract of a letter from London, dated May 22, 1767, *N.-Y. Jour.*, July 30, 1767; Franklin to Galloway, June 13, 1767, Original Letters to Joseph Galloway.

78. Franklin to Galloway, May 20, 1767, Original Letters to Joseph Galloway. See also Hinkhouse, *Preliminaries of the American Revolution*, 141–142.

79. Whatley to John Temple, May 22, 1767, *The Bowdoin and Temple Papers* (Mass. Hist. Soc., *Collections*, 6th Ser., IX [Boston, 1899]), 84.

insisted that assemblies would demand the right to "appropriate the Interest themselves." The crown "might get a Share upon occasional Requisition . . . by voluntary Appropriations of the Assemblies; but they would never establish Funds as to make themselves unnecessary to Government." The arguments seemed to satisfy the ministers, and the agents and merchants pushed ahead with their plans to petition Parliament for repeal.[80] Franklin and the others, however, failed to include the factor of chance in their political calculus.

During routine hearings on the annual budget late in January 1767, Charles Townshend presented the House of Commons with estimates of the cost of continuing the military establishment in America. Grenville, for one, took exception. In a move to embarrass the ministry and advance his own political fortunes, he called for an immediate reduction of such expenses. However it was Townshend, not Grenville, who captivated Commons with promises of cutting colonial costs, drawing a revenue from American trade nearly sufficient to meet the Treasury's colonial expenditures, and satisfying the American objections to parliamentary taxation. Former chancellors William Dowdeswell and Grenville took Townshend at his word, and on February 25, with the support of the landed gentry, they defeated a ministerial motion offered by Townshend to maintain the land tax at the wartime rate of four shillings in the pound. The Commons then easily passed an amendment slicing the rate to three shillings and called upon Townshend to make good any deficits by raising a revenue in America.

The defeat of his ministry was enough to stir Lord Chatham from his bed of pain in an attempt to replace Townshend with Lord North at the Treasury. Townshend refused to resign, however, and North, preferring to see which way the political winds would blow, declined the offer. The effort proved altogether too much for Chatham, who was again taken to bed with an attack of the gout and the "Melancholy," while a triumphant Townshend went on with his plans. At a cabinet meeting on March 12 the chancellor demanded that, before the budget came before the Commons, ministerial support must be given to plans for reducing American costs and taxing colonial trade. Shelburne objected. As the man directly responsible for American affairs, he had been working for some months on a project of his own to rationalize the colonial establishment and raise a revenue from quitrent collections and land-grant

80. Franklin to Galloway, June 13, Aug. 8, 1767, Original Letters to Joseph Galloway.

fees. He wanted and got some time for reactions to his plan to come in from America. The information arriving by the end of the month was hardly encouraging. Nevertheless Shelburne asked for and got another reprieve. "The affairs of America cannot suffer much by going on one more year in the Channel they have hitherto done," Shelburne declared, "and that year is short enough time for furnishing a Plan capable of correcting past, and preventing future, Abuses."[81] The truth was that time had run out and the initiative had passed to Townshend.

The House of Commons was scheduled to consider on May 5 both New York's refusal to obey the Mutiny Act and Townshend's "grand American budget of Resolutions, Regulations, and Duties." The two questions were postponed, however, when Townshend became indisposed. Meanwhile the cabinet met in emergency session to hammer out a joint policy on New York and the American revenue, and this time it was Townshend who carried the day while Shelburne sat quietly by. On May 13, the day the House of Commons gave the bill suspending the New York General Assembly a first reading, Townshend presented his plan for duties on American imports and for an American board of customs to facilitate their collection.[82]

Historians have generally argued that Townshend's plan met little opposition. But the fact is that immediately after Townshend's speech on the thirteenth, Grenville arose and, waving aside the chancellor's imposts as trifles, claimed, "I will tell the honorable Gentlemen of a Revenue that will produce something valuable in

81. "Reasons for not diminishing American Expense, Mar. 30, 1767," Shelburne Papers, LXXXV, 103–110. See also Chatham to the king, Mar. 7, 1767, Grafton to Chatham, Mar. 13, 1767, Shelburne to Chatham, Friday morning [Mar. 13], 1767, Taylor and Pringle, eds., *Correspondence of Pitt*, III, 230–236; W. R. Anson, ed., *The Autobiography . . . of . . . Duke of Grafton* (London, 1898), 126–127, 137. For a discussion of Shelburne's plans see Norris, *Shelburne and Reform*, chap. 3.

82. On the various meetings of the ministry see Norris, *Shelburne and Reform*, 48–49. Details of the meeting of May 13 are not given in the *Jours. of Commons*, but they can be reconstructed from the correspondence of the time. See especially Franklin to Galloway, June 13, 1767, *Original Letters to Joseph Galloway*; Garth to S.C. Comm. of Corres., May 17, 1767, Barnwell, ed., "Garth Correspondence," *S.C. Hist. Gen. Mag.*, XXIX (1928), 223–230; William Samuel Johnson to William Pitkin, May 16, 1767, in *Letters of William Samuel Johnson* (Mass. Hist. Soc., *Colls.*, 5th Ser., IX [Boston, 1885]), 228–235; William Strahan to David Hall, postscript to a letter of May 9, 1767, in "Correspondence between William Strahan and David Hall, 1763–1777," *PMHB*, X (1886), 322–323. The essential details were also published in the newspapers; see, for instance, the extract of a letter from London, dated May 16, 1767, *N.-Y. Jour.*, Sept. 3, 1767.

America; make Paper Money for the colonies, issue it upon Loan there, take the Interest, and apply it as you think proper." Seeing that the idea stirred some interest, Townshend stood up again and said "that was a Proposition of his own which he had intended to make with the rest, but it had slipped his Memory, and the Gentlemen who must have heard of it, now unfairly would take Advantage of that Slip, and make a Merit to himself of a Proposition that was another's." And as proof of it, he assured the Commons that "a Bill was prepared for the purpose and would be laid before them." The chancellor apparently went ahead to outline his plan, which included repeal of the Currency Act of 1764 and the creation of a loan office in each colony to lend bills of credit on good security with the interest to be appropriated to the king's service. But whether the appropriation was to be made by act of Parliament or by acts of the various assemblies in America was unclear. Such details were omitted as all points were not yet settled. At a meeting between Townshend and the Commons Ways and Means Committee on June 1, the major points were cleared up. The colonies were to establish their own loan offices, and the interest was to be appropriated for crown use by act of Parliament. Part of the interest return was to be used to defray the expenses of emission and management, while the remainder would go towards defraying the expense of defending, protecting, and securing the colonies.[83]

The measure never came to a vote. Townshend could not bring in a repeal bill without grounds or introduce a measure for an American loan office and tax without removing the Currency Act from the books. Presumably the grounds were to be furnished by the London merchants who, as was well known, were on the eve of petitioning Parliament for repeal, while Garth and Jackson were preparing to bring in a suitable repeal bill. But on learning of Townshend's intentions the merchants and agents drew back and refused to give the chancellor a saddle to put "upon their Backs." They felt that time was on their side. Almost everybody in and out of the

83. The quotations are all taken from Franklin's account in his letter to Galloway, June 13, 1767, Original Letters to Joseph Galloway. See also Garth to S.C. Comm. of Corres., May 17, 1767, Barnwell, ed., "Garth Correspondence," *S.C. Hist. Gen. Mag.*, XXIX (1928), 228; John Huske to Charles Townshend, Apr. 9, 1767, Namier and Brooke, *Charles Townshend*, 187–188. On Townshend's character and colonial aims in general see *ibid.*, 184–186. For a detailed and also a much different discussion of this problem see P. D. G. Thomas, "Charles Townshend and American Taxation in 1767," *Eng. Hist. Rev.*, LXXXIII (1968), 33–51.

ministry agreed to repeal, Garth informed the South Carolina assembly, "though widely differing in the manner" of it.[84]
Early in June, just after the House of Commons approved a series of resolutions embodying the Townshend duties, the chancellor informed the agents that he knew perfectly well why they and their merchant allies had dropped the application for repeal of the Currency Act. He insisted, however, that delay was pointless, since if he remained in office, he personally would offer the loan office plan at the next session.[85]

PENNSYLVANIA AND THE REPEAL MOVEMENT, 1750–1767

In the interim Franklin began to work out a different paper money plan. His reasons were varied. In the first place he had grown indifferent to the need for repeal, if only because of the unfortunate connection with his continental currency and tax scheme. Moreover feelings in Parliament were running so high against the colonies that anything smacking of a favor to America, such as the repeal of the Currency Act, would meet with strong opposition. Most important of all, recent experiments with paper currency at home demanded Franklin's immediate attention and another kind of action.[86]
Sometime towards the end of 1766, eight Philadelphia mercantile houses, weary of waiting for the promised repeal of the Currency Act, took matters into their own hands and issued some £30,000 of short-term interest-bearing promissory notes to provide payment for "Wheat and other Country Produce." The emission was prompted by the shortage of a local circulating medium and the recent and sharp drop in sterling exchange rates below a par of 167. In itself the fall in exchange was the result of the virtually unlimited credit given by English merchants for the purchase of local produce and the consequent spurt in the cash price of flour and grain, the contraction of the currency supply, and the abundance of sterling exchange following heavy shipments of grain, flour, and bread to Britain and flaxseed to Ireland.[87]
The sudden, sharp dip in exchange rates penalized merchants in

84. Garth to S.C. Comm. of Corres., June 6, July 5, 1767, Barnwell, ed., "Garth Correspondence," *S.C. Hist. Gen. Mag.*, XXIX (1928), 297, 300. See also Franklin to Galloway, June 13, 1767, Original Letters to Joseph Galloway.
85. Garth to S.C. Comm. of Corres., July 5, 1767, Barnwell, ed., "Garth Correspondence," *S.C. Hist. Gen. Mag.*, XXIX (1928), 300.
86. Franklin to Galloway, June 13, 1767, Original Letters to Joseph Galloway.
87. *Pa. Gaz.*, May 7, 1767.

the commodities trade. Since they customarily drew sterling bills on British correspondents to convert into local purchasing power, the depressed rates effectively raised the price they paid for farm goods. As a result the eight houses in question sought to take advantage of bullish conditions by buying produce with personal notes, the notes payable within nine months in sterling bills. In other words Pennsylvania currency was not only in short supply but also expensive. The merchants were issuing money of their own making, gambling that there would be a rise in exchange rates before their notes came due.[88]

Nearly two hundred other provincial merchants bought space in the *Pennsylvania Gazette* of December 11 to announce their unwillingness to take the promissory notes in "any payment whatsoever." Such notes, they claimed, would only prejudice trade and cheapen the public money. A month later a similar complaint from the inhabitants of the city and county of Philadelphia came before the General Assembly. The petitioners argued that the right to strike money of any kind belonged to the legislature alone and that the "partial Schemes of private Men" would only undermine the general welfare. Their point was that the personal notes would surely depreciate and that once the legislature relinquished the exclusive right of striking money anyone "actuated by Motives of private Gain" could issue notes. In the long run the fear of depreciation was real enough. For the moment, however, it was generally recognized that in a period of monetary stringency private notes would be readily taken up and would give the issuing houses an edge in the highly competitive business of buying up grain for foreign export or flour milling. After brief consideration the house ruled in favor of the remonstrants on every count. About the same time the boycotting merchants petitioned the assembly for help, they sought a legal opinion from the king's attorney general and solicitor general. A

88. "House of Representatives," *Pa. Archives*, VII, 5952–5953, and Richard Waln, Jr., to David Barclay and Sons, Dec. 12, 1766, in Richard Waln, Jr., Letterbook, Hist. Soc. Pa., Philadelphia. Marc Egnal has pointed out to me that of the eight firms that issued the notes, all but one seem to have owed their allegiance to the Presbyterian party and that quite a few were signers of an agreement in 1775 fixing the value of foreign coins in Pennsylvania. More interesting is the fact that many of the same houses were investors in Morris's Bank of North America and that Willing and Morris were among the eight firms in the first place. It just may be, as Egnal has suggested, that this episode in 1766 taught Morris an invaluable lesson, namely that to establish a bank it is necessary to make many more of the local firms "insiders." Even in the 1780s Morris had trouble with Philadelphia merchants who were excluded from his list of bank subscribers.

month or so later the officers replied that issuing private notes was probably not illegal, although under the South Sea Bubble Act as applied to America, any debts payable in such money were recoverable. In any event, in the face of general opposition in the colony, the notes were apparently withdrawn from circulation. The creation of private banks of issue awaited developments growing out of the War for Independence.[89]

Three months after ruling against the use of private money, the assembly took matters into its own hands and voted to strike £20,-000 in promissory notes. A number of elements had combined to convince the legislature that monetary and financial conditions had reached near crisis proportions and that the government had to act. Most important were the nearly successful efforts of the eight mercantile houses to create a private medium of local exchange, the widening call by the citizenry for an additional paper currency emission, and the urgent need to pay off an overdue public debt. The sources of the last problem, the payment of the public creditors, were buried deeply in past controversies over money and politics.

In 1723 Pennsylvania established a loan office system that provided the General Assembly with annual interest returns of some £2,500. The money accounted for nearly all of the public revenues for the next couple of decades. The executive share in the fund was nil, and although the loan office was renewed from time to time, the assembly never relinquished its hold on the purse strings. Then in 1746 the legislature augmented its income by laying a tax on imported liquors, which returned upwards of £2,000 a year over a ten-year period. A portion of the money was pledged to the redemption of a £5,000 treasury note appropriation. The remainder was at the disposal of the House of Representatives and was used to finance about half of the regular charges of government during the next decade. The interest payments from the loan office covered the other half. In 1756 the house renewed the excise in order to fund an additional £30,000 treasury issue. The action effectively wiped out the surplus. As for the remaining provincial taxes on property and polls, they were fully committed to other treasury note issues. By the middle of the century, consequently, ordinary expenses of government came out of the loan office fund. In the meantime a proposed extension of the loan office ran into opposition from pro-

89. *Pa. Gaz.*, May 7, 1767. See 3 and 4 Anne, Ch. 9, Pickering, ed., *Statutes of Great Britain*, XI, 106–108, for the law involved in the decision.

prietary and crown interests. The major source of public revenue was under attack.

Before the French and Indian War, the Penn family had sharply contested the doctrine of legislative supremacy in financial affairs. But after the fighting began, British requisitions for men and supplies took precedence over any other considerations. During the early part of the war, the General Assembly had a virtually free hand in currency matters and granted the military nearly £450,000 in fiat money. The volume of paper currency in circulation jumped 600 percent over former levels. The money itself was placed in the hands of house committees wholly beyond the reach of the executive. Similarly when the House of Representatives levied new excise and property taxes to redeem the wartime appropriations, it monopolized the appointment of all tax officials. During these years the crown also waived any question of possible violations of proprietary rights and of British monetary policies governing the tender, tenure, and volume of paper currency outstanding. In full control of the purse strings, the house pressed its claim of financial independency even further.[90]

During the spring and summer of 1759 the Pennsylvania General Assembly took advantage of continuing British requests for military aid and of the recently enacted parliamentary grant of £200,000 sterling as reimbursement for earlier colonial wartime expenditures to pass three additional measures bearing on the currency question in an effort to complete the rout of the Penns. To secure executive support for the move, the representatives bought off Governor William Denny by paying him his back salary, then more than two years in arrears, after he signed the three bills into law. The first of the acts granted an emergency loan of £50,000 to General William Stanwix. In return the legislation authorizing this grant also contained a promise to extend the old loan office for another sixteen years. The extension of the loan office was in contention because Thomas Penn, who had assumed the principal reins of proprietorship in 1746 and who desired to reestablish the executive control of finances, had personally blocked any earlier moves to renew the

---

90. The problem is dealt with at length in Yoder, "Paper Currency in Colonial Pennsylvania," chap. 4. In general the following discussion is dependent on Yoder's work. For an analysis of the political significance of this issue during the period 1751 to 1758, see James H. Hutson, *Pennsylvania Politics, 1746–1770: The Movement for Royal Government and Its Consequences* (Princeton, N.J., 1972), 6–59.

loan office issue of £80,000. By 1759 the representatives felt in a strong enough position to revive the question.

The second of the acts approved by Denny supplemented an earlier law, passed in the spring of 1758, that provided for a £100,000 treasury issue in support of the war. That appropriation had been prompted by an urgent plea by William Pitt for men and material in return for a promised "proper Compensation" by Parliament at some later date. As it turned out, the appropriation hinged on the settlement of a dispute over the taxation of proprietary land, a controversy that had broken out early in the war when the General Assembly had informed the Board of Trade that a number of proprietary restrictions against paper currency were hindering defense efforts. After repeated and unsuccessful complaints to the Board, the assembly—without consulting the governor—dispatched Benjamin Franklin to England in 1757 as colonial agent for the specific purpose of indicting the Penns for prohibiting the taxing of their estates. Franklin argued that the proprietor was depriving the province of a much needed source of funds for the redemption of the various wartime currency emissions. There the matter rested until the summer of 1759, when the House of Commons, at Pitt's request, passed a Supply Act authorizing the £200,000 parliamentary reimbursement. The measure, however, came just a few months too late to prevent the Pennsylvania General Assembly from passing its own Supply Act in April, which levied a property tax on all holdings, including the Penn estates, ostensibly to secure the £100,000 treasury issue of 1758. When Governor Denny affixed his signature to the measure, the Penn lands were subject to taxation for the first time in Pennsylvania history.

The last of the three measures designed to destroy the vestiges of proprietary power over money and taxes was the so-called Agency Act.[91] In effect the Agency Act authorized Franklin to receive the £27,000 sterling allotted to Pennsylvania out of the parliamentary reimbursement and to deposit the money in the Bank of England, where it was subject to the drafts of the trustees of the provincial loan office. The drafts were ultimately to be converted into bills of exchange and sold in Pennsylvania for paper currency, the proceeds to be turned over to the assembly committee of public accounts for sinking or burning. At issue was the exclusion of the proprietary voice on that committee, which, as Thomas Penn looked

91. See Hutson, "Benjamin Franklin and the Parliamentary Grant for 1758," *WMQ*, 3d Ser., XXII (1966), 575–595.

at it, was therefore free to divert the money from the sinking fund to any project of interest to the assembly only.

Penn was outraged at the renewed and all-out attack on his prerogative. He promptly sacked Denny for taking a bribe and overstepping his instructions and then petitioned the king for the repeal of the three acts in question. In June 1760, after three days of hearings, the Board of Trade upheld Penn's claims and cited the Pennsylvania General Assembly for encroaching on the rights of both the proprietor and the crown. The Board singled out for criticism the assembly's monopolistic control of taxes and of the tax machinery, the application of the excise and loan office funds, the appointment of all tax officials, and the taxation of proprietary property. By such means the commissioners warned, "The most sacred and inviolable parts of the executive power are transferred from the proprietaries and drawn into the hands of a popular assembly."

Faced with an urgent need for military aid and the negative recommendation of the Board of Trade, the Privy Council assumed the role of honest broker. It quickly arranged a compromise between Penn and the assembly agents Franklin and Richard Jackson. As a result the king rejected the proposed loan office extension and the emergency loan to Stanwix. On the other hand he approved the Agency Law and the Supply Act of 1759, which taxed the proprietary estate. The deal, which Franklin put into writing, was that as part of the bargain the House of Representatives would pass a supplemental act securing the Penns a future share in the power of the purse. The assembly never formally honored that agreement. In 1764 Pennsylvania's new governor, John Penn, a nephew of Thomas, had to wring a concession from the house. He obtained the long-sought-after executive voice in the determination of taxes in exchange for his approval of the province's last paper money issue before the passage of the Currency Act of 1764.[92]

The royal veto in 1760 of the proposed renewal of the loan office was followed by continued opposition of the proprietary. Accordingly the old loan expired in 1762, which effectively eliminated the interest fund just as the French and Indian War came to an end. Financial disaster, however, was still a few years in the future. In the fall of 1761 persistent rumors of peace and the growing scarcity of sterling exchange prompted the assembly to draw on Franklin for some £25,000 sterling that had been invested in Bank of England

92. Yoder, "Paper Currency in Colonial Pennsylvania," chaps. 4–5; Hutson, *Pennsylvania Politics*, 59–121.

stock, or nearly the full amount of Pennsylvania's share of the parliamentary reimbursement of 1759. As a result of the heavy demand
for sterling remittances at the time, purchases were limited to £500,
and by the end of October 1761 Philadelphia merchants had bought
up all the available provincial bills of exchange. Despite the collapse of the stock market in London and the loss of a sizable portion
of the Pennsylvania investment, the bills were ultimately paid without a single protest, largely because of a timely advance made to the
colony by the British mercantile firm of Sargent and Aufrere. By
law proceeds from the sale of the bills were handed over to the house
committee of accounts, which used a small part of the money to pay
the public indebtedness in 1762 and 1763 in an effort to stave off a
financial crisis. The remainder of the funds was used for the abatement of taxes and the redemption of paper money.[93]

After 1764 Pennsylvania's public debt was no longer paid. The
House of Representatives had considered discharging the arrears
with money borrowed out of the treasury that had been set aside as a
sinking fund for a £100,000 issue made back in 1760. But this clearly
violated the Currency Act of 1764, which banned the extension of
paper money already in circulation. In the end the house turned to
a familiar device for a solution. It set the printing presses in motion
and struck £20,000 of debentures, albeit without the time-honored
protection of legal tender. Both the legislators and the Philadelphia
merchants agreed that with the scarcity of cash the new money
would be freely taken up in the marketplace. While the house
showed some faith in the rule of the market, it was not willing to
leave everything up to "the hidden hand." In an effort to place a
prop under currency values, the assembly extended the collection
period of an excise levied in 1756 and originally intended for the
wartime defense of Philadelphia. Returns were to be used to redeem
the debentures within four years of the time of their issue. More
important was a provision that the debentures could be legally exchanged at the treasury at any time in the period for older notes that
happened to be on hand, notes that would of course be a full legal
tender. The currency act met no opposition in England, and when
issued the debentures passed at par with specie.[94]

93. See Hutson, "Benjamin Franklin and the Parliamentary Grant for 1758,"
WMQ, 3d Ser., XXIII (1966), 589.
94. James T. Mitchell and Henry Flanders, eds., *Statutes at Large of Pennsylvania from 1682 to 1801* (Harrisburg, Pa., 1896–1911), VII, 100–107, 424–430. The
money passed at par with specie, as did every other emission in Pennsylvania in

Pennsylvania had found a temporary solution to a threatened financial crisis, but it had by no means solved its money problems. The scant issue of £20,000 barely matched the amount of former notes sunk and burned that year or made up for recurrent losses of coin and sterling bills. Consequently the house directed its agents to press for repeal of the Currency Act.[95]

THE FAILURE OF THE REPEAL MOVEMENT, 1767–1768

Franklin had lost much of his enthusiasm for repeal, but he was well aware of the monetary needs of the province. And sometime during the late spring of 1767 he proposed that Richard Jackson bring a bill into the House of Commons allowing Pennsylvania, and Pennsylvania alone, to issue legal tender bills of credit *on loan*. Franklin knew of course of the continuing desire for a currency emission and the growing demand for a source of public credit at a time when the Pennsylvania economy was experiencing "a booming export trade, revival at home, and increasing domestic investments in large-scale industries," such as flour milling, and potash and iron manufacturing.[96] Jackson agreed, provided that the English merchants trading to the province would support such a measure. When approached, the "Pennsylvania merchants," though sympathetic, indicated that the rest of the London committee, "having gone Hand in Hand with us in all American Affairs," might be piqued by any separate action. A general meeting of the merchants was felt to be in order.[97]

At that meeting, which took place sometime at the beginning of June, Franklin argued that, since most colonies were out of favor for the moment, perhaps Pennsylvania, which "stood in a pretty good light," might have more success if it went it alone. Then when the resentment against the remaining colonies had abated, the Pennsylvania act would provide the others with a precedent. After much debate the proposal was shelved on the assumption that any petition would only serve Townshend's purposes; some merchants, however, simply opposed any special dispensation for Pennsylvania. Franklin

the period 1767 to 1775; see Franklin to Galloway, Dec. 1, 1767, John Bigelow, ed., *The Works of Benjamin Franklin...*, IV (New York, 1904), 335.

95. See Yoder, "Paper Currency in Colonial Pennsylvania," chap. 5, and chaps. 7, 9, and 10 of the present work.

96. Sachs, "Business Outlook," chap. 4.

97. Franklin to Galloway, June 13, 1767, Original Letters to Joseph Galloway, 105.

was not optimistic about the future of the repeal movement, but he was willing to wait. He hoped that at the next session of Parliament "the Complexion of Ministers and Measures" might change completely.[98]

After Parliament broke up early in July, the duke of Grafton tried to shore up the ministry by allying the existing members with the three great parties of the duke of Bedford, Rockingham, and Grenville upon a "broad Bottom." William Samuel Johnson wrote: "How it will end, requires more Skill in the Doctrine of Chances than was possessed by Newton."[99] It ended with a whimper, as the Pitt-Grafton ministry dragged on to its death a year or so later.

At this point the agents appeared to lose all hope of a repeal. Garth, for instance, in July advised the South Carolina Commons House of Assembly to issue some form of non-legal tender currency as the way out of its money problems, a course of action that the Commons House had already chosen when in April it voted to issue some £60,000 to pay for a new watchhouse and customhouse in Charleston. The measure provided that the money would be a legal tender for all public obligations for a five-year period, and it passed without a hitch and without a suspending clause. But because of the governor's neglectfulness, the provision was never sent to England for review. South Carolina thus managed, despite the Currency Act, to get into circulation some £60,000 of treasury notes.[100]

Franklin shared Garth's pessimism, and it was with some reluctance that he renewed his efforts to obtain ministerial support for a repeal of the Currency Act with no strings attached. Sometime at the end of August he found himself engaged in a dinner conversation over paper money with the minister Shelburne and Henry Conway. Shelburne complimented Franklin on his recent defense of the need for a legal tender currency in his reply to the Board of Trade and declared himself fully convinced by it. The prospects for repeal seemed to brighten somewhat with the report a few days later that the president of the Board, Lord Clare, had also "come over." There

98. *Ibid.*
99. Johnson to Pitkin, July 13, 1767, *Letters of William Samuel Johnson*, 242.
100. Garth to S.C. Comm. of Corres., July 5, 1767, Barnwell, ed., "Garth Correspondence," *S.C. Hist. Gen. Mag.*, XXIX (1928), 300; Apr. 19, 1767, Jours. of S.C. Commons House; Thomas Cooper and David J. McCord, eds., *The Statutes at Large of South Carolina* (Columbia, S.C., 1836–1841), IV, 257–261. See also Purdie and Dixon's *Va. Gaz.*, Oct. 29, 1767. The act passed during the governorship of Lord Charles Montagu, who was often remiss in sending acts and journals of the assembly to Britain. Regular reports began again with the administration of Lt. Gov. William Bull.

was some difficulty, however, with the four other commissioners, who had signed the Board recommendation against paper money back in 1764. As Commissioner Soame Jenyns whimsically put it, *"I have no kind of objection to it, provided we have heretofore signed nothing to the contrary."*[101]

Whatever the chances for repeal at that moment, all was lost when events once more turned against the colonies. The first omens were favorable. On September 4 Charles Townshend was obliging enough to die and take with him his plans for a continental currency and tax. During the cabinet shuffle that followed, Hillsborough became secretary for colonial affairs, a new office designed to ease Shelburne out of the Southern Department and American affairs and ultimately out of the ministry. This action effectively ended the Currency Act repeal movement. It will be recalled that three years before, when serving as president of the Board of Trade, Hillsborough had drafted a vigorous recommendation against colonial paper currency. The intervening years had not softened his views.[102]

With Townshend out of the way the London merchants finally delivered their long-expected petition for repeal of the Currency Act, but it elicited from Secretary Hillsborough no more than a promise to read Franklin's answer to the Board of Trade's recommendations of 1764. On February 17, 1768, Franklin personally waited on the secretary for a reply. Hillsborough reluctantly agreed to let the matter of repeal "take its course, without opposing it as last year he had determined to have done," although he still found it in the American interest to be rid of all paper money. He pointed with pride to the New England colonies, who, he said, "lately, on the rumor of an intended application for taking off the restraint [on paper currency], petitioned that it might be continued as to them." The facts in the case led to a more modest conclusion. A newspaper story that Dennys de Berdt, a prominent London merchant and agent for Massachusetts, had discussed the currency question with the London committee the previous spring served to convince the

101. As quoted in Franklin to William Franklin, Aug. 28, 1767, Smyth, ed., *Writings of Franklin*, V, 46–47.

102. See Garth to S.C. Comm. of Corres., June 6, July 5, 1767, Barnwell, ed., "Garth Correspondence," *S.C. Hist. Gen. Mag.*, XXIX (1928), 297–300; Franklin to Galloway, Aug. 8, 1767, Original Letters to Joseph Galloway; Edmund Fitzmaurice, *Life of William, Earl of Shelburne* . . . (London, 1875–1876), II, 67–77. Townshend also seems to have considered establishing a colonial currency by means of a private bank to be incorporated in Britain and located in London with agencies in each colony and to be capitalized at £1,000,000 sterling. See Townshend Papers, VIII, 39.

governor of Massachusetts, Francis Bernard, that de Berdt was plot-
ting the repeal of all laws governing currency. An avowed enemy
of fiat money, Bernard hurriedly obtained a petition from his Council against any revision of the Currency Act of 1751.[103]

By now Franklin's hopes for repeal had again worn thin. Nevertheless events taking place back in Pennsylvania led him into another
caucus with the merchants and the London committee. The Pennsylvania House of Representatives had closely followed the progress
of the Currency Act repeal movement and during the early summer
of 1767 had learned that the merchant-agent alliance had held up
its repeal petition because of fears that the ministry would move to
create a British loan office in America only to appropriate the interest charges. Franklin naturally concealed his hand in the plan,
and when the representatives met again the following October, he
received a commendation for his prudence at a time when the rights
and privileges of Pennsylvania were at stake.[104] The London merchants also received recognition for their part in the controversy.
Above all else, however, the representatives emphasized the continuing distress from the want of an adequate currency and credit
supply and urged renewed efforts at repeal.

When the merchants and agents met in London in January 1768,
they agreed that any repeal bill must be proposed by the merchants
alone; "in the light of a favour" to them, and not from the agents as
a "favour to America."[105] They decided to wait until the short
spring session of Parliament before trying to introduce any measure.
But by that time Hillsborough succeeded Clare as president of the
Board of Trade—without relinquishing his post as secretary of colonial affairs. The arch foe of American paper money practices now

103. See Franklin to Galloway, Feb. 17, 1768, Smyth, ed., *Writings of Franklin*,
V, 97–98; "Extract of a letter from a Merchant in London, April 11, [1767]," Crane,
ed., *Franklin's Letters to the Press*, 92–93; Bernard to the earl of [?], Aug. 25, 1767,
Bernard, *Select Letters*, 46–47; de Berdt to Samuel Dexter, Dec. 23, 1767, Albert
Matthews, ed., *Letters of Dennys de Berdt, 1757–1770* (Cambridge, Mass., 1911),
328; Richard Jackson to William Pitkin, Nov. 8, 1766, *Pitkin Papers...1766–1769*
(Connecticut Historical Society, *Collections*, XIX [Hartford, Conn., 1921]), 51. It
should be noted that there was some thought of New England becoming actively
involved in the currency question if the repeal of the Currency Act of 1764 proved
possible. See, for instance, William Samuel Johnson to William Pitkin, Mar. 19,
1767, *Letters of William Samuel Johnson*, 219, and James Bowdoin to Thomas
Pownall, May 10, 1769, *Bowdoin and Temple Papers*, 139–140.
104. Committee of Correspondence to Franklin and Jackson, Oct. 17, 1767,
"House of Representatives," *Pa. Archives*, VII, 6069–6071.
105. Franklin to Galloway, Feb. 17, 1768, Smyth, ed., *Writings of Franklin*, V,
97.

had almost the entire management of the colonies in his hands. After a couple of meetings with the merchants and their agent allies, Hillsborough positively declared himself against paper currency. Shortly afterwards the protagonists gave up the struggle for a general repeal. They knew nothing could be done if Hillsborough was dead set against it. In addition, a more important issue commanded their attention: the repeal of the Townshend Act.[106]

The American agents and their merchant allies failed to repeal or revise the Currency Act for reasons having little to do with the problem of colonial paper money practices. From the beginning the currency question had been entangled in the dispute over parliamentary taxation and the search for an American revenue. Further, the brief and fitful alliance of London and Glasgow merchants so essential to the passage of the Currency Act collapsed in 1764. Reestablished a year later within the even more powerful coalition of North American merchants and West Indian planters and traders, it shared in the repeal of the Stamp Act. The new bloc divided over the revision of the Revenue Act, and what remained after 1766 was a rump lobby of London merchants whose political effectiveness in working for repeal of the Currency Act and for other colonial reforms was greatly diminished. Shortly after, the repeal movement ran afoul of the rising antagonism between the British government and the colonies over the failure of the New York General Assembly to obey the Mutiny Act. Even the London merchants were alienated following the New York merchants' petition against the Revenue Act of 1766 and early in 1767 briefly considered dropping their demands for repeal altogether. More important, throughout the period the Board of Trade retained its "hard money" bias and resisted most of the attempts to relax currency controls. The twisting and turning of British politics in these years was also a factor in upsetting the plans for repeal. And when as a result of a series of political deals, Lord Hillsborough, an avowed enemy of all paper money, became secretary for colonial affairs early in 1768, the alliance of agents and merchants dropped its plans altogether. In the years ahead the Currency Act would be revised, but the changes would come in response to the actions of the individual assemblies.

106. See Franklin to Pa. Comm. of Corres., Apr. 16, 1768, Smyth, ed., *Writings of Franklin*, V, 120. See also *N.-Y. Jour.*, May 19, June 10, 1768.

Part *Two*
Alternatives to Repeal
1764-1768

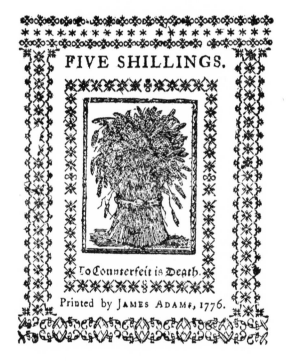

FIVE SHILLINGS.

To Counterfeit is Death.

Printed by JAMES ADAMS, 1776.

Chapter 5

Interpreting the Law
Money and Politics in
Maryland and Georgia

The American response to the news of the Currency Act was that the new regulation was in general ill-adapted to colonial realities, an impression later events failed to erase. For a time the repeal movement kindled some hope of redress, and the colonies generally deferred other action pending the outcome of that struggle. In the interim there was widespread discussion of currency matters and even some makeshift attempts to satisfy local demands for a medium of exchange without recourse to paper money. The discussion tended to center on a single question: lacking the right to strike fresh issues of fiat money, how were the middle and southern colonies to finance the future operation of government or to soften the effects of the rapid contraction of existing supplies of treasury and loan office notes? A related question facing those colonies caught in the midst of a postwar business depression was how to relieve the growing stringency of credit and coin.

Serious efforts to meet local demands for an increased circulating medium in the period, other than through the use of the printing press, were few. None proved especially new or interesting.[1] The business community, for instance, despite some talk of creating private banks of issue, did little more than expand the use of barter exchange and of private credit instruments.[2] Predictably more ambi-

1. That the colonists did not come up with any alternatives to a system of paper money points up the importance and general acceptance of that system.
2. See, for example, the discussions in "Pennsylvania and the Repeal Move-

tious were the proposed public schemes for relief. They included the purchase of copper farthings and silver three-penny pieces from England; the exploitation of rumored silver deposits in and around New York City, and the establishment there of a mint for striking a continental currency; the introduction of a large number of bank notes of an "inferior value" bearing a "small premium," to be printed in England and regulated by imperial authorities; and the creation of a "sterling paper currency over the whole continent" or some other variation on Franklin's loan office scheme.[3] Ultimately places like New York, Pennsylvania, Maryland, Virginia, and South Carolina did import great quantities of "coppers."[4] The remaining plans, however, were abandoned in favor of older and more familiar measures. Colonies that had not already done so extended the use of foreign coin to the discharge of debts previously payable in paper alone, a condition initially imposed to create a demand for bills of credit.[5] Other provinces simply enlarged the list of local commodities receivable for public obligations.[6] Finally, counterfeiters everywhere were busily pursuing a "solution" of their own throughout the period by injecting into the monetary stream their special kind of liquidity. They were very often successful.[7]

Collapse of the repeal movement dashed expectations of redress at the hands of the British government and forced Americans to confront the full implications of the Currency Act. But before then

---

ment, 1750–1767," and "The Politics of Scandal, 1765–1766," in chaps. 4 and 6 of the present study.

3. See, for example, the discussion in "Money and Economics in New York, 1766–1768," in chap. 8 below.

4. See, for example, the discussions in "The Initial Response to the Currency Act, 1764," "The Maryland Response to the Currency Act, 1764–1767," and "Money and Economics in New York, 1766–1768," in chaps. 4, 5, and 8 of the present study.

5. See, for example, the discussions in "North Carolina, 1768–1770," and "Money and Economics in New York, 1766–1768," in chaps. 7 and 8 below.

6. See, for example, the discussion in "The British Response: North Carolina, 1764–1768," in chap. 7 below.

7. See, for example, the discussion in "Virginia, 1772–1773," in chap. 10 below. The subject of colonial counterfeiting has yet to be fully studied. See the pioneering work of Kenneth Scott: *Counterfeiting in Colonial America* (New York, 1957); *Counterfeiting in Colonial New York* (New York, 1953); "Counterfeiting in Colonial New Jersey," New Jersey Historical Society, *Proceedings*, LXXV (1957), 170–179; "The Great Epidemic of Coining in the Jersies," *ibid.*, 112–127; *Counterfeiting in Colonial Pennsylvania* (New York, 1955); "Counterfeiting in Colonial Virginia," *VMHB*, LXI (1953), 3–33; "Counterfeiting in Colonial Maryland," *Md. Hist. Mag.*, LI (1956), 81–100; "Counterfeiting in Colonial North Carolina," *N.C. Hist. Rev.*, XXXIV (1957), 467–482. See also Harold Gillingham, *Counterfeiting in Colonial Pennsylvania* (New York, 1939).

Maryland and Georgia, colonies that took no part in the struggle for repeal and enjoyed a certain exemption from British monetary controls, had already struck new paper issues in seeming disregard of parliamentary law. Though receivable for public obligations, in the strict sense the Maryland emission was not a lawful tender and was not therefore a violation of the act of 1764. Barring all references to legal tender, the acceptability of the Maryland paper depended instead on the heavy demand for any kind of circulating medium at the time and the public's confidence in a provision for finally redeeming the money in sterling bills of exchange at a discount of 33⅓ percent, an arrangement peculiar to that province. By contrast the Georgia issue, secured in the usual way by taxes, *was* a lawful tender for public obligations and hence a clear breach of parliamentary law.

ORIGINS OF MARYLAND'S CURRENCY SYSTEM, 1733–1764

Paper currency has generally proven to be a troublesome subject in the writing of American history. Nonetheless scholars know far less about fiat money systems before the Revolution than after, despite the fact that colonial currency practices were far simpler than those of nineteenth- and twentieth-century America. The difficulty, it seems, stems from our unfamiliarity with the early practices and with the economic and political background that lend them meaning. Maryland is a case in point.

Seventeenth-century Maryland had essentially a one-crop economy with all its attendant ills. Whether or not it suited the needs of English mercantilism in the period, a concentration upon tobacco forced Marylanders to lay out hard cash for their meat, beer, and bread, much of which was purchased from Pennsylvania. The drain on specie was chronic, and when tobacco prices declined sharply at the turn of the century, the legislature banned the import of provisions and encouraged the local production of foodstuffs.[8] The continuing crisis in tobacco markets furthered the policy of diversification and self-sufficiency so that by the mid-eighteenth century Maryland had reversed the flow of foodstuffs and exported sizable amounts of grains and meats, not to mention wood products and iron. "A new Face seems to be overspreading the Country," one observer noted at the time. "Like their more Northern Neighbours,"

8. See the suggestive article by Gary B. Nash, "Maryland's Economic War with Pennsylvania," *Md. Hist. Mag.*, LX (1965), 231–244.

Marylanders "in great Numbers have turned themselves to the raising of Grain and live Stock of which they now begin to send great
Quantities to the *West Indies.*"[9]
After the middle of the century diversification continued as tobacco exports began to level off and slave imports dropped. Doubtless low returns dampened the enthusiasm for tobacco—especially
after the enactment of a quality-control measure in 1749 failed to
raise prices. On the other hand the new law did produce selective
cuts in export and production that chiefly affected marginal producers. Small planters saw a substantial portion of their crop turned
back at the public warehouses as "refuse" unfit for shipment abroad.
Likewise the measure hastened the abandonment of the "weed" in
those counties that had already begun the shift to wheat and other
grains. While in the past all fees and most other public debts were
payable in tobacco alone, a clause in the new act authorized those
growing little or no tobacco to use paper currency instead, thereby
eliminating any need to raise small amounts of tobacco as a means
of payment.[10]
In striking contrast to the relatively slower expansion of tobacco
culture was the rapid growth in the production of foodstuffs and
raw materials in response to generally favorable prices. At the close
of the French and Indian War the export value of grain, breadstuffs,
meats, lumber, and pig and bar iron possibly amounted to as much
as half that of tobacco.[11] Contemporaries recognized the economic
trends and generally applauded them, and as in other colonies, many

9. "Itinerant Observations in America, Reprinted from The London Magazine,
1745-6," Georgia Historical Society, *Collections*, IV (1878), 35. It should be noted
that despite a burgeoning export trade in foodstuffs, Maryland nevertheless continued to import sizable amounts of Pennsylvania produce.
10. The best discussion of general economic conditions in this period is Barker,
Revolution in Maryland, chap. 3. See also Paul H. Giddens, "Trade and Industry
in Colonial Maryland, 1753-1769," *Journal of Economic and Business History*, IV
(1932), 512-583, and Clarence P. Gould, "The Economic Causes of the Rise of
Baltimore," *Essays in Colonial History Presented to Charles McLean Andrews...*
(New Haven, Conn., 1931), 225-251. The best discussion of the tobacco problem
in the period is also Barker, *Revolution in Maryland*, chap. 3.
11. "Questions relating to His Majesty's Colony in America," *Md. Archives*,
XXXII, 24. Such estimates are of course highly impressionistic, and existing statistical records for the period are incomplete and fragmentary. Nonetheless a comparison of customhouse records for 1753 and the period 1768 to 1771 reveals that
grain exports had at least doubled during these years. In addition it should be
remembered that since the marketing charges for tobacco were substantially higher
than for wheat and corn, grain exports were relatively more valuable. See Newton
D. Mereness, *Maryland as a Proprietary Province* (New York, 1901), 125, and
C.O. 16/1, P.R.O.

a local writer urged even greater efforts at achieving self-sufficiency and independence, an attitude of mind that at least one historian has described as expressing a "spirit" that also "dominated politics and sentiments" in the period.[12]

The most spectacular economic change was the gain in wheat production. By the beginning of the Revolution, Maryland's entire Eastern Shore, apart from those southernmost counties that continued to produce limited amounts of low-grade tobacco and were heavily engaged in lumbering, had turned to the planting of wheat, and to some extent corn, for export.[13] (At mid-century a tobacco factor in Kent County on the Eastern Shore plaintively cried that the planters in his neighborhood now raised scarcely more than one hogshead apiece, which left him facing certain bankruptcy by the "visible decline of the trade wherein I am embarked.")[14] Other major centers of wheat production in the period were the Monocacy Valley in northwestern Maryland and the counties at the head of the Chesapeake in the northeast.[15] Wherever grown, much of the wheat ultimately found its way to the Philadelphia market. There, according to Maryland's governor, Horatio Sharpe, the price was "always higher." Local merchants could "always load their Vessels at once" and therefore "give more for the Cargoes than Merchants in this Province can give, because ours must be a long time collecting a Cargo for even a small Vessel."[16] Of the markets in Maryland, Sharpe thought Baltimore transacted the most business. Even so he found the town, in "both its Trade and Buildings," to be "almost as much inferiour to Philadelphia as Dover is to London."[17]

No doubt the governor's assessment of conditions in the grain trade was accurate enough for the period down to the end of the

12. Barker, *Revolution in Maryland*, 116.
13. See the sketchy but original work of Gaspare J. Saladino, "The Maryland and Virginia Wheat Trade from Its Beginnings to the American Revolution" (M.A. thesis, University of Wisconsin, 1960). On the trade in low-quality tobacco see the Wallace, Davidson, and Johnson Letterbooks, Maryland Hall of Records, Annapolis.
14. Quoted in Lawrence C. Wroth, "A Maryland Merchant and His Friends in 1750," *Md. Hist. Mag.*, VI (1911), 239. Compare the Reverend Richard Peters to the Proprietaries of Pennsylvania, Oct. 30, 1756, Letters of the Reverend Richard Peters to the Proprietaries of Pennsylvania, 1755–1757, Gratz Collection, Hist. Soc. Pa., Philadelphia.
15. A useful description of the regional character of agriculture in Maryland is to be found in Ronald Hoffman, "Economics, Politics, and Revolution in Maryland" (Ph.D. diss., University of Wisconsin, 1969), chap. 1.
16. To Calvert, Sept. 25, 1762, *Md. Archives*, XIV, 71–72.
17. To Calvert, Aug. 22, 1764, *ibid.*, 173.

French and Indian War. On the other hand his remarks tended to underestimate the growing importance of Baltimore after 1763. As early as the 1740s the town appears to have provided a ready market both for wheat grown in its immediate vicinity and for grain carted down a newly completed roadway from the recently settled Monocacy Valley in the west. A couple of decades later Baltimore also offered a burgeoning market to grain producers on the Eastern Shore, an area that provided the major impetus to its growth. By then, too, its markets had even begun to tap frontier areas of Virginia, Kentucky, and Pennsylvania, where farmers in the Shenandoah and Susquehanna valleys, attracted by the town's relatively favorable inland location, sent down the bulk of their grain, hemp, and garden products. Such developments did not go unnoticed. And in an effort to offset Baltimore's advantage, a group of Philadelphia merchants who had previously dominated the Susquehanna trade petitioned the Pennsylvania General Assembly to provide them with a competitive transportation system to the area.[18] Others chose to join the opposition and began investing heavily in the trading establishments, flour mills, and other industries springing up in and around the town, a decision that played a major role in the final emergence of Baltimore as the "grand emporium" of the Chesapeake grain trade.[19]

In short, by the beginning of the Revolutionary Era, Maryland had become a transitional zone between the middle and southern colonies. As one author has recently observed, "In the predominance of white rather than Negro labor, in the importance of bar iron and pig iron production, in the increasing emphasis upon wheat, in the variety of crops produced, in the growth of a port city flourishing on the basis of an increasingly widespread use of wagons for carriage to and from the interior—in all these respects conditions in Maryland resembled those in Pennsylvania."

18. See the discussion in Gould, "Rise of Baltimore," in *Essays Presented to Andrews*, 236–237, 246. Hoffman, "Economics, Politics, and Revolution in Maryland," chap. 1, also provides valuable information. On the Philadelphia question Charles H. Lincoln, *The Revolutionary Movement in Pennsylvania, 1760–1776* (Philadelphia, 1901), 57–65, remains a standard source.

19. Hoffman, "Economics, Politics, and Revolution in Maryland," chap. 4. See in addition the suggestion by Gould, "Rise of Baltimore," in *Essays Presented to Andrews*, 242. These developments are reflected as well in the letters of the Baltimore merchant William Lux; see Letterbook of William Lux, 1763–1768, New-York Historical Society, New York City. It is important to note that Baltimore did not provide a major market for the sale of British goods at the time.

Still tobacco remained the chief export and continued to draw heavy amounts of British credit and capital to the shores of the Chesapeake. And this plus "tidewater plantations and the presence of a political aristocracy were features more characteristic of Maryland's southern neighbors."[20]

A practical effect of Maryland's unique situation was that, apart from having difficulties of its own, the province came in for a share of the problems plaguing both its northern and southern neighbors. At the end of the French and Indian War much the same short-run economic conditions affected Maryland and Virginia alike. An adverse balance of trade, the rapid withdrawal of British credit, growing demands for sterling remittances to pay off former debts, dwindling supplies of specie, and rising exchange rates comprised one common set of factors; generally heavy tobacco yields but unexpectedly depressed tobacco prices abroad, high marketing charges, and the advanced price of British imports made up another. The upshot was a slump in the tobacco market and in the sale of British goods.[21] In consequence the buyers and factors for the great English and Scottish firms that dominated the trade began to retrench and press for the payment of local debts. "For God's sake Sandy, do your utmost in Settling, Securing, and Remitting me, so as I may be relieved of this dismal situation," became an increasingly common cry. The end results were much the same as described for Virginia,

20. H. Roy Merrens, *Colonial North Carolina in the Eighteenth Century: A Study in Historical Geography* (Chapel Hill, N.C., 1964), 10.

21. These remarks are based upon both the discussion of economic conditions in the period in the works cited in nn. 9, 10, and 15 above and in the mercantile correspondence cited below. Other sources that I have found useful but have not had occasion to cite include: the Charles Ridgely Papers, James Rogers Papers, Thomas Hyde Papers, and the Corner Collection, all from the Maryland Historical Society, Baltimore, and the John Reynell Letterbook, Hist. Soc. Pa., Philadelphia. See also the discussion in "The Debate over Rising Exchange Rates, 1762," in chap. 3 above. A detailed and careful analysis of short-run economic conditions in Maryland at the time is badly needed. The best account is Hoffman, "Economics, Politics, and Revolution in Maryland," chap. 3. Aubrey C. Land in a recent article, "Economic Behavior in a Planting Society: The Eighteenth-Century Chesapeake," *Journal of Southern History*, XXXIII (1967), 469–485, misses the significance of the impact of such short-run factors as British credit flows. More important, on the basis of a static analysis of wills and inventories, he assumes that there existed at the time a native creditor and capitalist class independent of the British colonial credit structure. Compare Wilbur C. Plummer, "Consumer Credit in Colonial Philadelphia," *PMHB*, LXVI (1942), 385–409, and Richard B. Sheridan, "The British Credit Crisis of 1772 and the American Colonies," *Jour. Econ. Hist.*, XX (1960), 161–182.

and there was no significant improvement in the overall economic situation before 1766.[22]

Affected by conditions more common to Pennsylvania were the Maryland grain merchants. To be sure the French and Indian War seriously impaired the West Indies trade, at least during the early war years, when wheat tended to be generally low in price. Then in 1759 prices suddenly shot up, remaining at high levels through the winter of 1762/1763. The spurt in prices proved deceptive, however; its causes involved an increase in the military demand for provisions, plus overcompetition, especially among the growing number of flour mills in the colony. More important, it seems, was dry weather. For nearly two years after 1761 droughts reportedly cut wheat yields. And as the fields dried up so too did farm income and local markets for high-priced British goods. Consequently when demand slackened again and grain prices slumped as they did early in 1763, the economic outlook began to look bleak to grain handlers and farmers alike.[23]

It was only a short time before the dip in the grain trade, the contraction of credit, and the universal need to repay sterling balances abroad combined to force the grain buyers, like the tobacco merchants, to retrench and to dun the local debtors. The people had been backward in their payment, the Baltimore grain merchant, William Lux, informed his English correspondents in 1764. "I cannot send you any orders, as it is impossible in the present uncertain state of our trade to be punctual."[24] "All ranks of people here, the people in general seem to be in a state of bankruptcy, and not little of the fraudulent kind," affirmed the tobacco merchant Henry Callister the following year. "It is madness now to sue for debts. If people are not able to pay, you must let them walk off or stay to defy you."[25] As in Virginia complaints that local courts and justices were partial to debtors began to pile up. "The laws are for them in both theory and practice," was Callister's acid comment.[26] It offered small comfort that the grain and tobacco merchants were not alone

22. James Lawson to Alexander Hamilton, Jan. 31, 1764, Alexander Hamilton Papers, 1760–1801, Md. Hist. Soc.

23. This discussion is based on my reading of the Lux Letterbook and of William S. Sachs, "Business Depression in the Northern Colonies, 1763–1770" (M.A. thesis, University of Wisconsin, 1950), chap. 4. See also n. 21 above.

24. To Russell and Molleson, Oct. 2, 20, 27, 1764, Lux Letterbook.

25. To Sir Ellis Cunliffe and Robert Cunliffe, Esqrs., Sept. 8, 1765, in Callister Papers, Maryland Diocesan Library Collection, Peabody Institute, IV, 736–737, Baltimore.

26. *Ibid.*

in their misery. Iron dealers could be heard voicing many of the same complaints.[27] Benedict Calvert, the secretary of the province, lamented, "Our trade is ruined, We are immensely in debt and not the least probability of getting clear. Our gaols are not half large enough to hold the debtors; upon every road you ride you meet people going from different Parts of the Province to get out of the way of their Creditors."[28] In brief, by the end of the French and Indian War, Maryland, like her neighbors to the north and south, was suffering from the effects of a serious slump in business, trade, and agriculture.

At war's end economic indexes seem to have been universally down, a condition greatly exacerbated by a stringency of cash. "There is no record, since the province was called Maryland, of such a scarcity of money, whether real or imaginary, as at this juncture," Callister declared in late 1764, echoing a widespread complaint. Coin, or "real" money, had been swept off to settle sterling accounts in Britain; paper, or "imaginary" money, on the other hand, had virtually disappeared from circulation. Unlike Virginia and Pennsylvania, where wartime currency supplies remained relatively undiminished, Maryland suffered a severe contraction of paper after the war. By 1765 all notes would be sunk, and the provincial fiat money system would be at an end.[29]

Recent historians have considered Maryland's venture into paper currency to have been highly successful, a view commonly held by many eighteenth-century observers as well. The Maryland system, runs the argument, enjoyed conservative management and good security. Except for a brief period at the beginning of the experiment, sterling exchange rates showed unusual stability, and fluctuations remained within acceptable levels. Maryland, in short, "had solved the problem of a paper currency."[30] As already suggested, however, an exaggerated concern with the rate of exchange and depreciation serves only to obscure the operation of a colony's paper

27. See the discussion in Barker, *Revolution in Maryland*, 106–109. See also Charles Carroll to Messrs. Capel, Osgood, and Hanbury, Sept. 28, 1762, "Letters of Charles Carroll, Barrister," *Md. Hist. Mag.*, XXXII (1937), 374.

28. To Cecil Calvert, June 24, 1765, "The Calvert Papers, Number Two," Md. Hist. Soc., *Fund-Publications*, X (Baltimore, 1894), 261–262, hereafter cited as "Calvert Papers, Two."

29. To Sir [?] White, Dec. 17, 1764, Callister Papers, IV, 703.

30. Quoted in Ferguson, "Currency Finance," *WMQ*, 3d Ser., X (1953), 160. For a more detailed discussion of Maryland paper money before 1764, see Brock, "Currency of the American Colonies," chap. 8, and Clarence P. Gould, *Money and Transportation in Maryland, 1720–1765* (Baltimore, 1915).

currency system. Maryland is no exception. Success as well as failure marked the provincial system. If the weight of the evidence suggests anything, it is that Maryland's experience with paper money was as complicated as any other at the time.

Maryland initiated its paper money system in 1733 with the authorization of a £90,000 loan. The issue was to pass as lawful tender for most public debts, with the notable exception of officers' and ministers' fees. Secured by Bank of England stock purchased out of the proceeds of a continuing tax on exported tobacco, the money was scheduled to be fully redeemed some thirty years later. In 1749, however, in conformity with a provision in the act of 1733, the loan office withdrew the entire issue from circulation, paid off roughly one-third in sterling bills drawn against accumulated Bank of England funds, and exchanged the balance for new bills to circulate for the remainder of the term of the original loan.

Only two additional currency issues were forthcoming prior to passage of the Currency Act of 1764. One was a small appropriation of £6,000 for military aids in 1754 to be drawn from a fund of uncirculated bills lodged in the loan office. Two years later came a treasury emission of £40,000 for the same purpose including £34,000 in new paper and the reissue of almost £6,000 borrowed from the loan office again. Duties on a wide range of imported luxuries from billiard tables to horse carriages were to supply the necessary funds to sink the 1756 issue. There was also provision for an emergency land tax to cover possible deficits. The bills themselves, under the control of the commissioners of the loan office, were to be expended from time to time as the need arose, a policy that effectively kept within narrow limits the available supply of paper money in actual circulation. Political considerations, as well as a conservative approach to all fiat money systems, ruled out additional wartime appropriations.[31]

The impact of the paper currency system on the local economy is difficult to gauge. Nonetheless one of the essential aims of the new system, to free Maryland from the grip of tobacco money and all the familiar problems connected with commodity exchange, did meet with some success. By mid-century local merchants reportedly began keeping their accounts in current money instead of pounds of tobacco and increasingly making their payments in paper. "Our method is new," Henry Callister explained, "we rate every article

31. See Brock, "Currency of the American Colonies," chap. 8, for a full discussion.

in Paper Mony at about 300 Percent advance on the prime Cost and buy Tobacco with this Mony debt discounted as above or with Paper Mony bought the same way. By this method we shall lessen our Tobacco debts, and all our dealings will be more certain, we shall know what we are doing and make them [the planters] know likewise."[32] Equally apparent is the growing importance of paper money to the grain trade. Unlike tobacco, which was purchased locally for sterling bills, cash, or credit, or some combination thereof, wheat could be bought for the most part for cash only, making paper currency a vital factor in the evolving system of diversified agriculture.[33]

Precisely what role paper money played in the formation of the Maryland economy must remain unclear until we have a better understanding of the structure and of the dynamics of economic life in the province. Still two things seem certain: Marylanders held paper currency to be absolutely indispensable to their well-being, and the rapid contraction of paper after 1763 provoked a major debate over monetary policy that had important economic and political ramifications.

By the end of the French and Indian War the treasury issue of 1756 had largely disappeared from circulation. Even so the Maryland General Assembly found it politically impossible to replace the retired issue with additional notes. The difficulty stemmed from an unresolved conflict over tax "reform," a word to be taken in the Pickwickian sense. Beginning in 1757 and for eight successive legislative sessions thereafter, the lower house had passed a supply or assessment bill authorizing a new treasury emission of some £45,000. But each time the upper house rejected the measure. For one thing the bill proposed to tax both the personal property and the income of the chief officers of state and of the professional and and mercantile classes. For another it would tax all landholdings, including the proprietor's, whose were the largest of all.

The question of tax "reform" and the assault on proprietary interests arose for the last time early in 1762. That April, Governor Sharpe informed General Amherst that the taxes levied against the treasury emission of 1756 were about to lapse. Further appropriations for the king's service would require legislative approval.

32. Quoted in Gould, *Money and Transportation in Maryland*, 71–72.
33. The need for cash for the purchase of grain is clearly revealed in the pages of the Lux Letterbook: see, for example, Lux to William Molleson, Nov. 7, 1766, *ibid.*

Sharpe intended to seek that approval in an effort to meet the Maryland troop quota assigned earlier in the war, even though, as he remarked, it would mean playing "again the old Game." Play he did; and this time the governor came close to winning.[34]

As expected the lower house responded to the latest request for aid by passing the familiar supply bill. Included was the disputed provision for a treasury issue secured by a tax on income and land. When the upper house therefore once more rejected the bill, supporters of Sharpe and of the proprietary interest were led to substitute for the proposed grant of £45,000 of new money a plan for an appropriation of £10,000 out of unexpended funds that had accumulated in the loan office over a period of time. This motion was defeated in the lower house by a vote of 25 to 19, was apparently then resurrected in some way or other, and was defeated again, this time by the slim margin of one vote. At this point Sharpe made one effort to have his supporters bring in yet another substitute measure calling for the use of the £2,000 remaining from the treasury appropriation of 1756 as a means of raising a bare minimum of troops. New taxes would not be necessary in this case, and it was hoped that with that question out of the way some accommodation would be possible. It was not, and this measure also failed.[35]

The Maryland assembly was at an impasse. After five contentious years the antiproprietary faction finally called off the drive for tax "reform." And with the abandonment of the supply bill the monetary situation became critical. The amount of paper and coin in circulation had been drastically reduced, and there was little prospect of striking additional currency issues. In the face of increasing British demands for remittances the local stock of coin rapidly drained away. All but a small portion of the remaining loan office bills of 1749 continued "locked up in the chests of the Wealthy" in anticipation of their final redemption in 1765. "If I am right," Secretary Calvert wrote, "the present Loan to be paid is £6,000 Sterling." Paid to whom? "To the most infamous Jobbers; Little currency has

34. The quote is from Sharpe to St. Clair, Mar. 13, 1762, *Md. Archives*, XIV, 32. See also Egremont to Sharpe, Dec. 12, 1761, Amherst to Sharpe, Feb. 21, 1762, Sharpe to Amherst, Mar. 8, 16, Apr. 7, 1762, *ibid.*, XIV, 13–14, 28–29, 29–30, 33–34, 37–38.

35. For a general discussion of this problem, see *ibid.*, LVIII, xxxviii–xlvi, 157–170. See also Sharpe to Calvert, Apr. 15, 1762, Sharpe to Egremont, Apr. 25, 1762, Sharpe to Amherst, Apr. 25, 1762, Sharpe to Calvert, Apr. 25, 1762, *ibid.*, XIV, 38, 47–48, 48–49, 51–53.

had circulation, the utility prevented, Lock'd up in the hands of merciless wretches that grind the very Poor."[36]

Speculation in currency was a familiar practice in Maryland. It stemmed from a provision in the act of 1733 designed to bolster the value of the loan office bills by providing for their redemption in sterling exchange at the proclamation rate of 133 ⅓. By 1748, just before the £90,000 loan was to be redeemed partly in sterling bills and partly in new notes, free exchange rates hovered at 150, finally falling to a par of 133. At this point self-interest prompted speculators, swindlers, and anyone else with the means to hoard as much paper as possible. Such action guaranteed a share in the distribution of sterling bills on redemption day as well as an advantage in connection with the temporary spread between the market and proclamation rates of exchange. Loan office bills were becoming too valuable to circulate as cash.[37]

Much the same thing occurred in 1763. And to Calvert and others it smacked of stockjobbing. There was a difference, however. This time sterling exchange rates did not fall to 133 ⅓ as redemption approached; instead they *rose* to between 163 and 170 in seeming violation of both economic "law" and contemporary expectations.[38] The would-be difference was more apparent than real. Actually Maryland had two currency systems (and two sterling exchange rates at the time), with neither having much bearing on the other. To understand that development, it is necessary to go back a few years.

Following the passage of the tobacco inspection act, in 1747 all official fees and most other public debts became payable either in the warehouse receipts and commodity notes introduced by the act or, as a service to those growing little or no tobacco, in paper at a rate of ten shillings per hundred pounds of tobacco.[39] The new move not only gave an added twist to an already complicated system but provided local speculators in currency with the means of turning an extra dollar. As Governor Sharpe noted: "Every Person that did not

36. To Lord Baltimore, Jan. 10, 1764, "Calvert Papers, Two," 218–219.
37. For an extended discussion see Brock, "Currency of the American Colonies," chap. 8, and Gould, *Money and Transportation in Maryland*, 44–45, 96–98. The Gould study is quite good but is condensed to the point of being virtually incomprehensible. It requires therefore a very careful reading.
38. See graph 3 in Appendix 2.
39. See Brock, "Currency of the American Colonies," 414; Gould, *Money and Transportation in Maryland*, 68–69; *Md. Archives*, XLIV, 595–638.

make Tobacco (which numbers do not)" had to pay his fees and taxes in paper, "which many being oftentimes not Masters of (as there is not £60,000 issued and most of that in the hands of the wealthy) they were obliged to pay their Gold and Silver at any Rate their Creditors would please to affix or on such Occasions be obliged to recur to any Person that would advance paper Cash which the Possessors would not often do but on hard Terms."[40]

Obviously something had to be done to remedy the mistake, and in 1753, on renewing the inspection and fee act, the General Assembly added silver coin to the growing list of acceptable currencies. Consequently those producing insufficient amounts of tobacco might thereafter pay all or part of their public obligations in paper *or* coin. The allowed rate was twelve shillings sixpence per hundred pounds of tobacco, or the equivalent of seven shillings sixpence per dollar, the value for silver coin in neighboring Pennsylvania.[41] The point is that Maryland lay on the rim of a regional trade area whose hub was Philadelphia, so that in ordinary business transactions such money tended to pass at the Pennsylvania exchange rate on sterling of 166 ⅔. This was not invariably the case, of course, since the commercial value of coin was a matter of practice, not law. In this sense the Maryland action can also be interpreted as an attempt to stabilize local monetary conditions: that is, to fix the value of coin, to keep hard money from draining north, and to help create a homogeneous money supply. Certainly the move to bring the value of paper and hard money into line for all public purposes suggests such an interpretation. In any event, because coin did pass at values prevailing in Pennsylvania, local exchange rates on coin *and* paper fluctuated just below the 166 ⅔ mark—except at those times when paper went into hiding in anticipation of its redemption in sterling at proclamation rates.[42]

By now Maryland's General Assembly had piled complication on complication. The latest remedial action flew in the face of the parliamentary act of 1706 limiting the inflation of foreign coin to 133 above sterling, and the proprietor threatened repeal. Calvert also opposed the new measure out of fear that the assembly had jeopardized the currency system by depreciating the value of paper.

40. Sharpe to Calvert, Aug. 8, 1754, *Md. Archives*, VI, 85.
41. *Ibid.* The act is printed *ibid.*, L, 303–367. See also Gould, *Money and Transportation in Maryland*, 106.
42. Maryland's regional trade connections with Philadelphia are discussed at some length in Hoffman, "Economics, Politics, and Revolution in Maryland," chap. 4. See also nn. 37, 40.

The governor and Council, on the other hand, stuck by the legislature and argued that, as the "Tender proposed" was not general "but intended only for the Officers fees and the particular Uses of that Act, this Board did not apprehend It was contrary to the Act of Queen Ann for regulating Coins." In addition it was thought to be "better to suffer a Little Inconveniency by the Chance of Lowering the Value of the Paper Currency than a Certainty of losing the Advantages to the Province by the passing so advantagious a Law as the Inspection Law."[43] In the end Calvert relented and approved the extension, not only in 1753 but again in 1758, without any change in the tender of hard money.[44] The assembly's only concession was to make the taxes covering the treasury emission of 1756 payable in paper alone.[45]

Predictably the latest assembly move proved to be another disaster. When the inspection act once more came up for renewal, in the fall of 1760, the legislators voluntarily dropped the disputed clause permitting the optional use of coin. In return they obtained an agreement to a two-year extension of the treasury issue of 1756 to 1763, a move made necessary by the discovery of a £14,000 shortage in the redemption fund. Prolonging the life of the money made it possible to attempt to meet the deficit with an emergency tax on items other than land and, for the time being, to defeat the designs of "the Few who had got the Paper Money into their hands conceiving that those who should want it to pay their Tax with must purchase it at any Rate," had "immediately raised its price," and incidentally lowered sterling exchange rates.[46] But within two years, as redemption again drew near and some paper still remained outstanding, the monetary situation once more became uncertain. As before, paper fell into the hands of speculators, and there was nothing to do but restore coin as a limited tender at the former value of 166 ⅔ above sterling. Months later, after the treasury issue of 1756 was finally laid to rest, the legislature again reversed itself. This time it omitted forever the inflationary clause governing coin

43. Calvert to governor and Council, governor and Council to Calvert, Dec. 10, 1754, *Md. Archives*, XXXI, 55–57. See also Sharpe to Calvert, Aug. 8, 1754, Calvert to Sharpe, Dec. 10, 1754, *ibid.*, VI, 85–86, 131.

44. *Ibid.*, L, 366–367, LVI, 128–129.

45. For a brief discussion of the act of 1756 see Gould, *Money and Transportation in Maryland*, 102–103, 106. See also Sharpe to Calvert, Oct. 12, 1760, *Md. Archives*, IX, 453–454.

46. Sharpe to Calvert, Oct. 12, 1760, *Md. Archives*, IX, 454. See also *ibid.*, LVI, 386–390; Gould, *Money and Transportation in Maryland*, 102–103.

in response to repeated complaints from proprietor and crown about the breach of parliamentary law. Thereafter coin became lawful for most public debts at the mint par of exchange, or at the actual sterling value of its silver content. To conform to the new rate, the fee table was necessarily adjusted downward.[47]

Clearly Maryland's paper money practices were complicated by shifts in local monetary policies as well as in underlying economic conditions, a fact reflected in the periodic swings of sterling exchange rates. Responsibility for the fluctuations in rates, however, rested to a large extent on local redemption laws and practices. In the decade after 1750, for instance, at a time when no redemption took place, exchange rates for paper and hard money alike hovered just below 167, the Pennsylvania rate for coin.[48] Beginning in 1760, however, the impending destruction of the treasury and loan office issues gradually lowered the exchange on both kinds of paper and gave rise to separate quotations on coin and currency.[49] The confusion in exchange dealings was short-lived. Within just a few years the exchange rate had climbed back up to 167 and higher because of the British credit crisis at the end of the Seven Years' War as well as the depression in tobacco and grain markets in the period. Single quotations were again the rule.[50] By this time the province had virtually sunk all its own paper and depended on varying amounts of gold and silver coin, copper farthings, promissory notes, tobacco receipts, and Pennsylvania currency to fill the local stream of circulation. Apart from coin, the only important medium in exchange transactions was Pennsylvania paper, which, though it had no legal status, enjoyed wide acceptance because of the stringency of hard money.[51] "I said Currency," remarked Henry Callister to one of his correspondents late in 1763 in an obvious effort to clear up the confusion, but, he continued, it does "not imply Maryland money, of which there is hardly any current."[52]

Before 1764 the currency question in Maryland probably was more significant as an economic rather than as a political issue. In Revolutionary Maryland, on the other hand, political imperatives

47. Gould, *Money and Transportation in Maryland*, 106; Kathryn L. Behrens, *Paper Money in Maryland, 1727–1789* (Baltimore, 1923), 46.
48. See graph 3 in Appendix 2.
49. See *ibid.* and Gould, *Money and Transportation in Maryland*, 45–46.
50. See, for instance, the quotations in the Lux Letterbook in the period.
51. See, for instance, the discussion of "Zedikiah Homminy" in the *Maryland Gazette* (Annapolis), May 13, 1762.
52. Quoted in Gould, *Money and Transportation in Maryland*, 106.

seem to have been equally important, and it would be impossible to grasp the nature of monetary problems in the period without recognizing that fact. To examine the interplay of the economic and political pressures as they affected the currency question is to discover that the history of the Revolution in Maryland is more deeply fissured than generally imagined.

The Maryland Response to the Currency Act, 1764–1767

By the end of the French and Indian War, the attack on proprietary interests had spent itself. For a brief moment Marylanders were free to attend to the accumulation of economic ills that beset the province. The remedies proposed naturally centered around long- and short-run considerations. Contemporaries with an eye to the long view tended to support one of the two more popular mercantilist solutions of the age. The first advocated that government actively encourage trade and agriculture. In the nature of things this was expected to create jobs, enhance the price of crops and lands, and generally to spur the growth of the economy. The emphasis was on a diversified system of commercial agriculture and the resulting production and export of a variety of profitable commodities and raw materials—not just of staple tobacco. But priority was also given to the manufacture of such items as flour, rope, iron, lumber, and ships in an effort to take advantage of the "value added" and to maximize returns as well as to exploit new markets. The market question was an important one. On one hand greater attention was to be paid to the problem of expanding the British market in order to relieve the vexing business of making sterling remittances. On the other hand, because it was commonly held that commercial growth was directly related to urbanization, there was growing talk of having the government act to "restrain the whole Trade of the Province to one or two Ports" in an effort to create a great urban marketplace like Philadelphia.[53]

The second view was much like the first. However, it gave greater stress to the need to establish a balanced, self-sufficient economy in which industry and shipping would take their place alongside agriculture and commerce as a specific for advancing economic growth and redressing the adverse trade balances with both the mother country and neighboring provinces. It also emphasized the need for freer

---

53. Sharpe to Calvert, Sept. 25, 1762, *Md. Archives*, XIV, 71–72.

trade as opposed simply to expanding the British market.[54] Long- and short-run considerations were not mutually exclusive, of course. But those who opted for the short run placed the greater emphasis on the immediate need for retrenchment and cutbacks in imports as the best way to reduce the commercial and financial distresses of the day.[55]

Despite all other differences, advocates of the several approaches to economic growth and well being after 1763 universally agreed on the necessity of increasing the local supply of hard money as the best way of alleviating the growing shortage of a circulating medium. Many of the same writers, however, also agreed that the recent and heavy drain on coin left no alternative other than to strike a new issue of paper currency. The subject did not want for ideas. To cite but one example, in the spring of 1763 one "Zedekiah Homminy" outlined a unique giveaway plan in the columns of the *Maryland Gazette* under which the General Assembly would dole out some £150,000 of new paper to the fifty thousand or so taxpayers in the province. The money was to be repaid over a twenty-year interval at 5 percent interest and thereafter lent out on good security in amounts up to £500.[56]

For the moment relief was to come from another quarter. Between 1762 and 1764 Marylanders privately imported nearly two million copper farthings from Philadelphia and an unknown number from New York for service as token money in the retail store trade.[57] Though overvalued and hence less satisfactory than had been hoped, the "coppers" seemed to have satisfied the local demand. When Lord Baltimore offered therefore to introduce a copper coinage into the colony a couple of years later, he received a polite but firm refusal.[58] An ancillary source of fractional money in the period was provided by the increased use of promissory notes. As one merchant, Stephen West, announced in April 1761 to the readers of the *Maryland Gazette*: "As I daily suffer much Inconvenience in my Business for Want of small Change, which indeed is a universal Complaint of almost every Body in any Sort of Business,

54. See, for instance, "Philopatris," *Md. Gaz.*, Mar. 11, 1762, and Lux to Molleson, June 15, 1766, Lux Letterbook.
55. See, for example, the discussion in Hoffman, "Economics, Politics, and Revolution in Maryland," chap. 2, and "A Countryman," *Md. Gaz.*, Apr. 8, 1762.
56. *Md. Gaz.*, May 13, 1762.
57. *Ibid.*, July 17, 1766.
58. See *ibid.*, and John A. Kinnaman, "The Internal Revenues of Colonial Maryland" (Ph.D. diss., University of Indiana, 1954), 477–478.

I intend, if no better Method is proposed, to Print, for the Convenience of my Neighbours and Myself, a Parcel of small Notes, from Three Pence to Two Shillings and Six Pence each, to pass Current at the same Rate as the Money under the Inspecting Law, and to be Exchanged by me, or any Person doing Business for me, upon Demand, for good *Spanish* Dollars at Seven Shillings and Six Pence each Dollar." West apparently only circulated limited amounts of such money, which he offered to withdraw as soon as "the Legislature or any Society of Gentlemen" agreed to make small money available for public use.[59] Greater relief derived from the greatly expanded circulation of Pennsylvania currency.[60]

An extended use of token money, promissory notes, and neighboring currencies hardly sufficed to meet the general need for a means of domestic exchange. As early as 1762 the dearth of "Circulating cash" seems to have placed real and personal property in danger of becoming nonliquid assets. "The value of land, slaves, and all manner of property ... [has] sunk within these two or three years about one hundred percent," one observer claimed.[61] In addition there were increasing reports that the monetary stringency was ruining business and driving some merchants and traders from the province.[62] As already noted the general depression in business and agriculture at this time had less to do with money than with market and credit conditions. A fresh emission of paper promised some relief, however, and its need now seemed obvious to all but a very few.[63]

Predictably, the arrival of news late in 1763 of a plan to extend the Currency Act of 1751 to all the colonies produced a generally unfavorable response in Maryland. Reports of the popular mood soon reached the ear of Cecil Calvert in London. Calvert remained unmoved. Like most educated Englishmen of his generation, he believed paper currency to be a form of imaginary wealth that must inevitably drive coin out of circulation. And it was axiomatic that the consequence would be wide fluctuations in sterling exchange

---

59. *Ibid.*, Apr. 2, 9, 16, Aug. 20, 1761. See also Jerman Baker to Duncan Rose, Feb. 15, 1764, *WMQ*, 1st Ser., XII (1903–1904), 240.

60. See Daniel Dulany to Secretary Calvert, Sept. 10, 1764, "Calvert Papers, Two," 246.

61. Callister to Sir Ellis Cunliffe, Sept. 8, 1765, Callister Papers.

62. See the discussion in Giddens, "Trade and Industry in Colonial Maryland," *Jour. Econ. Bus. Hist.*, IV (1932), 535–536.

63. On the opposition to currency at the time see Sharpe to Calvert, Dec. 21, 1765, *Md. Archives*, XIV, 251.

rates, which could only redound to the disadvantage of trade and
of all sterling creditors. Even more disturbing from Calvert's point
of view, much of the paper had fallen into the hands of "stock-
jobbers" who stood to make a handsome profit when the money
was redeemed and converted into sterling bills of exchange. That
practice seemed but another example of the evils of paper money,
a point Calvert stressed when called before the Board of Trade early
in February 1764 to testify on the possibility of enlarging the scope
of the 1751 act.[64]

Far more sympathetic to paper money were the government leaders in Maryland, and they eventually persuaded Calvert to tone
down his opposition. Even Governor Sharpe, who had no particular
love for paper money, questioned the wisdom of tightening monetary controls. On learning of the Currency Act of 1764, Sharpe
wrote Calvert that he wished Parliament had not thought it necessary "to prohibit absolutely any more Emissions." Although he felt
that Virginia and some of the other provinces had perhaps given
reason for the move, Sharpe believed that colonial trade in general
"must flag much from the Want of paper Currency." Nonetheless,
like the Board of Trade, the governor concluded that "unless the
Paper Money can be fixed at a certain and invariable Value I think
it must be best or at least most just to have none at all emitted."[65]

The defense of paper money was led by Daniel Dulany, an outspoken critic of the new parliamentary regulation. Recently returned to Maryland after a two-year stay in England, he was a chief
spokesman for the provincial Council and a man to whom Calvert
listened. Dulany admitted that Virginia had indeed issued more
than enough paper money, but he wondered whether, "because a
sore appears on some part of it," the limb must be amputated "before a milder Application is tried." He emphasized that in the past
Maryland's laws, unlike Virginia's, had not forced anyone to receive
paper notes in payment of sterling debts—unless specifically contracted for in paper. His chief point, however, was that paper was
indispensable. With the importation of British money banned by
statute "and much more effectively by the balance of trade being
against us," there was an absolute need for paper to supply a medium
of "internal intercourse." Old paths could be blocked, "but a new
channel" would be made. Dulany insisted that if Parliament pre-

---

64. Cecil Calvert to Lord Baltimore, Jan. 10, 1764, "Calvert Papers, Two," 218–
229; Calvert to Sharpe, Feb. 29, 1764, *Md. Archives*, XIV, 141–142.
65. To Calvert, Aug. 22, 1764, *Md. Archives*, XIV, 173–174.

vented "our emitting Bills of Credit under one Denomination, we shall have a paper Circulation under another, if not under a public law...[then] upon the Bottom of private Security." As for "stock-jobbing," Dulany found little wrong with the practice. From his point of view, one shared by a number of the Council's wealthy members, many rich people had invested "a good deal of their property" in paper, and the risks involved entitled them to any profit that might accrue.[66]

By the autumn of 1765 Maryland virtually depended upon Pennsylvania for a supply of paper money. What little remained of the loan office bills were either retired or shortly to be retired. The coin situation was hardly better. In addition popular opinion held that a fresh emission of paper would help ease the depressed economic conditions that had by now continued for four long years. Thus, at the opening of the fall General Assembly session, Sharpe raised the question of the need for a new currency issue. He had learned by this time that the Currency Act of 1764 did not, as he had originally feared, "prohibit absolutely any more emission." He urged therefore that while the legislators went about the business of settling up the old loan office account, they consider using any surplus funds to back an issue of treasury notes that would serve both to pay off the public debt and to supply a badly needed circulating medium without violating the ban on legal tender paper. The need seemed undeniable. And the plan was certainly feasible. But the governor was not to have his way without a struggle. There was some objection that new paper notes would drive the last remaining coin from the province. Essentially, however, the conflict was political in nature and, as will be explained shortly, revolved around one of the enduring questions in Maryland politics: the payment of the clerk of the Council.[67]

The struggle involving Sharpe's proposed issue of treasury notes began when in October 1765 a joint committee of the legislature completed a three-year inspection of the loan office and treasury accounts. Compared with Virginia, the report revealed, Maryland had managed the currency system fairly well. And losses were few. Only one major defalcation had occurred, involving some £5,000, although some sheriffs and tax collectors were in arrears and would never make good on their debts and at least a few public mortgages

66. Sept. 10, 1764, "Calvert Papers, Two," 245–246.
67. *Md. Archives*, LIX, 16–17; Sharpe to Calvert, Dec. 21, 1765, Sharpe to Baltimore, Dec. 24, 1765, *ibid.*, XIV, 251–253, 254–256.

were suspect. More important, a balance remained after the last loan office notes were converted into sterling bills— £25,000 sterling in Bank of England stock and nearly £10,000 sterling in cash.

A scant month later an ad hoc house committee charged with reviewing the matter of the bank holdings came up with a plan. Any surplus funds in the loan office and treasury were to be used to purchase extra bank stock so that within a decade a £50,000 sterling investment would be available as security for additional currency issues. On this basis the house was to consider authorizing a ten-year loan of £40,000. The insistence upon a loan, as distinguished from the treasury issue Sharpe had suggested, unquestionably reflected the need of the planters who dominated the house. They hoped to replace with public credit the supply of private British credit that had been drastically curtailed in the face of a European financial crisis and depressed tobacco markets. Another interesting feature of the committee's plan was that this time the money would be struck in paper dollars instead of the usual pounds and be rated at 4s. 6d. each, equal to a total of $135,000. Since the work-a-day coin in Maryland was the Spanish dollar, the new notes would presumably simplify commercial transactions.[68]

When the committee proposal came to a vote at the end of November, Sharpe's supporters in the lower house turned it down. Instead they offered a plan similar to the one the governor had alluded to in his opening address to the assembly: surplus funds were to be used not for a loan but for a treasury issue amounting to $140,000 that would be payable "to such of the Public Creditors who will accept of the Same." Faced with a demand for a circulating medium of any kind, the advocates of the loan office took what they could get and voted for the treasury emission.[69] Sharpe was delighted. And he had his reasons. In effect he had exploited a monetary and financial crisis to strengthen the claims of the Council in a long-standing contest with the lower house over the power of the purse. He had managed, too, to find a way of paying the public creditors who as victims in that contest had gone without any recompense since 1756.[70]

Conflict over the control of the public purse strings grew out

68. *Ibid.*, LIX, 183–184, 191–193.
69. Sharpe to Calvert, Dec. 21, 1765, *ibid.*, XIV, 251–253, LIX, 191–193.
70. Sharpe to Lord Baltimore, Dec. 24, 1765, *ibid.*, XIV, 255. See also *ibid.*, 251–253.

of a question that had first taken shape in the seventeenth century. Who should pay the Council—the proprietor or the people? Payment out of treasury funds was mandatory whenever the councillors sat as members of the upper house, but their payment for sitting as Council members was not. Before 1748 the question ordinarily arose in connection with the payment of official fees. In that year the legislature finally settled upon a fee table as part of the tobacco inspection act and specifically omitted any provision for paying the councillors as councillors. As a result for a number of years the Council rejected any account of the public debt unless it contained an allowance for the Council members.[71] In 1756 the impasse was broken. The Council suddenly dropped its demands and agreed to pass the journal of accounts and to pay off the debt "for the ease of the good people of this province"—provided that the clerk of the Council received compensation for his services. This new demand provoked a spirited exchange of views. But in the end the delegates to the lower house made their own concession to the "good people" and voted the clerk a stipend for his services up to 1756. No such provision was to be made in the future, however, and until September 1765 the nagging question of who should pay the clerk of the Council had tied up the public debt for nearly a decade. Public creditors went without a penny.[72]

Sharpe sent a detailed explanation of his treasury scheme to Secretary Calvert and Lord Baltimore in December 1765. According to the governor, the proposed emission was perfectly consistent with the rules laid down by the Currency Act of 1764. The notes were not to be declared a lawful tender. And the public creditors would be given the option of taking the money or leaving it. Earlier fears that paper money would drive coin out of circulation and out of the province seemed to have been forgotten, and Sharpe blamed the loss of specie on the adverse trade balance with the mother country. Lord Baltimore agreed entirely and gave the plan his blessing.[73]

Actually nothing had been settled. The currency proposal faced yet another legislative challenge, one signaling the resurgence of an antiproprietary movement that had dominated the war years. Charles Carroll of Carrollton cynically appraised the new political

71. See the discussion in Mereness, *Maryland as a Proprietary Province*, 362–363.
72. May 1, 4, 15, 1756, *Md. Archives*, LII, 271, 284–285, 404, 424, and Kinnaman, "Internal Revenues of Colonial Maryland," 456–473.
73. See nn. 69, 70 above.

stirrings as reflecting "the want of a sufficient number of lucrative offices to gratify the avarice or the ambition of the 'Outs.' "[74] Assembly elections in 1764 had in fact been bitterly contested. Party fevers were running high when the new legislature sat for the first time at the end of 1765 in the aftermath of the Stamp Act riots.[75] Carroll, for one, reported a move afoot to petition the crown to make Maryland a royal colony, a ploy that seemed far less attractive after Benjamin Franklin's failure to bring about a similar transformation in the government of neighboring Pennsylvania.[76] Then in November, Sharpe's currency scheme ran afoul of a sudden revival of the clerk fight. Soon after they agreed to cover the public debt with an issue of treasury notes, the delegates took up and passed the journal of accounts. But the Council insisted upon a number of changes. Payment was to be given the clerks of the upper house for services during the period from 1761 to 1765, to the late clerk of the Council for better than eight years, and to the present clerk, Mr. Ross, for eleven months. After much trouble the need for compensating the upper-house clerks was grudgingly accepted, though the delegates remained adamant in their refusal to provide for Ross. As they viewed it, the clerk, like the councillors themselves, was a creature of the proprietor, to be paid out of his revenues.[77]

While the delegates resurrected the musty arguments of the past in support of their refusal to pay Ross, the antiproprietary faction bruited that three to four hundred well-armed members of the Maryland Sons of Liberty were about to descend upon the capital from the back counties to "intimidate the council and force them into a compliance with the lower house in rejecting Mr. Ross' claims."[78] Likewise "stories were industriously spread of threats and menaces" against the property of Ross and of some of the leading members of the "court party." The move had limited success. A threatened renewal of the Stamp Act riots was enough to frighten

74. To Mr. Jennings, Nov. 23, 1765, in Thomas Meagher Field, ed., *Unpublished Letters of Charles Carroll of Carrollton, and His Father, Charles Carroll of Doughoregan* (New York, 1902), 98.

75. The best discussion of politics in this period is Hoffman, "Economics, Politics, and Revolution in Maryland," chap. 3.

76. To Daniel Barrington, Mar. 17, 1766, Field, ed., *Unpublished Letters*, 112.

77. Dec. 5, 7, *Md. Archives*, LIX, 203, 213. See also *ibid.*, xxvi–xxvii, xxix–lvi. For a detailed account of this episode see Kinnaman, "Internal Revenues of Colonial Maryland," 471–474.

78. Carroll of Carrollton to Barrington, Dec. 22, 1765, Field, ed., *Unpublished Letters*, 105.

the clerk into asking for a waiver of his claims.[79] And with the example of Maryland's Stamp Act collectors fresh in everyone's minds, it was generally believed that the journal would be passed. It was even given out that Dulany, as spokesman for the Council in this as in other affairs, had solemnly made just such a promise.[80] Instead the Council refused to honor Ross's request and again rejected the journal. The Council's determination to resist at this time seems to have been largely the work of Dulany. In the past Sharpe had found him all too ready to serve the people rather than the proprietary, but Dulany's new stance, and a pamphlet he penned in defense of the clerk's claim, elicited from the governor the remark that he appeared to have made "for once, a sacrifice of popularity to principle."[81]

As for the threatened violence, it failed to materialize, at least for the moment. "If any such design was ever intended," Charles Carroll explained, the people who were mostly men of some property were too sensible to carry it into execution.[82] A "considerable body of people" did come into Annapolis from the "Upper Part" of Annapolis and Prince Georges counties. Their chief efforts were directed at petitioning the assembly to defer the Ross claim to some future time so that the journal could be passed, the claims against the public satisfied, and the money that was desperately needed put in circulation.[83] No action on the petition was forthcoming, and the assembly broke up "in an angry and discontented temper."[84]

When Governor Sharpe prorogued the house on December 20, the legislature was deadlocked not only over the currency and debt question but also over a number of other issues raised during that session in an effort to broaden the attack against the proprietary. One involved the appointment of special house committees to ascertain the amount of provincial revenue the proprietor drew each year and his right to do so. The committees were also to discover the profits that attached to the great offices of state. The other con-

---

79. *Ibid.*; Sharpe to Calvert, Dec. 21, 1765, *Md. Archives.*, XIV, 253.

80. Carroll of Carrollton to Barrington, Mar. 17, 1766, Field, ed., *Unpublished Letters*, 111–112.

81. The quote is from Aubrey C. Land, *The Dulanys of Maryland: A Biographical Study of Daniel Dulany, the Elder, and Daniel Dulany, the Younger* (Baltimore, 1955), 250. See also Kinnaman, "Internal Revenues of Colonial Maryland," 476–477.

82. To Barrington, Dec. 22, 1765, Field, ed., *Unpublished Letters*, 105.

83. Sharpe to Calvert, Dec. 21, 1765, *Md. Archives*, XIV, 253.

84. Carroll of Carrollton to Barrington, Mar. 17, 1766, Field, ed., *Unpublished Letters*, 111.

cerned the renewal of house demands for a colonial agent, an issue that developed over the supposed need to submit the constitutional controversy involving Ross's salary to a crown decision.[85] But questions involving the colonial agency and the revenues and profits of the lord proprietor and of the chief officers of state could not be settled at the moment. As Charles Barker has shown, the antiproprietary movement ran out of steam at the end of the sixties only to be revived with renewed vigor and great success some years later.[86]

One tangible and forgotten reason for the armistice was that political advantage had to be surrendered to economic necessity. The shortage of cash had become a general complaint. On one hand the recovery of tobacco markets and the sudden jump in the European demand for wheat and flour beginning in late 1765 greatly increased the demand in Maryland for an adequate means of domestic trade. On the other it was reportedly increasingly difficult to dispose of property at anything near market value and "to get in small sums from people who are in very good circumstances, and this difficulty can be owing to nothing but a scarcity of circulating money." Equally important was the continuing need to pay off the public debt.[87]

Just before the General Assembly sat for the spring session in March 1766, some 450 inhabitants of Frederick County petitioned Governor Sharpe to help settle the journal of accounts. Western militiamen who had recently seen service in Pontiac's Rebellion had not been reimbursed since the last journal was passed in 1756. The alternative was another threatened march on the capital and seizure of the money owed.[88] In light of historians' recent efforts to establish the importance of the politics of deference and diffidence in the colonial period, it is interesting to note that when the legislature met, the upper house quickly voted to accept the various allowances claimed by the angry militiamen. Commenting on the new "politics of the street," Sharpe advised Calvert, "The Truth is that from the People's succeeding so far by their riotous Meetings and Proceedings in the several Colonies as to force the Persons who had been

85. See Barker, *Revolution in Maryland*, 333–334.
86. See the discussion, *ibid.*, chap. 10. But compare this with the account in Hoffman, "Economics, Politics, and Revolution in Maryland," chap. 3.
87. The quote is from Carroll of Carrollton to Jennings, May 29, 1766, Field, ed., *Unpublished Letters*, 119. The Lux Letterbook for 1765/1766 gives a good impression of short-run economic conditions at the time.
88. Mar. 29, 1766, *Md. Archives*, XXXII, 124–125.

appointed Destributors of the Stamps to resign their Offices they begin to think they can by the same Way of Proceeding accomplish any thing their Leaders may tell them they ought to do, and really I know not whether the Civil Power in any of the Colonies will be sufficient of itself to re-establish Order." Nevertheless the senior house again refused to pass the journal until provision was made for the clerk of the Council. The action seems to have been expected. In fact, according to one observer, it was counted on. Approval of the militia claims in addition to the other public debts was simply a way "to satisfy the clamours of the publick" while the delegates turned their full attention to the Stamp Act crisis. Talk of another visit "from the back woods" was dissipated for the time being, but it was plain that the public debt would be the first order of business when the legislature reassembled that fall.[89]

Before the General Assembly met, news arrived from Britain that cinched the case for passing the journal of accounts. The recent parliamentary review of the state of the American trade, prompted by the agitation over the Stamp Act, had raised hopes in Maryland and elsewhere in the colonies that the Currency Act of 1764 was about to be repealed or revised, but in August word came that Parliament had refused to do either. In addition it was learned that Lord Baltimore had approved the governor's scheme for paying the journals by emitting paper. Of central importance, however, was the fact that the pressure on the local medium of trade had become increasingly burdensome. European markets for wheat and flour were better than ever, and the exchange of sterling bills into local purchasing power only aggravated the need for cash while driving exchange rates far below par. Likewise the added demands on the existing stock of money affected the Philadelphia and New York money markets as well as making it increasingly difficult to loan or otherwise raise any cash there, as was the custom, and also drying up the supply of neighboring currencies. Finally by 1766 the tobacco trade had recovered from its postwar slump, thus adding its share to the local clamor for money.[90]

Given the economic pressures at the time, it was expected that the two houses would quickly resolve their differences. But shortly after the General Assembly reconvened in November, the word

89. See Sharpe to Calvert, Dec. 21, 1765, *ibid.*, XIV, 253. See also Carroll of Carrollton to Barrington, May 29, 1766, Field, ed., *Unpublished Letters*, 122.

90. See the discussion in the Lux Letterbook covering this period. See also the discussion in chaps. 7 and 8 following.

from Annapolis was that the legislators might continue to disagree about "Words in the Money Bill and do nothing." This drew from one merchant the comment that it would be "a Great Pity that so much good should be frustrated unless for some material Reasons." Nevertheless the same writer held out the hope that the assembly could be prevailed upon to settle everything by the close of the session and "give us a Medium which every Man in Business so sensibly feels the want of."[91] The hope was not unjustified and "the publick necessity" did ultimately force the houses into a compromise. The main stumbling block to a settlement remained the allowance due the clerk of the Council, and the Council was adamant about the need to pay Mr. Ross. Nevertheless at a conference called by the lower house an agreement whereby money for that purpose would be appropriated and then set aside pending an appeal to the king for a decision on the matter received quick approval. The other and smaller differences over claims met with similar treatment.[92]

Only one other question caused any trouble. After all the major items in the journal had been nailed down on December 4, the lower house returned the money bill to the Council accompanied by a claim to an inherent, unquestionable, and fundamental right to form any and all such legislation. The upper house was to approve or reject the document without any further changes. Other imperfections could be adjusted at a later time. As one historian has pointed out, this statement proved to be the most extreme declaration to date of the right of the lower house to initiate money bills "and almost declared that the upper house had merely the negative or assertive right but no real power to amend." Even so the Council passed the bill as it stood. It did, however, append a detailed statement to show that the lower house's claim was both "inconsistent with Our Constitution" and "repugnant to the Usage of the Province." The Council, it seemed, had no wish to obstruct further the "Course of Public Business." It put the lower house on notice that "we shall lay this Subject before his Majesty in Council, at the same time with our Representation on the affair of the Clerks of the Council, in order that both Points may be settled."[93]

The struggle was over. "The Journal is at length passed," Charles

91. Thomas Ringgold, Jr., to [?], Dec. 6, 1766, Letters of Samuel and John Galloway, Box I, "Correspondence 1739–1769," N.Y. Pub. Lib.
92. See the discussion in Kinnaman, "Internal Revenues of Colonial Maryland," 479–484.
93. The quote is from Kinnaman, "Internal Revenues of Colonial Maryland," 482. See also Barker, *Revolution in Maryland*, 336–340.

Carroll explained to a friend in England. "A medium of trade," he continued, "is absolutely necessary to a trading people, and such has been found the want of it in this province, that even the resentment and spirit of party has given way to so useful a measure."[94]

The "Act for the payment of the Public Claims, for emitting Bills of Credit, and for Other Purposes therein mentioned," authorized an emission of some $174,000, or £65,000, rated at seven shillings sixpence. Anxious to avoid any conflict with the provisions of the Currency Act of 1764, the assemblymen included in the new law an express declaration that the money was not a lawful tender for any debt except such "as shall or may be made expressly and specifically for... the delivery of such bills of credit." The value of the notes depended rather on the promise to redeem them in 1771 in sterling bills of exchange drawn on Maryland's account with the Bank of England. To a lesser extent their value rested on the fact that the provincial treasury readily received the notes for all public obligations as a matter of course.[95]

Under the terms of the Maryland charter, Lord Baltimore and not the crown enjoyed sole responsibility for reviewing acts of the provincial legislature. Still the proprietor was careful to avoid giving any grounds for royal interference in Maryland affairs. His governors had standing instructions to pass no paper currency laws without his approval. But Baltimore found no fault with the proposed issue. For that matter neither did the commissioners of trade—once they had a chance to look at it. Not until 1770 did the governor finally get around to sending the law off to the Board. Even the avowed enemy of all paper currency systems, Lord Hillsborough, thought the law the best of its kind and held it up as an example for the rest of the colonies.[96]

THE MARYLAND LOAN OFFICE ACT OF 1769

At this point much of the criticism in Maryland of the Currency Act of 1764 quieted down. Sharpe went so far as to argue that it was

94. Carroll of Carrollton to Jennings, Mar. 9, 1767, Field, ed., *Unpublished Letters*, 141.

95. *Md. Archives*, LXI, 264–275. See also William Franklin to Lord Hillsborough, Sept. 29, 1770, *N.J. Archives*, X, 200.

96. Hugh Hamersley to Sharpe, Mar. 22, 1766, Sharpe to Hamersley, Dec. 8, 1766, June 9, 1767, Hamersley to Sharpe, Aug. 13, 1767, *Md. Archives*, XIV, 282, 356, 390, 416; Hillsborough to Governor Tryon, Mar. 1, 1769, *Col. Recs. N.C.*, VIII, 18. Hamersley, who became secretary to the province on the death of Calvert, also approved of the measure: *Md. Archives*, 416.

to the colony's advantage to have the measure remain on the books, "since our Mercantile People have now money for the purposes of Trade while those in the neighboring Colonies are stinted . . . and if necessity makes them receive and circulate our Money, they must in fact pay us Interest for it, as in that Case we are to them in the nature of Bankers." He also believed that the continued scarcity of specie, due to the recent heavy exportation of dollars to England, would serve as an additional support for the credit of the bills.[97]

A feeling of optimism over the future of the new currency issue was widespread, if undue. William Lux crowed that "as our town increases in its trade daily and the importation of European goods much enlarged and as we have lately had a currency emitted we are of opinion that in the future near as good an exchange can be got for bills here as at Philadelphia."[98] The new currency did hold its value and generally passed at par with silver dollars in all payments. But it did not satisfy Maryland's need for an adequate circulating medium. Nor did it provide funds for loans to neighboring colonies. The growing clamor abroad for American grain, flour, and breadstuffs only boosted the demand for a local means of trade. Money remained relatively scarce, and Maryland's sterling exchange rates dropped far below par. Nonetheless the injection of treasury notes into the monetary stream did make it easier to sell sterling bills and raise cash. It also seems to have given Marylanders some slight advantage in the selling price of those bills.[99]

Hardly more than six months after the treasury issue of $175,000, voices could again be heard favoring the creation of an additional supply of paper money. Even Sharpe urged a further £30,000 emission, though it meant a jump in taxes, in order to expand Bank of England stock holdings.[100] The need, it seems, stemmed from the general economic buoyancy in the late sixties, at least in the export sector. Except for a small dip in 1767, tobacco prices, for example, tended to be favorable, though total returns probably remained about the same as production fell off. By contrast grain

97. To Hamersley, June 9, 1767, and Hamersley to Sharpe, Aug. 13, 1767, *Md. Archives*, XIV, 385, 416.

98. To William Alexander and Sons, Jan. 29, 1767, Lux Letterbook. See also Lux to Isaac and John Simon, Jan. 15, 1767, Lux to Reese Meredith, Feb. 4, 1767, *ibid.*

99. See the entries for Nov. 1766, *ibid.*, and especially the letter to Reese Meredith, Dec. 1, 1766, *ibid.*

100. To Hamersley, June 9, 1767, *Md. Archives*, XIV, 390.

production and exports stayed relatively heavy. Prices also held their own at least until 1768, when they fell to moderate levels. More important, the British credit pinch that had characterized the years 1762 to 1765 had passed, and imports bounded upwards again. The upshot was a business boom that explains not only the growing demands for a circulating medium at the time but also Maryland's great reluctance to enter into the nonimportation movement associated with the Townshend Acts.[101]

As in the past the columns of the *Maryland Gazette* spelled out the familiar long- and short-run analysis of underlying economic problems. And as before no solution appeared more popular than the creation of more public money and credit. "I have understood, our late Emission of Money, was regulated by too much Prudence," a correspondent from Cecil County informed the editor of the *Gazette* in the fall of 1769, ". . . that it was Deemed, upon an accurate Examination, to be unexceptionable in every Respect. The Difficulty was in finding out an Expedient, by which all the clashing with the Act of Parliament might be avoided; but it was happily found out, and, since the Efficacy of it has been experienced, it may again be adopted with Safety. The Money, however, of this Emission, has proved to be very short of the Occasions of our trade, and other intercourse; a great deal of it has been locked up from time to time, by some of the Possessors of it, 'til an opportunity of making a convenient Purchase of Land or Negroes has brought it again to Light." Ergo another paper money issue was in order. It was only a matter of time before Maryland again turned to the printing press for relief.[102]

The House of Delegates on November 29 brought in a bill for a public loan of $300,000 "for the improvement of the Province and the advancement of trade." This time, however, the governor had no pet schemes to substitute, and the Council no clerk to pay, so that despite the same contentiousness over "officers fees" the measure quickly passed both houses and was signed into law a month later.

101. For an excellent summary account of economic conditions at this time and of their effect on the Maryland response to the Townshend Acts and the nonimportation movement, see Hoffman, "Economics, Politics, and Revolution in Maryland," chap. 4. See also the Lux Letterbook for the period and especially Tobias Rudolph to Hollingsworth and Rudolph, Apr. 6, 1769, Hollingsworth Manuscript Correspondence, Box Jan. 1769 to Jan. 1770, Hist. Soc. Pa., Philadelphia.

102. Letter to the Printer, Cecil County, Nov. 1, 1769, *Md. Gaz.*, Nov. 16, 1769.

Lord Baltimore, too, easily gave his consent. Nor was there any difficulty with the commissioners of trade and secretary of state, who chose to overlook that the new bills, together with the treasury notes of 1766 and coin, were specifically made a lawful tender for any and all loan office obligations. Imperial authorities had already given their blessing to Maryland's earlier plan to back its paper money with its stock holdings in the Bank of England, and when essentially the same procedure was applied to the issue of 1769 they presumably saw no reason to change their mind.[103]

Maryland's new loan office was a typical "land bank scheme." The $300,000 was to be lent out in amounts of not less than $100 and not more than $4,000 on a first mortgage of double value. Annual interest rate on the loan was 4 percent. Any cash paid into the loan office, except for the notes of 1766, could be put out on loan again for eleven of the twelve years of the period of the original loan. This provision covered any monies received in the repayment of mortgages in addition to that arising from ordinary and peddlers' licenses. However, a fund for rebuilding the "Stadt" House in Annapolis had first call on the latter. Finally, the act also provided that any Bank of England stock not needed to redeem the issue of 1766 was to be sold and converted into sterling bills, which were to be remitted to Maryland, where they could be purchased on the open market at interest.[104] As for the money itself, it appears to have been in great demand. The commissioners of the loan office lent out well over half the bills before a year had passed.[105]

In sum, by the beginning of 1770 Maryland had struck nearly $500,000 currency. While not declared a legal tender, the money in fact was receivable for all public obligations. The practice was at best questionable, at worst illegal. But for the moment, at least, it caused no trouble on either side of the Atlantic.[106]

---

103. *Md. Archives*, LXII, xxxv–xxxvi, 53–54, 133–151. Between 1763 and 1770 the journals and acts of the Maryland General Assembly were rarely sent to the Board of Trade. This policy was changed at the request of Secretary Hillsborough; see Hillsborough to Governor Eden, Feb. 12, 1770, "Correspondence of Governor Eden," *Md. Hist. Mag.*, II (1907), 233, and Barker, *Revolution in Maryland*, 181–190, 314–315. Accordingly the currency act of 1769 did come before the Board; see Nov. 16, 1770, June 12, 1771, *Jour. of Comm. Trade, 1768–1775*, 213, 258. Even so there was reluctance to intervene in proprietary affairs, since the Maryland charter specifically denied the king in Council the right to review acts of the assembly.

104. *Md. Archives*, LXII, 53–54.

105. See Behrens, *Paper Money in Maryland*, 54.

106. See the discussion in chap. 10 following.

THE GEORGIA EXPERIENCE, 1759–1768

Another province exempted from the stricter requirements of parliamentary law in the period was Georgia, the boom colony of the eighteenth century. After the Treaty of Paris eliminated the French and Spanish threat to its borders, Georgia negotiated a peace treaty and land cession with the local Creek and Cherokee that brought ten years of harmony and trebled the colony's size. But the subsequent rapid advance of population, agriculture, and trade did not hinge entirely upon a successful arrangement with the Indians. A £3,000 loan office issue in 1759 provided some of the required capital for the purchase of slave labor and for the improvement and expansion of plantation agriculture.[107] Investment funds from abroad also helped. "Observing the province safe, and advancing to a hopeful and flourishing state," British merchants "were no longer backward in extending credit."[108] Four years later Governor James Wright initiated an effective program of internal improvements and of public regulation of markets, commodity prices, and exports that did much to advance trade. Even so it fell short of the desired goal of making Savannah a competitor of Charleston in the handling of Georgia's exports.[109]

As an integral part of Georgia's economic expansion, plans called for a new public loan in 1760 of some £7,500 currency.[110] Notwithstanding the Board of Trade's objection to a legal tender provision in connection with the loan, the crown recognized that the province's current exports supplied barely enough specie to meet the local demand for a medium of exchange. In consequence the king in Council allowed the act to stand. Accordingly, when news of the Currency Act arrived in the summer of 1764, Georgians asked only that their new loan office be left unmolested. "If we lost that," Governor Wright assured the commissioners of trade, "twill reduce

107. Gov. Henry Ellis to B.T., May 5, 1757, printed in Percy Scott Flippin, "The Royal Government in Georgia, 1752–1776. IV. The Financial System and Administration," *Georgia Historical Quarterly*, IX (1925), 205–206. The best study of the economy of colonial Georgia remains Milton S. Heath's *Constructive Liberalism: The Role of the State in Economic Development in Georgia to 1860* (Cambridge, Mass., 1954), 13–69.

108. Rev. Alexander Hewatt, *Historical Account of the Rise and Progress of the Colonies of South Carolina and Georgia* (South Carolina Historical Society, *Collections* [New York, 1836]), I, 483.

109. W. W. Abbot, *The Royal Governors of Georgia, 1754–1775* (Chapel Hill, N.C., 1959), 95–96.

110. Allen D. Candler and Lucian Lamar Knight, eds., *The Colonial Records of the State of Georgia* (Atlanta, 1904–1916), XVIII, 435–437.

us to the greatest distress, for it's scarce possible to carry on the common occurrences in life, even with the currency we now have."[111]

The money question came up again in March 1766 over a small treasury issue of nearly £2,000 to be used to spur immigration and settlement and to pay for rebuilding the Savannah courthouse. The new act contained no suspending clause. In addition it specifically made the currency lawful for public debts. The measure proved unacceptable, however, and the crown subsequently vetoed it. But by then the courthouse was "very near finished," and people had come "to settle under the Faith and encouragement of this Law." Obviously the money had accomplished its purpose. Still the legislature worried that the royal veto badly served future needs. Deprived of the privilege of issuing additional currency receivable for taxes, no public works, "however necessary," could be carried on. Nor, according to the Commons House, could any encouragement be given to the further settlement of the province. Moreover the existing fiat money supply did not exceed £7,000, "Much, very much too little to answer the present Medium of Trade." In short the house was protesting the necessity for some kind of limited legal tender paper currency, issued on a continuing basis, to finance public improvements, to support immigration, and to provide an adequate medium of local exchange.[112]

As it turned out, legislative fears were ill grounded. The crown's disallowance bore no relation to the money question. It reflected instead Britain's desire to limit emigration to America, not Georgia's paper money supply. In reviewing the new treasury issue, the Privy Council referred to the thoroughly "commendable and expedient" earlier policy of encouraging Protestants to settle in Georgia. But conditions had changed since then. When so "great a number of useful inhabitants" of Britain, many of whom were manufacturers, were daily emigrating to the colonies, the Council ruled that a policy such as Georgia's could only be looked upon as detrimental to the interests of the mother country. The Privy Council also took ex-

111. Dec. 15, 1764, in Correspondence of Board of Trade, XXI, 125ff, P.R.O. (transcripts in Hist. Soc. Pa.), and Wright's comments in a letter to B.T. dated Apr. 15, 1761, Flippin, "Georgia," *Ga. Hist. Qtly.*, IX (1925), 209–210. See also the address of the assembly in Candler and Knight, eds., *Col. Recs. Ga.*, XIII, 509–511, and *Acts of Privy Council, Col.*, Unbound Papers, 334–335.

112. James Habersham to William Knox, May 19, 1768, *The Letters of Hon. James Habersham, 1756–1775* (Georgia Historical Society, *Collections*, VI [Atlanta, 1913]), 71–73; Candler and Knight, eds., *Col. Recs. Ga.*, XVIII, 745.

ception to the practice of providing immigrants with public lands without the specific approval of the governor. He and he alone had the right to dispose of the king's property.[113]

Despite the royal veto the Georgia legislature made no effort to recall the £1,815 out of circulation. And the king in Council raised no further objections. As a consequence the Commons House felt itself to be on safe grounds when in December 1768 it appropriated an additional issue of £2,200 to finance another round of internal improvements, including the rebuilding of a lighthouse and the surveying of the coastline. Accompanied by comments from the governor urging approval, the law came up for review in December 1769. But it was never reported out of the Board of Trade—though the money was once more made lawful for all public obligations. Well acquainted with the inadequacy of Georgia's specie supply, the commissioners presumably were pleased that the province could shoulder so large a share of its expenses. Certainly Georgia's shaky financial situation had given the ministry cause for concern, and Parliament appropriated some £3,500 sterling annually in support of the fledgling economy in the years between 1758 and 1776. Money raised in Georgia was money saved at home. Thus, at a time when Hillsborough and the Board of Trade were attempting to use the Currency Act to ban any kind of lawful paper money from the other colonies, Georgia got away with striking the small amount of £4,000, which was explicitly designated a legal tender for public debts.[114]

Less successful was the effort to extend Georgia's loan office system. That move became hopelessly entangled with a Commons House effort to appoint a colonial agent of its own choosing. Early in 1767 the Savannah merchants petitioned the assembly for relief from the growing scarcity of money. According to the merchants, "the very great addition of Inhabitants" and the "extraordinary increase of Commerce" alone warranted an enlargement of the loan office. They also cited as evidence the great extension of the province that had taken place since the war's end and the settlement of East Florida, "where the Bills of Credit of this Province are taken in payment." But the most important reason given for expanding the supply of bills of credit was that men in trade who had "very considerable Debts lying out in the hands of the Best persons in the

113. *Acts of Privy Council, Col.*, V, 112–113.

114. Candler and Knight, eds., *Col. Recs. Ga.*, XIX, 83–87; *Jour. of Comm. Trade, 1768–1775*, 150.

Province" could not command the smallest payment on the "most urgent Occasions."[115] In sympathy with the merchants' demands, the Commons House promptly voted to petition Parliament for the privilege of trebling the size of the public loan. The Council proved to be no less enthusiastic and readily agreed to help further the scheme.[116] Meanwhile, in a related action, the Commons House voted to make South Carolina's colonial agent, Charles Garth, the Georgia agent as well in order to have him take charge of the intended petition.[117] At this point the Council suddenly lost interest in the loan office.

The Garth issue had first come up during the Stamp Act crisis at a time when William Knox still served Georgia as provincial agent. Knox's tenure began in 1761, and the Commons House had reappointed him from time to time with the approval of the governor and Council. Then in the fall of 1765 the Commons House abruptly suspended Knox on its own initiative because of his outspoken support of the stamp tax. In an attempt to counter the move, the Council promptly gave Knox a vote of confidence. The house was nonplussed. It bypassed Knox and sent a remonstrance against the Stamp Act in the care of Garth for presentation to Parliament. Only later did the South Carolina agent receive pay for his services. The Commons House simply requisitioned the public treasurer to advance the necessary sum shortly after the assembly reconvened in late 1766. Here matters rested until March 1767, when the house voted to replace Knox with Garth.[118]

The Council rejected the Garth appointment out of hand. It argued that the same man could not reasonably serve two masters who came into continual conflict over questions of boundaries and the like. Still the Commons House decided to send the petition for expanding the public loan to Garth, designating him "Agent for this Province."[119] But the petition never came before Parliament.

115. Feb. 4, 1767, Candler and Knight, eds., *Col. Recs. Ga.*, XIV, 427–428. It should be noted that although Georgia's currency circulated in East Florida, South Carolina's circulated in Georgia. Georgia gained more than it lost in this exchange. See Comm. of Corres. to Garth, Sept. 4, 1764, Gibbes, ed., *Documentary History of the American Revolution*, I, 2, and Thomas Rasberry to Josiah Smith, Feb. 9, 1761, Lilla M. Hawes, ed., "The Letter Book of Thomas Rasberry, 1758–1761, Part VII," *Ga. Hist. Qtly.*, XLII (1958), 293.

116. Feb. 10, 1767, Candler and Knight, eds., *Col. Recs. Ga.*, XIV, 431–432.

117. Feb. 3, 1768, *ibid.*, 527.

118. James Habersham to Samuel Lloyd, Sept. 5, 1767, *Habersham Letters*, VI, 58–60.

119. Candler and Knight, eds., *Col. Recs. Ga.*, XIV, 469–474.

The governor and Council made certain of that. The Council resolved that it knew of "no Agent being appointed to sollicit the affairs of this Province in Great Britain." It asked Wright to use his influence in London to see "that no Person may be received at the public Boards under the Character of Agent for this Province who is not duly appointed and authorized by an Act of the whole legislative Body." On more than one occasion Wright requested the British government to refuse Garth recognition. His efforts proved successful. The proposed extension of the loan office was lost for good.[120]

Long before the collapse of the Currency Act repeal movement, Maryland and Georgia had successfully managed to issue varying amounts of treasury notes. The Georgia money was made a legal tender for specific public obligations in seeming disregard for the letter of the Currency Act. The British government chose to ignore the illegality. Georgia's issues were small and posed no threat to creditor interests on either side of the Atlantic. Further, the colony received a parliamentary subsidy, and money raised locally could only ease the burden on British taxpayers.

In Maryland treasury notes were not in fact a lawful tender. However, they were receivable for public debts as a matter of practice. Ultimately redeemable in sterling bills of exchange, the treasury issue could hardly have been considered a violation of parliamentary law. And it was not. Hillsborough found the Maryland practice to be exemplary and held it up to the other colonies for their instruction. Maryland's public loan issue of 1769, on the other hand, was legal for all loan office debts. Once again Hillsborough chose to overlook the question, presumably because the bills were redeemable on essentially the same basis as the treasury notes. In any event the fact remained that the possibility of redeeming paper with sterling bills was unique to Maryland. No other colony had such large sterling holdings in the Bank of England to draw upon.

In brief, both Georgia and Maryland found it possible to get around the restraints imposed by the Currency Act of 1764 and to support existing paper currency systems. They could plead special circumstances. Other provinces, as will be seen, were not so favorably situated.

120. "Journal of the Upper House," *ibid.*, XVII, 372, 374; Gov. Wright to Commons House, Feb. 2, 1768, *ibid.*, XIV, 520. See also Abbot, *Royal Governors*, 140.

Chapter 6

The Robinson Scandal Redivivus
Money and Politics in Virginia

In anticipation of a successful conclusion to the Currency Act repeal movement, most colonies shelved the paper money question during 1765 and 1766. This was not so in Maryland and Georgia, where small amounts of treasury notes were pumped into the local stream of circulation. And not so in Virginia. There the monetary practices most responsible for the act of 1764 precipitated another crisis whose roots were buried deep in past controversies over money problems.[1]

THE POLITICS OF SCANDAL, 1765–1766

On May 11, 1766, John Robinson died of the "Torments of the Stone." For over a quarter century, as treasurer of the colony and Speaker of the House of Burgesses, Robinson wielded more power than any of his countrymen, and as Edmund Randolph later noted, his passing marked the end of an era.[2] But no sooner did his obituaries appear than a scandal spilled over into the columns of the *Virginia Gazette*. The man renowned for his "sound political knowledge," "benevolence," and "sincerity" turned out to have "had no great command of his fingers."[3] In his last ten years Robinson had embezzled some £100,000 of the public's money, most of which he lent to friends and political supporters.

1. See chap. 3. The present chapter appeared as "The Robinson Scandal Redivivus: Money, Debts, and Politics in Revolutionary Virginia," *VMHB*, LXXVII (1969), 146–173.
2. *Jours. of Burgesses, 1766–1769*, xiii–xiv.
3. "Plutarch," Purdie and Dixon's *Va. Gaz.*, Aug. 15, 1766.

Historians have generally shied away from delving into the scandal, feeling perhaps that writers should "Revile not, like profane and wicked elves, / Th' expir'd, *who cannot answer for themselves.*"[4] If Robinson's foibles were all there was to the story, the matter would be of little more than sordid interest. However, when properly understood, the scandal helps to clarify the intricate relationship among paper money, debts, and politics in Revolutionary Virginia, a problem that has lately intrigued a number of historians.[5] It also reveals why the old-line tidewater aristocrats came to share power with a group of young politicians and Revolutionaries such as Patrick Henry and Richard Henry Lee.

During a recess of the General Assembly early in 1765, Lieutenant Governor Francis Fauquier issued a proclamation declaring that some £212,000 worth of notes issued in 1757 and 1758 would be redeemable on March 1, when they would cease to be legal tender. Holders of the notes were invited to exchange them at Williamsburg for those bearing a later date. Most of the money arrived in April during the meeting of the General Court, at which time the merchants normally settled their accounts, but the treasury proved unable to replace the notes, which raised talk of bankruptcy and caused "a great deal of noise."[6] Robinson's excuse was that considerable sums of later emissions had been burnt "which ought to have been preserved" for the purpose of exchange, a matter he claimed the General Assembly had neglected when it passed a redemption law several years before under the prodding of Richard Henry Lee.[7]

In plain fact Virginia law only permitted destroying the money that was to be sunk in 1765; notes bearing a later date were specifically exempt. Nevertheless, because the laws were less accessible then than they are today, Robinson's story was not altogether discredited. Certainly some knowledgeable merchants believed that the treasurer had been too lenient with certain sheriffs and other tax collectors, who, it was claimed, were illegally lending out tax money that could not now be "commanded at pleasure." The practice was

---

4. *Ibid.*, Sept. 19, 1766. The best-known account is Mays, *Pendleton*, I, chap. 11.
5. See Evans, "Planter Indebtedness," *WMQ*, 3d Ser., XIX (1962), 511–533; Gipson, "Virginia Planter Debts," *VMHB*, LXIX (1961), 259–277; Robert E. and B. Katherine Brown, *Virginia, 1705–1786: Democracy or Aristocracy?* (East Lansing, Mich., 1964), chap. 5.
6. Corbin to Capel and Osgood Hanbury, May 31, 1765, Corbin Letterbook, Col. Williamsburg Research Lib., Williamsburg, Va.; Allason to Alexander Walker, May 21, 1765, Allason Lettterbook, Va. State Lib., Richmond.
7. Allason to Alexander Walker, May 21, 1765, Allason Letterbook.

not unknown in Virginia and was commonplace in neighboring North Carolina. Others observers of a less generous nature held that the Speaker himself had appropriated the funds. They censured Robinson's conduct, then "censured the House of Burgesses; and gave it as their opinion that the Speaker would not have dared to embezzle the publick money if he had not obtained an influence in the House by indirect methods."[8] The matter was certainly serious enough to be laid before the Board of Trade, and shortly after the April court ended, rumor had it that some of the principal factors and merchants would lodge just such a protest. They never did, for reasons that in retrospect seem perfectly clear.[9]

By April 1765 sterling exchange rates in Virginia, under the joint pressure of heavy British demands for sterling remittances and a short supply of bills of exchange, had climbed to their highest point in provincial history. Many Virginians placed responsibility for the situation on the large wartime currency emissions, and not a few blamed the mismanagement of the treasury as well. Whatever the cause assigned, everyone recognized that cash was desperately short and debt collections had slowed to a trickle. Under the circumstances, when the merchants were offered any of the estimated £50,000 or so that was still illegally circulating, they seldom refused it.[10] Legal tender or not, paper of every sort served as a medium of exchange in a difficult situation, a fact that gave the merchants pause. Moreover, by the time the next court met in October, the high exchange rates had already slipped a few points (for reasons discussed later). At the year's end sterling rates would again reach the moderate levels of 1757.[11]

The crisis over the default of the treasury still had a way to go. Somebody—the treasurer, the sheriffs, the taxpayers—had to redeem the £50,000 that remained outstanding. In an elaborate defense of

8. "A Freeholder," Purdie and Dixon's *Va. Gaz.*, Oct. 17, 1766. See also the comments of William Nelson to Edward and Samuel Athawes, Nov. 13, 1766, Letterbook of Thomas and William Nelson, 1766–1775, Va. State Lib., Richmond. It seems that some £15,000, which was redeemable after 1765, actually was burned because the Board of Trade only got around to reviewing the act of 1761 in Feb. 1763; see the discussion in "The 'Quiet Years,' 1760–1761," in chap. 3 above.

9. Allason to Alexander Walker, May 21, 1765, Allason Letterbook.

10. See, for example, Corbin to Capel and Osgood Hanbury, Mar. 15, 31, 1765, Corbin to Robert Cary and Co., Aug. 1, 1765, Corbin Letterbook; Allason to his brother, May 21, 1765, Allason Letterbook; "To Messrs. Thomas Parramore and Southy Simpson, Representatives for the county of Accomack," Purdie and Dixon's *Va. Gaz.*, Oct. 17, 1766.

11. See table 5 in Appendix 1.

paper money back in May 1763, the House of Burgesses had been at pains to prove that existing taxes sufficed to sink all the paper in circulation and had put its honor behind every existing note. If for any reason redemption funds proved inadequate, the Burgesses promised to levy additional taxes. Something also had to be done about the stringency of credit and cash, which had plagued the colony ever since 1762. Finally, all those who wanted to help Robinson out of his predicament, including those debtors and friends who either had known all along of his peculations or who after the April court had at least begun to suspect, had to come up with a new source of public funds.[12] A solution satisfying all requirements was the creation of a loan office. On May 17, shortly after the opening of the legislature, a writer who identified himself as a distressed planter outlined the advantages of just such a scheme for the readers of Royle's *Virginia Gazette*.[13] A few days later leading house members received a letter urging their attendance at the Burgesses, where the session was being extended a few days to consider a bill for a new currency issue backed by a British loan.[14]

When the house sat again on May 24 to deal with the money question, Richard Henry Lee, who was the chief obstacle to any plans to extricate Virginia from "its present deplorable Circumstances," was absent.[15] Robinson had received compromising evidence from John Mercer, an avowed enemy of Lee's, about Lee's attempts to become Stamp Act collector for Virginia, and Lee, who had played such a prominent and violent role in local opposition to the act, seems to have chosen the better part of discretion and stayed away the entire session. With Lee gone, the house committee appointed at his insistence two years before to investigate the treasury and to give a full disclosure of the monies burnt and on hand made the kind of perfunctory report that had been all too common before 1763. Just before the session ended, Chairman Archibald Cary, one of Robinson's three or four heaviest debtors, gave the treasury a coat of "whitewash."[16]

12. See the discussion in "Threats of Parliamentary Intervention, 1762–1763," in chap. 3 above.

13. The issue is no longer extant, but see Thomas Jefferson to William Wirt, Aug. 14, 1814, in Paul Leicester Ford, ed., *The Writings of Thomas Jefferson* (New York, 1892–1899), IX, 466.

14. Charles Carter of Corotoman to Landon Carter, May 20, 1765, in Landon Carter Papers, Alderman Lib., Univ. of Va., Charlottesville.

15. *Ibid.; Jours. of Burgesses, 1761–1765*, 314.

16. John Mercer to the Printer, Purdie and Dixon's *Va. Gaz.*, Sept. 25, 1766; May 24, 29, *Jours. of Burgesses, 1761–1765*, 350, 356; Mays, *Pendleton*, I, 176–177, app. II.

The Burgesses passed a number of resolutions on May 24 embodying the loan office plan discussed in the pages of the *Virginia Gazette* the week before. British merchants were expected to lend Virginia £240,000 sterling at 5 percent interest, the money to be repaid within twelve years at a rate of not less than £20,000 yearly out of the proceeds of a new tax on polls and tobacco. The present levies on those two items were to be discontinued. Approximately £100,000 of the loan, to be drawn in bills of exchange, would be applied to the redemption of the existing paper currency supply. At the going rate of exchange an amount that large would almost cover Robinson's shortages, so that his debtors would have to pay no more than a few pennies on their accounts. The remaining £140,000 would be imported in specie to provide a deposit against which the colony could lend its own bank notes on permanent security at 5 percent interest.[17] In sum Virginia was about to consolidate its debts and make available a ready supply of credit and cash to every man of property, including the Robinson debtors.

Despite support from Speaker Robinson, his friends and debtors, and any of the other distressed and indebted planters in the house who could be expected to vote their own and their constituents' interest, the resolutions did not pass without opposition. Reportedly, "it had been urged that from certain unhappy circumstances of the colony, men of substantial property had contracted debts, which, if exacted suddenly, must ruin them and their families, but, with a little indulgence of time, might be paid with ease." Thereupon, as Thomas Jefferson recalled nearly a half-century later, a newly elected member of the Burgesses, one Patrick Henry, retorted, "What, Sir! . . . Is it proposed then to reclaim the spendthrift from his dissipation and extravagance, by filling his pocket with money?"[18] Henry's call for industry and frugality fell on deaf ears, and the triumphant Robinson quickly appointed seven conferees to meet with the Council over the Burgesses' proposal. Included were Edmund Pendleton, who prescribed "no bounds to his gratitude for his primary patron," Speaker Robinson; three of Robinson's heaviest debtors, Cary, Carter Braxton, and Lewis Burwell; two of his closest political advisers, Peyton Randolph and Benjamin Harrison; and John Fleming, who was reportedly "extremely attached to Robinson, Peyton Randolph,

17. May 24, 1765, *Jours. of Burgesses, 1761–1765*, 350.
18. Jefferson to William Wirt, Aug. 14, 1814, in Ford, ed., *Writings of Jefferson*, IX, 466. Jefferson's observations were made long after the event and contain certain errors, none of which have any direct bearing on the quotation cited.

etc., and at their beck, and had no independence or boldness of mind."[19]

Anti-paper money forces in the Council carried more weight than their counterparts in the house. A Council majority, including Richard Corbin and William and Thomas Nelson, had already taken a stand against past paper money issues as a source of a spirit of extravagance and ruin, and this time they took only three days to kill the plan. As Corbin later explained to his British correspondents: "To tax People that are not in Debt to lend to those that are is highly unjust, it is in Fact to tax the honest, frugal, industrious Man, in order to encourage the idle, the profligate, the Extravagant and the Gamester." He also identified the loan office as a scheme to restore the colony's shaky credit, revealed by the treasury deficits in March and April.[20] The moment the Council killed the Robinson bill, many of the loan office supporters departed Williamsburg and left behind them a half-filled House of Burgesses. Their absence played into the hands of Patrick Henry. A day later Henry and his followers pushed through the Burgesses the famous Virginia Stamp Act resolutions over the opposition of Robinson and what remained of the "cyphers of the aristocracy."[21]

Lieutenant Governor Fauquier lost no time in registering his disapproval of the Henry action and on June 1 dissolved the assembly and called for new elections. In July the voters returned forty-one new house members, reflecting in large part the general dissatisfaction with the stamp tax and their "private Distress" over the state of the economy. By the time the legislature met again in November of the next year, Robinson was dead, and the story of his peculations

---

19. See "Edmund Randolph's Essay on the Revolutionary History of Virginia (1774–1782)," *VMHB*, XLIII (1935), 127; Jefferson to William Wirt, Aug. 5, 1815, Andrew A. Lipscomb and Albert Ellery Bergh, eds., *The Writings of Thomas Jefferson* (Washington, D.C., 1903), XIV, 335–336. On the indebtedness of Cary, Braxton, and Burwell, see Mays, *Pendleton*, I, app. II.

20. See the discussions in "The Debate over Rising Exchange Rates, 1762," and "Threats of Parliamentary Intervention, 1762–1763," in chap. 3 above. Nelson to Capel and Osgood Hanbury, Feb. 27, 1768, Nelson Letterbook; Corbin to Capel and Osgood Hanbury, May 31, 1765, Corbin to Philip Ludwell, Aug. 2, 1765, Corbin Letterbook. While, generally speaking, the Council was opposed to the loan office in principle, Corbin was clearly voting his interest.

21. Jefferson to William Wirt, Aug. 5, 1815, Lipscomb and Bergh, eds., *Writings of Jefferson*, XIV, 336; May 29, 1765, *Jours. of Burgesses, 1761–1765*, 358. See also "Biographical Sketches of Distinguished Men: Peyton Randolph," Lipscomb and Bergh, eds., *Writings of Jefferson*, XVIII, 136–137; Jefferson to William Wirt, Aug. 14, 1814, Ford, ed., *Writings of Jefferson*, IX, 465–472; *Jours. of Burgesses, 1761–1765*, liv–lxxvi.

was spread across the pages of the Virginia newspapers for all to read. The scandal could conceivably have seriously undermined the dominion's paper money system, and so it seemed to some. Instead it proved to be a mainstay, and the chief effects of the embezzlement of over £100,000 turned out to be political.[22]

Late in May 1766, shortly after Robinson's death, his close friend Peter Randolph penned a hurried note to the former Speaker's protégé, Edmund Pendleton, informing him that he had been named an executor of the estate. The dead man's affairs were in great confusion, and according to Randolph there was a deficiency in the treasury of more than £70,000. For that reason, he explained, Mrs. Robinson wanted her husband's will probated at once, and to facilitate the collection of the estate's debts, Pendleton was to meet her in Williamsburg the second Monday in June at the next court of oyer. Also named as executor was the attorney general of the province, Peyton Randolph, who declined the responsibility. Brother Peter took the job instead, telling Pendleton that the attorney general had no wish to "prejudice his future views with respect to the Treasury"—and, he might have added, to the Speakership as well.[23]

The Robinson faction plainly intended to keep power. Pendleton's job was to bring the estate into some semblance of order, discharge its debts into the treasury as rapidly as possible, and dissuade the widow from publicly confronting the estate's debtors. In return the debtors, joined by Robinson's former allies, were to elect Attorney General Peyton Randolph as Speaker and treasurer. Every effort was made to handle the scandal with tact, grace, and ease. The memory of the dead would be honored, and the reputation of the living salvaged. It was a clever and ambitious plan, but Robinson's followers failed to give sufficient weight to the strength and determination of the anti-paper money forces and to the tensions arising out of the Stamp Act. Moreover they seriously underestimated the ambitions of opponents like Robert Carter Nicholas, Richard Henry Lee, and Richard Bland.

Lieutenant Governor Francis Fauquier had long-standing instructions, largely inspired by Robinson's enemies, to separate the offices of Speaker and treasurer in Virginia. Fauquier had done nothing to implement those orders. He had depended on Robinson to pre-

22. Corbin to Robert Cary and Co., July 1, 1766, Corbin Letterbook; Fauquier to the secretary of state, June 14, 1765, C.O. 5/1345, P.R.O.
23. May 25, 1766, in Circuit Court Book 120, U.S. Circuit Court, Va. District, Va. State Lib.

serve an "entire harmony" in government and, during the great struggle against France, to obtain needed military aids from a grudging House of Burgesses whose control over the purse had greatly enhanced its power and bargaining position. The alliance had proven successful. The Speaker and his friends had effectively supported the government position throughout the war, and the marriage of convenience soon gave way to friendship.[24] Following the war Fauquier continued to disregard repeated requests from home to remove Robinson as treasurer. Shortly after Robinson's death, for instance, he lamented to the Board of Trade that the king's service had received a shock from the recent death "of our late worthy Speaker." He went on to explain that the event would have been a sensible loss at any time, but more particularly so now, as he had promised himself great assistance from Robinson at the next assembly session. If the default of the treasury and the controversy over the Stamp Act did not cost Robinson his Speakership—a possibility the lieutenant governor did not discount—Fauquier had expected his ally to help quiet the people and to sustain the royal prerogative in Virginia. With Robinson dead Fauquier favored Attorney General Randolph for the Speakership as a man having the same "good qualities of his late most intimate Friend." The lieutenant governor wanted to appoint Randolph interim treasurer as well, but was prevented from doing so because such a move might have forced Randolph to vacate his house seat and put him out of the Speaker's race. Instead the treasury clerk, James Cocke, was to be put in charge of the office until the house met and made itself heard.[25]

Before Fauquier could act on his decision to fill in with Cocke, Robert Carter Nicholas, an old rival of the Randolphs, came forward to offer his services as interim treasurer even at the risk of losing his house seat, which he had just regained after a five-year hiatus. Nicholas's credentials were impressive. As a lawyer he had long been a chief debt collector for British mercantile houses and was thoroughly familiar with the legal side of the money question.

24. Fauquier to B.T., Nov. 19, 1764, in C.O. 5/1331, P.R.O. See also chap. 3 above and Jack P. Greene, "The Attempt to Separate the Offices of Speaker and Treasurer in Virginia, 1758-1766," *VMHB*, LXXI (1963), 11-18.

25. Fauquier to B.T., June 25, 1765, May 11, 1766, C.O. 5/1331, P.R.O. See also "Biographical Sketch of Peyton Randolph," Lipscomb and Bergh, eds., *Writings of Jefferson*, XVIII, 136-140. Fauquier also favored George Wythe to succeed Randolph as attorney general. See W. Edwin Hemphill, "George Wythe and the Colonial Briton: A Background Study of the Pre-Revolutionary Era in Virginia" (Ph.D. diss., University of Virginia, 1937), chap. 1.

As a burgess he was involved in one way or another with the colony's currency system from the day he entered the house in 1756. His first year he served on at least one committee charged with drafting a currency measure. Five years later he sat on another with Richard Henry Lee to conduct a semiannual examination of the treasury's holdings of any and all notes redeemable in 1765, to burn them, and to give Treasurer Robinson a receipt for the amount. He was also an original member of the General Assembly committee of correspondence created in 1759 to handle such things as the British merchants' complaints against Virginia's currency practices. In sum Nicholas could claim some expertise and experience in the general areas of money and finance. A reputation for "purity and propriety" may also have been of some help.[26]

Nicholas claimed to have solicited the treasury office "on the advice of conscience" alone. He had heard the late Speaker reflected upon, and he feared the loss of tens of thousands of pounds of retired paper. He also feared that as the money had gotten back into the stream of circulation it had driven up sterling exchange over the last couple of years. He admitted, however, that the conversation of friends had strengthened his desire to get to the bottom of such matters.[27] The friends behind Nicholas appear to have been Richard Corbin, Philip Ludwell, William Nelson, and Benjamin Waller. Corbin was an ancient and formidable foe of paper money as well as of Speaker Robinson. A Council member and collector of British merchant debts and of the royal quitrents, he had often lost money for his clients and himself as a result of the rise of sterling exchange rates.[28] Ludwell was the councillor who had first objected to the colony's currency system.[29] The great merchant William Nelson, another Council member, also believed that excessive amounts of circulating paper had boosted the price of exchange and was a stead-

26. See William J. Lescure, "The Early Political Career of Robert Carter Nicholas, 1728–1769" (M.A. thesis, College of William and Mary, 1961); "Randolph's Essay on Revolutionary History of Virginia," *VMHB*, XLIII (1935), 126–127.

27. Nicholas to the Printer, Purdie and Dixon's *Va. Gaz.*, June 27, 1766. Longstanding animosities between the Nicholas and Randolph families may also have motivated Nicholas; see the autobiographical sketch of Edmund J. Randolph in the form of a letter to his children, Mar. 25, 1810, Alderman Lib., Univ. of Va., Charlottesville. I am indebted to John Selby for this reference. See also n. 10 above; Philip Ludwell's will, printed in *VMHB*, XIX (1911), 288.

28. See the discussion in "The Debate over Rising Exchange Rates, 1762," in chap. 3 above. See also William Minor Dabney, "John Robinson: Speaker of the House of Burgesses and Treasurer of Virginia" (M.A. thesis, University of Virginia, 1941).

29. Nov. 19–20, 1759, McIlwaine, ed., *Leg. Jours. of Va. Council*, III, 1227–1228.

fast opponent of paper money.[30] The key figure in the group, however, was probably Benjamin Waller. In his public life Waller served at different times as a burgess and member of the assembly committee to destroy outdated treasury notes, a county judge, and a clerk of the General Court and of the house. Above all he was a lawyer and bill collector.[31] Clearly the friends and forces behind Nicholas were mercantile, and in this sense it is possible to view the Robinson scandal as a continuance of earlier efforts to protect British investments in Virginia against the risks in any fiat money system.[32]

On the advice of Council, Fauquier withdrew Cocke's name and gave Nicholas the interim appointment. The next move fell to Nicholas and his friends, who now had to arrange for the separation of the two offices and the election of their man as *permanent* treasurer. If the move proved successful, it would be agreeable to Fauquier.[33]

Immediately after his appointment, Nicholas openly pledged to investigate fully the rumors about the treasury and to reestablish the public credit on a sound footing. Equal justice was to be meted out to his country and to the memory of his late and worthy predecessor. Nevertheless by his own testimony Nicholas had had no time to examine the state of the treasury when he publicly called for a prompt settlement by the many sheriffs and collectors said to be in arrears. In the future they were to account regularly with the treasury or feel the full weight of the law. Whether necessary or not, the move smacked of politics, a suspicion Nicholas seemed to confirm when he concluded his remarks with as rousing a political cry as

30. See the discussion in "The 'Quiet Years,' 1760–1761," in chap. 3 above. Nelson to Edward and Samuel Athawes, Nov. 13, 1766, Nelson to Capel and Osgood Hanbury, Feb. 27, 1768, Nelson Letterbook.

31. See "Sketches of his own family, written by Littleton Waller Tazewell for the use of his children," Norfolk, Va., 1823, MS, Tazewell Papers, Va. State Lib., Richmond. Tazewell claims that it was through Waller's exertions that "the enormous fraud committed upon the Treasury by Speaker Robinson was first detected; and his efforts upon this occasion drew down upon him for a time, the resentment of many of the speaker's friends, some of whom were amongst the most conspicuous men in Virginia at that day" ("Sketches," 101). The Tazewell statement was brought to my attention by Lynda Rees, who is presently editing the "Sketches" as an M.A. thesis at the College of William and Mary. See also Mays, *Pendleton*, I, 336, n. 5; Hening, ed., *Statutes of Va.*, VII, 465–466; James A. Servies and Carl R. Dolmetsch, eds., *The Poems of Charles Hansford* (Chapel Hill, N.C., 1961), xvii–xix.

32. See the discussion in "The 'Quiet Years,' 1760–1761," in chap. 3 above.

33. Fauquier to B.T., May 22, 1766, C.O. 5/1331, P.R.O.

dignity and Virginia tradition allowed: "If I should be fortunate enough to give the wished for satisfaction to the publick, I shall think myself extremely happy, and own that I then shall not be without some hopes of being continued in the office."[34] Doubtless Nicholas was guardedly calling for the separation of offices and his election as treasurer. And if there was any doubt that the campaign was under way, it was quickly dispelled when Nicholas wrote to every burgess personally soliciting votes the same day that his paid political announcement went off to the newspapers. The letters were somewhat more strongly worded and less veiled than the newspaper release, but the message was the same.[35]

A few days later Nicholas wrote a somewhat different letter to Richard Henry Lee, who was already in the race for Speaker on the strength of his recent opposition to the government. Disclaiming any political ambition, Nicholas vaguely alluded to the several incidents that drove him to offer his service to the public. He then got to the point. During Robinson's life, Nicholas like Lee had often declared that the powerful offices of Speaker and treasurer ought to be separated, but he never attempted a change out of respect for the old gentleman. With Robinson gone, it now seemed a "proper season for a separation." Nicholas knew that it was often objected that the treasury gave an undue weight to the chair, and he promised that if the places should be divided "it is my steadfast Purpose, if it continues in my Hands, that it shall have no Influence, whether I am in or out of the House of Burgesses, which I know may be at my Option, though I must not tell everyone this."[36] An alliance between Nicholas and Lee was plainly one of convenience based on shared political ambitions and a belief in the need for separating the offices. However, they also held a principle in common, although it went unmentioned at the time. Both were fundamentally opposed to all fiat money systems, and both considered paper currency to be behind the rise of sterling exchange and the touted extravagance of the Virginians. As they saw it, industry and frugality, not currency and credit, would save the planters. Nicholas later changed

34. Purdie and Dixon's *Va. Gaz.*, May 23, 1766.
35. Nicholas to Colonel Preston, May 21, 1766, Preston Papers, Draper Collection, 2QQ97, Wisconsin State Historical Society, Madison, Wis. (microfilm available at Col. Williamsburg Research Lib.); Nicholas to the Printer, Purdie and Dixon's *Va. Gaz.*, June 27, 1766.
36. May 23, 1766, Revolutionary Lee Papers. See also Fauquier to B.T., Apr. 7, 1766, C.O. 5/1331, P.R.O.

his views. Lee would always remain an unyielding opponent of paper money.[37]

About the time the Nicholas letter arrived, Lee received a similar note from Richard Bland. Widely known as "the most learned and logical man of those who took prominent lead in public affairs," Bland won his spurs in the controversies over the Pistole Fee and the Stamp Act. Like Lee and Randolph, he was also running hard for the chair, and he wanted Lee to know that, win or lose, their friendship would not be impaired. On the matter of the treasury, Bland declared that in the public interest the office should be put into more hands than one. He desired the offices of Speaker and treasurer divided and the treasury placed under the rule of a commission. Although Bland gave little credence to the popular suspicions that the public trust had been converted to private use, he nevertheless wanted the treasury funds placed upon a new footing. He believed this was also Lee's view and hoped that the two of them could now unite for the public good.[38] Bland was obviously angling for the support of the Lee, not the Nicholas, faction. However he also had something to offer the Robinson debtors and others who supported the demand for a public loan office plan: he revealed to Lee the outlines of a bank scheme that in a few years would enable Virginia to discharge the public debt without any further taxes. The plan was to be completed after the legislature had finally cleared up the facts about the public income and state expenditures.[39]

Another letter making the rounds in the spring of 1766 was the work of Archibald Cary, a chief debtor to the Robinson estate. A strong supporter of the loan office, Cary was one of the house managers of the recent bill for that purpose, as well as chairman of the committee that had just completed an audit of the treasury accounts and reportedly found nothing amiss. Cary was canvassing for Peyton

37. See, for example, Nicholas to the Printer, Purdie and Dixon's *Va. Gaz.*, June 27, 1766; copy of an article prepared for the *Virginia Gazette* by Richard Henry Lee on paper money, "Lee Papers," *So. Lit. Messenger*, XXX (1860), 136; Robert Carter Nicholas, "Paper Money in Colonial Virginia," *WMQ*, XX (1911–1912), 244–256. See the discussion in "Threats of Parliamentary Intervention, 1762–1763," in chap. 3 above.

38. See Jefferson's sketch of Bland in letter to William Wirt, Aug. 5, 1815, Lipscomb and Bergh, eds., *Writings of Jefferson*, XIV, 338; Richard Bland to Richard Henry Lee, May 22, 1766, Revolutionary Lee Papers, Alderman Lib., Univ. of Va.

39. Bland later announced his candidacy as well as his support of the move for the separation of offices, in Purdie and Dixon's *Va. Gaz.*, July 4, 1766.

Randolph, a person for whom he claimed to be able to put hand to heart as the most proper man to succeed the late and worthy Speaker. His plea for this "firm friend to his Country," said to be devoid of both passion and prejudice, ended with a reminder that, since the first order of business in the new House of Burgesses was to choose a Speaker, it behooved Randolph's supporters to be in town for the opening of the General Assembly.[40]

An early meeting was of some importance in the tactics of the Randolph faction. It had organized quickly and could count on the fast-fading reputation of Robinson to pull in a few marginal votes if the house convened at once. Moreover such a meeting would take place before any further audit of the treasury could be made, since current taxes were not due until October. Any action on the Robinson scandal therefore could not be taken until after the legislature met again the following year. Accordingly Randolph supporters petitioned for a meeting in July on the pretext that this would give the house an opportunity to express its thanks for the recent repeal of the Stamp Act. But Fauquier decided against any such move in the belief that legislative tempers needed time to cool. As it turned out, just the opposite happened. A series of reports appearing in the *Virginia Gazette*s during the legislative recess only raised passions to a new pitch.[41]

Between 1736 and 1766 the *Gazette* was the only newspaper regularly appearing in Virginia. It generally followed an administration line, carefully selecting the news and suppressing any criticism of a government that employed the editor as printer to the colony. Then in May 1766 a Maryland printer, William Rind, established an opposition paper at the invitation of some of the "hot Burgesses" who opposed Fauquier. In the meantime Joseph Royle, the public printer and owner of the old *Virginia Gazette*, had died, and his former employees had taken up the newspaper in order to make "interest" with the assembly.[42] The "interest" was the public print-

40. Cary to Colonel Preston, May 14, 1766, in Preston Papers, Draper Coll., 2QQ95.

41. "Tit for Tat," and "An Unbiased Virginian," Purdie and Dixon's *Va. Gaz.*, July 4, 1766; Fauquier to B.T., Sept. 4, 1766, C.O. 5/1331, P.R.O. For an excellent discussion of these controversies, see J. A. Leo Lemay, "Robert Bolling and the Bailment of Colonel Chiswell," *Early American Literature*, VI (1971), 172–195.

42. See William Henry Castles, Jr., "*The Virginia Gazette*, 1736–1766: Its Editors, Editorial Policies, and Literary Content" (Ph.D. diss., University of Tennessee, 1962), esp. chap. 3. See also Bernard E. Mitchell, "History of Printing in Colonial Williamsburg" (M.A. thesis, College of William and Mary, 1929); Fauquier to B.T., Apr. 7, 1776, C.O. 5/1331, P.R.O.

ing business, and for the remainder of the year the rival *Gazettes*, one published by Rind and the other by Purdie and Dixon, vied for public support and popular subscriptions. The time was opportune for a newspaper war. The local stories that year were all newsworthy: the banterings of Lee and Mercer over the spoils of office under the Stamp Act, the Stamp Act crisis itself, the Chiswell murder case—and, above all, the Robinson scandal.[43] As one wag put it, "And it shall come to pass, after the People of V——n shall prevail against their Stamp Masters, that he who is over their Treasury, even the T——r of the great Assembly shall be gathered unto his Fathers; And he shall die an old Man, in a good old Age, and full of Days: And there shall be great Confusion in the Land. Party shall menace Party, and Dunce shall enflame Dunce; and the Gazettes of *Purdie* and of *Rind* shall contain Wonders."[44] Government and aristocracy were under attack, and readers of the two newspapers looked on as privileged and amused spectators. "Our writers," as one Virginian explained, "are generally such as have been very little used to Contradiction, and know not how to bear it from one another; and when they find their Writings not treated with the Respect they have been accustomed to in their private Characters, they grow angry, and sometimes abuse one another."[45]

Both newspapers printed an appeal on June 23 by Robinson's executors to the estate's debtors to honor the late Speaker's memory by promptly settling all accounts, even if it meant selling their land and slaves. A few days later Purdie and Dixon published a very different communication from Robert Carter Nicholas. Nicholas had clearly lost self-control. He told his readers that the appearance of his first piece the month before had been received with mixed

---

43. See Carl Bridenbaugh, "Virtue and Violence in Virginia, 1766; Or, The Importance of the Trivial," Mass. Hist. Soc., *Procs.*, LXXVI (1964), 3–29. Bridenbaugh overlooks the fact that the Robinson, Lee-Mercer, and Chiswell imbroglios overlapped in certain ways. For example, Corbin, who supported Nicholas in the Robinson scandal, sided with Lee in the Lee-Mercer affair; in addition Corbin backed Lee in his bid for a seat on the Council. And Lee, of course, also supported Nicholas. Chiswell, on the other hand, was Robinson's father-in-law and partner in a lead-mining venture. At the time of Chiswell's murder of Routledge, which roughly coincided with Robinson's death, Chiswell lost not only his honor but his angel as well; Robinson had pumped some £10,000 of embezzled treasury funds into the mining venture. Since the mine could not continue without additional infusions of capital, Robinson's death might have hastened Chiswell's own demise; see Pendleton to Preston, Feb. 6, 1768, in Preston Papers, Draper Coll., 2QQ103–104.

44. "A Prophesy from the East," Rind's *Va. Gaz.*, Aug. 15, 1766.

45. Letter from Virginia, Oct. 25, 1766, *N.-Y. Jour.*, Nov. 27, 1766. The letter provides a nice summary statement of the political climate in Virginia in the period.

feelings. Some had supported his stand, others had disagreed with it, and a few had accused him of being "the head" or "the tool" of party, ostensibly the Lee faction, which was already notorious for its opposition to Robinson. Nicholas protested that a sense of civic responsibility alone had motivated him to apply for the interim appointment as treasurer, for he had great reason to suspect mismanagement of the treasury. He did admit to having written every burgess. He insisted, however, that he had not asked for their vote, as others had done, but had instead suggested that they might favor him with their "countenance and regard" if they approved his conduct and supported a disunion of offices. In any case Nicholas wished to explore publicly the reasons why the offices should be separated. He only hoped that no one would later accuse him of aspersing the memory of Robinson. Generally speaking, Nicholas's position was that a union of the offices gave too much weight and influence to the Speaker, whether or not such power was consciously sought. The argument was developed at some length before he got around to attacking Robinson directly. Following his interim appointment as treasurer, Nicholas asserted that he had decided to remain silent until the legislature met, not to conceal anything but to avoid inflaming the country and turning any circumstance to his private advantage. Finding that many people already knew of things to which he had until recently been a stranger, he came to feel that silence would be of little use. Consequently, when any questions came his way, he gave the best account of the matter possible. Even at present he could not say what the exact deficiency of the public money was, but he supposed it to be not more than £80,000 or £90,000. The Robinson scandal had broken.

The polemic was not yet done. It seemed to Nicholas that the loss of so much of the public money must have been a growing evil of many years standing. He thought it could only have taken such deep root from "too implicit a confidence, which had, through a considerable tract of time, imperceptibly wrought itself into the minds of a set of Gentlemen whose own integrity, as is often the case, kept them above suspicion." In some circles this was called influence, in others "universal benevolence"; whatever the cause, the "dismal consequences" to the country were the same: the rapid rise in sterling exchange rates. He assumed that everyone knew that money was more or less valuable according to the quantity in circulation and that, as annual taxes siphoned off a portion of the currency, exchange rates should have fallen. Instead, he pointed out, rates continued to fluctuate between 60 and 65 percent from court to court without apparent good reason. Clearly the money, "squeezed from the people for their taxes instead of being sunk at our Treasury as it ought to have been, was thrown back into circulation." The reasons behind the violent opposition to the appointment of burning committees were revealed at last.

Nicholas's remark about exchange is a curious one. He and his readers certainly knew that exchange rates had recently fallen to par, their lowest point in the last twenty years or more. Yet by his own testimony a large volume of currency continued in circulation because of the infusion of £100,000 of embezzled money. In Nicholas's mind at least the theory of money had plainly triumphed over the reality, and the jibe about taxes at a time when taxpayers bitterly complained of the difficulties of paying existing levies showed that politics had triumphed over all. Nicholas pursued the tax question at some length, pointing out that the defalcations of Robinson would probably mean another tax hike. Of the money redeemable in March 1765, he believed there was upwards of £50,000 in circulation. An identical amount of other notes was to be redeemed that coming September, and there was, as Nicholas put it, "not four thousand pounds in the Treasury."

No man of less weight than the former Speaker and treasurer would have dared to take such liberties, Nicholas said. He concluded that the two offices had to be separated, if only because continuing the business of the treasury in the old way would raise a hue and cry in Britain against Virginia and in favor of taking the treasury appointment away from the Burgesses altogether and of giving it to the Council. As for the argument that the treasuryship must support the dignity of the chair, Nicholas found it entirely possible to substitute instead a stipend to the office of Speaker. Nicholas ended his attack by protesting that he had no itch for writing and had waited weeks for another man to speak out. It was only to acquaint his countrymen with the real situation that he finally took pen in hand, and he would continue to tell the truth so long as he had "tongue to speak or fingers to write."[46]

Predictably Nicholas's condemnation of Robinson and his blatant appeal for election as treasurer provoked a bitter controversy that filled the two *Gazettes* all that year and occasionally showed up in later years as an ugly reminder of the scandal. The leading supporters of Robinson at the time, although they sometimes masked their

46. "To the Printer," Purdie and Dixon's *Va. Gaz.*, June 27, 1766.

identity, were Benjamin Grymes, a chief debtor to the estate, and John Randolph, who was busy promoting his brother for the Speakership.[47] Their responses were often as long and biting as Nicholas's original piece, but apart from the irrationalities they boiled down to a few major assertions. The first was that if the charges against Robinson were indeed true—and they were as yet unproven—he could only have erred because of his great charity and the recognized need to augment the currency supply at a time when cash was desperately short. In any event, ran the argument, his estate and securities were sufficient indemnity against any public loss. As for the possibility of private suffering from the increase in paper, it was suggested that the only conceivable losers were a few rich British merchants with sterling debts to collect. Moreover sterling exchange rates had recently fallen to par, which signaled the correctness of Robinson's views that more, not less, money had to be put into circulation. Another common assertion was that Nicholas's political ambitions had led him to expose Robinson in an effort to disunite the two offices and gain the treasuryship. In the meantime his promise to be severe with all those indebted to the public would only break the planters. Finally, whatever Robinson had or had not done, his performance gave no basis to argue that the offices of Speaker and treasurer should be separated.[48]

John Randolph vehemently supported the last position. Upon it rested the political fate of Peyton Randolph, who, if the argument held up, could be expected to succeed Robinson and secure the power of the old clique. If not, political control in Virginia would be divided among a number of factions, one of which centered around Richard Henry Lee and Patrick Henry and contained the "hot, young and giddy Spirits" so feared by the anxiety-ridden and hard-pressed senior burgesses. As one contemporary noted, the Randolph argument had little that was solid in it, yet it was "artfully interlarded with saving maxims, plausible doubts, and insinuations of apprehensions" and was therefore "well calculated to deceive the unthinking many." The gist was that innovation was

47. "A Key to the Virginia Gazettes, 1766," *ibid.*, Jan. 1, 1767. Those interested in the full debate should consult the following issues, *ibid.*: May 23, June 27, July 4, 11, 13, 25, Aug. 1, 15, Sept. 5, 12, 19, Oct. 4, 10, 17, 30, Nov. 6, 27, Dec. 4, 11, 1766, Jan. 1, 8, Feb. 12, Apr. 9, 1767; also Rind's *Va. Gaz.*, May 16, Aug. 8, 15, 1766.

48. See Nicholas to the Printer, Purdie and Dixon's *Va. Gaz.*, Sept. 5, 1766; Arthur Lee, n.d., Revolutionary Lee Papers; Benjamin Grymes to the Printer, Purdie and Dixon's *Va. Gaz.*, Oct. 10, 1766; William Nelson to Edward and Samuel Athawes, Nov. 13, 1766, Nelson Letterbook.

dangerous. Separation—not the lack of it, as Nicholas prophesied—was more likely to provoke the home government into taking the treasury appointment out of the Burgesses' hands altogether and awarding it to the Council.[49]

Randolph and the other Robinson supporters appear to have failed to convince the majority of readers of either *Gazette*.[50] Attacks upon the old "Christian Gentleman" and his allies not only continued but grew into a general assault upon the "confederacy of the great in place, family connections, and that more-to-be-dreaded foe to public virtue, warm and private friendship."[51] Before the paper war and public passions had subsided, many Virginians had come to agree with Arthur Lee that the chief lesson to be learned was that to trust in the integrity of the ruling powers was a chimera which unfailingly led to ruin and slavery.[52] Thus on the eve of the opening of the new General Assembly late in the fall, the freeholders of Accomack and James City counties publicly instructed their representatives to vote for the separation of offices.[53] "Vox populi" was not to be ignored that year. During the elections earlier in the summer, which turned in part on the Stamp Act controversy, many of the members who had ignored the popular outcry against the tax had been turned out of office.[54]

When the House of Burgesses finally convened the first week of November, Fauquier avoided any mention of the private distresses and party feuds that had soured the people's blood. In his opening address to the legislature he focused instead on the good news of the Stamp Act repeal and on the loyalty owed the king. In addition he stressed the need for a high common purpose and recommended to the consideration of the Burgesses "a poor, unhappy set of People" who, deprived of their senses, wandered about

49. See Arthur Lee to Richard Henry Lee, n.d., Revolutionary Lee Papers. See also Benjamin Grymes to the Printer, Purdie and Dixon's *Va. Gaz.*, Oct. 10, 1766.
50. Meanwhile the Robinson faction was circulating among the burgesses a secret letter predicting the most dire consequences if the offices were separated; see "To the Author of a Manuscript Circular Letter," *ibid.*, Sept. 12, 1766.
51. David Boyd to Richard Henry Lee, n.d., "Lee Papers," *So. Lit. Messenger*, XXVII (1858), 118. See also "The Freeholder" and "The Sick Lady's Case," Purdie and Dixon's *Va. Gaz.*, Oct. 4, 17, Nov. 27, 1766; William Nelson to John Norton, Sept. 6, Nov. 12, 1766, Nelson to Edward and Samuel Athawes, Nov. 13, 1766, Nelson Letterbook; James K. Owen, "The Virginia Vestry: A Study in the Decline of a Ruling Class" (Ph.D. diss., Princeton University, 1947), 210–217.
52. To Richard Henry Lee, n.d., Revolutionary Lee Papers.
53. Purdie and Dixon's *Va. Gaz.*, Oct. 17, 30, 1766.
54. The best published account of politics in Virginia in this period is Lucille B. Griffith, *The Virginia House of Burgesses, 1750–1774* (Northport, Ala., 1963).

the country terrifying their fellow creatures. Legal confinement and proper provision were needed for such miserable objects in order to help them find their lost reason.[55] Happy news and high purpose, however, had to wait their turn. Without losing any time, the house elevated Peyton Randolph to the Speaker's chair—even though the Lee-Bland forces presented Bland as their single candidate for the office.[56] Lee then spoke out in favor of separating the chair and treasuryship, arguing that wise and good men in all ages had sought to divide the places of honor and profit for the security of liberty.[57] After lengthy debate the Lee-Bland clique, with an assist by the Nicholas faction and a helping hand from Patrick Henry, severed the offices by an equally impressive vote of 68 to 29.[58] Serious discussion of Bland's commission plan followed, but the house ultimately elected Nicholas treasurer; it then compensated the Speaker for his loss by voting the chair an annual salary of £500.[59] The campaign begun nearly ten years before was over, and it was said that Randolph was chagrined by the outcome.[60] Well he might have been. The old-line tidewater aristocracy had lost a substantial measure of authority, and as the Revolutionary movement gathered momentum even more power would have to be shared with the dissidents, the Northern Neck planters, and the Tuckahoes.

THE ECONOMIC ISSUES

Readers of David J. Mays's sympathetic biography of Edmund Pendleton are familiar with the rest of the story.[61] Less well known

55. Nov. 6, 1766, *Jours. of Burgesses, 1766–1769*, 12; Fauquier to B.T., Sept. 4, Oct. 8, 1776, C.O. 5/1331, P.R.O.

56. Nov. 6, 1766, *Jours. of Burgesses, 1766–1769*, 11.

57. Undated rough draft in Revolutionary Lee Papers; Nov. 11, 1766, *Jours. of Burgesses, 1766–1769*, 23.

58. See Paul Carrington to William Wirt, Oct. 3, 1815, in Letters of Patrick Henry, Library of Congress (available on microfilm at Col. Williamsburg Research Lib., Williamsburg, Va.); also Nov. 11, 1766, *Jours. of Burgesses, 1766–1769*, 23.

59. Fauquier to Shelburne, Nov. 10, Dec. 18, 1766, C.O. 5/1331, P.R.O. Apart from the general feeling of confidence in Nicholas, another factor in the decision to drop the commission plan was the expense of paying the five or so commissioners. See *Jours. of Burgesses, 1766–1769*, xiv. An additional reason for voting Randolph a salary as Speaker was the need to compensate him for the loss of the lucrative post of attorney general. See Robert Carter to James Buchanan and Co., [Nov.] 27, 1766, Letterbook of Robert Carter of Nomini Hall, 1764-1768, Col. Williamsburg Research Lib., Williamsburg, Va.

60. William Nelson to Edward and Samuel Athawes, Nov. 13, 1766, Nelson Letterbook; Fauquier to Shelburne, Apr. 27, 1767, C.O. 5/1331, P.R.O.

61. Mays, *Pendleton*, I, chap. 11.

is the fact that the Robinson scandal, unlike Virginia's paper money crisis of the early 1760s, did not lead to any repercussions in Britain. For that matter the effects in Virginia were hardly as serious as might have expected from the tone and severity of Nicholas's public charges. What had happened?

Any explanation must begin with the fall of sterling exchange rates to par in 1766. This not only helped strengthen the public credit but also greatly advanced the value of local debts and currency. Under the circumstances Virginia's merchants had little reason to grieve, and the chief complaint reaching England concerned the dearth of cash, including paper notes.[62] Ironically Robinson had done the public a good turn by illegally recirculating over £100,000 of paper.[63] True, he siphoned off nearly 10 percent of the total to advance his own interests in a lead mine. He made a series of unlawful and unsecured loans to friends and others, few of whom were able to pay back the money. There also seems to have been a smaller number of equally illegal loans to desperate credit risks who were clearly not friends and who paid him an outrageous interest of 15 percent by "selling" Robinson sterling bills of exchange that were bound to be protested in Britain. "Racehorses," the Virginians called them.[64]

Nevertheless the larger truth remains that the expanding economy and broadening credit and currency system of the 1750s, which were outgrowths of increased British investments in Virginia and to a lesser extent of wartime issues of paper money, collapsed in the early 1760s. Given such conditions, lending out some £100,000 was a move that shrewdly anticipated a revival of the economy and repayment of the loans. Another fact often ignored is that Robinson made the bulk of his loans to entrepreneurs and practical businessmen interested in lessening the subordination of Virginia and them-

62. See, for example, Fauquier to secretary of state, June 14, 1765, C.O. 5/1345, P.R.O.; Allason to his brother, May 21, 1765, Allason Letterbook; Dudley Digges to William Dabney, Nov. 11, 1766, in Charles W. Dabney Papers, 1744–1940, Southern Historical Collection, University of North Carolina Library (microfilm available at Col. Williamsburg Research Lib.); John Snelson to Cust and Innes, Sept. 1, 1766, Letterbook of John Snelson, 1757–1775, So. Hist. Coll. (microfilm available at Col. Williamsburg Research Lib.); J. E. Tyler, ed., "Colonel George Mercer's Papers," *VMHB*, LX (1952), 419.

63. See, for example, "To Messrs. Thomas Parramore and Southy Simpson, Representatives of the county of Accomack," Purdie and Dixon's *Va. Gaz.*, Oct. 17, 1766.

64. Mays, *Pendleton*, I, app. II; chap. 3, n. 2, above; "C. R. to Mr. Rind," Rind's *Va. Gaz.*, Apr. 26, 1770.

selves to the British mercantile system. In effect they hoped to change the balance of payments through diversifying agriculture, building industry, and broadening the channels of commerce. In fact such changes were already taking effect; the idea was to hurry them up. The continuing economic decline and Robinson's death unfortunately aborted the scheme.[65]

The usual, opposite interpretation sees the Robinson loans as greatly aggravating economic conditions by increasing the currency in circulation and boosting exchange rates after 1761. Nicholas, so goes the argument, then restored the public faith and credit, and exchange rates dropped to normal again.[66] As has already been shown, the abrupt rise in sterling exchange rates after 1761 had less to do with the volume of circulating paper than with the excessive demand for sterling remittances, the shortage of coin, and the stringency of British credit. This was equally true of the sudden decline in rates in the autumn of 1765.

At the time the treasury defaulted on its payments in the spring of 1765, exchange rates had climbed to 165. Six months later the courts began to shut down in protest against the Stamp Act and in an effort to provide a moratorium on debts. Many remained closed for nearly a year. Debt collection, already slow, came to a virtual standstill, either because executions could not be completed until the courts reopened or because without the threat of court action few of the distressed inhabitants willingly parted with their money.[67] A

65. The questions raised here have as yet only been briefly explored. See, for example, Coulter, "Virginia Merchant," chap. 4; William G. Keener, "Blair-Prentis-Cary Partnership: The Store and Its Operation," unpubl. report to the Research Department, Col. Williamsburg Foundation, Apr. 1957; Mays, *Pendleton*, I, chap. 11.

66. See, for example, Gipson, "Virginia Planter Debts," *VMHB*, LXIX (1961), 259–277, and Evans, "Planter Indebtedness," *WMQ*, 3d Ser, XIX (1962), 511–533. It is also generally assumed that the increased volume of paper money in circulation drove up the general price level. There is little evidence for this. The old assumption that the colonial price level usually rose and fell according to the volume of money, and especially paper money, in circulation needs to be carefully reexamined.

67. See, for example, Richard Henry Lee to Landon Carter, Feb. 24, 1766, James C. Ballagh, ed., *The Letters of Richard Henry Lee* (New York, 1911–1914), I, 15; Allason to his brother, Dec. 8, 1765, Allason Letterbook; Corbin to Robert Dinwiddie, July 12, Nov. 10, 1765, June 3, 1766, Corbin Letterbook; Snelson to Edward Harford, Jr., May 11, June 12, 1766, Snelson Letterbook; Fauquier to B.T., July 26, 1766, in C.O. 5/1331, P.R.O. See also Snelson to Cust and Innes, Sept. 1, 1766, Snelson Letterbook; Fauquier to B.T., Nov. 3, 5, 8, 11, Dec. 17, 1765, C.O. 5/1331, P.R.O. That even before the moratorium certain courts and sheriffs were already employing delaying tactics in the collection of debts out of sympathy for the planters is revealed in the letters of Allason to Robert Shaw, Apr. 3, 1764, and to James Aimley, Aug. 30, 1764, Allason Letterbook. This was common practice in times of

few years before, the chain of credit had collapsed, driving exchange rates to new highs. Now the chain of payment had given way with predictable and opposite results. The demand for sterling bills to repatriate British assets and investments fell precipitously at about the same rate as sterling exchange rates. Moreover the years of heavy liquidation of British holdings in Virginia were past. This also eased the demand for sterling bills; the drastic fall in British imports during the Stamp Act helped too. In short the demand side of the supply and demand curve for sterling exchange had collapsed. In June 1765 exchange rates stood at 165. In October they had slipped to 150, and by the time the court of oyer met in December they were down to 140. Three months later they were at par, which helped wreck at least one scheme to corner the paper money market and set off rumors that sterling bills would be sent to Philadelphia, where exchange was higher.[68] Meanwhile the Robinson scandal was just beginning to roil the waters of Virginia politics.

All during this time the paper currency supply was contracting. In fact it started to contract noticeably at the very moment sterling rates began to rise. Contrary to what most writers on the Virginia economy believe, the currency supply continued to dwindle as exchange rates reached their peak and finally fell to par. This shrinkage of the stock of paper as well as coin began to be felt and was widely reported early in 1764. Two years later, in 1766, the monetary stringency was acute enough to force sheriffs to receive payments for judgments partly in cash and partly credit.[69] A series of short tobacco harvests after 1764, compared with relatively heavier

---

economic crisis; see the discussion in "British Merchant Protest, 1757–1760," in chap. 3 above.

68. See table 5 in Appendix 1; Allason to his brother, May 13, 1764, Jan. 8, Oct. 16, 1766, Allason Letterbook; Greene, ed., *Diary of Landon Carter*, I, 395. The volume of British imports into Virginia is given in Robert W. Coakley, "Virginia Commerce during the American Revolution" (Ph.D. diss., University of Virginia, 1949). The fact of the matter was that sterling exchange rates had generally taken a tumble in all the colonies because, as one merchant put it, the Stamp Act "put an entire stagnation to all Trade and Business and made those who have any Money unwilling to part with it." See Lux to Russell and Molleson, Sept. 17, 1765, Lux to Col. Robert Taylor, Nov. 12, 1765, in Lux Letterbook, N.-Y. Hist. Soc., New York City. For a discussion of the speculation attempt, see Soltow, *Economic Role of Williamsburg*, 169.

69. See, for example, table 5 in Appendix I and Allason to Alexander Walker and Marshall Keith, June 24, 1764, and Allason to his brother, May 21, 1765, Allason Letterbook; Alexander Cunningham to Neil Jamieson, Feb. 9, 1766, Hector Colchester to Neil Jamieson, June 24, 1766, Papers of Neil Jamieson, 1757–1787, Lib. of Congress; Snelson to Cust and Innes, Sept. 1, 1766, Snelson Letterbook.

yields in earlier years, only aggravated the situation. In the first place the volume of tobacco notes, which provided a supplementary medium of local exchange, was greatly reduced. This increased the pressure on available currency. In addition more tobacco than usual was sold within Virginia to the larger buyers who paid a high cash price for the short commodity.[70] Finally, the European market for American wheat in the period turned favorable, and in Virginia as elsewhere commodity merchants were forced to purchase the grain for cash at advanced prices. The upshot was a spurt in the demand for currency, while paper, and probably coin as well, began rapidly contracting.[71] These general conditions in the demand and supply of paper money persisted even after the opening of the courts in the fall of 1766, and—in addition to the sharp drop in demand for sterling remittances, the more favorable terms of trade, and the gradual return of British credit—they largely explain the precipitous fall of exchange rates and the fact that rates remained at par or lower for the rest of the decade. Sterling rates failed to rise to any appreciable extent until the next English credit crisis in 1772.

One year after the Robinson scandal the dearth of cash inspired a number of moves to augment the paper currency supply and to keep a large part of the existing stock of paper in circulation beyond its redemption date—including some of the money Robinson had unlawfully pumped into the monetary stream. The events that had given rise to the Currency Act of 1764 had been turned on their head. As one merchant put it, "I suspect we shall be as fond of having our Assembly authorized by Parliament, to Emit more paper Currency, as we was sometime ago of preventing it."[72] Like many others he had come to realize that the balance-of-payments question held the key to the fluctuation of exchange rates.

70. Snelson to Edward Harford, Jr., May 11, 1766, Snelson Letterbook; John Syme to Farrell and Jones, June 4, 1765, June 20, 1766, in *Jones' Exor. v. John Syme*, U.S. Circuit Court, Va. District (1797)—Ended Cases, Restored, Va. State Lib., Richmond; Allason to his brother, May 13, June 24, 1764, Sept. 6, 1765, Allason to Alexander Walker and Marshall Keith, June 24, 1764, Allason Letterbook; *Yearbook of the United States Department of Agriculture*, 1908 (Washington, D.C., 1909), 131; James H. Soltow, "Scottish Traders in Virginia, 1750–1775," *Econ. Hist. Rev.*, 2d Ser., XII (1959), 89–92. For a discussion of tobacco notes as a medium of local exchange, see Sheick, "Commodity Currency in Colonial Virginia." It is important to note that by 1766 a growing amount of cash was spent on local purchases of other crops, especially wheat; see Fauquier to Shelburne, Nov. 10, 1766, C.O. 5/1331, P.R.O.

71. See the entries for 1766 and 1767, Lux Letterbook.

72. See Allason to his brother, Oct. 29, 1767, Allason Letterbook.

Chapter 7

Reworking the Law
Money and Politics in the Carolinas, Pennsylvania, and Virginia

By the end of 1767 Pennsylvania and South Carolina had joined Maryland and Georgia in issuing small amounts of treasury notes. Sometimes the money was made a legal tender for specific public obligations. More often it was not. In any event practice dictated that the local treasurers receive the money for taxes and other public payments. They could hardly have done otherwise. To have refused paper currency would have amounted to a destruction of the public credit at the hands of the very officials appointed to preserve it. Even so the feeling persisted that it was imperative to safeguard paper emissions by the use of a legal tender clause that at the very least covered all public transactions. Then as now men placed little faith and less trust in the essential goodness of governments or of government servants. And for good reason. In the past a number of public treasurers had shown themselves to be all too willing to sacrifice the public credit for private gain. Besides, a legal tender provision was traditional. Rightly or wrongly most Americans appear to have held that no paper currency system could function properly without it.

By contrast British officials tended to feel just as strongly that a legal tender provision was a device for cheating the creditor interests of a country. And despite admitted ambiguities in the meaning of the Currency Act of 1764, they further believed that a legal tender provision violated parliamentary law. Nevertheless the Currency Act at first received a liberal reading, but within a few years

197

British policies noticeably stiffened. Early in 1768 Hillsborough replaced Shelburne in the American Department, and he immediately let it be known, in connection with a petition from North Carolina for an addition to the fiat money supply, that in his reading of the law any paper issue infused with even the smallest degree of legal tender was not to be tolerated. In general the position reflected Hillsborough's well-known aversion to paper money. Doubtless it reflected as well growing ministerial determination in the period to have obedience paid to all acts of Parliament respecting America, and during the next two years the Hillsborough interpretation slowly gained ground. In February 1770 it finally acquired official stamp in the Privy Council's rejection of a New York loan office act.

There were limits, though, to how far the ministry would go in following Hillsborough's lead. Thus an attempt to expand the meaning of the Currency Act to cover events taking place in Pennsylvania failed to elicit any support from fellow ministers. The situation in question developed during Lord Clare's term as president of the Board of Trade. Pennsylvania, followed shortly by a number of other colonies, had successfully led the way in paying current and contingent expenses with treasury notes that, though not specifically declared a legal tender, were nevertheless taken up by local officials as a matter of course for all public payments. In the spring of 1770, citing the Currency Act of 1764 as his authority, Hillsborough induced the commissioners of trade to challenge the legality of that practice. But after Board solicitor Richard Jackson strongly advised that Pennsylvania's paper money laws violated neither the letter nor the spirit of the Currency Act, the commissioners ultimately dropped their challenge. The Privy Council refused to take any stand on the question at all. For all practical purposes then, by the summer of 1770 the British government had grudgingly conceded that Pennsylvania, and by extension other colonies as well, could meet expenses with treasury notes receivable for public obligations—providing that currency laws drop all reference to legal tender.

An important departure in monetary policy had taken place. Nor was Pennsylvania the only province immediately affected, for the new policy received confirmation from a British response to three other currency emissions struck before 1770—two small issues in North Carolina and Virginia and a larger issue in South Carolina. It might be said that British policy had lapsed into a kind of empty formalism.

THE BRITISH RESPONSE: NORTH CAROLINA, 1764–1768

Hillsborough's announcement of a tougher stand on currency came in the spring of 1768. The occasion was the arrival in London of a petition from North Carolina soliciting royal support for a legal tender issue of £100,000 in treasury notes, a simple request that masked an involved story of money and politics.

The postwar depression that had ravaged the Virginia economy in the early sixties seems to have had a less serious impact on North Carolina. To be sure, the province's northern counties, engaged as they were in the shipping of tobacco to Petersburg, Virginia, or to the Albemarle ports of Currituck and Roanoke for export to Glasgow and London, showed some symptoms of the crisis. But the relatively limited agricultural and commercial development of the areas in question and the diversification of the local crops offered real protection against the effects of weakening tobacco markets. Similarly in the south, where naval stores, wood products, and grains constituted the major exports and a relatively prosperous Charleston the chief trade center, market conditions appeared only marginally better. As for the one postwar economic problem reportedly common to both sections, the stringency of money, the northern counties appear to have enjoyed a distinct advantage. And over the next decade the south would take the lead in pushing for additional and heavy emissions of paper money.[1]

By the end of the war hard cash was in short supply throughout North Carolina. Late in 1765 Governor William Tryon reported home that while a few coins still passed in the maritime counties

1. My analysis of economic conditions in North Carolina during the late colonial period derives from a careful reading of the several sources cited and from long discussions with H. Roy Merrens, my colleague and friend and the author of *Colonial North Carolina in the Eighteenth Century*. Business correspondence for North Carolina is skimpy in the extreme as compared with the sources available for the other colonies. The one economic history of the province is Charles C. Crittenden, *The Commerce of North Carolina, 1763–1789* (New Haven, Conn., 1936). Unfortunately it employs a static and categorical approach to economic conditions and for my purposes proves to be useless. An older but still valuable study of North Carolina's currency practices is Bullock, *Essays on the Monetary History of the United States*, 125–204. See also the excellent article by Robert M. Weir, "North Carolina's Reaction to the Currency Act of 1764," *N.C. Hist. Rev.*, XL (1953), 183–199.

scarcely any circulated in the backcountry. And the situation promised to get worse as local merchants continued to remit what little specie came to hand to British and foreign markets. As for the effect of the recently enacted stamp tax, the governor asserted that the duties to be paid in the province's five superior courts alone would in a year's time consume the available stock of hard money, not to mention the demand generated by the twenty-nine inferior courts and the various legal instruments in the hands of sheriffs and other civil officials that were also subject to the tax.[2] Paper currency proved equally scarce. Contraction of wartime issues had taken a heavy toll, and in 1765 not more than £70,000 passed among a population that had already exceeded two hundred thousand and was rapidly increasing. Like coin much of the paper outstanding circulated in the more heavily commercialized areas of the east and especially the northeast, where sizable quantities of Virginia paper money entered the local monetary stream.[3]

If generally speaking the less-developed and poorer western counties suffered most from the straightened supply of coin and currency, neither did they derive much comfort from the provincial system of commodity notes and commodity payments. In 1764, for example, the General Assembly renewed quality-control legislation that made inspectors' notes for tobacco and indigo lawful for all county and vestry levies. But provincial taxes remained unaffected. They continued to be paid in coin and currency in order to service the redemption of the colony's various paper money issues. Moreover tobacco notes generally circulated only within the tobacco-producing areas of the northeast and the commercial centers of the Albemarle, while indigo remained a negligible crop throughout the province. In short the 1764 law made no provision for inspecting and rating commodities grown in the west and south. In the absence of cash, rated commodities from these areas would at least have facilitated the payment of local taxes.[4]

Not surprisingly the overall record suggests that the more highly

2. Tryon to Sec. Henry Conway, Dec. 26, 1765, *Col. Recs. N.C.*, VII, 143–144. See also the *North-Carolina Gazette* (Wilmington), Nov. 27, 1765.

3. See table 6 in Appendix 1 and the discussion below. See also the comments in the news item from Williamsburg dated Oct. 8, 1767, *N.-Y. Jour.*, Nov. 5, 1767.

4. On the sectional and regional implications of this point see Merrens, *Colonial North Carolina in the Eighteenth Century*. On the matter of taxes and money see Marvin L. Michael Kay, "The Payment of Provincial and Local Taxes in North Carolina, 1748–1771," *WMQ*, 3d Ser., XXVI (1969), 218–240, and esp. 235–239. See also by the same author, "Provincial Taxes in North Carolina during the Administrations of Dobbs and Tryon," *N.C. Hist. Rev.*, XLII (1965), 440–453.

commercialized areas around the Albemarle received special favor in the distribution of the local supply of money and credit. But the larger fact remains that North Carolina's developing economy generated a greater demand for cash and credit than capital sources could supply. Commerce, agriculture, government, all were affected.

Little was done to remedy North Carolina's monetary problems until after the Stamp Act turmoil had subsided. The General Assembly met only briefly in 1765, but early in the fall session of the following year the lower house received a petition from Pasquotank, a northern maritime county, setting out the many hardships engendered by the scarcity of paper money and coin.[5] The petition appears to have triggered a full review of the subject. After considering the grievance in committee of the whole, house members agreed to two separate recommendations that revealed the essential outlines of the colony's money problems and went some distance towards solving them. The recommendations favored making an extensive number of commodities receivable for local taxes in addition to petitioning the king for repeal of the Currency Act, permission to emit legal tender paper money, and for such "other relief as he, in his Royal Wisdom, shall think meet."

Barely a week later and without a word of explanation, the house dismissed the committee appointed to draft the petition. Possibly the persistent newspaper rumors of impending repeal and/or reform of existing British monetary policy dissuaded the legislature from taking any remedial action. Ostensibly the same reason lay behind a subsequent move that killed the bill to rate commodities. Reports of widespread crop failures for the second year in a row may also have exerted some influence on that decision.[6]

Following the adjournment of the legislature, late in January 1767 Tryon informed Secretary Shelburne of the Pasquotank complaint and of the pressing need for a "larger Medium of trade." Barely enough money remained to pay taxes and quitrents, Tryon asserted, and in the opinion of local merchants, who reported great difficulty in getting in their debts, an additional emission of £150,000 would be hardly sufficient "under the present state" of commerce. Tryon also alluded to another kind of money question that at the

5. Nov. 20, 1766, *Col. Recs. N.C.*, VII, 386.
6. Nov. 22, 27, 1766, *ibid.*, 393–394. See also *ibid.*, 417; Nathaniel Williams to [?], Feb. 22, 1767, Nathaniel Williams Letterbook and Accounts, 1758–1768, Duke Univ. Lib., Durham, N.C.; Robert Hogg to Robert Sterling, June 9, 1766, Hogg and Clayton Letterbook and Accounts, 1767–1771, Duke Univ. Lib.; and the discussion in "Petitions for Repeal, 1766–1767," in chap. 4 above.

moment seems to have caused him as much and perhaps more concern. He claimed that the sheriffs and tax collectors, whether through neglect and peculation or from the deficiency of coin and paper currency, had paid into treasury hands less than one-third of the public levies.[7]

Unfortunately for the province Tryon's information reached Shelburne at a bad time, just after recent events in New York had led the secretary to reverse his position on the necessity of repealing the Currency Act. Shelburne never bothered to reply or even to go through the formality of turning the correspondence over to the Board of Trade for review.[8]

That summer Tryon repeated his charges against the sheriffs and tax collectors. He advised Shelburne that, on the average, sheriffs had embezzled over half of their tax collections. That amounted to more than £40,000, about as much, given the respective size of the two colonies, as Robinson had pocketed in Virginia. And that figure probably reflected a conservative estimate, since in 1770 an auditor's report showed the sheriffs owed well over £65,000. In any event Tryon proved far less optimistic than Virginia's governor about the possibility of recovering the stolen money. He judged that not more than £5,000 would ever be returned. Sheriffs and their sureties would either skip the province or declare bankruptcy before they would pay. In addition the governor found the public treasurers to be far too lenient with the embezzlers, if only because, "by not suing the sheriffs in arrear," the treasurers obtained "a considerable weight of interest among the connections of these delinquent sheriffs and which generally secures them a re-election in their offices when expired." Still Tryon hoped to obtain better regulation of the sheriffs when the assembly reconvened. Meanwhile he solicited crown support for a move to replace the elected and corrupt treasurers with executive appointees.[9]

As planned the governor opened the General Assembly in December 1767 with an address underscoring the abuses of the sheriff's office and requesting tighter controls. The representatives, many of them sheriffs or former sheriffs, willingly admitted that the office cried aloud for correction. Any recommendations the governor might make, they said piously, were most welcome. Their chief

7. Jan. 31, 1767, *Col. Recs. N.C.*, VII, 433.
8. See the discussion in "Petitions for Repeal, 1766–1767," in chap. 4 above.
9. July 4, 1767, *Col. Recs. N.C.*, VII, 497. See also *ibid.*, VIII, 278–281, and *North-Carolina Gazette* (New Bern), Mar. 24, 1775.

concern, however, remained the shortage of an exchange medium, and they declared their intention of taking every "laudable measure" to prevent further scarcities.[10] As a result early in January the house appointed Maurice Moore, Jr., Cornelius Harnett, and Robert Howe, all members from the Cape Fear region, to serve on a committee to consider the problem. Two councillors, also from the Cape Fear, joined the group shortly after.[11]

Clearly the movement to expand the currency supply had come into the hands of a group of southern leaders, which caused no surprise then or later. In the area around the lower Cape Fear and Wilmington, local merchants appear to have been indigenous. Largely independent of control by firms in Charleston, the nearest great market, they were also somewhat less firmly attached to the great Scottish and English houses that dominated the Albemarle and the western tier of counties in the north—like Edgecombe, Northampton, and Granville—which were an economic appendage of nearby Virginia. In addition the Cape Fear area had developed rapidly after 1760, so that while British credit remained in relatively shorter supply there than elsewhere, local demand for credit was greater among all the elements of the population. In competing with Charleston for backcountry trade, Cape Fear merchants found themselves also handicapped by the shortage of cash as well as credit. A few years later the governor would describe the "majority from the southern region" as a people "almost universally necessitous and in debt."[12]

Within a month the joint committee of the General Assembly presented Tryon with a petition to the king explaining the urgent need for a lawful £100,000 currency issue to facilitate both trade and the payment of local taxes. Amounting to some sixteen shillings sterling for each inhabitant, the money would remain in circulation sixteen years as a full legal tender for all domestic debts—except those due to the crown and to British creditors.[13] As things stood the proposed emission clearly violated parliamentary law. Still the assembly had good reason to believe its petition would meet with success. In the first place the stipulation that the new bills should

10. Dec. 7, 11, 1767, *Col. Recs. N.C.*, VII, 551–552, 570. On the shortage of money at the time see Alexander Stewart to the secretary of the Society for the Propagation of the Gospel, June 28, 1768 (1767), *ibid.*, 495.
11. Jan. 13, 1768, *ibid.*, 661.
12. This statement derives from my reading of the various sources cited in this chapter as well as from conversations with H. Roy Merrens. See also Gov. Josiah Martin to the earl of Hillsborough, Dec. 26, 1771, *ibid.*, IX, 76.
13. Jan. 16, 1768, *ibid.*, VII, 681–683.

not be lawful for any debts owed to the crown or to British creditors would placate those merchants trading to North Carolina who ten years before had protested to the Board of Trade about being forced to receive as legal tender paper already depreciated in value. That grievance, it will be recalled, had played an important role in the passage of the Currency Act and in the subsequent move to bring about its repeal.[14] Moreover another of the merchants' gripes that had won Board support had also been settled recently. In the summer of 1767 Tryon reported to the commissioners of trade that local courts no longer awarded sterling judgments in paper at face value, as British merchants had earlier charged. Current practice compelled payment in paper money at the actual or market rate of exchange.[15]

Most promising of all was the timely arrival of a letter from Henry McCulloh, the merchant and land speculator who had returned to England to play a role in the making of the Stamp and Currency Acts and who now aspired to become provincial agent. McCulloh wrote of a move afoot from within the ministry to take monetary affairs "out of the hands of Parliament and place them in their Old Channels, that is under the direction of the Crown and the Great Boards." Parliament would assign to each colony a proscribed amount of paper currency not to be exceeded without crown permission. In addition, he wrote, currency issues were to be properly secured at the time of emission, while sterling debts would be specifically exempted from any legal tender laws.[16]

At the General Assembly's request Tryon strongly recommended the petition in his dispatches home. Actually he needed no urging; he had already accepted the need for an increased currency supply as part of a larger and far-ranging plan for encouraging the economic growth of the colony. This point has not received sufficient attention. From the beginning of his term Governor Tryon, with active assembly support, had initiated an ambitious program of internal improvements including the building and repairing of roads, ferries, and bridges, and the clearing of rivers and streams. Also scheduled for improvement in the general effort to advance agri-

14. See the discussion in "The Currency Act of 1764" in chap. 3, the discussion in chap. 4, and B.T. to Tryon, Nov. 29, 1765, *Col. Recs. N.C.*, VII, 132.

15. Tryon to B.T., July 15, 1767, *Col. Recs. N.C.*, VII, 511.

16. To John Harvey, Sept. 13, 1767, *ibid.*, VIII, 516–518. See also the discussions in "The Currency Act of 1764" and "Franklin's 'Paper Money Scheme,' 1765–1766," in chaps. 3 and 4 above.

culture and commerce were harbor and port facilities. To prevent
backcountry trade from being siphoned off to Charleston was an
added goal, although there markets and prices were better and transportation generally easier. Similarly Tryon was deeply involved in
an attempt to promote North Carolina's forest industries and commodities trade by opening up new markets for naval stores and
lumber in England, obtaining an increase on existing bounties, and
tightening the quality controls over exports.[17]

A final and equally important reason for Tryon's endorsement
concerned his desire for improved government. Knowing this and
hoping to whet his ardor for paper money, the lower house accepted
all of the governor's recent suggestions for stricter regulation of the
sheriffs and treasurers.[18] The legislature also appropriated £15,000
to erect a governor's residence at New Bern, another pet favorite
project of the governor's. In this instance Tryon anxiously sought
to rapidly build a great capital and port city both for the easier
administration of the colony and for the creation of a central market that would offset the economic advantages of Charleston.[19]

Tryon's dispatches home tended to place greater emphasis on the
urgent short-range need for an additional emission of fiat money
than on long-range plans to encourage agriculture, trade, and industry. As he explained to Secretary Shelburne, the current liber-
ality of the legislature in better establishing and supporting government had no parallel in the annals of North Carolina. In recognition
of this new-found willingness to cooperate, Tryon hoped that the
king would move to relieve "the great inconveniences his subjects
here labor under as well for want of a medium to pay the public
taxes, as to carry on trade." A lack of an adequate circulating medium already forced sheriffs and tax collectors to distrain on personal effects and to sell them at public auction, though the monetary
stringency meant that they rarely sold at their real value or commanded money enough to cover the overdue taxes. The governor
insisted the result would be the ruin of small property holders. He

17. The point is developed by Frances Long Harrold, "Governor William Tryon
of North Carolina, 1765–1771" (M.A. thesis, University of Wisconsin, 1954), esp.
chap. 3. See also Tryon to Shelburne, Feb. 2, 1768, Tryon to Messrs. Drummond
and Co., Feb. 2, 1768, *Col. Recs. N.C.*, VII, 678–680.
18. See Tryon to Shelburne, Mar. 5, 1768, *Col. Recs. N.C.*, VII, 693–698.
19. The matter of the governor's "Palace" has been written up any number
of times in connection with the Regulator Movement, but this particular side to
the question tends to be overlooked. See Harrold, "William Tryon," chap. 4.

concluded his case by citing the rash of counterfeiting that had plagued the province during the last few years; a new and carefully printed issue would largely eliminate that problem.[20]

Tryon's observations gave a fairly good impression of the monetary problem facing North Carolina at the time, and they found an echo in other writings, some of which were far more explicit. For instance an unidentified Wilmington man, apparently a merchant, cited the decline of exports in the period as a contributing cause to the dearth of specie. He estimated that the total currency in circulation, including paper and coin, did not exceed five shillings per person, though the poll tax alone stood at seven shillings sixpence and would shortly advance at least another shilling. "Exclusive of this," the writer went on, "we have a duty on spirituous liquors of 6d per gallon, besides County, Parish, and other internal taxes." People would pay taxes if they could, but the monetary pinch was already such that the propertied people had begun to turn down the position of sheriff in several of the counties because of the impossibility of collecting the public debt. The end result could only be a shortage of executive officers to serve processes and make executions and thus a stop to all credit and business.[21]

By the time the petition for an additional fiat money issue and the governor's letters reached England, Hillsborough had replaced Shelburne in the American Department. The new secretary lost no time in making his feelings known in the matter. He wrote Tryon in mid-April 1768 acknowledging that the petition had come to hand but noting that the question of legal tender currency did not fall within the competency of the crown. The petition would have to go before the House of Commons. Unfortunately Parliament stood adjourned at the moment, though Hillsborough added that in his view the petition stood little chance of a sympathetic reading, since the matter had already received "so full a Discussion at the Board of Trade, at the Privy Council, and in each House of Parliament" and legal tender paper currency had been found to be "big with Frauds, and full of Mischief to the Colonies, and to Commerce in general."[22] By the time the Hillsborough reply arrived in North Carolina it was already widely held that McCulloh's optimism rested on shaky

20. Mar. 5, 1768, *Col. Recs. N.C.*, VII, 692–693. On the counterfeiting question see *ibid.*, 551, 680.

21. "Extract of a letter from Wilmington in North Carolina," *S.-C. Gaz.*, Mar. 14–21, 1768.

22. Apr. 16, 1768, *Col. Recs. N.C.*, VII, 709.

grounds. Prospect of obtaining leave for a legal tender currency emission seemed slight indeed.[23] The latest news only confirmed suspicions and thus blighted the promise of political harmony.

By the spring of 1768 Hillsborough had begun showing a strong hand in his administration of American affairs. In consequence his announced opposition to any kind of fiat money scotched lingering rumors in America of an impending repeal of the Currency Act and a return to more traditional monetary policies and practices. Events created a logic of their own, however. A scant year later Hillsborough found it expedient to soften his position in the face of another currency emission in Pennsylvania.

PENNSYLVANIA, 1767–1770

Despite the successful effort of Pennsylvania in 1767 to pay its backlog of debts with £20,000 of "indented bills," the clamor for public credit and a more adequate medium of domestic exchange grew increasingly strident. Twenty thousand pounds proved far too small a sum to satisfy popular demands for cash, and the fact that the bills passed freely in trade only fired popular enthusiasm for a large loan office issue. By late 1767 and through the next year numerous newspaper articles appeared citing the great scarcity of money and the difficulty of carrying on trade for want of a proper medium of exchange. All classes were reportedly affected. Farmers lost their plantations by executions, merchants went broke, and people of all walks jammed the debtors' prisons. According to the anonymous newspaper writers, the future promised little more than barter, declining trade, bankruptcy, poverty, and want.[24] Business correspondence only echoed such complaints.[25]

There is little doubt that popular opinion held the source of the people's "very great Distress" to be exactly as Philadelphia mer-

23. See, for example, letter from "New Bern (in North Carolina)," June 10, *N.-Y. Jour.*, June 31, 1768.

24. See, for example, *Pa. Chron.*, Dec. 21, 1767, Jan. 4, Oct. 10, 12, 1768.

25. See, for example, entries in the Pemberton Papers, XXVIII, Clifford Correspondence, Letterbook, 1767–1773, and the John Reynell Letterbook, Folder Feb. 1767–Apr. 1769, both in Hist. Soc. Pa., Philadelphia. See also Sachs, "Business Outlook," chap. 7. I should like to acknowledge here that my analysis of conditions in Pennsylvania owes a great deal to the work of Marc Egnal, my colleague and friend, who is presently completing a study of the political economy of Pennsylvania in the mid-eighteenth century. I have greatly benefited from our conversations and from my reading of advance copies of chapters of his forthcoming dissertation.

chant John Reynell put it in the spring of 1768: "We have not the Pleasure of having any quantity of Paper money made, only a small matter for the Support of Government."[26] "Were you here to see the scarcity of cash, you would be amazed," another firm reported from that same city; "not a person has purchased a single article . . . but [has preferred to keep his] money—in short, the case with everybody."[27] In reality the matter seems to have been more complex than these and similar letters suggest.

Following termination of nonimportation associated with the Stamp Act, Pennsylvania again began to absorb increasing amounts of British goods. Payment for the growing imports came partly out of returns from the heavy exports of domestic commodities in the period and partly out of the supply of short-term credit liberally provided by British merchants anxious to recapture and even expand their American markets. As a consequence, by mid-1767 several reports from Philadelphia spoke of overstocked inventories, excessive competition among sellers, and dull sales, particularly of dry goods. Near the end of the year the trickle of complaints had swelled to a torrent. By this time the balance-of-payments problem also threatened to get out of hand, for wheat prices in the Mediterranean area had suddenly begun to slacken, while the West Indies continued to offer a poor market for agricultural products. In addition commodity prices at home declined in late 1768, and not until 1770 did they resume their upward swing. The overall effects of the various forces at play were the weakening of the domestic market, retrenchment, and a growing demand for debt payment on both sides of the Atlantic—attended by a spreading wave of bankruptcies. Another, related result was a growing tightness of money and credit that only aggravated general conditions.[28]

That the trading community, sensing a correlation between the monetary stringency and the business slump, should under the circumstances opt for a public loan was predictable enough—particularly since some kind of monetary analysis of trade conditions formed part of the conventional wisdom. Thus Pennsylvanians typically believed that experience taught that the former loan office had helped breathe life into business before the French and Indian War. It was also common knowledge that since then the economy had considerably expanded, creating even greater demands for a cir-

26. To Andreas Groth, May 11, 1768, Reynell Letterbook.
27. Quoted in Sachs, "Business Outlook," chap. 7, 200.
28. See n. 25 above.

culating medium. But not everyone fell back upon traditional reasons to account for the "embarrassed" state of the economy. "We find ourselves poor and much straitened for cash," one observer commented in the *Pennsylvania Chronicle* in October 1768. "I think the reason is pretty plainly this, that we are badly paid for what we sell, *i.e.*, our wheat, flour, iron, lumber, hemp, etc. etc. are paid for in lace, cambricks, lawns, top knots, hoses, shoes, silks, cloths, linens, buckles, buttons, china, tea, trinkets, and gewgaws innumerable." Just a few months later another observer commented, "I am . . . not in the least against the petition now on foot for emitting a large sum in bills of credit, at a proper time, for a public loan." Nonetheless, he continued, large "emissions of paper money in this province are not the only requisites to a real amendment of our circumstances, for these incidents are no otherwise desireable than as they may increase the practicability of such amendment, but 'tis economy and industry that must effect it."[29]

Ultimately the question of whether or not the dearth of money lay at the root of the economic problems gripping Pennsylvania in 1767 and 1768 has little to do with the wisdom of issuing a large sum of paper money on loan—though some people at the time thought that it did. Merchants supporting a loan generally recognized the complexities of economic reality. Most merely hoped that a sizable infusion of currency would facilitate the movement of goods, provide a source of public credit and cash sufficient to help them gather in their debts and settle their accounts, and shore up property values, which reportedly had declined as much as one-half or more because of the monetary stringency. The last consideration proved especially important at a time when most debts were secured by land in one form or another.[30]

Doubtless monetary remedies would go some way towards reviving business. But few merchants—or anyone else for that matter—believed they would go far enough. Other solutions came up for consideration as well. As a result of the Townshend Acts, late in 1767 fresh proposals were made for another nonimportation movement. After the happy experience with the last such movement, the possible economic advantages to the businessmen could not be discounted. "You will have a good price for all your dead stock which

29. "To the Farmers and Tradesmen of Pennsylvania," *Pa. Chron.*, Oct. 10, 1768; "Colonus," in *Pa. Jour.*, Jan. 12, 1769.
30. See the succinct statement by Sachs and Hoogenboom, *Enterprising Colonials*, 92–96. The statement is drawn from Sachs, "Business Outlook."

have always been unprofitable," an anonymous writer publicly reminded the merchants. "You will collect your debts, and bring your debts in England to a close, so that balances would hereby be brought about in your favour, which without some such method, must forever be against you."[31] In the face of a persistent business slump such arguments proved increasingly attractive, and by the end of 1768 the Philadelphia merchants had agreed to join their brethren in New York and Boston in suspending British imports during 1769.[32] That year Pennsylvania's imports declined by half; as ever, retrenchment proved to be a harsh but effective cure for overtrading.[33] Nevertheless something still had to be done about the money question.

On reconvening early in 1768 following its Christmas recess, the General Assembly received a petition from the city and county of Philadelphia requesting a new public loan to provide an adequate medium of local exchange as well as funds "for the cultivation and improvement" of the province.[34] The house tabled the document, however, postponing any action until the possible arrival of news of the expected repeal of the Currency Act. One money question that did come up that session involved the alleged embezzlement of some £20,000 by Charles Norris, the deceased treasurer of the old loan office. But Mary Norris, widow and executrix of the estate, quickly settled the matter. In the meantime the representatives repeated their earlier instructions to agents Franklin and Jackson to continue working for currency reform and revision of the parliamentary law.[35] At first the agents' reports were hopeful. That spring, Franklin advised, the repeal movement would be reactivated during the short session of Parliament that began in May. Instead, shortly after, Hillsborough became secretary of state for the colonies and president of the Board of Trade, whereupon Franklin notified Joseph Galloway that the agents and merchants had given up virtually all hope of repeal.[36]

31. *Pa. Gaz.*, Nov. 17, 1767.
32. The best account of the colonial response to the Townshend Acts is Leslie J. Thomas, "The Non-Consumption and Non-Importation Movements, 1767–1770" (M.S. thesis, University of Wisconsin, 1949). For a different view of the merchants' response, see Jensen, *Maritime Commerce of Colonial Philadelphia*, 172–195.
33. *Historical Statistics of the United States*, 757, Z21–34.
34. Feb. 4, 1768, *Pa. Archives*, VII, 6134–6135.
35. Feb. 20, 1768, *ibid.*, 6168–6169. For a general discussion of the administration of the loan office, see Yoder, "Paper Currency in Colonial Pennsylvania," chap. 6, and esp. 243–244 for the Norris story.
36. To Pa. Comm. of Corres., Apr. 15, 1768, Smyth, ed., *Writings of Franklin*, V, 120. See also the discussion in "Pennsylvania and Repeal, 1750–1767," in chap. 4 above.

Early the following year the house received over fifty petitions from throughout the province calling for the restoration of the loan office. With their assets frozen, merchants, farmers, and mechanics found themselves at the mercy of their creditors and of "those few Persons who stood possessed of the principal Part of the Gold and Silver in the Colony." Under the circumstances an increase in the supply of cash and the creation of a source of public credit appeared to offer some relief. Encouraged by the success of the treasury issue of 1767, the petitioners expressed a willingness to take up the proposed loan office bills in discharge of all contracts with the "utmost Chearfulness."[37] The way would have been clear for authorization of a public loan, notwithstanding the failure to repeal the Currency Act of 1764, if everyone had acquiesced in the need for such a measure. But those who feared the inflationary effects of a large paper issue, together with those who held up the superior benefits of nonimportation and even domestic manufacturing, raised loud and serious objections. "I am very far from being an enemy to the using paper as a medium of traffic," wrote one disarming critic to the readers of the *Pennsylvania Journal*. "I consider it as a very useful, and, at the same time, a very dangerous expedient." The general standard of emission, he went on to say, should be

the price given for the general produce of our soil, and the relative value which our currency may have to sterling coin. By this standard I imagine our emissions of paper currency may generally be regulated with safety. Particular circumstances may indeed intervene, and render this rule fallacious. Such circumstances are now the interesting objects of our attention, and the more attentively we consider them, the more readily we shall be induced to believe, that—while we are loaded with heavy debt to Great-Britain, and while we imprudently pursue such measures as must annually increase this debt, we cannot with propriety —We cannot indeed with safety sollicit any considerable emission of paper currency; since the progress of our internal economy must receive a fatal check from the extension of our public credit.[38]

Economy and industry, not simply repeal of revenue acts and emissions of paper money, would advance prosperity, added another correspondent. "I know it is a prevailing opinion, that the want of money among us hath been a principal cause of the difficulties we complain of, and I believe it has some foundation; for we must allow

37. Jan. 4–6, 10–11, 13–14, 17–19, 1769, *Pa. Archives*, VII, 6293–6295, 6300–6305, 6307–6308, 6311, 6313, 6317–6318, 6320.
38. "The Citizen. No. IX," *Pa. Jour.*, Jan. 26, 1769.

that a currency of some sort is very convenient in every community so far as it is wanted for a medium of commerce." Nonetheless this writer found that it was "unquestionably our highest interest to manufacture for ourselves so far as we have materials, and can do it without much interruption to agriculture."[39]

The petitioners and their critics received their answer on January 19 when the house members resolved that a currency issue on "solid Funds" was indeed necessary but then postponed any action on the matter until their next sitting.[40] The paper money question was not entirely ignored, however. During the discussion of the public loan, a representation came in from the overseers of the poor of Philadelphia and of the surrounding townships and requested a £14,000 loan to refinance a mortgage on some property in "old Almshouse Square." In ordinary times the overseers would have sold off the poorhouse holdings and cleared their own debts. The present scarcity of cash and the accompanying collapse of realty values made any such move unthinkable. In addition the petitioners pointed out that the money would give employment to the growing number of indigents and other victims of the business recession without entailing any increase in the local poor tax. The house honored the petition by granting the full loan, payable in annual installments of at least £1,000, with the funds to be drawn from a new treasury issue.[41] In a related move the representatives authorized an added £16,000 emission to cover current public expenses. To provide the required sinking fund for the money, they stretched the old excise tax to its limits, extending it another four years.[42] It was now abundantly clear that any further steps in that direction would necessitate an increase in the excise or the reestablishment of the loan office interest fund.

The question of legal tender arising out of the latest treasury issue was quickly tackled. In line with practices recently established, the house guaranteed that the full £30,000 of non-legal tender currency could be exchanged at the treasury at any time prior to redemption for whatever lawful paper happened to be on hand. Governor John Penn, a member of the proprietary family, prompt-

39. "Colonus," *ibid.,* Jan. 12, 1769.
40. *Pa. Archives,* VII, 6321–6322.
41. *Ibid.,* 6314, 6322–6324, 6343–6344, 6369.
42. *Ibid.,* 6359, 6369; "Minutes of the Provincial Council of Pennsylvania," *Colonial Records of Pennsylvania, 1683–1790* (Philadelphia, 1852–1853), IX, 578–580.

ly signed both currency measures and dispatched them to the Board of Trade for review.[43]

Pennsylvania's treasury issues of 1769 were the only paper money laws enacted before 1772. Despite continued interest in a public loan, the "land bank" proposal simply fizzled.[44] As promised, on reconvening in May 1769 the assembly placed the loan office question at the top of its agenda and after brief consideration approved an issue of £120,000. But the governor withheld his signature. The forty-page bill came back to the legislature within a week accompanied by some twenty-seven amendments. They embraced two major objections. The first dealt with the problem of legal tender, and Penn asked the representatives to strike a provision making the money lawful for all public debts. He also wished to drop the wording "directed to be emitted" in favor of the phrase "were to be made current" and to add a disclaimer in language lifted directly from the Currency Act of 1764 to the effect that "nothing in this act contained, shall extend or be construed to make the bills of credit hereby directed to be emitted, a legal tender in payment of any bargains, contracts, debts, dues, or demands whatsoever." For all his concern over legal tender, however, Penn found nothing wrong with retaining a provision making the bills lawful at the loan office.

A second and more important objection involved the failure to give the executive a share in nominating the trustees of the loan office and in applying the interest returns. These issues, it will be recalled, had brought down the old loan office. At the moment, the legislature was in no mood to relax its grip on the purse strings, though it did give way on the legal tender question. When therefore Penn insisted on full compliance with his demands, the house again postponed final action on the loan and resolved to answer his objections in full when it met again at the end of the year.[45]

That reply was not forthcoming. Whatever doubts there may have been before, the fall elections finally convinced the delegates that a public loan was of vital concern to the economic well-being of their constituents. "The very distressed situation of this province, occasioned by the great scarcity of a circulating medium, calls most

43. Mitchell and Flanders, eds., *Statutes of Pa.*, VII, 197–212.
44. *Pa. Jour.*, Apr. 13, 1769.
45. May 10, 12, 17, 23, 1769, *Pa. Archives*, VII, 6376, 6378, 6381, 6387; "Minutes of the Provincial Council," *Col. Recs. Pa.*, IX, 589–596.

seriously for instant relief," as one writer put it at the time. "The country being much in debt to the merchants in this city [Philadelphia], and these to the merchants at home, so soon as these begin to press for remittances, we are obliged to do the same with our debtors in the county. Lands given in security there, are put up to sale, and are often sold at one third their value. The reason of this is the great scarcity of money—for the poor debtor cannot procure cash to pay off his creditor, though he should offer six times the value in security." "I am sorry," he concluded, that "the assembly, I mean those members of it who voted against paper money in the last session, were not so far governed by this reason as to sacrifice to it any trifling unimportant consideration whatever."[46] When the assembly reconvened in January 1770, it offered a major concession: the governor was to have a share in the interest fund but not in the nomination of the trustees. Penn held out for both.[47]

Political fortunes had clearly changed since the war years. Then the proprietary had come under pressure to surrender its claim over finances. At the present moment it was the assembly's turn, and Penn showed himself to be an able adversary and as much an opportunist as his opponents. After a few weeks of sparring, the representatives dropped the loan office until conditions were more to their liking. Ironically it would have failed in any event. As Franklin later remarked to Speaker Galloway, as long as the money was made a tender "even to the loan office in discharge of the mortgages it would have been repealed" in London.[48]

Two years would pass before the General Assembly attempted to revive the plan. In the meanwhile the treasury issues of 1769 received sympathetic treatment at the Board of Trade when they came up for consideration in July 1770. Years before, when an earlier and similar Pennsylvania measure had come up for review, Matthew Lamb had served as Board solicitor. But Lamb had died in the autumn of 1768, and the office remained vacant for nearly eighteen months until in the spring of 1770 Richard Jackson, erstwhile agent for Pennsylvania and a leading protagonist in the Currency Act repeal movement, took the post. Like Lamb before him, Jackson found no objection to a paper money act that scrupulously avoided any mention of legal tender. Hillsborough was of another

46. See "Mercator" in *Pa. Jour.*, Sept. 14, 1769.
47. *Pa. Archives*, VII, 6392, 6473; Jan. 30, 1770, *Col. Recs. Pa.*, IX, 648–649.
48. June 11, 1770, Carl Van Doren, ed., *Benjamin Franklin's Autobiographical Writings* (New York, 1945), 94.

mind. On July 13 he had the commissioners of trade call Jackson in for "some discourse," whereupon the new counsel promised to reconsider his original opinion. Five days later Jackson returned, with Franklin at his side acting as Pennsylvania's agent. The Board's position at the time was that the laws in question appeared "to relate merely to the internal economy of that province in matters no ways affecting the trade and commerce of this kingdom or His Majesty's authority or prerogative." Still the wording of the law struck the commissioners in some ways as inconsistent with the intent of the Currency Act of 1764. After consulting with the Board, however, Jackson announced that the measure was not contrary "either to the letter or the spirit of that act of parliament." The commissioners relented and offered no further objections. Neither did the Privy Council, which took no action at all on the matter.[49]

By mid-1770 the British government had made an important concession to American demands. Colonies falling under the Currency Act of 1764 could meet current and contingent expenses with new emissions of treasury notes receivable for all public debts—providing the enabling legislation dropped any reference to legal tender. British responses to three other currency emissions struck before 1770 helped to establish the new policy. The first was a large issue in South Carolina; the others, far smaller issues in North Carolina and Virginia.

SOUTH CAROLINA, 1764–1768

For nearly forty years South Carolina had a permanent fund of £106,500 of legal tender currency outstanding. It will be recalled that the law lacked any provision for the redemption of this money, though in time some of the notes got lost, became worn out, or were otherwise destroyed.[50] Thus in 1771 probably not more than £99,000 remained in circulation.[51] Because of such losses the legislature had replaced the entire issue from time to time, and late in August 1769 the Commons House authorized yet another reprint

49. This information may be found in Mitchell and Flanders, eds., *Statutes of Pa.*, VII, 617–626. The quote is from 626. Three months later Hillsborough learned from Gov. William Franklin that all Pennsylvania emissions were in effect tender at the treasury. Perhaps Hillsborough knew this already. More likely he did not, and one wonders if he had known, whether the Privy Council would have rejected the measures.

50. See the discussion in "Petitions for Repeal, 1766–1767," in chap. 4 above.

51. See table 7 in Appendix 1.

in an effort to return the full supply of lawful currency to the monetary stream. The reissue was prompted by the desperate shortage of cash that affected the fortunes of two major economic interests: the debt collectors for the great British mercantile houses trading to the colony and the commission merchants who dominated the staple trade in rice, indigo, lumber, naval stores, and certain other preferred commodities. "The situation of the Province is very distressful for want of a Medium of Trade," was the way one of the leading debt collectors, Peter Manigault, put it in the spring of 1769: "We have but little Currency and all the Gold and Silver is swallowed up by the new Duties. Bills of Exchange go a Begging, and there is nobody to purchase them. In short the Scarcity of Money is so great that they make 5 ½ per Cent difference between Ready Money and 3 Months Credit in the Sales of Rice. The stagnation here is surprising, for though our Rice has sold at a great Price not a fourth Part of it is paid for. . . . I heartily wish for better Times." [52] That summer commission merchant Henry Laurens declared himself to be so strapped for cash and so deeply in debt to the local rice factors and planters that he was considering a delay in plans to leave the colony for an extended trip to England. [53]

A monetary stringency seems to have developed sometime in the late fall of 1767. Following disastrously short grain crops in 1765, which led to greatly diminished commodity exports the following year, the assembly took the extraordinary step of actually banning rice shipments. The poor rice harvest partially accounted for the move, but more important was the failure of the corn crop. "There is no corn in the province," reported one merchant in June 1766, "and the planters are obliged to give their Negroes Rice, and it is imagined that there is not more Rice in the Country then will be consumed before the new Crops." [54] The upshot was that by late 1767 the unusually heavy demands for rice from grain-starved markets abroad gave the planters an opportunity to demand cash for

52. To Isaac King, May 1, 1769, Peter Manigault Letterbook, 1763–1773 (unpublished document in possession of Old Salem, Inc., Winston-Salem, N.C.; microfilm of typescript by Maurice A. Crouse).

53. To William Fisher, Aug. 10, 1769, Henry Laurens Letterbook, Papers of Henry Laurens, South Carolina Historical Society, Charleston. See also Laurens's letters to Fisher, Aug. 24, 1769; to John Tarleton, Sept. 25, 1769; to George Appleby, Sept. 26, 1769; and to William Cowles, Oct. 4, 1769, *ibid.*

54. Robert Hogg to Robert Sterling, June 9, 1766, Hogg and Clayton Letterbook. See also *Historical Statistics of the United States*, 767, Z262–266. Rice exports dropped nearly one-third in 1766.

their product instead of sterling bills of exchange and credit.[55] Bills were a bad commodity, Laurens remarked at the time, for they could only be sold at a heavy discount, if at all.[56] When demand and prices for rice continued favorable through 1768, the clamor for an adequate medium of local exchange reached alarming heights, a situation seriously aggravated by dull markets for British manufactures.[57]

Of far greater significance among the causes of the monetary pinch in the period was the effect of levying a prohibitory tax on slaves in 1766, 1767, and 1768. Negro imports declined from nearly seven thousand in 1766 to a mere trickle in the next couple of years.[58] The ban on slave imports meant that the planters who ordinarily invested heavily in slaves whenever the price of rice was up, and thereby channeled into circulation large amounts of cash, now had surplus funds on hand. Thus they enjoyed the unusual position of being creditors to the commission merchants.[59] "Our Planting Gentlemen," Laurens recorded late in 1768, were very much in the "ascendent" over the merchants and had gotten "most of the Currency hoarded in their Coffers." The situation was not hopeless, however. Laurens fully expected that the arrival of "a few Guinea Men" after January 1, 1769, when the prohibition of slave imports would be lifted, would "turn the Tables" on the planters. Money desperately needed in trade would quickly return to the stream of circulation. The planters were "full of Money," Laurens continued in a cynical vein, and if they could not lay out cash for Negroes they would only spend it "in Horse Races."[60]

55. The demand reflected, of course, not only the drop in rice exports in 1766 but also the general shortage of grain in European markets at the time.

56. See Laurens's letters to Henry Bright, Dec. 11, 1767; to James Habersham, Jan. 25, 1768; and to Edward Brice, Feb. 5, 1768, Laurens Letterbook.

57. See the entries for 1768 in Laurens Letterbook. To cite but a few of the more important examples, see the letters to James Habersham, May 27, 1768; to Dr. Andrew Turnbull, Nov. 14, 1768; and to Champignon and Brice, Nov. 22, 1768, *ibid.*

58. *Historical Statistics of the United States*, 770, Z303. The best general study of the subject of the slave trade is Kenneth W. Stetson, "A Quantitative Approach to Britain's American Slave Trade, 1770-1773" (M.S. thesis, University of Wisconsin, 1968).

59. On the relationship between the price of rice and slave purchases see, for example, Laurens's letters to William Stork, Nov. 21, 1767; to William Greening, Dec. 24, 1767; to William Fisher, May 28, 1768; to Ross and Mill, Sept. 2, 1768; and to Habersham, Nov. 17, 1768, Laurens Letterbook.

60. Laurens's letters to Turnbull, Nov. 14, 1768; to Habersham, Nov. 17, 1768; to Campbell and Hayes, Dec. 2, 1768; to James Harford, Dec. 19, 1768; to Ross and Mill, Dec. 24, 1768, *ibid.*

"Guinea ships" did arrive and in great numbers. Between January 1 and July 1 over four thousand Negroes were imported, as compared with an average of only two thousand yearly between 1756 and 1766.[61] Nevertheless, to the great dismay of the mercantile community, cash became even scarcer, while sterling bills were so plentiful that they sold for part cash and part credit on the longest of terms and at heavy discounts. Apparently, persistent heavy demands and high prices for rice and other commodities had simply outpaced the local supply of coin and paper currency, even though the purchase of slaves had indeed emptied the planters' coffers into the monetary system. In addition the rapid increase at the time in the backcountry trade only added to the pressure on money and quickly led to the development of a system of credit and barter exchange between the backcountry and the Charleston market.[62] In this situation it seemed more important than ever to get the full amount of the permanent fund of £106,500 lawful tender currency back into circulation. A final way to relieve conditions, of course, was to enter the association against the Townshend Acts, a course that, whatever its other advantages, also had the effect of plugging the drain on coin and easing the demand on paper.[63]

When the act for reprinting the £106,500 came before the Privy Council in November 1770, it was promptly disallowed. According to Garth the objections to the measure were many, though the inclusion of a clause making the money legal tender for all contracts, public and private, proved the most damaging. In his testimony before the Board of Trade, Garth had tried to counter that objection by presenting the measure as "a mere matter" of exchange and arguing that many Carolinians had already turned the old bills in for new ones. Nevertheless Board solicitor Jackson found the legal tender clause "repugnant" to the letter of parliamentary law. The crown agreed.[64]

Arrival of news of the royal veto in February 1771 provoked an immediate reaction in South Carolina. Laurens, for instance, viewed the disallowance as "downright Robbery." He thought that the money could not "with any colour of Justice be taken from us—

61. *Historical Statistics of the United States*, 770, Z303.
62. The analysis is based on figures in C.O. 16/1, P.R.O., the Laurens Letterbook, and conversations with H. Roy Merrens.
63. See, for example, *S.-C. Gaz.*, Mar. 2, 1769, and Leila Sellers, *Charleston Business on the Eve of the American Revolution* (Chapel Hill, N.C., 1934), 203–220.
64. Garth to S.C. Comm. of Corres., Nov. 24, 1770, Barnwell, ed., "Garth Correspondence," *S.C. Hist. Gen. Mag.*, XXXIII (1932), 118–119.

if the Repeal proceeds as some apprehend from mistake the Evil will soon be remedied—if from a Determination to Scourge us, we must fall upon ways to counteract the Attempt."[65] A method was indeed found to nullify the veto or rather to turn it to the advantage of the province. Before word of the disallowance reached South Carolina, the public treasurers had already replaced some £25,000 of the original emission and had destroyed £7,000. Obviously the net balance favored the province. Though the treasurers did obey the royal command after a fashion and later burned those new bills that came into their hands, they nevertheless also connived at keeping the replacement money in circulation as long as possible. They did so with the full approval of the Commons House.[66] In consequence by 1774 most of the reissued bills were reportedly still outstanding. Meanwhile the Commons House had pledged itself to redeem the new money at some future date. As for the individual house members, including many of the great Charleston merchants, they readily lent their support by agreeing to accept the money in common trade.[67]

Even before the South Carolinians learned of the failure of the act to reissue the £106,500, the Commons House had voted another currency emission of £70,000. The occasion was the building of the backcountry courthouses and jails provided by the circuit court act of 1769. Though political considerations were plainly involved in the move, it is probably no coincidence that the timing, in the spring of 1770, coincided with the onset of another period of monetary stringency. "I am so very poor," Laurens wrote in May of that same year, "that I am hardly able to get Cash enough in this time of uncommon Scarcity to pay my Butler and my Baker."[68] By the fall the situation was even worse. Laurens reported heavy demands for rice and the other major Carolina exports, large discounts on sterling

65. The quote is from Laurens to John Hopton, Jan. 29, 1771, Laurens Letterbook. See also the letters to Ashburner and Hind, Oct. 18, 1770; to Cowles, Jan. 15, 1771; to Reynolds, Feb. 4, 1771, *ibid.*

66. Bull to the secretary of state, Aug. 26, 1773, C.O. 5/380, P.R.O.

67. See Laurens to Hopton, Jan. 29, 1771, Laurens Letterbook, and the discussion in "South Carolina, 1770–1775," in chap. 10 below.

68. To L. MacKintosh, May 10, 1770, in Laurens Letterbook. For details leading up to the passage of the act see Joseph A. Ernst, "Growth of the Commons House of Assembly of South Carolina, 1761–1775" (M.A. thesis, University of Wisconsin, 1958), 63–94. From my point of view this is but another way in which the political leaders used the grievances arising out of the Regulator Movement to their own advantage. For a very different view of the matter see Richard Maxwell Brown, *The South Carolina Regulators* (Cambridge, Mass., 1963).

bills, and a growing scarcity of cash. "Our whole circulating Currency," he declared, "including a large computed Sum for Gold and Silver which are indeed become very scarce commodities, does not exceed one-fifth part of the amount of our crop of Rice and Indigo in the present year from December 1769 to December 1770."[69]

A circulating medium was obviously too valuable to defer issuing the £70,000 in treasury notes. Consequently the new currency law made no provision for a suspending clause. The measure did go to London for review, however, and once again the Board of Trade recommended a disallowance because the act specifically declared the money to be lawful for all public debts. But the wheels of administration moved slowly, and the crown only got around to vetoing the act in January 1772.[70] By then the money was spent and the buildings were nearing completion. As before the treasury made little effort to withdraw new currency from circulation; exports continued heavy at the time, and cash remained extremely short.[71] In the spring of 1775, when the issue was originally to have been sunk, some £35,000 remained outstanding.[72] The Carolinians had a way of squeezing as much as possible out of defeat.

NORTH CAROLINA, 1768–1770

In North Carolina a modest effort to increase the currency supply proved still more successful. In early November 1768, Governor Tryon confronted the members of the General Assembly with Hillsborough's discouraging response to their recent petition for a currency emission of £100,000. But by then the provincial government, with the active support of Tryon, had contrived to expand the currency supply in another way. Before the month was over the legislature voted a treasury issue of £20,000 to defray the costs of a recent expedition against the Regulators.[73]

69. To Reynolds, Getley, and Co., Sept. 20, 1770, Laurens Letterbook.
70. June 20, 1771, *Jour. of Comm. Trade, 1768–1775*, 261–262; Jan. 15, 1772, *Acts of Privy Council, Col.,* V, 319–320.
71. See Bull to secretary of state, Aug. 26, 1773, C.O. 5/380, P.R.O., and Laurens to Grubb, Sept. 5, 1772, Laurens Letterbook.
72. Mar. 1, 1775, Jours. of S.C. Commons House.
73. Accounts of the Regulation in North Carolina are legion. However, a definitive study has yet to be done. The best analyses of the movement that I have encountered are James B. Schick, "Regionalism and the Revolutionary Movement in North Carolina, 1765–1776: The Administrations of Governor William Tryon and Governor Josiah Martin" (M.S. thesis, University of Wisconsin, 1963), chap. 2, and Marvin L. Michael Kay, "The Institutional Background of the Regulation in

Though widespread civil disturbances had plagued the province for a number of years, it was not until the spring of 1768 that a voluntary organization centered in the northwestern counties and known as "the Mob" or "the Regulation" announced that it would stop the collection of all further taxes until satisfied that such levies were legal. Nor would members pay official fees other than those the law specifically allowed. Sheriffs, tax collectors, and other law officers were warned away. That April, after Regulators in Orange County "liberated" a mare distrained for nonpayment of taxes, the governor called out the militia and proclaimed the area to be in a state of insurrection. The threat of force encouraged a shift in Regulator tactics.

In small ways over the last few years Tryon had shown himself to be a friend to honest government. Consequently, when he suggested that the Regulators acquaint him with their problems, they willingly drafted a petition for redress of grievances. Their chief complaints concerned the extortionate fees and practices of local officials and the fear that the local tax collectors pocketed most of the taxes for themselves. An aggravating factor was the lack of money of any kind, which made it virtually impossible to pay taxes or fees, whether lawful or not. Likewise the seizure and public sale of property to cover delinquent payments was found to be especially burdensome because the monetary stringency had depressed property values. The inevitable result was the bankruptcy of the poor taxpayer and the enrichment of the "monied men," the local merchants and crooked officials who bought up valuable assets for a pittance. This was a development former governor Arthur Dobbs had warned against more than eight years before. In sum the Regulators rightly claimed to be suffering from a system of unlawful and heavy taxes, excessive fees charged by a corrupt bureaucracy, unwarranted and unwise seizures of property, the scarcity of a means of local exchange, and a freeze on assets.

Tryon proved sympathetic to the petition. After all, he too had complained of the want of money, and just the year before he had publicly aired the problem of the embezzlement of tax funds. On the other hand no governor could hold that any grievance, however just, gave cause for a subversive act against the public order and public safety. Tryon therefore advised the Regulators to begin

Colonial North Carolina" (Ph.D. diss., University of Minnesota, 1962). I have leaned heavily on both accounts in the following discussion.

promptly paying their taxes and to desist from further illegal acts. The practical effect of such advice was to further the spread of the movement into other back counties. Again the governor called out the militia, and again the Regulators petitioned for redress. This time Tryon seemed more conciliatory. That summer, after promising to punish all proven extortionists, the governor undertook a personal tour of the backcountry ostensibly to ease tensions and to learn about conditions firsthand. Actually Tryon's intention was to suppress what he could only see as a lawless rabble opposed to all government. He quickly gathered around him a volunteer army of some fifteen hundred, including many of the same corrupt officials that had caused the trouble in the first place, and for the moment the Regulators, who numbered about four hundred activists, fell silent. From his viewpoint Tryon had enforced the law and his authority at a small cost—about £5,000 currency and nothing in blood. The only difficulty was in finding a way to raise the £5,000.

That November the lower house responded to the recent display of violence with a ringing statement about the dire need for a new paper money issue to save the country from ruin. The legislators had just received the depressing news of the rejection of their petition for an additional £100,000 fiat money issue, and they argued that without a new source of funds it would prove impossible to pay the volunteers who had rallied to march against the insurgents.[74] Tryon agreed. And he hinted at the possibility of finding some "expediency" that should compensate the brave militiamen and still ease the payment of public and private debts.[75] Whatever scheme Tryon might have had in mind, the only "expediency" the house could think of was paper money. At a time when merchants reported a scarcity of coin, a slowness in payments, and a shortage of good sterling bills because of the slackening demand for the province's chief exports, it surprised no one when the legislature immediately began debating the merits of another currency appropriation to defray public expenses, including the cost of reimbursing the militia.[76]

In the meantime, in an effort to facilitate payment of public and private obligations pending passage of another currency measure, the lower house took a number of ancillary actions. It voted to make

74. Nov. 12, 1768, *Col. Recs. N.C.*, VII, 931.
75. Nov. 15, 1768, *ibid.*, 933–934.
76. This statement is based on my reading of the entries in the Hogg and Clayton Letterbook from the summer of 1767 through the summer of 1769.

foreign coin a lawful tender for all domestic transactions, passed a debtor-relief law to take effect in periods of monetary stringency, and provided for the importation of copper halfpence as legal tender for small obligations. As it turned out, however, the last two laws were subsequently disallowed—the debtor law on grounds that it prejudiced creditor interests and the currency measure on grounds that the intrinsic worth of such coins fell far below the assigned legal value and that the use of copper halfpence only opened the way to widespread counterfeiting.[77] As a final move in the direction of easing the demand for local means of trade, the legislators instructed the public treasurer, over the objection of the governor and Council (except for the Cape Fear men), to cease collecting taxes levied against the £32,000 paper currency issued in 1760 and 1761. The argument was that these levies had already achieved their purposes, and whether true or not, the resulting tax cuts did slow down the contraction of the existing supply of legal tender paper while taking the pressure off beleaguered taxpayers.[78] Despite initial objections to this violation of the provincial tax laws, Tryon in time relented. He had been mistaken in his original judgment. After all, money was short, and the move proved popular with the country. In 1770 he went so far as to consent to a measure indemnifying those sheriffs who had failed to make their tax collections after 1768.[79]

More significant than any of the various amelioratory measures taken at the time was the lower house reaction to the petitions that kept coming in from the back counties and the centers of Regulator activity. Even before the fall session began, popular opinion held that the people's chief complaints would be favorably received and their grievances redressed. Such was not altogether the case. For instance the petitioners from Halifax demanded either "an Act of Assembly to make more money" or a broad extension of the warehouse and inspection system and a provision for paying provincial and county taxes in commodities.[80] Given the choice, the legislature opted for more money. Lack of a staple in the backcountry, the difficulty of rating or imposing quality controls over a wide range

---

77. *Col. Recs. N.C.*, VII, 934, 941; Walter Clark, ed., *State Records of North Carolina*, XXIII (Raleigh, N.C., 1907), 781–782.

78. Tryon to Hillsborough, Feb. 10, 1769, July 2, 1770, *Col. Recs. N.C.*, VIII, 10, 211–212. See also *ibid.*, VII, 922, 924.

79. See the discussion in Weir, "North Carolina's Reaction to the Currency Act of 1764," *N.C. Hist. Rev.*, XL (1953), 191.

80. *Col. Recs. N.C.*, VII, 866–867; Tryon to Hillsborough, Dec. 24, 1768, *ibid.*, 884–886.

of products, and, most important, the control of government by eastern interests that demanded an increased paper money supply rather than an expanded system of commodity payments and inspectors' notes militated against any other move. As in South Carolina the groups in control of the lower house willingly used the Regulator movement to their own advantage. Without a boost in the use of commodity exchange and commodity notes, the house could and did argue that a fresh issue of paper served a wider community interest.[81]

After receiving an estimate of the costs of the Regulator expedition, the lower house rapidly completed a plan to emit £30,000 of "indentures," or debenture notes. Though the militia expedition "afforded a pretext of emitting Notes of Credit," the resulting measure was a catchall. It was to pay for the militia volunteers, provide for running a Cherokee boundary line, supply the frontier garrison at Fort Johnson, discharge the salaries of public officials for the years 1767 and 1768, furnish funds for a hemp bounty designed to ease the balance of payments, and, finally, allocate £10,000 to complete the so-called governor's "Palace."[82] But the Council balked. The house was attempting to issue more money than was needed, a ploy it had unsuccessfully tried some years before under similar circumstances. The councillors thought £20,000 sufficient to defray the various public expenses. So large a sum as the projected £30,000 might provoke a royal veto and jeopardize plans for a later currency issue that was specifically designed to supply an adequate circulating medium but that had to be preceded by a petition to Parliament. As for the £10,000 application for the governor's house, that money was already covered by existing legislation and was to be paid out of future tax collections. Paying it off in debentures would only violate the security of the original grant. Other conflicts between the two houses of the legislature involved the redemption period for sinking the issue, the proposed tax rate, and the Council's right to amend money bills. In stating its position, the Council made clear its desire to forego discussion of the rights and privileges of the respective houses. The various recommendations were to be taken as just that and were not to be viewed as formal amendments.[83]

81. Compare Ernst, "Growth of the Commons House of Assembly of South Carolina," chap. 4.
82. *Col. Recs. N.C.*, VII, 912–916; Samuel Johnston to Alexander Elmsley, Jan. 21, 1769, *ibid.*, VIII, 9.
83. *Ibid.*, VII, 915–916.

The lower house quickly satisfied the Council's major objections, and on December 1, 1768, a bill authorizing a £20,000 debenture issue passed both houses. It lacked only Tryon's signature to become law. But that signature was crucial, and the celerity and the apparent ease with which the house members had accommodated themselves to the wishes of the Council obscured the existence of a regional division in the legislature over the contradictory demands of political idealism and economic interest.

Sometime during the month of April that same year, Speaker of the House John Harvey had received a copy of the Massachusetts circular letter in connection with the Townshend Acts. Harvey had postponed action on the matter, however, until the legislature reassembled in November, when news of the circular and of Hillsborough's rejection of the currency petition became generally known. In some quarters strong feelings existed that the circular deserved prompt and prior attention. Nevertheless that question was laid aside while the house and Council hammered out a compromise measure for issuing debentures, which it was hoped would also command the governor's support. Only after the debenture bill was safely out of the way did the lower house take up the Massachusetts circular and on December 2 resolve to petition the crown for repeal of the Townshend duties.[84] But the debenture bill still lacked Tryon's signature, so the house carefully avoided taking the kind of forthright stand against the Townshend legislation that in other colonies had led to dissolution of the assembly and the termination of the public business. As for the circular, Harvey received only verbal instructions from the house to answer it at a later date.

Despite such political precautions, to everyone's consternation the governor rejected the debenture measure on December 3 as contrary to the Currency Act of 1764. The money, it seems, was to have some of the qualities of fiat money. Under the circumstances it is possible the assembly had believed that its moderate stand on the Townshend question would induce Tryon to overlook a violation of parliamentary law. Then, too, perhaps Tryon was being overly fastidious in his interpretation. In any event the governor promised his support only after the deletion of what he construed to be a legal tender provision. Significantly he did not see fit to dissolve the legislature in connection with the house response to the Massachusetts circular as demanded by Secretary Hillsborough. As he later explained the matter to the secretary, the "moderation"

84. *Ibid.*, 685–689, 917, 921, 931, 973.

of the lower house made it unnecessary even to prorogue the assembly until all the public business was concluded.[85]

Tryon had his way with the legislature. A member of the lower house reportedly rushed to the governor to find out his objections, after which the properly amended version of the currency bill was voted through the required three readings. As Samuel Johnston later remarked, while the £20,000 "are not a tender in payment," they would "answer the purposes and have the effect of a Currency."[86] Good as his word, Tryon then signed the bill into law. The governor was not above making a concession of his own, however. The suspending clause specifically required of such legislation by royal instruction was conspicuously missing. That Tryon nevertheless passed the measure required some explanation to the home authorities. According to the governor the omission was a matter of expediency; the province was in immediate and dire need of public funds to pay the militiamen. "On the one hand," the governor related, "I was sensible and it was no secret in the country that many of the volunteers, who stood up in arms in support of the laws of the country had declared if they did not get their services allowed by the General Assembly they would be as indifferent about Government as the insurgents, and that they would turn out no more in the same cause; on the other hand had these troops and Commissaries received no security for the discharge of their services it would have raised the hopes and expectations and much forwarded the intentions of the discontented through the whole government. It was therefore, my Lord [Hillsborough], on principles of public good and a sense of the justice due to the troops that my conduct was governed in this instance."[87]

That North Carolina's response to the Townshend Acts and the Massachusetts circular proved to be the most temperate of all the colonies was clearly attributable to the compromises and adjustments over the debenture bill. The Cape Fear representatives exemplified this when, after having provided the fiery leadership in the resistance to the Stamp Act, they simply deferred to the conservative Albemarle men in the protest against the Townshend Acts. The Cape Fear group wanted paper money. For the moment at

85. *Ibid.*, 979; Tryon to Hillsborough, Dec. 13, 1768, Jan. 10, 1769, *ibid.*, 880–881, VIII, 5.
86. Johnston to Elmsley, Jan. 21, 1769, *ibid.*, VIII, 9.
87. Tryon to Hillsborough, Jan. 10, 1769, July 2, 1770, *ibid.*, 6, 212.

least, abstract concepts of liberty had to give way to the concrete demands of the moment.[88]

In addition to striking a £20,000 debenture issue at the close of the year 1768, the lower house also renewed its application for "permission to emit a paper currency" as a lawful tender. To support the petition the house, albeit without approval of Council, finally gave Henry Eustace McCulloh the job he had long coveted, that of "Agent to this Colony." At the same time McCulloh received orders to join with the other colonial agents in working for repeal of the Currency Act.[89] If anything, the monetary pinch in North Carolina had become even more acute by 1769 following a fall in the price of naval stores and consequently in the supply of sterling exchange. Thus the small debenture issue only whetted local appetites for a far larger treasury emission.[90]

The petition and news of McCulloh's appointment arrived in London early the following summer. Notwithstanding his rejection by the Council, McCulloh decided to take up the agency. He warned his countrymen, however, that Hillsborough "is at present of opinion, that giving the American Assemblies a power to make their Notes a Tender is repugnant to the Idea of a Paper Circulation and highly improper." Others in the ministry, he had reason to believe, held a different view. But as minister for America, Hillsborough had great weight. Nevertheless McCulloh promised to "impress his Lordship with the reasons that make this circumstance necessary in your Paper Emissions; and further to shew that no injustice to any, but great good to all, would result from granting the liberty requested." In the meantime he would solicit the assistance of the merchants trading to North Carolina in obtaining a parliamentary dispensation for the colony alone from the provisions of the Currency Act of 1764. A general repeal was out of the question.[91]

McCulloh's unfavorable impression of Hillsborough's views on the paper money question proved quite correct. As early as mid-December 1768 Tryon had informed the secretary that the assem-

88. See the discussion in Schick, "Regionalism and the Revolutionary Movement in North Carolina," chap. 2.

89. John Harvey *et al.* to McCulloh, Dec. 12, 1768, *Col. Recs. N.C.,* VII, 878–879; Tryon to Hillsborough, Feb. 25, 1769, *ibid.,* VIII, 11–12.

90. Hogg to McGhie, June 26, 1769, to Sterling, July 1, 1769, in Hogg and Clayton Letterbook.

91. To Comm. of Corres. of the lower house, July 14, 1769, *Col. Recs. N.C.,* VIII, 56–57; to John Harvey, Jan. 26, 1770, *ibid.,* 172.

bly had renewed the petition for a currency emission.[92] But the following March, Hillsborough simply reiterated the position he had taken on the first petition. "The Commendable Conduct of the Assembly in the present disturbed situation of North America disposes His Majesty to shew them every indulgence in His Power," he wrote. But "you must however be sensible from what I have already wrote you upon the subject of Paper Currency, that it is not in His Majesty's Power to dispense with the Act of Parliament respecting the Legal Tender, and therefore no Petition that prays for Paper Currency as a Legal Tender can meet with the success you wish." He concluded by suggesting that the province learn from the experience of the New England colonies and of Maryland in establishing "a Paper Currency upon a just foundation of Credit without making it a legal Tender."[93]

Despite renewed rumors of an impending revision of the Currency Act of 1764, by the beginning of 1770 McCulloh had given up all hope of obtaining any kind of dispensation. Lord Hillsborough, he wrote home, "is your bitter enemy."[94] As if in confirmation the secretary wrote Tryon later that year that he considered the £60,000 or so then outstanding to "be fully sufficient to answer the purpose of circulation, until the prejudices of the People shall admit, and the circumstances of the Colony induce, a currency of better credit and greater stability."[95] Exchange rates at the time had fallen below par, while the treasury notes were widely counterfeited, a fact the governor had pointed to as a prime reason for a new replacement issue.[96]

News of Hillsborough's adamant stand on the currency question did not sit well with the newly elected assembly that met in the fall of 1769. Demands for an additional paper money supply were greater than ever, with petitioners to the lower house asking not only that no future tax be laid "in Money, until a Currency is made," but also that there be a public loan.[97] The new house would prove to be less tractable than the previous legislature.

By that autumn a political storm was gathering over the Virginia resolves of May 1769 that branded as tyrannical the recent par-

92. Dec. 13, 1768, *ibid.*, VII, 880–881.

93. Hillsborough to Tryon, Mar. 1, 1769, *ibid.*, VIII, 17–18.

94. "Extract of a letter from London, Dec. 6, 1769," *Pa. Jour.*, Mar. 22, 1770; McCulloh to John Harvey, Jan. 26, 1770, *Col. Recs. N.C.*, VIII, 172.

95. Oct. 3, 1770, *Col. Recs. N.C.*, VIII, 247.

96. To Hillsborough, July 2, 1770, *ibid.*, 212.

97. *Ibid.*, 76–78, 86–89.

liamentary proposal to try Americans accused of treason in English courts. And despite Tryon's hopeful news that if Americans everywhere remained calm the Townshend duties would soon be repealed, the lower house immediately adopted the resolves with only minor changes. In addition it prepared an address to the king roundly condemning the very suggestion of trying Americans in Britain and instructed McCulloh to have the document published in the English press. Visibly shaken by the turn of events, Tryon quickly dissolved the assembly in effort to put an end to such proceedings. But the house merely convened informally on its own authority and, after the fashion of the Virginia House of Burgesses, promptly entered into the association against the Townshend Acts.[98]

Clearly the assembly in 1769 had little in common with the legislature that had temporized over the Massachusetts circular letter the year before. The critical difference was that, with the possibility of obtaining a legal tender currency no longer likely, the Cape Fear "radicals" were again free to pursue the "disinterested and patriotic" course they had adopted at the time of the Stamp Act crisis.[99]

All during that time Hillsborough had pointedly refrained from commenting on the debenture act, which did not come before the Board of Trade until December 1770. By then the notes had been circulating "as freely as the proclamation money" for some time. The delay followed the death in late 1768 of the former solicitor to the Board, and no legal opinion became available until Richard Jackson took over the office in the spring of 1770. When the Board did review the act, it was accepted as a matter of necessity—as Tryon had anticipated. Still, as in the earlier case of the Pennsylvania issue, the feeling existed that apart from its aims the act was "certainly liable to objection." Existing records do not reveal the precise nature of the Board's misgivings, but they might well have had something to do with the provision for redeeming the £20,000. To be sure, the debentures were not specifically made lawful for public obligations. They would, however, obtain some degree of legal tender after June 10, 1772. On that day, and anytime during the following two years, anyone holding debentures could redeem them at the treasury for whatever lawful currency was on hand,

98. See the discussion in Schick, "Regionalism and the Revolutionary Movement in N.C.," chap. 1. See also *Col. Recs. N.C.*, VIII, 121–124, 134, 151, and *Cape-Fear Mercury* (Wilmington, N.C.), Nov. 24, 1769.

99. See the discussion in Schick, "Regionalism and the Revolutionary Movement in N.C.," chap. 1.

be it coin or paper. That the money was convertible into coin remained largely irrelevant. Coin was too useful and expensive an item normally to be paid into the treasury. But the desperate need for a means of local trade and the fact that the money was convertible into lawful paper guaranteed its continued circulation.[100]

Obviously the North Carolina plan represented another variation on the Maryland and Pennsylvania schemes. And the position of the Board of Trade and the ministry remained perfectly consistent with the policy laid down in July 1770 in connection with the treasury note emission in Pennsylvania.

VIRGINIA, 1767–1770

In Virginia the disruption of the money supply and the shaky condition of the public credit continued to be a major economic concern. Before the fall of 1765 these problems had centered on the spurt of sterling exchange rates to record highs, a consequence, it was later said, of the Robinson scandal and the massive glut of paper in the monetary stream. By the end of that year, however, the exchange market underwent a dramatic and sudden reversal. In response to several economic factors, including most notably the easing of the British credit crisis and the closing of the courts in connection with the Stamp Act, exchange rates tumbled to par, where they generally held until the end of the decade. Virginians were delighted. Though puzzled by the turn of events, they nonetheless viewed the falling rates as a clear sign that the public credit was on the mend. And they confidently expected that, as the paper currency supply continued to contract under the twin pressures of taxes and the forced payment of the Robinson debt, it was but a matter of time before credit would be fully restored to its "former Lustre."[101]

Currency did contract. In the spring of 1767 the House of Burgesses reported a drop in the circulation of treasury notes from a high in 1765 of possibly as much as £300,000 to a current low of some £205,000, including the approximately £100,000 owed by the Robinson estate. And exchange rates did remain at par.[102] But as quickly as cash supplies diminished, the demand for money in-

---

100. B.T. to Tryon, Dec. 12, 1770, *Col. Recs. N.C.*, VIII, 264–266.

101. See the discussion in chap. 6 above.

102. See table 6 in Appendix 1. Sterling bills were scarce; see the Corbin Letter-book for 1767.

creased in response to a gathering boom in wheat exports and the unusually heavy cash purchases of tobacco at the time. Money was reportedly becoming "exceeding scarce"—the "chief coin being bonds and promises"—with depressing effects not only on the commodities trade but also on the sale of British goods and the collection of local debts.[103] By the fall of 1767 the growing monetary stringency had been widely commented on, eliciting from one merchant, William Allason of Falmouth, Virginia, the remark noted earlier that "we shall in some time be as fond of having an assembly authorized by Parliament, to emit more paper money, as we was of some time ago of preventing it."[104]

Despite the increasing concern over the shortage of a local medium of exchange, no merchant, not even Allason, actually advocated an increase in the circulation of treasury notes. It was hard to shake off the impact of the Robinson scandal, which had only served to confirm the merchant community's worst fears about the ill effects of a surplus currency supply. After suffering in their pocketbooks from the former rise of exchange and then making considerable profits on the current fall, Virginia's merchants and factors were in no mood to tamper with the existing currency system.[105] They agreed with their colleague William Nelson, who early in 1768 informed his London suppliers that, "you really mistake me. You write as if you thought me one of those who are clamoring for Paper Money; I never liked it in my Life: and I would now rather Struggle with our Difficulties than have any more emitted. I have observed that when We have a large Quantity of Money in Circulation and it is easily obtained it serves only to promote and cherish that Spirit of Extravagance which hath been our Ruin. No I think the Man that could introduce and establish a new Spirit of Frugality, which alone can save us, would deserve more Thanks from us than if he were to make us a present of £200,000."[106] Likewise most merchants agreed with the collector of the quitrents, Richard Corbin, who a few months earlier had noted that "as exchange keeps

103. See the discussion in "Pennsylvania, 1767–1770," above in this chapter. See also Allason to his brother, Oct. 29, 1767, Allason Letterbook, Va. State Lib.; and L. Savage to John Norton, June 3, 1767, Norton-Savage Correspondence and Papers, 1757–1770, Box 18, Brock Collection, Huntington Library, San Marino, Calif.

104. Allason to his brother, Oct. 29, 1767, Allason Letterbook.

105. See the discussion in chap. 6 above. See also Savage to Norton, Aug. 27, 1767, Norton-Savage Correspondence.

106. To Capel, Osgood, and Hanbury, Feb. 27, 1768, Nelson Letterbook, Va. State Lib.

fluctuating between 25 and 27 percent it is pretty clear evidence that the present sum of existing currency [£200,000] is Nearly Sufficient for the Medium of business in this Country."[107] But neither Corbin nor the merchant community, whatever the state of exchange, felt any real need to keep that sum of paper in the monetary stream. Instead they tended to believe that creating a paper currency in the first place had largely helped "banish Gold and Silver from amongst us" and that as the present paper supply diminished "Specie in great plenty" would again return to normal circulation.[108]

In sum before the end of the decade the farthest that the merchants and factors of Virginia would go in interfering in the local paper money supply was to consent to a legislative move in the spring of 1768, taken at the request of acting Governor John Blair, for repealing the land and poll taxes for the current and following year. Even then the move was designed to relieve the heavy burden of taxes rather than the pressure on the currency supply.[109] The repeal after all only slowed the pace of taxing the existing treasury notes out of existence; by 1768 circulation was down to £170,000, and by November 1769 the sum had fallen to £130,000.[110] On the other hand, it should be noted that after the tumble of exchange rates in 1766 merchants who just a short while before had responded to the Robinson scandal by refusing to receive any outdated or overdue treasury notes in payment now gladly accepted any and all paper that fell into their hands. Not only was money of any kind increasingly hard to come by, but Robinson's successor at the treasury, Robert Carter Nicholas, facilitated such transactions by willingly exchanging all expired or torn notes that came to him for good bills bearing a later date or for specie when available. After the fall of 1769 matters were complicated because all Virginia paper had legally expired. Nonetheless slightly over £100,000 actually remained outstanding, owing, as Treasurer Nicholas delicately put it, to "the great Difficulties attending the Collection" of the debts due the Robinson estate and of the arrears of the public tax col-

107. To John Robert, May 15, 1767, in Corbin Letterbook, Col. Williamsburg Research Lib.

108. Corbin to John Robert, May 15, 1767, *ibid.*

109. Savage to Norton, Feb. 13, 1768, in Norton-Savage Correspondence; William Dabney to Edward Ambler, Apr. 6, 1768, Dabney Papers, 1744–1940, So. Hist. Coll., Univ. of N.C. Lib., Chapel Hill; *Jours. of Burgesses, 1766–1769*, 158; William Zebina Ripley, *The Financial History of Virginia, 1609–1776* (New York, 1893), 41.

110. Table 6 in Appendix 1.

lectors. And as Nicholas further noted, the General Assembly made no move to impose new taxes. In addition the mercantile community conspired to keep the overdue notes out of treasury hands and in circulation. "Most of the merchants as well as others," Nicholas explained, were aware of the scarcity of money and "sensible of the Goodness of the Foundation, on which the Security of these Notes is established and have generally . . . preferred them either to Gold or Silver, as being more convenient for transacting the internal Business of the Country."[111] The expired notes continued to pass current. Ironically a half-dozen years earlier these same merchants had called for stricter controls over the redemption of the existing currency supplies.[112]

Not all members of Virginia society faced the gradual shrinking of the currency with such equanimity. A series of short tobacco crops in the late sixties had reduced production by a third or more and cut deeply into the profits of many a planter, especially in the tidewater, where some crop yields had fallen as much as two-thirds. In the piedmont, by contrast, overall production seems to have increased.[113] In addition, though the easing of the British financial crisis after 1765 had led to an increased flow of trade goods to Virginia and hence the reestablishment of business credit by Scottish and English suppliers, new credit was not so readily available to the planters as it had been before the great financial collapse in 1762. Instead British merchant-creditors began consciously to bond their old debts in Virginia in an effort to better protect their investments while continuing to press for payment, although somewhat more gently than earlier.[114] Under the circumstances, then, a number of hard-pressed tobacco planters joined with the Robinson sureties to renew demands for the establishment of a loan office. A public loan still offered the sureties and the indebted planters the best chance

111. Nicholas in Purdie and Dixon's *Va. Gaz.*, July 16, 1773, in "Paper Money in Colonial Virginia," *WMQ*, 1st Ser., XX (1911–1912), 234–235.
112. See chap. 3 above.
113. Terrence L. Mahan, S.J., "Virginia Reaction to British Policy, 1763–1776" (Ph.D. diss., University of Wisconsin, 1960).
114. Compare Hemphill, ed., "John Wayles," *VMHB*, LXVI (1958), 305, and *William Jones, surviving partner of Farrell and Jones* v. *Richard Taylor, surviving partner of Taylor, Neusam, and Wray*, U.S. Circuit Court Record Book, 2, B, Va. State Lib. I am indebted to Harold Gill of the Colonial Williamsburg Research Department for calling the Farrell and Jones correspondence to my attention. The two sources cited above provide the single best guide to an understanding of the credit problems in Virginia between 1765 and 1772.

of meeting overdue obligations and finding the necessary cash to help shift their investments from tobacco to wheat—or to some other more salable commodity.

In the spring of 1766 Richard Bland, who at the time aspired to succeed Robinson as Speaker of the House of Burgesses, had written Richard Henry Lee about a scheme for a loan office or "public bank," which in a very few years would enable Virginians to settle their own accounts and to "discharge the public debts and expences, without any tax for the future."[115] Details still had to be worked out, but the plan was to be made available by the next assembly session. Either Bland was not ready in time for the fall meeting or he dropped his plan altogether after losing his bid for the Speakership. In any event it appears to have received no further mention. Bland's was not the only bank plan discussed in the period, however. Thus London merchant Robert Cary also communicated thoughts "on the establishment of a Virginia Bank" early in 1766 to Richard Corbin. Certainly no friend to paper money, Corbin nonetheless seems to have thought well of the idea, for he wrote back that "something must be done to restore Credit, and I think a Scheme may be formed from your plan, effectually to answer the desireable purpose." Whatever its merits, the Cary scheme, like Bland's, seems to have been lost in the growing "Confusion" over the Robinson scandal.[116]

Not until the spring of 1767 did the House of Burgesses move to create a public bank. And then it was "chiefly the Securities of the late Speaker who proposed it," not Bland or someone connected with Corbin or Cary.[117] On April 7, 1767, the Burgesses resolved to petition the king for relief from the scarcity of a local circulating medium, which was having such bad effects on business. Under present conditions, the house protested, trade was dangerously obstructed, the poor liable to "very dangerous oppressions," and commodity values much diminished. Soon the dominion would be unable to pay heavy balances owed to Britain. Four days later the Burgesses voted to establish a loan office.[118]

While similar in purpose and outline to the scheme proposed in 1765, the 1767 measure differed greatly in its details. In general, however, it was but another variation on the Maryland loan office of

115. Bland to Lee, May 22, 1766, Revolutionary Lee Papers, Alderman Lib., Univ. of Va.

116. Corbin to Cary and Company, July 16, 1766, Corbin to Roberts, Dec. 22, 1766, Corbin Letterbook.

117. Savage to Norton, Aug. 24, 1768, Norton-Savage Correspondence.

118. Apr. 7, 11, *Jours. of Burgesses, 1766–1769,* 128–129.

1733. The central idea was that as soon as Virginia could obtain crown permission—which the Burgesses hoped to do before the next spring— £200,000 currency was to be lent out "on sufficient security" at 5 percent annual interest. To preserve the credit of its paper, Virginia would borrow from British merchants some £100,000 sterling, also at 5 percent, to be paid off by means of an additional duty of two shillings sterling on exported tobacco. The principal was to be sunk in three five-year installments beginning in April 1773. In case of any deficiency the Burgesses pledged the public faith to make it good.[119]

A difficulty quickly arose when the Council would not give its support to the plan. As William Nelson, the merchant and councillor, wrote to his British correspondent John Norton, "You will observe that the Council did not join in it. Why? Because they did not like it, and why did they not like it? Why, because they thought it was designed to serve a few (or rather not a few) improvident men who ran in debt whilst they could get credit and they likewise thought it unjust to load the whole country with taxes to answer the purpose of the comparatively few; besides, they thought it too soon again to mortgage their estates, after having just emancipated themselves and posterity from the state of bondage to pay off the debt contracted by the last war." As to the question of the additional taxes needed to finance the loan, Nelson declared, "I think that the benefits which ought to be expected from a general taxation of a country ought to be defusive and general, or it will not be just; however, the Council not agreeing, did not discourage the other House from recommending it to the agent; in hopes I suppose, that if the money could be procured, they might hereafter be brought over, in which I persuade Myself they would be mistaken."[120] Nelson might also have added that the merchant community greatly feared a recurrence of the rise in exchange rates that had plagued the colony in the early sixties.[121]

Notwithstanding the Council's action, the Burgesses went ahead to have the colonial agent petition the king for approval of the bank and to sound out the British merchants trading to Virginia about the possibility of extending the sterling loan necessary to underwrite the

119. *Ibid.*, 125–128.

120. Aug. 27, 1768, Frances Norton Mason, ed., *John Norton and Sons: Merchants of London and Virginia* ... (Richmond, Va., 1937), 66–67.

121. See, for example, Savage to Norton, Aug. 27, 1767, Norton-Savage Correspondence.

issue. But the British merchants showed no great interest in the project, while the Board of Trade upon receiving the request in June 1768 rejected it forthwith. The commissioners judged it improper to consider any document lacking the support of the upper house of the Virginia legislature.[122]

Refusals at home and in London to countenance a public loan seem to have discouraged the Robinson debtors and their planter allies from further action, and nothing more was done on the matter, although proposals for loans kept popping up in the pages of the *Virginia Gazette*. For the next couple of years schemes for improving the economy turned instead on the need to redress adverse trade balances with Britain.[123] True, a few Virginians persisted in their advocacy of a larger currency supply, but the memory of the Robinson scandal was still too fresh in everyone's mind to win much public support for the scheme, such as that expressed in other colonies at the time. Rather the favored means for accomplishing the revival of the economy were: cutting back the purchase of British manufactures; exploiting new markets through the diversification of agriculture; producing new and selected raw materials; encouraging secondary production of such items as flour and breadstuffs; manufacturing cheap cloth to replace British dry goods; prohibiting slave imports, and developing local cooperative stores to beat down the high prices of British goods.[124]

There was even talk of totally reorienting the local economy by accelerating the shift out of tobacco and into foodstuffs through the creation of a highly commercialized urban marketplace. The idea was to lessen the dependence on resident British merchants and factors, especially the hated Scottish storekeepers, through the establishment of great urban-commercial hubs, like Philadelphia (a city already engrossing a large part of the booming Virginia wheat trade), which were thought to be in themselves a major spur to economic growth. This was far easier said than done, of course, though the later efforts of George Washington and other Virgin-

122. Apr. 11, 1767, *Jours. of Burgesses, 1766–1769*, 129; May 31, June 3, 10, 1768, *Jour. of Comm. Trade, 1768–1775*, 29–32, Savage to Norton, Aug. 24, 1768, Norton-Savage Correspondence.

123. See, for example, Rind's *Va. Gaz.*, Mar. 3, 1768. This question of trade balances needs to be carefully explored. See the discussion in chap. 1 above.

124. These generalizations are drawn for the most part from my reading of the *Va. Gaz.* for the years 1766 through 1772. Historians familiar with such schemes have with few exceptions dismissed them as mere political weapons employed at the time of the crisis over the Stamp Act and the Townshend duties.

ians to locate Washington, D.C., in the Chesapeake were very much an outgrowth of such thinking.[125] In fact, although all the various schemes and remedies appeared worthwhile, they produced few material results. The one important economic action taken at the time, the setting up of a nonimportation movement associated with the Townshend Acts, was designed at best to produce only temporary economic relief and at first was aimed for the most part at the ailing tobacco planters. That the outcome proved disheartening as compared with similar efforts in the north—the Virginia merchants actually increased the volume of goods purchased in the period—was proof of the ready availability of British credit.[126]

What is most significant about the contemporary debate over monetary expansion and the other economic remedies in the period is the conscious awareness of the need for constructive economic change. At bottom this awareness was perhaps more a result of the boom in the wheat trade at the end of the 1760s than of the short-term slump in tobacco production and exports. It would not be incorrect to say that Virginia by 1770 had virtually two separate economies—one wheat, and the other tobacco. The spread of what might conveniently be called the "Wheat Belt" into Virginia after the middle of the eighteenth century is a matter of some importance to students of colonial economic history. Nonetheless it is hardly mentioned in the literature. In the absence of any adequate summary, only a bare and tentative outline of the subject can be sketched in here.[127]

Doubtless the spread of the "Wheat Belt" into Virginia and its subsequent growth resulted mainly from the settlement and expansion of the piedmont after the 1730s. In tidewater Virginia, on the other hand, the evidence suggests that it was not until the severe depression in the tobacco trade in the mid-1750s that the planters seriously attempted to shift to new market crops such as indigo, hemp, and, to a lesser extent at first, wheat. But poor crops, poor techniques, or poor markets—or some combination of such factors—plus a revival of the tobacco trade after 1759 quickly led to the

125. See, for example, Purdie and Dixon's *Va. Gaz.*, Mar. 22, 1770. Kenneth Bowling of the University of Wisconsin is presently preparing a study of the Washington, D.C., question.

126. The best discussion of the economic aspects of the nonimportation movement is to be found in Thomson, "Merchant in Virginia," 319–339.

127. The following discussion of the growth of Virginia's wheat production is based almost entirely on Saladino, "Maryland and Virginia Wheat Trade." See also Soltow, *Economic Role of Williamsburg*, 77–98.

abandonment of nearly all such experiments.[128] Indigo seems to have been dropped early in the 1760s. In the case of hemp Virginia soon became the leading colonial producer, a negligible achievement when it is considered that exports averaged hardly more than five thousand tons annually.[129]

Wheat production, by contrast, increased steadily in response to favorable European market conditions. By the 1760s the progress of wheat cultivation in Virginia had caught the attention of newspaper commentators on both sides of the Atlantic. Similarly the somewhat slower growth of flour milling led Lieutenant Governor Fauquier to report to the Board of Trade in 1766 that the Virginians "daily set up Mills to grind their wheat and the flour for exportation."[130] After that year the quantum jump in demand for American grain and flour from British and southern European markets seems to have spurred Virginia's wheat producers to prodigious efforts. At the end of the decade the colony's wheat exports exceeded that of Maryland, and in 1770 Roger Atkinson, a leading tidewater merchant, would declare that "the article of wheat, a kind of second staple, is a prodigious addition. . . . It will enrich the people and add greatly to the value of the land."[131] Two years later, he wrote that "We have now got another staple . . . viz. Wheat, which will, I believe in a little time be equal if not superior to Tobacco. . . . We shall in a few years make more in Virginia than all the provinces of Pennsylvania put together."[132]

Thus by the 1760s towns that in earlier periods had owed their very existence to the tobacco trade—Fredericksburg, Alexandria, Petersburg, and Norfolk—were turning more and more to wheat. In a parallel development the local Scottish factors and storekeepers, who just a few decades before had trafficked so heavily in tobacco, also began to diversify their operations and move into the wheat trade. A few even severed their connections with their British masters to become indigenous produce merchants. In the absence of a warehouse system for wheat, backcountry stores readily served to

128. For a brief discussion of Virginia's indigo production see Coulter, "Virginia Merchant," chap. 5.

129. On Virginia hemp production see George M. Herndon, "The Story of Hemp in Colonial Virginia" (Ph.D. diss., University of Virginia, 1959).

130. Fauquier to B.T., Dec. 17, 1766, C.O. 5/1331, P.R.O.

131. To James Hicks, Sept. 4, 1770, Roger Atkinson Letterbook, 1769–1776, Alderman Lib., Univ. of Va. (microfilm available at Col. Williamsburg Research Lib.).

132. To Lyonel and Hyde, Aug. 25, 1772, *ibid.*

collect grain and other produce from throughout Virginia—and to some extent from neighboring North Carolina and Maryland as well. The center of the new trade was the port of Norfolk, which as early as 1763 drew from Fauquier the remark that the town had "almost wholly engrossed the West India and Grain Trade." The reason, according to merchant Neil Jamieson, was that "the Expence of Country freight was lower to Norfolk than from one River to another, so that by loading at Norfolk when the Cargo laid in different Rivers, was cheaper and Sooner performed than if the ship lay in any other part of the Country."[133] Norfolk was by no means independent of outside control, however, and local merchants purchased quantities of wheat for houses in Philadelphia, the chief grain and flour market in North America.[134] So conscious were the Virginians of both their dependency on that northern city and of the growing importance of their "second staple" that articles soon appeared in the *Virginia Gazette* decrying the connection, bemoaning the loss of profits, and stressing the need to build a local and competitive metropolitan hub before the dominion fell prey to the Philadelphia merchants as it had earlier fallen prey to the great tobacco houses of London, Glasgow, and Liverpool.[135]

The failure of the public loan in 1767 led to a hiatus in the debate over money. But the boom in wheat, the continuing heavy cash purchases of tobacco, the slump in the sale of British goods, the persistent difficulties in collecting debts, and the gradual contraction of the currency supply soon combined to increase the strains on the existing supply of money to the breaking point.[136] By late 1769 sterling exchange rates had slipped below par, and a number of the larger merchants left the province for Philadelphia to sell their bills of exchange for coin. They came back to the South empty-handed, for there was no hard money to be had. The expanded grain trade in the middle colonies had greatly increased the domestic demand for

133. The Fauquier quotes are from Saladino, "Maryland and Virginia Wheat Trade," 30; The Jamieson quote is from Soltow, *Economic Role of Williamsburg*, 90. For additional information about Norfolk see *ibid.*, 79, 89, 96, 183–185. For an important discussion of this development see also Robert Spoede, "William Allason: Merchant in an Emerging Nation" (Ph.D. diss., College of William and Mary, 1973).

134. See especially Soltow, *Economic Role of Williamsburg*, 86–88, and Saladino, "Maryland and Virginia Wheat Trade," 74–75.

135. See, for example, Purdie and Dixon's *Va. Gaz.*, Mar. 22, 1770.

136. This statement is based on my reading of Virginia's mercantile correspondence cited in chaps. 3, 6, and 7 of the present study.

coin to cover the heavy purchases of wheat from local farmers.[137] Not surprisingly therefore, by the end of the decade Virginia's merchants, or a large part of them, suddenly changed their minds and along with the planters opted for an additional if moderate issue of treasury notes. In December 1769 the House of Burgesses won the approval of the Council and the new governor, Lord Botetourt, for a treasury issue of £10,000. A small part of the money was to be used to survey a boundary line between Virginia and the Cherokee territory; an even smaller part was to go towards defraying the costs of importing £2,500 in copper coin as small change in the retail trade, a matter of some concern to the local merchants and factors. The new notes were slated to be redeemed within the short period of two years by a duty on imported slaves and a tax on carriages, ordinary licenses, writs, petitions, tobacco, and caveats. Because no suspending clause was attached, the short-lived act would become effective immediately. And among such persons as were willing to receive it, the money would "pass current." Nothing was said about the notes being lawful for public debts, though in Virginia as elsewhere the treasury customarily accepted the money in discharge of all public obligations, a practice agreeable to the various economic groups.[138] Meanwhile the newspapers once more began to carry a number of letters raising anew the question of the need for a public loan. That solution to the monetary stringency continued to be rejected, however, as far too extreme. It would, it was felt, threaten the exchange market.[139]

Virginia's new currency act came before the Board of Trade late

137. Allason to his brother and John Gray, May 2, 1769, Allason Letterbook; Piper to Dixon and Littledale, Jan. 7, 1769, Harry Piper Letterbook, 1767–1776, Alderman Lib., Univ. of Va. (microfilm available at Col. Williamsburg Research Lib.; Edward Stabler to Israel Pemberton, Dec. 15, 1768, Pemberton Papers, XX, 1768–1769, Hist. Soc. Pa., Philadelphia.

138. Hening, ed., *Statutes of Va.*, VIII, 343–348. See also Nicholas to Purdie and Dixon's *Va. Gaz.*, July 16, 1773, in "Paper Money," *WMQ*, 1st Ser., XX (1911–1912), 236–237, and *Jours. of Burgesses, 1766–1769*, 353. In Mar. 1773 some £6,800 were still circulating. As for the copper coin, Botetourt promised to use "all his interest" to obtain it, but as long as Hillsborough remained president of the Board of Trade and secretary of state, permission to import the "coppers" was held up. The request was finally granted under Lord Dartmouth, and some five and one-half tons of half pennies was put into circulation as lawful tender for small debts in Feb. 1775. See Mason, ed., *Norton and Sons*, 115, 205, 230–231, 236, 244–245, 265–267, 272, 287–288, 313–314, 332, 336, 342, 344, 352, and 378.

139. See, for example, Rind's *Va. Gaz.*, Mar. 6, Apr. 26, June 7, 14, 1770. These issues of the *Va. Gaz.* are most important for an understanding of the complicated ties between the economic boycott associated with the Townshend duties and the serious concern over the long- and short-run problems of the Virginia economy.

in November 1770. After only brief consideration the commissioners recommended it for disallowance because of the excessive duty on imported Negroes. Between 1755 and 1769 the battle over the restriction of slave imports had seesawed back and forth between Virginia's larger and smaller planters, with the great slaveholders anxious to restrict the expanding production of their rivals in the tobacco industry. Then in an attempt to secure the £10,000 treasury issue of 1769 the Burgesses added 5 percent to the existing 10 percent duty on African slaves. Six months later the merchants of Lancaster and Liverpool vigorously protested this latest move on the part of "sinister" men to discourage "this valuable branch of commerce" and to interfere with "the general good." Both the Board and the Privy Council supported the petitioners' view, and in December 1770 the king in Council sent additional instructions to the Virginia governor forbidding any increase in the duty on slaves above 10 percent. In addition to the tax question an objection was raised to the lack of a suspending clause. Still the crown permitted the currency act to stand, if only because it had already been in operation for twelve months and had but another year to go. Nothing was said about paper money.[140] As for the issuance of the £10,000, it did little to relieve the dearth of cash in Virginia, and as will be seen, in only a short while the dominion again turned to the printing press and to the paper money expedient.

Between 1768 and 1770 Secretary Hillsborough and the Board of Trade made a concerted effort to tighten British monetary policy by enforcing what they took to be the letter of the Currency Act of 1764. Colonies could still issue paper money. But it could not be made a legal tender for any payments, public or private. Such a system was of course possible in theory. Even without any other means of security, the great demand for a circulating medium in these years, as a number of observers pointed out, would probably have sustained paper currency values. In practice the new policy threatened an existing arrangement whereby the colonies typically met their public expenses by issuing treasury notes in anticipation of future taxes payable in the notes of issue. This had the double advantage of creating a use and therefore a demand for the money and

140. Nov. 7, 14, 1770, *Jour. of Comm. Trade, 1768–1775*, 209–210, and Dec. 9, 1770, in *Acts of Privy Council, Col.*, V, 286–288. An excellent discussion of the economic interests behind the fracas over slave imports is to be found in Coulter, "Virginia Merchant," chap. 5.

of providing a method to secure its ultimate redemption. To inspire confidence in a system so susceptible to political abuses, the assemblies regularly made their treasury notes lawful for all public obligations. Holders of the notes had a kind of warranty from the government.

In effect, while Hillsborough accepted the need for a system of "currency finance," he was working to cancel the warranty. In his zeal to eliminate all legal tender clauses and, in the long run, to place the credit of paper money on another foundation altogether, the secretary helped knock out an essential prop to the credit of paper money. Consequently the colonists carefully rewrote their warranties around the letter of the law and forced the reluctant Hillsborough to give the practice his stamp of approval.

Part *Three*
Revising the Law
1770-1775

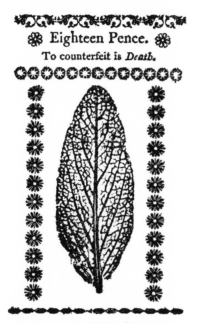

Eighteen Pence.
To counterfeit is *Death.*

Burlington in NEW-JERSEY,
Printed by Ifaac Collins, 1776.

Chapter 8

The Currency Act of 1770
The Loan Office Question
in New York and New Jersey

Heavy demands for military aids and the rapid growth of a market economy had led to the development in America of an uncertain and inefficient monetary system. Made up of unequal parts of paper currency, coin, promissory notes, bonds, bills of exchange, and book credit, its only recommendation was that it worked. When therefore the Currency Act of 1764 threatened to choke off the supply of fiat money to the area south of New England, the colonies affected fought back to preserve an essential element in a familiar if complex system. Later, following an unsuccessful attempt to repeal the act, they bent their efforts toward circumventing it. In one way or another, by 1770 most had managed to issue small amounts of treasury notes that, while not a legal tender, were still receivable for public debts. In time the Board of Trade came to accept this makeshift practice as consistent with the letter, though perhaps not the spirit, of the Currency Act of 1764.

In comparison with the other provinces, Maryland, New York, and New Jersey had opted instead for a public loan. This had the added advantage of providing a source of badly needed credit as well as currency. In Maryland a proposal in November 1769 for a $300,000 loan to facilitate local trade met with scant opposition.[1] The commissioners of trade and the secretary of state chose to overlook the fact that the new bills were specifically made a legal tender for all loan office obligations. That response contrasted sharply with

1. *Md. Archives*, LXI, 53–54, 65, 69–70, 118, 133–151.

the opposition of those same officials to a similar move in New York and New Jersey.[2]

British resistance to public loans in New York and New Jersey served to spotlight the contradictions in the official interpretation and handling of the Currency Act of 1764 and the ambiguity of the law itself. It also testified to the persistence of earlier royal policies. Following the passage of the Currency Act of 1751, the Board of Trade had sought to use royal instructions and the suspending clause as a means of extending throughout America the limitations on the volume, tender, and tenure of paper money that applied to New England. Focused on New York and New Jersey, this drive was blunted by the French and Indian War.[3] Military claims had precedence over monetary controls, and in support of the fighting the two colonies issued paper without let. After the war and the passage of the Currency Act of 1764, the Board simply revived its earlier policies for use as a yardstick in rejecting the creation of the public loan offices.

In 1770 Parliament abruptly revised the Currency Act and authorized New York to issue £120,000 on loan as legal tender for all debts. Though unexpected, the amendment reflected no break with old principles. Instead it was a pragmatic response to a postwar depression and monetary stringency in New York that preceded and then merged with a local political crisis. The same money question also became ensnared in the tangled web of local economic and political issues in neighboring New Jersey. Results were not the same.

MONEY AND ECONOMICS IN NEW JERSEY, 1762–1767

Though a tributary of Philadelphia and New York, the New Jersey economy nevertheless escaped some of the economic squalls that struck the northern seaboard cities after 1762. To be sure, the province shared in the general financial distress of the area. The shortage of British credit and the rapid contraction of the heavy wartime stock of coin in the neighboring ports created a vacuum that quickly siphoned off specie supplies in New Jersey. Even so the province was in a relatively better financial position than her larger neighbors. With one of the smallest populations in America, New Jersey emerged from the war with over a quarter of a million

2. See the discussion in chap. 5 above.
3. See Keyes, "New Jersey Paper Currency," chaps. 8–9.

pounds of fiat money in circulation. Issued for periods up to twenty years, the currency was to be taxed out of existence at the gradual rate of some £15,000 annually, beginning in 1763. But despite the reported scarcity of coin and despite short crops in 1761 and 1762, the province was not really in bad shape. At war's end commodity production was still down, but crop prices were high and land "advanced in value." Consequently, when news of the Currency Act arrived in mid-1764, New Jersey had less reason for immediate concern than did her neighbors. Nonetheless any curb on fiat money issues was seen as "a very great provincial hardship" that would ultimately cramp trade, impede settlement, and obstruct the king's service "upon any future Emergency."[4]

By 1765 the drain on cash had begun to depress real estate values of every kind. Assets had suddenly become nonliquid, and defaulting debtors filled the local jails. "There is such a general scarcity of Cash that nothing we have will Command it," New Jersey resident

4. The quote on crop and land prices is from J. W., *An Address to the Freeholders of New-Jersey, on the Subject of Public Salaries* (Philadelphia, 1763), no. 9532 in Charles Evans's *American Bibliography*. There is no economic history of colonial New Jersey. Much useful information, however, may be gleaned from Sachs, "Business Outlook"; Sachs, "Agricultural Conditions in the Northern Colonies before the Revolution," *Jour. Econ. Hist.*, XIII (1953), 274–290; Donald L. Kemmerer, *Path to Freedom: The Struggle for Self-Government in Colonial New Jersey, 1703–1776* (Princeton, N.J., 1940); Samuel Smith, *The History of the Colony of Nova-Cæsaria, or New-Jersey...* (Burlington, N.J., 1765); Leonard Lundin, *Cockpit of the Revolution: The War for Independence in New Jersey* (Princeton, N.J., 1940); Wheaton J. Lane, *From Indian Trail to Iron Horse: Travel and Transportation in New Jersey, 1620–1860* (Princeton, N.J., 1939); and Francis Bazley Lee, *New Jersey as a Colony and as a State: One of the Original Thirteen* (New York, 1902), I–II. Useful local histories include Joseph S. Sickler, *The History of Salem County, New Jersey...* (Salem, N.J., 1937), which has a good discussion of the Wistar glass works and Salem trade; William Shaw, *History of Essex and Sussex Counties* (Philadelphia, 1884); William A. Whitehead, *Contributions to the Early History of Perth Amboy and Adjoining Country, with Sketches of Men and Events in New Jersey during the Provincial Era* (New York, 1856); Carl Raymond Woodward, ed., *Ploughs and Politics: Charles R. Read of New Jersey and his Notes on Agriculture* (New Brunswick, N.J., 1941); Lucius Q. C. Elmer, *History of the Early Settlement and Progress of Cumberland County, New Jersey, and of the Currency of This and Adjoining Colonies* (Bridgeton, N.J., 1869). The paper currency question receives inadequate treatment by Kemmerer in his article "A History of Paper Money in Colonial New Jersey, 1668–1775," N.J. Hist. Soc., *Procs.*, LXXIV (1956), 106–130. Far better is the account by Keyes, "New Jersey Paper Currency." Specialists will also want to look at Miriam R. Waxberg, "Money in Morris County, 1763–1782," N.J. Hist. Soc., *Procs.*, LIII (1935), 20–26, and Edward A. Fuhlbruegge, "New Jersey Finances during the American Revolution," *ibid.*, LV (1937), 167–190. On the reported shortage of cash at the war's end see Stayce Potts to John Stayce, Dec. 12, 1763, in *Journal of American History*, III (1908), 99.

James Parker explained in November. "Debtors that were a year or two ago responsible for £1,000 can not now Raise a fourth part of the sum and those who had putt out their money upon Land Security of double the Value are unable to get the principal as there is an Entire Stop to all sales by the sheriff for want of Buyers." Men of the best estates could barely maintain themselves, while country stores were "all shutt up," the proprietors "either broke or obliged to decline that Business from a Real Inability to carry on which obliges the farmers to supply their familys as far as they are able with our own Manufactures." Parker concluded that it was impossible to "describe the distress."[5] "Discontent was painted in every man's face," added Cortlandt Skinner, an assembly leader of the Perth Amboy faction and sometime Speaker of the house, "and the distress of the people was very great from an amazing scarcity of money."[6]

The reasons for the shortage of money and the accompanying collapse of realty values seem clear enough. An adverse trade balance with its two major entrepôts at Philadelphia and New York drained New Jersey of quantities of commodities, coin, bills of exchange, promissory notes, and bills of credit. Although Jersey's paper money was not lawful beyond the confines of the province, neighboring merchants and land speculators who dealt in the produce, lands, and industries of New Jersey always had a ready market for its paper currency.[7] Even in normal periods the neighboring provinces sluiced off as much as one-third of New Jersey's paper currency supply.[8] And at tax time many Jerseyites had to obtain their provincial notes in New York and Philadelphia in order to meet obligations at home.[9] A more important indication of the colony's regional status was that western New Jersey's sterling ex-

5. Quoted in Kemmerer, "Paper Money," N.J. Hist. Soc., *Procs.*, LXIV (1956), 137–138.
6. Oct. 5, 1765, as quoted in Whitehead, *Perth Amboy*, 102.
7. The question of regional economic patterns and functions has not received the attention it deserves; but see the suggestive article by Sachs, "Interurban Correspondents and the Development of a National Economy," *N.Y. Hist.*, XXXVI (1955), 320–335; Joseph A. Ernst and H. Roy Merrens, "The View From Philadelphia: An Interdisciplinary Approach to the South Carolina Economy of the Middle of the Eighteenth Century," a paper read at the Southern Historical Association Meeting, Oct. 29–Nov. 1, 1969, Washington, D.C.
8. See Fuhlbruegge, "New Jersey Finances," N.J. Hist. Soc., *Procs.*, LV (1937), 167–190.
9. John Rutherfurd to a Member of the New Jersey House of Assembly, May 16, 1783, Letters from John Rutherfurd, New Jersey Historical Society, Newark.

change rates on currency paralleled Pennsylvania's while eastern New Jersey's followed New York's.[10]

Given the normal pressures on money at the time, the collapse of British credit and the contraction of the wartime supply of specie in the neighboring metropolitan centers after 1762 placed an impossible demand on the provincial stock of coin and currency. Within three years an excessive amount of New Jersey's money supply had drained away to New York and Pennsylvania. What remained was insufficient to provide either liquidity or an adequate medium of exchange, a situation that only aggravated the existing slump in the sales of British goods in markets throughout the middle colonies. But while the shortage of cash adversely affected the trade in British goods, it appeared to have only a minor effect on commodity markets. Commodity prices, for instance, were far more dependent on shifts in short-terms conditions in shipping and in the world agricultural market, and they reacted only slightly to immediate but weak local demands or to fluctuations in the volume of paper money or coin. The use of money was not so widespread nor the pull of the domestic market so strong that the quantity of paper currency outstanding provided any yardstick for gauging price movements. On the other hand, if farm prices were high, so were the farmers' liabilities. The cumulative effect of scanty harvests near the end of the war, the increase of taxes after 1763, and the recent fall in land values were to drive a growing number of farmers to the edge of bankruptcy.[11] Creditors, land speculators, and all others holding realty assets were scarcely better off. As elsewhere in the middle colonies, they found their investments not only greatly diminished but frozen.[12]

As a result of the widespread financial disruptions, the grand jury

10. See *N.J. Archives*, VII, 383–400, and Elmer, *Cumberland County*, 124.

11. On the question of the relationship between commodity prices and farmers' liabilities see Sachs, "Agricultural Conditions in the Northern Colonies," *Jour. Econ. Hist.*, XIII (1953), 274–290. The question of the determination of commodity prices has yet to be fully analyzed. Readers of the business correspondence of eighteenth-century merchants know that the availability of cash did at times influence agricultural prices. Nonetheless domestic price levels for farm products were essentially a reflection of European and American market factors. See, for instance, the discussion in Bezanson *et al.*, *Prices in Colonial Pennsylvania*, chap. 12. Readers are also referred to the related discussion of this point in chap. 1 above.

12. See nn. 5 and 6 above. See also the letter of Richard Stevens to Walter Rutherfurd, Phila., Dec. 12, 1765, Rutherfurd Collection, N.-Y. Hist. Soc., New York City.

of Hunterdon County petitioned the General Assembly in the early summer of 1765 for a loan office act for relief from the shortage of money. Other demands included the need for new laws to regulate the volume of retail credit and to cut down on costly legal fees.[13] Although a measure was quickly enacted barring high legal fees, the credit and currency proposals were temporarily shelved, possibly because the assembly had already acted to ease financial pressures by redeeming a part of the existing paper currency supply with the latest of the parliamentary reimbursements for the colony's wartime expenditures.[14] The last measure also provided a source of sterling remittances.[15] In a related move the house likewise rejected Governor William Franklin's appeal for a higher allowance for his own housing, but met his request for "bounties on hemp, flax, and mulberry trees, with a view of stimulating our inhabitants to future industry and wealth" and, in time, of providing "considerable in the article of remittance to the mother country."[16] Thus, according to the house, would the "purpose of paying our English debt . . . be answered; without parting with the little cash we have."[17]

Before further acts of relief and retrenchment could be taken, the Stamp Act crisis had engulfed the colony. From the fall of 1765 until the spring of the following year all other issues were eclipsed, although nonimportation and the closing of the courts took much of the pressure off both money and the debtor classes. Upon reconvening in the summer of 1766, the General Assembly did little more than thank Parliament for the repeal of the Stamp Act. The paper money question was held in abeyance in the expectation of a similar repeal of the Currency Act.[18]

Repeal was still a fond hope a year later, and impatient inhabitants from Somerset, Hunterdon, and Middlesex counties flooded the assembly with petitions for immediate relief from the growing scarcity of cash and its associated ills.[19] Before the house could officially receive the documents, however, the governor interrupted with news of a new British monetary policy in the offing, and the legislature once more tabled the currency question until the following session.

13. May 23, 1765, New Jersey General Assembly, Votes and Proceedings, Jenkins, ed., *Microfilm Records of the States*, hereafter cited as N.J. Gen. Assembly.
14. *Ibid.*
15. See chap. 4, n. 11, above.
16. June 6, 11, 1765, N.J. Gen. Assembly.
17. June 11, 1765, *ibid.*
18. See chap. 4 above.
19. June 11, 1767, N.J. Gen. Assembly.

The knowledge that the colonial agents, under the leadership of the governor's father, Benjamin Franklin, were busily lobbying for a repeal or revision of the Currency Act was good enough for the assembly. But the repeal movement fizzled, and the only palpable result was that in New Jersey the paper money question was laid aside for still another year.[20]

NEW YORK, 1766–1768

In New York news of the repeal movement's collapse arrived in the midst of a business depression. After a brief revival in 1766 the economy had foundered again. Export markets in the Caribbean had continued dull, and local merchants found increasing difficulty in moving West Indian products at anything near profitable prices. More serious, sales of British goods sagged. An easing of British credit and a spurt in grain and flour exports to the mother country and southern Europe had encouraged relatively heavy imports of manufactures with predictable results. By the late spring of 1767 merchants were once more complaining of top-heavy inventories, sluggish domestic markets, low prices, excessive competition, and impending bankruptcy. The situation had grown worse by the end of the year. Earnings declined following a brief but sharp drop in grain, flour, and bread prices, while British suppliers tightened up on credit again in order to protect their interests in a weakening colonial marketplace. That adjustment proved to be short-lived, and the year 1767 registered an increase of imports over previous years.[21]

Conditions showed little improvement in 1768. Early that year vendue houses were reportedly crowded with British manufactures of all kinds, selling at less than prime cost. Nonetheless the major complaint in 1768 as in 1767 was the stringency of money, a situation that was generally held to be directly connected with the slump in local trade, in realty values, and even in wages.[22] Merchant John

20. See chap. 4 above and also Lord Stirling to William Franklin, May 25, 1767, as quoted by W. A. Duer, *The Life of William Alexander, Earl of Stirling...* (New York, 1847), 87, and William Franklin to Benjamin Franklin, June 10, 1767, N.J. Hist. Soc., *Procs.*, 1st Ser., I (1845–1846), 103.

21. For the best discussion of economic events in the northern colonies in the period see Sachs, "Business Outlook," chap. 7. See also Harrington, *New York Merchant*, chap. 8, cited below.

22. The statement is based on my reading of the New York newspapers and of the business letters of the time that are cited below.

Van Cortlandt was only expressing a widespread feeling in the period when he informed his London supplier that "there is not enough Money Circulating to do Business."[23] Van Cortlandt and the other New York City merchants were not the only ones to feel the pinch: "the poor industrious tradesman, the needy mechanic, and all men of narrow circumstance" were said to face "impending ruin."[24] When money contracted, the "money'd men" held on to whatever cash came their way, refusing to pay their bills and bankrupting the small tradesman and artisan.[25] Few doubted that an infusion of money and credit into the flagging economy was the sovereign remedy. Common opinion held that additional amounts of paper money were necessary to spur the exchange of goods and services, to aid merchants and traders in meeting their obligations, and to bolster realty values.

The New York General Assembly finally despaired of the long-awaited repeal of the Currency Act and in December 1767 asked Governor Moore to consent to a bill authorizing an eight-year loan of some £130,000 without a suspending clause. Unwilling to violate instructions requiring inclusion of the controversial clause, Sir Henry agreed only to lay the matter before the crown, although a similar request in 1766 had come to nothing. Personally Moore was persuaded that the economic crisis was "very great" and growing worse. In his covering letter to Secretary of State Shelburne, he emphasized that before the year was out the circulation of all legal tender paper would cease, to the detriment of commerce and the ordinary services of government. Moreover compliance with the assembly's wish was politically desirable, since it would be repaid with "returns of duty and submission."[26]

Sir Henry's dispatch arrived just after Lord Hillsborough had replaced Shelburne in colonial affairs, and in Hillsborough's view

23. John Van Cortlandt to Thomas Shipboy, June 18, 1767, in Van Cortlandt Letterbook (A), 1762–1769, N.Y. Pub. Lib. For other examples in the period see also the Stirling Manuscript Collection, folder 3, dated 1764–1767, N.Y. Pub. Lib.; Van Cortlandt to John Richardson Herbert, Jan. 27, 1768, Van Cortlandt to John William Hoffman, Feb. 23, Sept. 30, 1768, Feb. 16, 1769, Van Cortlandt Letterbook; John Blanchard to Lord Stirling, Nov. 23, 1768, Alexander Papers, Box 1, folder: 1760–1769, N.-Y. Hist. Soc.; James Beekman to Samuel and Thomas Fluyder, May 4, 1768, Beekman to Peach and Pierce, Sept. 4, 1767, Philip L. White, ed., *The Beekman Mercantile Papers, 1764–1799* (New York, 1956), II, 715, 867. See also the discussion in White, *Beekmans of New York*, 361–383.
24. See "Probus to the Printer," *N.-Y. Jour.*, Nov. 19, 1767.
25. *Ibid.* As an example see the plaintive note to Lord Stirling dated Nov. 16, 1767, Stirling MSS.
26. Moore to Shelburne, Jan. 3, 1768, *N.Y. Col. Docs.*, VIII, 1.

the Currency Act gave the crown little discretion in matters affecting fiat money. Nor could the king be expected to decide any paper money question without careful study. Therefore, as long as New York persisted in its rejection of the need for the suspending clause in its legislation, the secretary insisted on having an advance copy of the loan office bill. Moore promptly complied with the request.[27]

In support of the loan office proposal, Moore's dispatches at the time presented a full range of arguments favoring an additional issue of paper money. Broadly speaking, the governor believed that "Commerce," "Cultivation," and "Population" were endangered by the monetary stringency, "and all Ranks greatly impoverished."[28] Doubtless Moore exaggerated in order to strengthen his case, though actual events in the period seem to bear out his contentions. At the first signs of a scarcity of cash, local businessmen were forced to increase the use of credit in the form of book debts and promissory notes. The principal backing for such indebtedness in America in the period was short-term realty bonds, which normally could be discounted. But as the various notes and mortgages came due, the existing pressure on cash only intensified, a condition that was seriously aggravated by the general tendency in times of distress to convert assets into cash and to hoard money. In consequence realty values, including realty mortgages and bonds, reportedly slipped 50 percent or more, to the point of breaking debtors and creditors alike. Bankruptcies soared, jail rolls swelled, and businessmen maintained their credit ratings only with the greatest of difficulty.[29] The financial shock was felt as far away as England. When bonds and book credits went unpaid, it was impossible, as James Beekman and several of the leading merchants complained to dunning British correspondents, to turn assets into remittances or to place further orders. To meet their sterling obligations, Beekman and others found it necessary to substitute commodity shipments wherever possible for the sterling bills ordinarily purchased with local currency.[30]

Hit equally hard by the dearth of cash and the decline of realty

27. Hillsborough to Moore, Feb. 25, 1768, Moore to Hillsborough, May 14, 1768, *ibid.*, VIII, 10–13, 72.

28. Moore to Hillsborough, May 14, 1768, *ibid.*, 72.

29. See, for instance, James Beekman to Peach and Pierce, Sept. 24, 1767, in James Beekman Letterbook, N.-Y. Hist. Soc., New York City. See also the discussion in Sachs and Hoogenboom, *Enterprising Colonials*, 95–96, and Harrington, *New York Merchant*, 336–337.

30. See the discussion in White, *Beekmans of New York*, 543–548, and Harrington, *New York Merchant*, 63–64.

values were the heavily mortgaged farmers of New York. They relied on what little money they could raise out of the profits of the land to pay off their debts. But as Moore noted, since money became scarce there were "numberless instances of Suits against Farmers, whose Estates have been sold upon Execution, and bought by the old Proprietor for less than the first purchase, after several years Cultivation and Improvement." Moore added that the problem was the more serious because nothing contributed as much to settlement as the purchase of farms and lands on mortgage.[31] Similarly affected by conditions were the ubiquitous land speculators, who saw their assets shrivel with each drop in the price of land.[32] As for the position of the "lower sort," Moore found that it had degenerated to a point "more easily perceived than described."[33]

Despite the governor's vigorous arguments in favor of a loan office, nothing came of the New York proposal. Hillsborough either forgot or more likely ignored his promise to lay the measure before the Board of Trade. He reportedly told Benjamin Franklin sometime in January 1768 that if the middle colonies, with their reputation for maintaining a stable currency, were to apply for dispensation from the legal tender provision of the Currency Act, they should have "fair play." By February, however, he had "expressed his Sentiments positively" against a paper currency, and not simply a legal tender currency. Nor did he again mention the proposal in his official correspondence.[34]

While the New York assembly awaited word of its ill-fated measure, less patient persons toyed with schemes promising more immediate, if limited, relief. In New York City the monetary strin-

---

31. Moore to Hillsborough, May 14, 1768, *N.Y. Col. Docs.*, VIII, 72. See also John Van Cortlandt's letters to Benjamin Golden, to George Carpenter, to Lawrence Fossee, to Joseph Golden, to John Wright, Nov. 9, 1768, Van Cortlandt Letterbook. On the cash earnings of farmers see Max G. Schumacher, "The Northern Farmer and His Markets during the Late Colonial Period" (Ph.D. diss., University of California, Berkeley, 1948), 136–139.

32. See the discussion in Harrington, *New York Merchant*, 135–136, and Sachs, "Business Outlook," 240–241.

33. Moore to Hillsborough, May 14, 1768, *N.Y. Col. Docs.*, VIII, 72. This general complaint was tied in with the move for domestic manufacturing and nonimportation; see, for instance, "A Tradesman to the Printer," *N.-Y. Jour.*, Dec. 17, 1767. The newspapers in the period were filled with such complaints and should be given credence. The business correspondence paints much the same picture.

34. Feb. 17, 1768, Sparks, ed., *Works of Franklin*, VII, 382; "Extract of a Letter from a Gentleman in London, to another in this City, dated Feb. 25, 1768," *N.-Y. Jour.*, May 19, 1768. See also "New Bern (in North Carolina), June 10," *ibid.*, June 31, 1768.

gency was especially acute. The concentration of business and a sudden spurt in population following the war had created an unusually heavy demand for money, particularly ready cash for the everyday store trade. Purchases in previous years of many tons of small copper coin from Britain proved to be an inadequate solution to the problem, and, according to one writer at the time, the continued "great Scarcity of small Change in this City, occasions much trouble and loss of Time, while Perhaps a whole Neighborhood is troubled to change a Bill or a Dollar, which sometimes cannot be effected; and thus both Buyer and Seller are disappointed."[35] In consequence as early as February 1768 a group of unknown local merchants advertised their intention of issuing "indorsed notes of hand" at interest and on good security. A similar, or perhaps the same, idea was developed at greater length a few months later when it was hinted that "a certain Number of Gentlemen of known Estates" should sign and make available to the public a "sufficient Quantity of small Tickets from Three Pence to Nine Pence Value" as small change, as was done "in one or more neighbouring Governments." The idea was probably modeled after a plan that had been tried out a short while before by eight merchants in Philadelphia, and their failure killed off any chance of success in New York.[36]

More ambitious was a rival scheme that also made its appearance in February. "Is it not a Pity in this Distressing Time," queried an anonymous author, that the corporation of the city of New York "should not embrace the Opportunity of doing something" about the dearth of cash rather than "to leave the advantage to a Number of able Gentlemen, who would vastly enrich themselves" by their "Undertaking?" The supposed alternative was to have the corporation take upon itself the lending out of some £100,000 in paper on municipal credit at 5 percent interest for twenty years. The principal on the loan would be payable in the notes of issue, the interest in specie. The accumulated coin would then be put out on further loan at nominal interest, with the returns to be applied to the support of local industries and the employment of the poor.[37]

More practical was the proposal put forward shortly after by the Chamber of Commerce of New York City, a merchants' organization founded in the spring of 1768. Anxious to procure "such laws and regulations as may be found necessary for the benefit of trade

35. "Hint to the Public," *ibid.*, Aug. 4, 1768.
36. *Ibid.*, Feb. 4, Aug. 4, 1768.
37. *Ibid.*, Feb. 4, 1768.

in general," the Chamber resolved to encourage a greater local circulation of Pennsylvania paper currency to offset the loss of New
York paper to the neighboring colonies of New Jersey, Connecticut, and Rhode Island. The Pennsylvania notes were to be advanced
6⅔ percent over the price of New York paper, or the difference
between the legal value of Spanish dollars in the two colonies. Already widely quoted in ordinary business transactions, the valuation
was meant to serve as a guideline for members of the Chamber of
Commerce. But the practice of attracting neighboring currencies
did not sit well with all members, and a similar proposal to advance
the value of New Jersey paper failed. Apparently the Chamber had
no better luck with its plan "to establish a paper money in the
City."[38]

Most of the private and local schemes for monetary relief in 1768
failed to get much beyond the talking stage. And at best, devices
like the extended use of copper coin, private credit instruments, or
neighboring currencies could only be viewed as stopgap measures.
The real problem, throughout the province, was how within the
existing imperial framework to provide a source of currency and
credit sufficient to meet the transaction and liquidity demand for
money. Beyond that problem there was also the possibility of alter-
ing or abolishing the framework.

At the moment few New Yorkers harbored serious thoughts of
overturning the empire as a solution to their problems. Rather they
hoped to ameliorate immediate conditions and ultimately to reform
the empire. The plans of the New York affiliate of the London-based
"Society for the Promotion of Arts, Agriculture, and Economy"
exemplified this attitude. Established with the bipartisan support
of New York's political leaders near the end of 1764, the society
had been inactive for several years. Then late in 1767 it was revived
for the purpose of encouraging by private means both the production of raw materials and industrial products for sale to Britain and
the fabrication of cheap linen cloth for local consumption and the
employment of the poor. Hemp, iron, potash, and the like already
commanded a ready market in Britain. But it was believed that increasing their output would provide a way to alter the balance of

38. See John Austin Stevens, Jr., ed., *Colonial Records of the New York Chamber of Commerce, 1768–1784* (New York, 1867), 1, 10, 15–16, 18, 84, 104, 151, 161,
171, 186–187, 308. The Chamber also established rates on foreign coin as well; see
ibid., 52, 56–57, 67, 102. This problem is handled in more detail and in a suggestive
way in Sachs, "Interurban Correspondents and the Development of a National
Economy," *N.Y. Hist.*, XXXVI (1955), 320–355.

trade within the empire and thereby relieve local pressures on money and remittances.[39] Similarly a paper manufactory was rushed to completion in the summer of 1768 in an effort to give employment to the poor and to ease an imbalance in the trade with neighboring Pennsylvania, which up to then had supplied New York with nearly all its paper.[40]

Such plans were perfectly sound. And they mirrored an actual economic trend, for exports of commodities and manufactures to Britain rose 30 percent between 1752 and 1767.[41] A pamphlet written for the society in 1767 developed the theme at some length. The anonymous author declared that New York faced three serious situations: debtor prisons were overcrowded, estates were sold to satisfy trifling debts, and all ranks of people cried out for money. It was not always understood, the writer argued, that each of these problems arose from a single cause—imports exceeded exports, and the unfavorable balance caused all the calamity. The solution was to build up sterling exchange and the stock of hard money by encouraging local manufacturing. The author stressed not only producing raw materials for British use but also manufacturing textiles and other items in direct competition with British industry. In this way imports could be substantially cut, and the drive to export expanded. The moneyed capital earned and saved could then be reinvested in native industries to cut imports and the outflow of specie even further. The pamphleteer lamented that instead of following good advice New Yorkers thought only to apply their "sovereign remedy": paper money with all its attendant evils.[42] Doubtless the explanation was a valid long-run analysis of New York's adverse trade balance with the mother country, but the talk "of the Americans establishing Manufactures among them," was overly optimistic. As another observer pointed out, the problem was that "nothing can be carried

39. See, for example, *N.-Y. Jour.*, Dec. 24, 31, 1767, Jan. 14, 21ff, and Sachs, "Business Outlook," 254–258. See also Milton M. Klein, "The American Whig: William Livingston of New York" (Ph.D. diss., Columbia University, 1954), 645.

40. *N.-Y. Jour.*, June 14, 1768.

41. Sachs, "Business Outlook," 188.

42. *The Commercial Conduct of the Province of New-York Considered, and The True Interest of that Colony attempted to be shewn In a Letter to The Society of Arts, Agriculture, and Economy* (New York, 1767), Bancroft Collection, England and America, 1766–1767, N.Y. Pub. Lib., New York City. On the effects upon manufacturing of the scarcity of cash whether as a medium of exchange or as moneyed capital, see Peter Hasenclever to Sir William Johnson, Jan. 6, 1768, Stokes, comp., *Iconography of Manhattan Island*, IV, 781; Gerard Bancker to Lord Stirling, Nov. 29, 1767, in Stirling MSS, folder 3; Robert Livingston to Lord Stirling, Oct. 20, 1767, in Alexander Papers, Box I, folder: 1760–1769.

into Execution (at least for the present) for the Want of Money, which greatly affects all Ranks."[43]

In addition to the lack of an adequate circulating medium, New York faced a number of related monetary problems. One was the peculation of its treasurer, Abraham de Peyster, which came to light after his death in September 1767. Although he apparently had appropriated some £50,000 of public funds for his own purposes, de Peyster so adroitly juggled his books that they were straightened out only after many adjustments and much expense. In the end the province had no choice but to distrain upon his estate, and even then the arrears could not be fully covered. Nearly £30,000 remained outstanding, a substantial part of which, as in the Robinson scandal, had been placed out on loan.[44] As Peter Van Schaack reported, it was widely argued that "unless we have an emission (which being by loan will enable the colony to replace this deficiency in a manner least burdensome) [it] must be supplied by a tax on the colony."[45] It went without saying, of course, that a loan office emission would enable the debtors to the de Peyster estate to mend their deficiencies as well.

More serious was the announcement by the customs commissioners at Boston in the summer of 1768 that for the future the collection of British customs duties was to be in specie. The action followed a recent Treasury decision to alter the existing system of paying royal troops in America; an effort was now to be made to take advantage of the new parliamentary duties payable in sterling. Under the old arrangements contractors for the English government who were charged with seeing that the soldiers stationed in America were paid in hard cash would remit from London sterling bills of exchange. Their American agents would sell these bills locally, wherever possible for coin, which was to be handed over to army paymasters. Under the new and simpler arrangements, however, the agents would receive their supply of hard cash directly from the collectors and receivers of customs in America. This transaction would appear

43. See the many entries in the John Van Cortlandt Letterbook for the winter of 1767/1768.
44. See Watts to General Monckton, Jan. 23, 1768, *The Aspinwall Papers* (Mass. Hist. Soc., *Colls.*, 4th Ser., IX–X [Boston, 1871]), II, 599; Moore to B.T., Feb. 23, 1768, *N.Y. Col. Docs.*, VIII, 14–15; William Smith, Jr., to Philip Livingston, Jan. 18, 1768, Philip Schuyler Papers, Box 23: Letters to Schuyler, 1761–1771, N.Y. Pub. Lib., New York City.
45. To his brother Henry Van Schaack, Dec. 20, 1769, Henry Cruger Van Schaack, *Memoirs of the Life of Henry Van Shaack* ... (Chicago, 1892), 18.

on the Treasury books back in London. In any event, because of the critical shortage of coin in this area, the customs official in New York had customarily either accepted paper money in lieu of specie or extended long-term credit. The new directive would play havoc with the economy, and Moore immediately protested. But the crown refused to interfere in Treasury affairs.[46]

Another monetary problem was the counterfeiting of coin and paper currency. Worst of all, in the fall of 1768 New York ran out of legal tender. Historically only the Lyon dollar and paper currency were lawful for payments within the province. First brought over by the Dutch, Lyon dollars turned up only rarely, while the £85,000 or so in paper notes still in circulation was redeemable in November, after which they would no longer be a lawful tender. The dearth of lawful money plainly exposed debtors to the "petulance and Malice of their Creditors."[47] For this reason in 1767 and again in 1768 the General Assembly considered the possibility of making all coins lawful at values set "in the common course of business." Moore agreed to the need for such a measure, and in May 1768 when he sent Hillsborough a draft of New York's loan office proposal, he added a note requesting crown permission to sign into law a bill governing the value of coin. No reply was forthcoming. In consequence the next time such a bill came across his desk, Moore perforce vetoed it as a violation of the parliamentary act of 1708. Characteristically Hillsborough shelved not only the loan office plan but everything connected with it.[48]

By the end of 1768 New York faced an economic crisis. The

46. Moore to Hillsborough, Aug. 18, 1768, Hillsborough to Moore, Oct. 12, 1768, *N.Y. Col. Docs.*, VIII, 96–97, 101. The problem began in Nov. 1765 when the deputy paymaster of the British army reported having difficulty receiving the various customs duties, a situation that led to a Treasury investigation. See abstracts from Treasury minutes and correspondence, Apr. 26, May 17, July 9, 10, Nov. 2, 1765, Bancroft Collection, England and America, 1764–1766. Cf. Jack M. Sosin, "A Postscript to the Stamp Act. George Grenville's Revenue Measures: A Drain on Colonial Specie?" *American Historical Review*, LXIII (1958), 918–923, and Shy, *Toward Lexington*, 242–244.

47. Moore to Hillsborough, May 14, 1769, *N.Y. Col. Docs.*, VIII, 72. For the story of the Lyon dollar see Fernow, "Coins and Currency of New York," in Wilson, ed., *Memorial History of the City of New York*, IV, 300–301, 314, 319. Regarding the market price of coin and specie see Stevens, ed., *Chamber of Commerce Records*, 56, 57, 316. Newspapers in the period are filled with accounts of counterfeiting, and the counterfeiting rings seem at times to have been well organized and continental in their scope. See, for instance, *N.-Y. Jour.*, Feb. 20, 1768.

48. Moore to Hillsborough, May 14, 29, 1769, *N.Y. Col. Docs.*, VIII, 72, 169–170; June 4, 1767, Nov. 4, 1768, Jour. N.Y. Assembly, Jenkins, ed., *Microfilm Records of the States*, hereafter cited as Jour. N.Y. Assembly.

tumble of agricultural prices, the absence of legal tender money, the shortage of paper currency, coin, and sterling exchange, a depressed West Indian trade, sluggish sales of high-priced British imports, and falling land values characterized a situation in which all classes suffered. The one bright light on the darkened horizon was the heavy grain and flour shipments to southern Europe that year. To ease monetary pressures and to buoy up the flagging economy, a number of solutions had come up for consideration in and out of the General Assembly. Most popular by far was the plan to provide public credit, fill the stream of circulation, and set trade in its proper channels by a timely issue of paper money on loan. All schemes had failed—save one.

That one effective way to alleviate pressures on money and exchange was to buy less. Absorbed during the last months of 1767 in internal politics, the province was slow to react to the Townshend Acts. But when Boston undertook a campaign against those measures on a platform of home industry, nonimportation, and nonconsumption of British goods, New York joined in for solid economic as well as political reasons. Such measures offered some relief from the business slump and monetary stringency while enabling the merchants to dispose of their "dead Stock" at a good price. In addition the measures promised to help ease not only sterling exchange rates but also that competition among merchants considered to be the death of trade.[49] The lack of money in turn insured the success of the nonimportation agreement, and as at least one writer has pointed out, that agreement was more rigorously enforced in New York than in New England or in Pennsylvania.[50] Nonetheless the widening demand for credit and a circulating medium had yet to be dealt with.

MONEY AND POLITICS IN NEW JERSEY, 1768–1769

The economic outlook in New Jersey in 1768 was equally dismal. Trade had slumped, and the general clamor for money was not to be denied. "*Money! Money!*" one dispirited Jersey man shouted above the din, "Money, it seems, is to do every thing for us, to clothe the sluggard, provide bread for the indolent, support the extravagant,

49. See the discussion in Sachs, "Business Outlook," 203–212.
50. An excellent and detailed account of the political side of the controversies surrounding the Townshend Acts, nonconsumption, domestic manufacturing, and nonimportation is to be found in Champagne, "New York Politics."

and supply the luxurious. In short, it is to help those who will not help themselves."[51] The General Assembly disagreed. Having waited in vain for the promised repeal of the Currency Act, committees from both houses met in April to answer the petitions carried over from the year before and resolved that an issue of paper money was imperative. The assembly quickly passed a loan office bill, which the governor refused to sign.[52]

That August, William Franklin wrote Secretary Hillsborough at length explaining his opposition to the assembly bill and offering a plan of his own. Franklin noted that the measure had passed without the suspending clause required by the crown of all such legislation after 1751 in conformity with the spirit of the Currency Act passed that year. Moreover, according to the legend on the new paper notes, they were to "pass current." Franklin felt this would have the effect, though unintentional, of making the money a lawful tender in violation of the Currency Act of 1764 and in opposition to the secretary's recent pronouncement against all fiat money systems. More important to the government, the assembly had failed to set aside a part of the interest returns from the proposed loan as a fund for increasing official salaries and freeing crown officers from their dependence on the legislature's power of the purse. As to the reasons favoring the act, Franklin merely referred the secretary to the law's preamble. He did note, however, that the Council shared his feeling that a reasonable sum of paper money would prove useful both to the province and to the mother country.

Franklin also discussed, at greater length, the related question of public finance and of his own plans for a loan office. According to the governor, before the French and Indian War, New Jersey had ordinarily paid public expenses out of loan office interest returns. Import-export duties were unknown, and on the few occasions when such funds proved insufficient, the legislature had levied a tax on real and personal estates; this "would shortly be the case again."

Given the financial situation of the province, the governor indicated that if any future interest fund were allocated to public purposes the Council would join in supporting a loan of as much as £100,000. The money was not to be a legal tender, of course. But Franklin was ready to dispense with the need for a suspending clause. In the general anxiety for a currency emission, the governor be-

51. "A Ploughman," *Pa. Chron.*, Jan. 18, 1768.
52. Apr. 23, May 10, 1768. N.J. Gen. Assembly; Franklin to Hillsborough, Aug. 24, 1768, *N.J. Archives*, X, 48–50.

lieved that the assembly members would not hesitate to embrace such a plan and that advantage should be taken of their "Disposition to bring them to make a more adequate Provision for the Officers of Government." To drive the point home, Franklin appended a schedule of the "scandalously low" salaries of government officers.[53]

Hillsborough made a cautious reply early in the fall. The Currency Act did not restrict paper money per se, he said. If "the whole merit of this measure depended upon" the notes being legal tender— if "it did require no other restriction and limitation"—"His Majesty's consent would seem to follow of course." But the king thought that "the necessity there is for so large a Sum as this is, the nature and extent of the public Services to be provided for, and the Fund and Security for the redemption of the Bills, are some, amongst many other material circumstances, necessary to be fully set forth and explained." The crown would withhold its judgment, Hillsborough said. The governor was not to sign any currency act without either forwarding an advance copy to the king or attaching a suspending clause.[54]

Franklin immediately sent back a draft of the assembly bill, accompanied by some personal comments, which reached London early in 1769. According to the governor, the "principal inhabitants" mostly desired the measure and would see to it that a similar bill passed at the next session. He added that the £100,000 loan would not endanger the value of the current money supply. On the contrary, the province badly needed the cash to provide local exchange and to improve lands. Such reasons were ancillary to Franklin's major concern, however, which remained that the crown insist that a portion of the interest returns on the loan be used to raise local salaries and free the king's servants from their subjection to the lower house.[55] This time the commissioners of trade replied. Franklin was correct, they felt. Since the bills of credit were "to pass current," a legal tender was implied, and this was cause enough to veto the act. The governor was instructed to pass no money measure without a suspending clause, although the province could strike £100,000 of non-legal tender currency for a five-year period.[56] In effect the Board extended to the New Jersey loan office proposal the same restrictions imposed on New York three years before.[57]

53. Franklin to Hillsborough, Aug. 24, 1768, *N.J. Archives*, X, 48–50.
54. Nov. 15, 1768, *ibid.*, 60–62.
55. Jan. 28, 1769, *ibid.*, 99–102.
56. May 2, 1769, *ibid.*, 107; *Acts of the Privy Council, Col.*, V, 196–197.
57. See the discussion in chap. 4 above.

The Board's new instructions arrived in September 1769, and Franklin, who had been waiting for an answer before convening the legislature, promptly called the General Assembly into session to pass along the news of the rejection of the first loan office bill and to recommend passage of a similar measure without the controversial legal tender clause. Convinced of the governor's good intentions, the legislators thanked him for his trouble, even though they found the latest terms "particularly hard." Nevertheless, unlike the New York assembly on a similar occasion in the past, the Jersey legislature early in October authorized a £100,000 issue in strict conformity with the Board's suggestions. No provision was made to raise official salaries, but the governor still seemed satisfied.[58]

Confident of success the house promptly shipped the act off to London in the care of New Jersey's new colonial agent, Benjamin Franklin, an acknowledged influence peddler in England and a man highly touted for his understanding of the currency question.[59] The governor was in a very different mood. Still fretting about salaries, he confided to Hillsborough that he had been "in hopes, at the last Session, to have prevail'd with them [the assembly] to appropriate a Part of the Interest Money, to arise from the Loan of the £100,000 proposed to be struck in Paper Bills of Credit, towards making a more adequate Provision for the Support of the Officers of Government; and I urged to them that it would be a means of . . . obtaining the Royal Allowance thereto." The house had respectfully declined even to listen. Accordingly Franklin hinted that the king might refuse confirmation of the act until the assembly provided a salary fund and stipulated the allowance to be made to each officer. Surely the legislators would then "be brought to a Compliance, especially as there is no Method can be devised for Raising Money for the Support of Government, which will be more agreeable to the People." In every other respect the governor felt that the new bill met all objections.[60]

Before New Jersey received word of the fate of its currency bill, events taking place in New York and London had led to a stiffening of ministerial attitudes to any loan office scheme. It would be five

58. William Franklin to Benjamin Franklin, May 11, 1769, N.J. Hist. Soc., *Procs.*, 1st Ser., I (1845–1846), 107; Oct. 11, 1769, N.J. Gen. Assembly; 10 Geo. III, c. 7, New Jersey Session Laws, Jenkins, ed., *Microfilm Records of the States*, hereafter cited as N.J. Session Laws.

59. Committee of the Assembly to Dr. Benjamin Franklin, Dec. 7, 1769, *N.J. Archives*, X, 136–137.

60. Dec. 24, 1769, *ibid.*, 144–145.

long years before New Jersey's loan office proposal received satisfaction at the hands of the Board of Trade. In the meantime the
initiative had again passed to New York.

MONEY AND POLITICS IN NEW YORK, 1768–1769

The currency question in New York prior to 1768 hinged on
problems associated with a postwar slump in business. But in that
year the question suddenly emerged as a major issue in connection
with local opposition to the Quartering Act and an ensuing battle
for control of the General Assembly. The antagonists in that battle
were New York's two major political factions: the Livingstons, who
were allied with the great Hudson landowners, and the De Lanceys,
who drew their support from the bulk of the mercantile community
in New York City. It was no chance occurrence that the De Lanceys
chartered a course in line with the merchants' interest concerning
the currency question, while the Livingstons took the opposite tack.
In time the British government was forced to intervene in the struggle in order to settle the controversy over the Mutiny Act, or the
Quartering Act as it is more commonly called. Under ministerial
prodding, and in direct support of the De Lanceys, Parliament voted
to grant the province dispensation from the Currency Act of 1764
in exchange for military aids under the terms of the Quartering Act.

In accordance with New York's septennial election law, Governor Moore dissolved the assembly on January 2, 1768, and called for
new elections. For the first time in seven years the "outs" in provincial politics, the De Lancey faction, had a chance to get in. In
the end the Livingstons won, but by so close a margin that a second
vote could easily have reversed the results. As a consequence, when
the new house assembled in October the two factions promptly
tangled over the Massachusetts circular against the Townshend Acts
and the instructions from Hillsborough demanding dissolution of
any legislature that answered the Bay Colony. To court favor with
the Sons of Liberty, the De Lanceys favored a quick reply to the
circular; as defenders of colonial rights, they anticipated success in
the next election. For their part the Livingstons sought to avoid consideration of the Massachusetts letter without losing their popular
following. The clan's assembly leader, Philip Livingston, moved a
petition against the Townshend Acts, but said nothing about the
circular. The ruse failed. Through a series of political maneuvers involving riots, instructions, and memorials, the De Lanceys forced

the house both to answer Massachusetts and to petition Parliament. Sir Henry Moore had no choice but to dissolve the assembly and call new elections. This time the Livingstons were routed, and with the positions reversed it was their faction that now worked to cut short the life of the house while courting popularity. Meanwhile, in an effort to protect their victory, the De Lanceys anxiously cultivated the provincial governors, first Moore and then Colden. They also tried as best they could to preserve their newfound popular following without losing their hold on the great merchants.[61]

Of the many issues facing the new House of Representatives, two of the more urgent were the need to supply the king's troops as provided by the Quartering Act and to establish a loan office. The first arose from a deficiency in the supply fund that had led in the spring of 1769 to the summoning of the assembly sooner than usual; the second, from "clamours raised in the Country" for quick relief from the stringency of money.[62] The Livingstons hoped to bend the first situation to party ends. Barely a month after the election, Peter R. Livingston wrote Philip Schuyler that the faction had a ready-made issue to bring on a dissolution: a need to appropriate supply funds, the very question that had led to the revival of the Sons of Liberty in 1767. Livingston noted that any such grant must prove unpopular, for the royal troops were in bad odor. A refusal to vote supplies, on the other hand, would violate the Quartering Act and give cause for immediate dissolution of the legislature.[63]

It came as no surprise to the De Lanceys that supply was a partisan issue, and they had their own ideas on the subject. In March, a month before the house convened, a scribbler reminded the readers of the *New-York Journal* that another supply requisition would be coming up shortly and that the citizenry would be "very averse to the making of new Laws for the Imposition of more Taxes" in support of a "Standing Army." But the writer went on to suggest that it would not be "ill timed" for the electorate in the different consti-

61. The foregoing discussion is largely based on the work of Champagne, "New York Politics"; see also and compare Roger Champagne, "Family Politics versus Constitutional Principles: The New York Assembly Elections of 1768 and 1769," *WMQ*, 3d Ser., XX (1963), 57–79; Bonomi, *A Factious People*, 237–257; Bernard Friedman, "The New York Assembly Elections of 1768 and 1769: The Disruption of Family Politics," *N.Y. Hist.*, XLVI (1965), 3–24; and Lawrence Leder, "The New York Elections of 1769: An Assault on Privilege," *Mississippi Valley Historical Review*, XLIX (1963), 675–682.

62. Moore to Hillsborough, Jan. 20, May 29, 1769, *N.Y. Col. Docs.*, VIII, 147, 169.

63. Feb. 27, 1769, Philip Schuyler Papers, Box 23.

tuencies to "hint to" their representatives "how to behave" in such a case. He warned, however, that there was talk of a plan to let the next assembly make, and not simply take, money.[64] It was the broadest of hints and the best of hopes. New York's monetary condition was perilous, and as a *quid pro quo*, the De Lanceys would offer to provision the soldiers in the hope of getting Governor Moore to agree to sign a loan office bill into law.

As expected, when the assembly opened Moore appealed for additional supply funds: the last dole had covered only the debts in arrears, and new deficits had accrued. A committee took the request under advisement. In the meantime, in a strictly partisan bid for popularity, Philip Livingston moved an emission of £120,000 on loan. Secretary Hillsborough still had the loan office proposal of 1767 under review, of course, so that the move was potentially embarrassing to the De Lancey majority.[65] Shortly after, the Livingstons contrived to end the life of the house. As members of the committee responsible for drafting a reply to the governor's opening address, Livingston partisans Philip Schuyler and George Clinton tried to turn back the request for troop funds. The De Lancey majority proposed instead that the request be honored—provided that the required funds could be raised. As the assembly later explained it, the decay of trade had trimmed revenues so low that they hardly covered government costs; an extra expense would only exhaust the treasury's small reserves. And the scarcity of money precluded new tax levies. Moore got the message. He informed the representatives that the king would learn of their willingness to vote the necessary aids and of the need for a fresh issue of paper.[66]

For the time being the life of the house had been preserved. The De Lanceys suddenly discovered that it was possible after all to make a small grant of £1,800 for troop supplies, and despite objections from the Livingstons, they pushed the appropriation through the legislature. The De Lancey rhetoric was patriotic: a donation when "we know not of the continuation of the Mutiny Act" showed a readiness to grant aid upon simple requisition and thus refuted any reason for compulsory taxation by Parliament. But their reasoning was political. With the provisions bill safely in his pocket, Moore

64. "A Countryman," *N.-Y. Jour.*, Mar. 16, 1769.
65. Apr. 4, 5, 1769, Jour. N.Y. Assembly.
66. Apr. 8, 9, *ibid.*; William H. W. Sabine, ed., *Historical Memoirs ... of William Smith* (New York, 1956–1958), I, 62.

might well be expected to sign a loan office measure similar to the one in the hands of Secretary Hillsborough.[67] While awaiting some sign of Moore's willingness to join ranks with them, the De Lanceys persisted in their strategy of removing the opposition leadership. On April 12 they sponsored a motion to expel Philip Livingston from the House of Representatives. A city member, Livingston had lost his seat in the last election to a De Lancey supporter, John Cruger, the great Bristol merchant, who in due course became the new Speaker. Livingston retained his place in the assembly, however, when he was subsequently returned as a representative of Livingston Manor. In consequence the De Lanceys sought his expulsion from the house on the technical grounds of nonresidency. In an effort to "pull down the house" before his ouster, Livingston requested the legislature to show the unity of the colonies by reaffirming the Townshend Acts resolution, an action that had led to the last dissolution of the assembly. The move misfired. The De Lanceys simply shelved the proposal before carrying out the expulsion, and when the manor returned Supreme Court Judge Robert R. Livingston to fill the vacant position, they resolved that no member of the court could legitimately sit in the house. Finally, when the residency requirements in the election act of 1699 proved ambiguous, raising questions about the legality of unseating Philip Livingston in the first place, the De Lanceys amended the law to suit their purposes. The most important point about the amendment, however, was that it was only made possible by effecting a compromise with Moore that, as it turned out, scotched whatever chance the loan office bill had of passing.[68]

Sir Henry Moore was the makeweight of political power in New York, and, as one observer put it, both parties "stood ready to court his Favor."[69] Ordinarily found in the Livingston camp, Moore nevertheless disclaimed any desire to act as political arbiter. He wished merely to make the "ferment subside." For this reason, as he explained to Secretary Hillsborough, while some "turbulent spirits" wanted a dissolution of the house, he made every effort to save it. When therefore the De Lanceys urged him to sign the bill amending

67. Apr. 14, 1769, Jour. N.Y. Assembly; Sabine, ed., *Smith*, I, 66.
68. For a contemporary view of these events see Sabine, ed., *Smith*, I, 59–71. Three modern accounts are Champagne, "New York Politics," 191–204; Klein, "William Livingston," chap. 15; and Bonomi, *A Factious People*, 257–260.
69. Sabine, ed., *Smith*, I, 51.

the election law of 1699, he did so only in the interest of peace and as the lesser of evils. Moore reported to London that "two bills were pressed upon me, one for emitting the sum of £120,000 in Bills of Credit, the other for regulating elections." The currency measure had a sugar coating. According to Moore the De Lanceys were well aware of his sense of duty, as demonstrated by his earlier insistence on the need for a suspending clause, and though there was still no provision for such a clause in the present bill, there was instead a stipulation that a "kind of Revenue" fund be created out of interest during the term of the loan, or a period of fourteen years. As Moore indicated, this was closer than any other governor had come to achieving the British goal of a permanent revenue under executive control, since the proposed fund could only be spent with the consent of the governor and Council.[70]

Confident that their scheme would be successful, the De Lanceys quieted the Sons of Liberty with the promise that the present treasury appropriation would be the last.[71] But Moore balked. He reminded the house that the king's instructions still forbade passing any currency measure without the controversial suspending clause. As for the amendment regulating elections, the governor declared that common sense militated against signing a bill calculated only to serve partisan ends. Nonetheless Moore preferred to have his understanding impeached rather than have his duty to the king called into question, and so he chose to pass the amendment after all, while postponing the currency question until the following assembly session. By then the copy of the loan office proposal of December 1767 would have long since reached England, time enough for the king to communicate his pleasure.

Caution aside, the governor remained a sincere advocate of a loan office. He willingly passed along to Secretary Hillsborough the now-familiar arguments in favor of the law, adding only that the present request for a loan would be the last for fourteen years and that the miseries of the people were almost beyond belief. If the crown could agree to a loan office, the troops would be guaranteed a source of future supplies, estates would be saved from ruin, "and such an impression made on the people in general as must be productive of the most favourable consequences to the Colony."[72]

70. Moore to Hillsborough, Apr. 13, May 26, 29, 1769, *N.Y. Col. Docs.*, VII, 157, 167–168, 169–170.

71. Moore to Hillsborough, May 29, 1769, *ibid.*, VIII, 169–170.

72. Moore to Hillsborough, May 26, 29, 1769, *ibid.*, 168–170; May 20, 1769, Jour. N.Y. Assembly; Sabine, ed., *Smith*, I, 51–53. According to Smith, Moore informed

The spring session of the General Assembly had yielded the De Lanceys a series of signal victories. One way or another, they had managed to keep the house alive, support the merchants' interest, placate the Sons of Liberty, oust the opposition leaders, and maintain the grudging support of Governor Moore. In sum they had managed everything but the whims of chance. On September 11, 1769, Sir Henry Moore died "of a Dissentory," and that astute octogenarian-politician, Lieutenant Governor Cadwallader Colden, moved back into the executive chair and the political spotlight.

No sooner had Colden taken office than he began rapidly replacing Livingston patronage holders with De Lancey partisans and his own sons in an apparent move to attach himself to the assembly majority and to reestablish former ties with the De Lanceys. As if to confirm that impression, on October 17 he informed the Council that there was need for yet another troop appropriation. When reminded of the acute shortness of treasury funds and of the province's inability to issue paper money or to levy new taxes, the old man reportedly turned sharply on his heel and declared "he would consult the City Members as to the Expediency." As councilman and Livingston stalwart William Smith, Jr., carefully recorded in his diary, the "City Members" were at the devotion of the De Lancey faction. Smith suspected that in return for their support the De Lanceys would not "lose the present House in which they had a Majority."[73]

A new *quid pro quo* was in the making. Following up Governor Moore's last dispatches home, Colden promptly wrote Secretary Hillsborough that he was in hopes that the king would permit him to sign the loan office measure recently sent over by Sir Henry. He took care to remind the secretary of the close connection between future troop appropriations and the need for an additional issue of paper currency. Colden was convinced that the crown would accede to his request, and he therefore bided his time before calling the legislature into session. The last of the recent £1,800 supply grant had already been spent in an effort to settle old accounts, and new debts had accumulated since then. Popular hostility towards the troops was still widespread and, if anything, had grown in in-

---

the Livingstons that he fully expected to have the election amendment "damned in England."

73. Sabine, ed., *Smith*, I, 53–56, 67. Jobs for his sons and favorites had always been a part of the price paid for Colden's support; see Siegfried B. Rolland, "Cadwallader Colden, Colonial Politician and Imperial Statesman, 1718–1760" (Ph.D. diss., University of Wisconsin, 1952), 389–413.

tensity in recent months. Nonetheless Colden guessed that when royal consent to loan office bill came through, a grateful legislature would lay aside all objections and speedily vote the additional aids required by the soldiery. It did not quite turn out that way.[74]

While Colden waited, New York's attitude toward the Quartering Act stiffened. On September 28 a special supplement of the *New-York Journal* carried the story of South Carolina's refusal to supply the king's soldiers under the terms of the Quartering Act. The Carolina assembly cogently argued that troop support was specifically provided for by the various parliamentary acts taxing America. If General Gage needed more money, let him apply to the Exchequer. New York's Sons of Liberty immediately hailed South Carolina's defiance and asked all America to subscribe to the southerners' argument.[75]

Colden could wait no longer. He summoned the house at the end of November after carefully leaking the story that, despite his instructions and British silence on the last loan office proposal, he was ready to sign a paper currency measure. Colden and the De Lanceys felt that their best chance of passing an unpopular supply bill was to attach to it a promise to enact the popular loan office without any mention of the offensive suspending clause. As expected Colden opened the fall session by asking for a supplementary troop supply grant. The De Lanceys, however, temporarily shelved the request in order to bring in a loan office bill almost identical to the one passed under Moore. In the meantime they attempted to drum up popular support for their actions. On opening day there lay on the house table the Virginia resolutions against the parliamentary proposal to have Americans accused of treason tried in England. A copy had arrived during the summer, and by the time the assembly met that autumn New Yorkers were aware that a number of other colonial legislatures had already approved the resolves. With another chance to pose as popular defenders of American liberties, the De Lancey majority quickly adopted the Burgesses' resolution; only then did they inform Colden that the house would give "serious consideration" to his request for troop money. Two weeks later, following a careful canvass of votes, the De Lanceys raised the supply question

74. Colden to Hillsborough, Oct. 4, Dec. 4, 1769, *N.Y. Col. Docs.*, VIII, 189, 191; Nov. 21, 1769, Jour. N.Y. Assembly.
75. Nov. 2, 1769, *N.-Y. Jour.* For the South Carolina story see Ernst, "Growth of the Commons House of Assembly," 114–117.

on the house floor. But first they cleared the galleries. Visitors might intimidate members overly sensitive to popular criticism.[76]

According to Colden's analysis, the De Lanceys "would willingly have given the whole [supply] Sum out of the Treasury." The Livingstons, on the other hand, were "unwilling that the assembly should at this time when They have not the Lead, gain too much Credit" and took great pains to get instructions everywhere in the colony against granting any troop money—unless it actually came out of a loan office issue. The makeweight of power in the situation was a group of independents who straddled the question and voted mainly with an eye to popular opinion.[77] As predicted the Livingstons proposed that Colden's request for £2,000 for supplies be taken exclusively from loan office monies. When the motion failed by a single vote, the De Lanceys affected a compromise. They asked for and received permission to bring in a supply bill providing that only one-half of the troop appropriation come out of treasury reserves. The remainder would be drawn from the anticipated loan office interest fund.[78]

Clearly the De Lanceys were in a bind. Before the session began, the Colden-De Lancey alliance had thought to use the paper money issue to win support for granting troop supplies out of treasury funds. Carrying water on both shoulders, Colden could then claim that with his aid the "Friends of government" faithfully supported the Quartering Act. A grateful Hillsborough was expected to acquiesce in the loan office plan to both the political and economic advantage of the De Lanceys and their merchant allies. But the need to compromise ruined the Colden-De Lancey bid to ingratiate themselves on both sides of the Atlantic. Colden ended up signing a currency act contrary to his instructions and accepting a supply bill with strings attached.

76. Nov. 21, 22, 23, 29, Dec. 6, 1769, Jour. N.Y. Assembly; Moore to Hillsborough, July 11, 1769, Colden to Hillsborough, Dec. 4, 1769, *N.Y. Col. Docs.*, VIII, 175–176, 191–192; Colden to Hillsborough, Dec. 16, 1769, Jan. 6, 1770, *The Colden Letter Books, 1760–1775* (N.-Y. Hist. Soc., *Colls.*, IX–X [New York, 1877–1878]), II, 195, 201, hereafter cited as *Colden Letter Books*; Sabine, ed., *Smith*, I, 69–70; "Open Letter from McDougall to the Public from New Gaol," *N.-Y. Jour.*, Feb. 15, 1770; *Col. Laws N.Y.*, 24–26. The De Lanceys also took care to evict the opposition leaders from the house; see Nov. 24, 25, 1769, Jan. 12, 1769, Jour. N.Y. Assembly.

77. Colden to Hillsborough, Dec. 16, 1769, Jan. 6, 1770, *Colden Letter Books*, II, 195, 199–201.

78. Dec. 15, 1769, Jour. N.Y. Assembly; n. 76 above; "Open Letter from McDougall," *N.-Y. Jour.*, Feb. 15, 1770.

While Colden prepared to defend his conduct to Hillsborough, the Livingstons organized a last-ditch assault on the provisions bill and the "Friends of government." The most significant thrust against the government came from an outsider. The day following the De Lancey move to supply the troops out of treasury funds, the celebrated tract by Alexander McDougall, "To the Betrayed Inhabitants of the City and Colony of New York," appeared on the streets. McDougall's broadside damned the lieutenant governor and his allies for asking impoverished citizens to supply troops kept there to enslave them and for implicitly acknowledging the authority that levied the Townshend duties. Such a sacrifice of both liberty and property could only be attributed to a "corrupt source," Colden himself, who had but one interest and that was to "make hay while the sun shines." In order to get a full salary from the house, assure jobs for his many sons, and supply the king's troops, he had agreed to sign a currency bill—a promise that was "only a snare to impose on the simple," for the measure would "not obtain the royal assent." However, if no troop money were voted, the assembly would be suspended, and Colden would be out of office. Therefore the De Lanceys "left no stone unturned to prevent a dissolution." The broadside called the citizens to meet in the open, vent their feelings, and to go to the city representatives and demand they join the opposition to the provisions bill.[79]

The polemics had just begun, and the Livingstons now made a headlong newspaper assault on the De Lancey-Colden alliance. In turn the De Lancey apologists, in a desperate effort to gag the critics, publicly assailed the Livingstons for opposing those who voted troop supplies in exchange for a currency issue meant to relieve their distressed constituents. Nevertheless some fourteen hundred New Yorkers answered the call of "To the Betrayed Inhabitants" and viva voce opted for no supplies.[80] But the De Lanceys were not easily cowed, and delegates sent to inform the city representatives of the people's sentiments were told that the majority doubtless favored a provisions bill. When the vote on the measure came up

79. Colden to Hillsborough, Jan. 6, 1770, *Colden Letter Books*, II, 201; The "Friends of government" tract is printed in E. B. O'Callaghan, ed., *The Documentary History of the State of New York* (Albany, N.Y., 1849–1851), III, 528–532. See the discussion of this episode in Bonomi, *A Factious People*, 267–275.

80. The polemical war can easily be followed in the abstracts of broadsides published in "New York Broadsides, 1762–1779," *New York Public Library Bulletin*, III (1899), 25–28, and Stokes, comp., *Iconography of Manhattan Island*, IV, 800–805. See also Bonomi, *A Factious People*, 270–271, and *N.-Y. Jour.*, Dec. 21, 1769, Jan. 18, Feb. 15, Mar. 5, 12, Apr. 19, and May 10, 1770.

before the house, it passed (again by a margin of one). Colden re-affirmed his pledge to favorably receive the currency bill despite the lack of a suspending clause. On January 5 he signed the supply and loan office measures into law. The next move fell to the British ministry.[81]

Shortly after taking office, as noted earlier, Colden had written for approval of the loan office bill sent to Hillsborough by Moore. Approval was to smooth the way for the supply appropriation. But when word had not arrived by the time the General Assembly met in late November, Colden and the De Lanceys decided that their only choice was to pass a loan office measure identical in every way to the Moore bill—but without a suspending clause. The Board of Trade's delay in considering Moore's proposal was a result of the long recess of the Board during the late summer and early fall of 1769. Upon reconvening the commissioners made a close study of every wrinkle and twist of the controversial plan and of the supporting documents sent by Moore, Colden, and the legislature. In the end a doubt arose over wording that possibly violated the meaning and intention of the Currency Act of 1764, and the Board turned for an opinion to the crown law officers, Attorney General William de Grey and Solicitor General John Dunning, who advised that the clause in question might be so construed.[82]

81. *N.-Y. Jour.*, Dec. 28, 1769, Jan. 4, 1770; Dec. 30, 1769, Jan. 4, 5, 1770, Jour. N.Y. Assembly; *Col. Laws N.Y.*, V, 24–26. Dorothy R. Dillon, *The New York Triumvirate: A Study of the Legal and Political Careers of William Livingston, John Morin Scott, and William Smith, Jr.* (New York, 1949), and Carl L. Becker, *The History of Political Parties in the Province of New York, 1760–1776* (Madison, Wis., 1909), offer a very different interpretation of the events in this period, since both focus on the Sons of Liberty and tend to play down the underlying conflict between the Livingston and De Lancey factions. The error of that approach is best seen in the *Original Papers of the Mercantile Library Association of New York City* (New York, 1861), 50–52, and more particularly in Champagne, "New York Politics," a study that in this author's opinion largely supersedes all previous work in the area. The most recent study, Bonomi, *A Factious People*, represents a fascinating attempt to write the political history of colonial New York as an example of interest-group politics. That the author fails to make a convincing case is due in the largest part to her decision to avoid the question of economics and thus of political economy.

82. Nov. 17, 24, Dec. 6, 1769, *Jour. of Comm. Trade, 1768–1775*, 110–114, 116. Available to the Board were Moore's letters of Oct. 21, 1769, Jan. 1, Mar. 30, Apr. 13, May 26, 29, July 11, 1769, and Colden's letters of Sept. 13, Oct. 4, 1769; also available were the New York Council's letters of Sept. 13, Oct. 4, 1769, and Moore's address to the house of May 30, 1769. The critical point is that the Board at this time had no knowledge either of the De Lancey-Colden scheme or of the second loan office act. A copy of the reports of the attorney general and solicitor general may be found in Barnwell, ed., "Garth Correspondence," *S.C. Hist. Gen. Mag.*, XXXI (1930), 289.

Generally speaking, the proposed measure was in no way irregular. Essentially it provided for the creation of a land bank and the issuance of some £120,000 in bills of various denominations. The bills would be distributed according to population quotas to bonded officers of would-be "branch banks" to be set up in the cities and counties of the colony. These "banks" would make loans to any local resident without favor, in amounts of not more than £300 and not less than £50, on a first-come, first-served basis. The loans would be secured by fourteen-year mortgages backed by lands, tenements, and hereditaments valued at double the amount of the principal and by houses at three or four times the amount. As for the clause in dispute, it simply stated that the loan offices would accept the new currency bills in the payment of mortgages for and during the term of fourteen-years; in addition the treasury would take the bills in any settlement of public debts for a fifteen-year period from the date of emission. But because the attorney general and the solicitor general interpreted the Currency Act of 1764 as possibly prohibiting paper money to be legal tender for any obligations, public or private, the clause was taken by the Board of Trade to be illegal. The provision making New York's loan office bills acceptable at the treasury and loan office in payment of debt may have accorded with the spirit of the law, but as Hillsborough later explained to Colden, it did violence to the letter.[83]

In December the Board of Trade reminded the Privy Council of the general policy statement covering the American currency question, which Lord Hillsborough had written in February 1764 as a rationale for the Currency Act. As to the principles underlying the Moore bill, the Board emphasized the doubt raised by the disputed clause and sent along all relevant papers. The commissioners were straddling the issue. They argued, on the one hand, that an emission of paper currency, especially for an extended period, was in principle objectionable and a specific clause in the New York proposal was in fact illegal. On the other hand local conditions in New York might conceivably warrant a fourteen-year issue of currency to be lawful for specified public debts. They vaguely concluded that the Privy Council should "give such advice to His Majesty upon the matter, as to your Lordships' wisdom shall seem expedient."[84] It is

83. *Col. Laws N.Y.*, V, 24–26; Hillsborough to Colden, Dec. 9, 1769, *N.Y. Col. Docs.*, VIII, 193.
84. "Representation of the Lords of Trade Regarding an Emission of Bills of Credit," Dec. 28, 1769, *N.Y. Col. Docs.*, VIII, 195–196. New York's colonial agent,

possible of course that the king in Council, by executive interpretation, might have altered the meaning of the Currency Act of 1764, at least as far as it applied to New York. But the point is altogether conjectural.

On February 8, 1769, two Colden letters came before the Board of Trade that killed any chances for approval of either the Moore or Colden bills. Although the first letter spoke of a new loan office, it noted only that the new measure was identical with the Moore proposal and would probably pass both the lower house and the Council. The other letter was a defense of Colden's having signed a second currency bill without attaching a suspending clause and without receiving any word from England concerning the fate of the earlier proposal. Colden justified his action in three principal ways. He alluded to an opposition party that had so effectively aroused popular feeling against the troop appropriation that the "Friends of government" had had to compromise and grant half of the supply funds out of the loan office measure. Even then the bill carried by a small majority, and it would not have carried at all had not the friends of administration received promises that the currency measure would have the lieutenant governor's signature. Colden reiterated his earlier claim that the first and second loan office proposals were essentially the same. He added as well that no bills of credit would be issued in any event until the middle of June, six months distant, sufficient time for the crown to veto the measure if that were deemed necessary. Thus as Colden saw it, he had ignored the form, not the substance, of the suspending clause. Finally, like Moore, Colden concluded that the loan office, by creating a fourteen-year reserve fund under the governor's control, would successfully eliminate for at least a decade any problem of troop supply.[85]

The Board was not persuaded. It immediately recommended a veto of the second loan office measure, emphasizing the lack of a suspending clause and Colden's failure to await a decision on the Moore bill. In addition the commissioners hinted that Colden might have signed the second measure knowing of the "difficulties which had arisen in point of law" over a clause in the original. If so, the lieutenant governor's action violated his trust. The Privy Council

---

Robert Charles, was partly responsible for the presentation of the two sides of the case; see Dec. 6, 1769, *Jour. of Comm. Trade, 1768–1775*, 116.

85. *Jour. of Comm. Trade, 1768–1775*, 167; Colden to Hillsborough, Dec. 4, 1769, Jan. 6, 1770, *Colden Letter Books*, II, 193–194, 199–202.

rejected the Moore bill at once. Colden's offering received equally short shrift.[86]

At this point Secretary Hillsborough received a letter suggesting that Colden had been unaware of any difficulties over the disputed clause. Like the Board of Trade, Hillsborough had fumed over Colden's early letters and had upbraided him for neglecting to instruct the assembly of the steps taken in London in connection with the first loan office measure. Had that been done, the assembly would not have had the "colour of a pretence" in framing another bill pending the king's consideration of an earlier and similar proposal. In fact, if Colden had not attempted to stop such proceedings, the crown would have learned of his "imprudence and want of attention."[87] But after the latest dispatch Hillsborough understood Colden's problem for the first time. More important, he approved of Colden's solution. In reply the secretary expostulated with the old man over the deletion of the suspending clause and the refusal to await official action on the original measure. Nothing was said about the loan's fourteen-year term. Hillsborough's chief point was that the crown was pleased with the troop supply act; the king considered "preserving the Colony in tranquility as a very desirable and commendable object." Despite the royal veto of New York's two paper money bills, such was "the paternal attention of His Majesty to the wishes of his subjects, in New York . . . that notwithstanding the steady opinion of all His Majesty's servants that it is against the true interest of the Colony to have a paper currency attended with any degree of legal tender, yet I have reason to believe, the Parliament will be moved to pass an Act to enable the Legislature of New York to carry into execution the Bill they appear so desirous of."[88]

86. Feb. 8, 26, 1770, *Jour. of Comm. Trade, 1768–1775*, 167, 173; Privy Council to king, Feb. 8, 9, 14, 1770, *N.Y. Col. Docs.*, VIII, 202–203, 215–216.

87. Hillsborough to Colden, Jan. 18, Feb. 17, 1770, *N.Y. Col. Docs.*, VIII, 201, 205–206.

88. Feb. 17, 1770, *ibid.*, 205–206. The dispatch was a letter of Dec. 16, 1769, and apparently Hillsborough received it just before the king vetoed the second loan office bill. The secretary explained to Colden that the letter did not permit him to inform the king as to why a part of the troop money was to come out of the new bills of credit. It should be noted that Colden had the cooperation of General Gage, who, satisfied that his troops could be provisioned, supported the second loan office proposal. It is most likely that Gage's letters to Hillsborough were also a factor in convincing the secretary that he should permit New York to strike money on loan; see Gage to Hillsborough, Dec. 4, 16, 1769, Feb. 21, 1770, Clarence E. Carter, ed., *The Correspondence of General Thomas Gage with the Secretaries of State, 1763–1775* (New Haven, Conn., 1931), I, 242–243, 248.

Whatever the feeling may have been in the situation, it is important to note that the new North ministry wished generally to avoid arousing the Americans any further. The "Quiet Period" had begun.

THE CURRENCY ACT OF 1770

By the fall of 1769 New York's political situation had fundamentally altered. The De Lanceys' stand on the supply issue had alienated the Sons of Liberty, who in a series of brawls beginning with the Battle of Golden Hill in January 1770 had since renewed the dispute with the soldiers. The De Lanceys reciprocated in kind. Early in March a broadside appeared favoring troop appropriations and abusing the American patriots as party tools. "The frequent Notices to meet at the Liberty Pole, the violent Rage and Resentment which some People have endeavoured generally to excite against Soldiers, pretended to proceed from a Love of Liberty, and or Regard to the Interests of the Poor"—may not all of this mean that "if we cannot breed a Disturbance, and kick up a Dust in one Way, we must in another. . . . And if we cannot render Mr. Colden's Administration odious, and breed Dissensions and Animosities amongst the People; and 'frighten the Assembly' . . . all our Hopes in a future Election will be blasted."[89] Immediately after receiving Hillsborough's conciliatory letter in late April 1770, Colden informed the Council that a parliamentary bill recognizing New York's need to create a land bank would soon become law.[90] That same day the newspapers carried a notice of the crown's veto of the two loan office measures along with an anonymous note to the effect that Parliament would shortly pass an act allowing the province to strike an issue on loan that was lawful for all public debts.[91] This promise together with the more important news of the repeal of the Townshend Acts, which arrived a few weeks later, apparently encouraged the city merchants to put an end to their nonimportation agreements of July.[92] The action fol-

89. Stokes, comp., *Iconography of Manhattan Island*, IV, 807.
90. Sabine, ed., *Smith*, I, 80–81.
91. Stokes, comp., *Iconography of Manhattan Island*, IV, 808.
92. See Champagne, "New York Politics," chap. 9; William Samuel Johnson to Jonathan Trumbull, May 21, 1770, *Letters of William Samuel Johnson* (Mass. Hist. Soc., *Colls.*, 5th Ser., IX [Boston, 1885]), 438; Fluydor, Marsh, and Hudson to James Beekman, June 17, 1769, in White, ed., *Beekman Mercantile Papers*, II, 720.

lowed strictly partisan lines. Meanwhile Colden regaled Hillsborough with further accounts of efforts by himself and the "Friends of government" to provision the troops and "check the promoters of discord."[93]

In London, New York's colonial agent, Robert Charles, set in motion a series of actions on behalf of the province that resulted in passage of the Currency Act of 1770. Early in April 1770, as a member of the Commons, Charles petitioned Parliament for the privilege of bringing in an amendment to the Currency Act of 1764 authorizing New York to issue bills of credit as legal tender for all public purposes. South Carolina's agent, Charles Garth, who also sat in the Commons, promptly moved the insertion of a clause making *all* colonial paper lawful for public transactions. But the motion failed on grounds that there was nothing to show that the other colonies even desired such a power, and "Doubts were entertained of the Propriety of departing at all" from the Currency Act. Therefore the Commons felt that "before such a general Amendment was come into, it was fit to try the Effect and Operation of this particular Departure."[94]

Nor did "poor Charles's" amendment pass without a hitch. As the agent told Benjamin Franklin, it was seen as a private bill for which he was to pay expenses amounting to nearly £2,000. Even then the measure was so altered that he feared that it might prove useless. Franklin later reported that "Charles was so bewildered and distressed with the affair, that he finally put an end to his perplexities— BY A RAZOR!"[95] Possibly out of a sense of condolence rather than conviction, or both together, Parliament finally did pass the act of dispensation in early May. New York was permitted to issue £120,-000 on loan to be legal tender in payments to the loan office for fourteen years and to the treasury for the same term plus one year.[96] A month later Hillsborough wrote Colden that he felt the lieutenant governor had "erred from real good intention" in signing the loan

93. Colden to Hillsborough, Apr. 14, 25, May 16, July 7, Aug. 18, Oct. 5, 1770, *N.Y. Col. Docs.*, VIII, 212–217, 245, 248–249, and Colden to B.T., May 16, 1770, *Colden Letter Books*, II, 219–220.

94. Garth to S.C. Comm. of Corres., May 14, 1770, Barnwell, ed., "Garth Correspondence," *S.C. Hist. Gen. Mag.*, XXXI (1930), 284–286, 290; *Jours. of Commons*, XXXIII, 895.

95. To Joseph Galloway, June 11, 1770, in Van Doren, ed., *Franklin's Autobiographical Writings*, 194.

96. *Jours. of Commons*, XXXII, 899, 908, 916, 921, 979, 982; Pickering, ed., *Statutes of Great Britain*, XXVII, 306.

office bill. If the legislature passed the sort of law Parliament had authorized, the crown would approve it.[97]

Hillsborough's letter arrived in New York in August together with the act of dispensation, which immediately appeared in the local press.[98] Opposition to the law began at once. On August 23 a correspondent to the *New-York Journal* deprecated the parliamentary measure because it allowed for legal tender in public transactions only. If currency were no good between man and man, a debtor could not pay his creditor and would end in jail. The political implication of this and similar items became clear shortly after Lord Dunmore arrived in the province as replacement for the late Governor Moore. In a public letter to the freeholders of the colony, a Livingston hack asserted that the Currency Act of 1764 banned only paper money that passed as lawful tender in private transactions. He argued that for some time Connecticut had accepted bills of credit at the treasury for payment of public debts; why should there now be such excitement when Parliament had clearly extended no rights the province did not already enjoy? The Currency Act of 1770 only encroached upon the rights and liberties of American assemblies. New York was to give England no precedent. No currency emission should be voted at the upcoming session of the assembly.[99]

Whatever the constitutional issue involved, there was no mistaking the political intent of such remarks. If a currency bill failed to pass, there would be no loan office money for the soldiers from that source. And after the appearance of the "Betrayed Inhabitants" broadside there was no possibility of voting provisions from existing funds. Governor Dunmore's remaining option would be to dissolve the house and order new elections. The Livingstons seemed to be ringing the changes on an old theme. "Rather suffer a little longer under the cruel gripings of greedy usurers," concluded one Livingston supporter, "then give up the command of your treasury into

97. June 12, 1770, *N.Y. Col. Docs.*, VIII, 215–216.
98. Colden to Hillsborough, Aug. 18, 1770, *Colden Letter Books*, II, 225–227; *N.-Y. Jour.*, Aug. 16, 1770.
99. *N.-Y. Jour.*, Nov. 8, 1770. There was no basis to the claim that New York, like Connecticut, had the right to strike paper money to be lawful in all public dealings. True, the New England colonies, falling under the Currency Act of 1751, could issue bills acceptable at the treasury for the payment of public debts. But in its New York decision, the Privy Council construed the Currency Act of 1764 to mean that the colonies outside New England were prohibited from issuing fiat money in any form, for any reason.

the hands of a set of men who if they continue in their present principles, will squander it away upon [the King's soldiers] that have it in their power to entail poverty and slavery on you and your posterity. Remember, the love of money is the root of all evil."[100]

Demand in New York for paper money was so general and intense by 1770 that the notion of blocking the loan office bill to cut off troop supplies seemed farfetched. Only rumors of impending war with Spain gave credence to the idea of stopping the bill as a means of pressuring the crown and Parliament to yield to provincial demands. Thus General Gage wrote to Hillsborough just before the New York General Assembly convened in December 1770 of a design to oppose any currency issue not lawful for all obligations. The colonials counted on the wartime need for military appropriations to emit paper money in the shape they chose. In brief the Livingstons were playing on expectations that the ministry would reinstate the lax monetary policies of the French and Indian War period.[101] The war scare quickly blew over. By the middle of January 1771, in the absence of news of any hostilities, the assembly gave in—although the legislators steadfastly refused to attach a suspending clause to the measure and got away with it.[102] The victory was short-lived, however. By 1772 the British credit system collapsed for the second time within a decade. America was plunged into another business depression, the worst to date.

Clearly the first parliamentary revision of the Currency Act of 1764 had little to do with any British understanding of economic realities in America. It had even less to do with an earlier attempt by a coalition of colonial agents and London merchants to have the ministry admit error and reform the colonial monetary system. Rather the act of 1770 was essentially a response to colonial political needs and to the British army's supply requirements. One aim was to ease tensions in New York. Another was to support the De Lancey-

---

100. *N.-Y. Jour.*, Nov. 8, 1770.

101. Dec. 7, 1770, in Carter, ed., *Gage Correspondence*, I, 284.

102. *Col. Laws N.Y.*, V, 149–170. The ministry did not formally approve or disapprove of the act. When a copy came before the Board of Trade, it was put aside for further consideration because of the provision permitting counterfeiters of New York's currency operating outside the colony to be brought to and tried in New York. Nothing ever came of the question. See Edmund Burke to the N.Y. Comm. of Corres., May 6, 1772, in Ross J. S. Hoffman, ed., *Edmund Burke, New York Agent, with His Letters to the New York Assembly* ... (Philadelphia, 1956), 205.

Colden mercantile alliance in its efforts to pass a troop appropriations bill under the general terms of the Quartering Act. But the
chief consequence was that the law served as a precedent in the next
revision of the Currency Act of 1764.

Chapter 9
The Currency Act of 1773

The administration of the Currency Act of 1764 struck many Americans as blatantly inconsistent, a fact Governor William Franklin of New Jersey underscored in an angry exchange with Secretary Hillsborough later in 1770. The circumstances were the rejection of a New Jersey public loan earlier that year because the proposed bills of credit would be lawful for all debts and mortgages. According to Franklin, "It was never imagined here that so extensive a Construction would be put upon the Act of Parliament for restraining paper Currencies." To expect a man to mortgage his estate for money which was not a tender to the loan office that issued it was the "Height of Absurdity." But what made New Jersey's situation unbearable, the governor asserted, was that neighboring Pennsylvania and Maryland had "for some Years past, and at this very Time, a considerable Sum of paper Money circulating, which, tho' not a legal Tender in common Payments . . . is nevertheless a Tender to the Treasuries from whence it issued."[1]

Admittedly Franklin was being somewhat disingenuous. It was clear that in Pennsylvania, unlike Maryland, treasury notes were not in fact lawful for public debts. They were receivable at the treasury, but this was a matter of practice, not law. They were a tender, perhaps, but not necessarily a lawful tender. Nonetheless the effect was the same. And Franklin bitterly concluded his remarks to Hillsborough with the observation that not one of the currency acts of either Pennsylvania or Maryland was ever disallowed. Nor was Franklin the only American to spot the contradiction. A few months earlier Joseph Galloway had registered his surprise

at the conduct of the administration, in regulation to the New York and New Jersey paper money bills. The reasons assigned for their rejection

1. Sept. 29, 1770, *N.J. Archives*, X, 200.

are really ridiculous, and can be accounted for on no other ground than that they are determined the Americans shall not have any paper medium at all. Is not every promiser in a promissory note obliged to receive his note, every banker to take his bill, and every drawer of a bill of exchange to take it back, if not paid; and yet I never understood that such notes or bills were ever deemed legal tender? When I lend or deposit with another, one hundred pounds, he gives me paper, or a promissory note for repayment. Is he not obliged to receive his paper and deliver me my deposit? Such is the case of a bank bill, and inland bill of exchange, as well as foreign. And the same is the case with respect to American paper money. A farmer pledges his land to the government, and takes paper. When he comes to redeem his pledge, ought he not to return the paper, and ought the government to be obliged to receive it in discharge of the land? To say that the statute intended to prevent this, is to say it prohibits all paper money in America. But how is their conduct on this occasion to be reconciled with what has passed heretofore. Several of our late laws for the support of government, and the act for payment of the debts of the House of Employment, were liable to the same objection, and yet they have been laid before the King in Council and passed unrepealed.[2]

As Franklin and Galloway suggested, imperial authorities did seem to be entangled in a curious sophistry. On one hand, the letter of the Currency Act was to be literally followed, and no paper money struck that was explicitly made lawful for any obligations, public or private. On the other, a colony could issue paper acceptable for all public debts as long as the act of emission omitted the objectionable term "legal tender." No sophistry was intended, however. Whatever lapses there may have been in the past, as long as Secretary Hillsborough was in charge of American affairs the letter of the currency law was to be applied. Opposed to fiat money of any kind and committed to the idea of parliamentary supremacy and to a strict interpretation of parliamentary law, the secretary began to press for tighter enforcement of the Currency Act of 1764 from the first day he took office early in 1768.

It is not surprising then that Franklin's outburst had a bad effect. After Hillsborough in the spring of 1770 had unsuccessfully disputed Pennsylvania's handling of its treasury issues, no further challenges to the colonies were forthcoming until after the arrival of the Franklin letter. That document, it appears, only strengthened the secretary's doubts about all the various dodges certain colonies had used to make paper money "a Legal Tender at the Treasury."

2. To Benjamin Franklin, June 21, 1770, Sparks, ed., *Works of Franklin*, VII, 482.

Consequently, in language reminiscent of Franklin's complaint, Hillsborough admonished Governor Josiah Martin of North Carolina late in 1771 to pay careful attention to the parliamentary law "as some Other colonies have, by framing their Acts for establishing a Paper Credit in such a manner as to make those Bills a Legal Tender at the Treasury of the Colony, laid the Privy Council under the necessity of advising the King to disallow them."[3] Likewise he warned the Virginians at the same time that he had learned that their treasury, like Pennsylvania's, regularly accepted any and all paper money for public debts, an expedient he deemed contrary to the Currency Act of 1764.[4]

But whatever plans were taking shape in the secretary's mind at the time, the fact was that by the end of 1771 Hillsborough had become persona non grata with the recently installed North ministry, for reasons that in retrospect seem perfectly clear. Though avowedly not an "amibitious man," the head of the new ministry, Lord North, had carefully calculated his chances before finally taking office in January 1770; Edmund Burke compared him to an oyster that "lay still, gasping for the tide, ready to receive it, whether it came from the east, west, north, or south, and taking it in, however muddy, foul, and dirty."[5] North was no less cautious after assuming the leadership of a bare parliamentary majority. He took every precaution to avoid being overthrown, while he went about the difficult task of winning over as many of the more than three hundred members of Parliament as possible. In this situation Secretary Hillsborough's insistence on roiling colonial waters over currency and other questions required his removal. It was only a short while therefore before the secretary found himself overruled by his ministerial colleagues, who finally drove him from the government in the late summer of 1772.[6]

Hillsborough's replacement in the American Department was Lord Dartmouth, a reputed "friend to America." In fact the new secretary turned out to be something less than friendly, although his reading of the Currency Act of 1764 was liberal enough. In only a few months he had Parliament give legal recognition to the monetary practices current in Pennsylvania and other colonies. Following

3. Dec. 4, 1771, *Col. Recs. N.C.*, IX, 65.
4. Dec. 4, 1771, C.O. 5/1375, P.R.O.
5. *Pa. Jour.*, Apr. 26, 1770.
6. See Lawrence H. Brown, "The Grafton and North Cabinets, 1766–1775" (Ph.D. diss., University of Toronto, 1963), 268–341.

years of unsuccessful lobbying by the American agents and their merchant allies, the Currency Act finally was revised by a ministry up to its neck in domestic problems and therefore anxious to allow colonial matters "to return to old channels."

THE BRITISH RESPONSE: NEW JERSEY, 1769–1772

The New Jersey legislature showed every bit as much anger as Governor Franklin at what it took to be the high-handed treatment of its second bid for a public loan. Following the Board of Trade's rejection of its first loan office plan because of an implied legal tender provision, the General Assembly had carefully excised the objectionable clause before resubmitting the legislation for royal approval early in October 1769. More important, while the government awaited word of the fate of the second plan, clamor for additional currency and a public loan had become greater than ever.[7] By the late fall of 1769 petitioners from Middlesex County had already pointed to the "deplorable state" of the province arising "partly from the excessive scarcity of money and the decay of trade: But chiefly from the multiplicity of Law Suits, mostly for debt, which like an overflowing stream have deluged the land, and ruined hundreds of families." They wanted a public loan "on land security," a reduction in the tax load, and a lowering of fee costs in debt actions.[8]

Those espousing a more direct form of action for redress of grievances were heard from that following spring, when a series of riots suddenly erupted in a number of the counties in an apparent effort to prevent the prosecution of hard-pressed debtors. "What is the Case of Two Thirds of the People" of New Jersey "and that of every Degree, more or less?" an anonymous commentator asked the readers of the *New-York Gazette* at the time. "They are in Want of Money; they are in Debt; and . . . cannot pay; they are sued; Judgments are obtained against them, they try to borrow, offer good Security for the Money, but all in vain, there is no Money, nor Money lenders; execution issues against them, a heavy Bill of Cost arises, the Sheriff levies, advertizes and sells them Effects for one fourth or fifth part of their Value. . . . A Man possessed of an Estate worth £5,000, will have it torn from him, tho' all his Debts amount to but £1,000, a Situation which will naturally make a man feel

7. Middlesex County petition to Franklin, Oct. 1769, printed in *N.J. Archives*, XXVI, 529–533.
8. *Ibid.*

desperate." It was this that led many "even of the better Sort of
People" to wink at and even to "secretly encourage the illegal Steps
that have been taken." Thus the problem did not lay with the
lawyers and heavy legal fees. Such fees were regulated by law, and
lawyers who exceeded fee schedules "were open to a Prosecution or
Complaint to the Court." The real issue at hand, the writer concluded, was the lack of money, a fact the assembly clearly recognized. The only solution was a public loan; the province was to
strike and dole out some £100,000 in amounts not exceeding £100
per inhabitant to be repaid in twenty years at 5 percent annual interest. Further, until such time as the scheme could be put into
effect, the assembly should suspend all forced sales by the sheriffs.

Against such a background, when word of the royal veto arrived
in the summer of 1770 in the middle of a monetary and political
crisis, Governor Franklin had good reason to worry that "a Party"
would "take Advantage of the Ill humour." Specifically Franklin
feared that a faction would prevail on the legislators to defy British
authority as represented in the Quartering Act of 1765.[9]

When first passed, the Quartering Act had had no effect on New
Jersey. Following the Treaty of Paris the province had closed down
all five of its barracks, rented them, and sold off the furnishings. But
after the Stamp Act riots and the march of troops through the colony
in the summer of 1766, the General Assembly canceled the barracks'
leases and appointed commissioners to refurbish the buildings and
supply firewood, bedding, blankets, and such other necessaries as
were customary. In brief, following the recent example of New
York, New Jersey agreed to provide most of the articles required by
parliamentary law, while refusing to insert "the very words" of the
act in its appropriations.[10] Likewise in June 1767 the assembly granted
a flat £500 per barracks. In the end the crown vetoed both measures
for not allowing all the necessaries specified by law. The assembly
refused to budge from its position, however, and the impasse was

---

9. Quoted, *ibid.*, XXVII, 80–85; Franklin to Hillsborough, Sept. 29, 1770, *ibid.*, X,
200–201. For a discussion of the riots see Lundin, *Cockpit of the Revolution*, 57–59,
and Richard S. Field, *The Provincial Courts of New Jersey* (New York, 1849),
171–172.

10. Franklin to Shelburne, Dec. 15, 1766, B.T. to the king, June 10, 1768, *N.J.
Archives*, IX, 577, X, 22–23. The New Jersey reaction to the Quartering Act was
unique: the law was judged to be "virtually as much an act for laying rates on the
inhabitants as the Stamp Act," except that the Quartering Act was more "partial."
That is, the army housed its troops in only a few of the colonies, exempting the rest
from any part of the expenses.

not broken until the new Quartering Act of 1769 dropped the provision requiring a colony to itemize troop supplies.[11]

During the winter of 1769/1770 the New Jersey legislature voted to provide for the king's soldiers as in the past—"notwithstanding endeavors were used to induce them to follow the example of South Carolina" and to refuse any support.[12] At the same time Governor Franklin blocked a design on the part of some assembly members to tack the supply question onto the bill for a public loan, as the New York legislature had done under similar circumstances. According to Franklin the house majority had proven tractable because it wished to avoid offending the crown, thus risking the loss of the loan office.[13] But when the king went ahead and scuttled plans for a second loan anyway, the currency and supply issues could no longer be separated. On receiving news of the royal veto of the latest loan office act, the assembly argued that it had waived every essential consideration in framing the measure to prevent such a thing from happening.[14] Unable to see how they could draft another bill answering the purpose of a currency and still meet ministerial objections, a majority of the members moved to tie the loan to the provisions question, as Franklin had feared. Late in October 1770 the house narrowly resolved not to appropriate any further supplies. Because of the closeness of the vote, Franklin immediately closeted with a number of the assembly leaders and, after threatening a parliamentary suspension of the legislature and promising strict economy, obtained a £500 treasury grant to be placed directly under his control—a concession to the fact that a recent exposure had proved fraudulence on the part of a barracks master responsible to the house. The only condition attached was that the grant was the last one he could expect. Any future provisions were to be raised by a tax to be levied only after increasing the paper money supply.[15]

Six months later, in the spring of 1771, the governor suddenly called the legislature back into session. He explained that despite

11. Franklin to Hillsborough, Nov. 23, 1768, William Franklin to Benjamin Franklin, May 11, 1769, *N.J. Archives*, X, 83, 111.
12. Dec. 6, 1769, N.J. Gen. Assembly, in Jenkins, ed., *Microfilm Records of the States*. On South Carolina's example see Ernst, "Growth of the Commons House of Assembly," 114-117.
13. Franklin to Hillsborough, Nov. 5, 1770, *N.J. Archives*, X, 202-203.
14. Oct. 18, 1770, N.J. Gen. Assembly.
15. Oct. 23, 1770, *ibid.*; Franklin to Hillsborough, Nov. 5, 1770, *N.J. Archives*, X, 202-203.

utmost care and frugality on his part the £500 grant had run out. He wanted more money. But he noted that the royal veto precluded any discussion of the possibility of another loan office bill. As a consequence the house said nothing about currency and simply reaffirmed its refusal to make further appropriations or to levy new taxes on a people already burdened with a heavy wartime debt.[16]

Franklin was not to be put off so easily. The governor discerned a great improvement of the province since 1763. He asserted that New Jersey could easily afford an additional tax, arguing that commodity prices had remained at relatively high levels since 1754. Nor were the colonists seriously burdened by their zeal for the king's service. Franklin noted that Jersey had financed its wartime operations and the cost of local government through the use of the printing press and the issuance of some £350,000 currency. The resulting debt was to be sunk over a twenty-nine-year period, which, according to Franklin, worked no hardship on anyone. He claimed that there was not a county in the province where taxes were over "Six-pence in the Pound on Land and Stock, and in many places not above Four-pence," though "none but profitable Land" was rated. This hardly compared with English taxes of "*Four Shillings* in the Pound, besides innumerable other Taxes unknown to the People" of New Jersey. But the more important question, Franklin declared, was, Could the province, without either a loan office or the imposition of new taxes, provision the king's soldiers? The governor paraded out an elaborate set of treasury figures to prove that it could, and "without calling in a farthing" of paper money.

An interesting twist to Franklin's argument turned on the fact that in New Jersey during the war all the paper money issued was "originally made current for His Majesty's Service only." In that case, the governor wondered, by "what Colour of Reason" could the assembly now refuse to apply such money for crown use upon a requisition again made in the king's name for just that purpose? Moreover, at the time of the Stamp Act repeal, the house members had assured the king "that as they have *heretofore* granted Aids to the Crown, suitable to their Circumstances; so *whenever* Requisitions are made for that Purpose, in the ancient and accustomed Manner, their Duty to His Majesty, and *Concern* for the *Glory* and *Interest* of *Britain*, will *ever* induce them *cheerfully* to *comply* therewith to the *utmost* of their *Abilities*." How then, Franklin

16. May 29, 31, 1771, N.J. Gen. Assembly.

queried, "consistent with the *Duty* you owe *your Constituents*," can you withhold money for provisions? Could the king ever pay regard to any future declarations of New Jersey if refused this needed appropriation?

After making a number of lesser points, the governor ended his polemic with a threat. If the legislators continued to oppose Parliament, they would "in the opinion of every sensible Man, act a Part extremely rash and imprudent, and big with Mischief."[17]

The house appeared unimpressed. It reminded Franklin that in the past the legislature had appropriated money in the expectation that the governor would use his influence to win approval for a public loan, not request "further aids" for the soldiers. And without a loan and a ready supply of credit, public debtors could not hope to pay the treasury short of selling their lands at a great loss, a clear proof of the distress of the colony. In addition invidious comparisons between England's taxes and New Jersey's taxes were irrelevant. Britain raised taxes on the pound value of annual rents. In New Jersey they were levied on capital. As for the state of the treasury, the governor had overlooked that most assets were frozen, that there were a number of debits that available cash could not cover. Nor was the "elaborate history of the appropriations to the late war" a persuasive argument. It proved only that a loyal citizenry had mortgaged itself to the year 1783 in support of the crown. Finally, the house blamed the high price of wheat and other commodities on short supplies resulting from crop failures and worn-out soil; the farmers got higher prices for their scarce crops, but profits were less. Besides, not more than a quarter of the population raised grain, while everyone who had to buy bread "was reduced to distress." The representatives concluded that "the reason your excellency and we give such different accounts of the riches of the province, is easy to account for: you see nothing but affluence, we see the distress of the people."[18]

17. Franklin to the General Assembly, Apr. 23, 1771, *N.J. Archives*, X, 243–251. The view that there had been a "great improvement" since the end of the war had been asserted in the so-called Quota Act of 1769, a fact that Franklin was quick to point out. That act placed a levy on "goods and chattels, lands and tenements" by county in "proportion and manner" as required by law. The proportions were fixed until 1769, when they were altered in accordance with the so-called "great improvement of the colony." But this reference had as much to do with the increased population in the period and the erection of a new county as with any other factor. See 10 Geo. III, c. 8, N.J. Session Laws, in Jenkins, ed., *Microfilm Records of the States*.

18. Apr. 25, 1771, N.J. Gen. Assembly. The remark about wheat prices seems dis-

Franklin had temporarily lost touch with reality. He was well aware of the recent riots and the growing clamor for paper money, and before bandying words with the legislators, he had been as outspoken as they were about the monetary crisis and the need for additional currency. Consequently he convinced no one of the justice of his remarks, except perhaps Lord Hillsborough and himself. Early in June, Hillsborough learned from Franklin that it was "a notorious Fact that the Colony was never in a more flourishing Condition than at present, and that there is now actually in the Treasury a greater Sum of Paper Money unappropriated . . . than is sufficient to answer the present Demand."[19] Certain that he had won over the legislators, Franklin promised the secretary that he would recall the assembly as soon as possible. But on reconvening, the house remained adamant in its refusal to vote troop supplies. And when a short time later Cortlandt Skinner, a Franklin supporter, brought in a bill to issue £100,000 on loan—which was *not* legal tender for mortgages—he was overwhelmingly defeated.[20]

A month before, the governor had refused to countenance any kind of public loan, and the Skinner measure was meant to salve assembly feelings. If it did not, it was seemingly because the house chose a course of action consistent with past behavior. Franklin, however, explained his defeat another way. He wrote Hillsborough that the representatives had expected that a dissolution would shortly take place. They therefore had voted against the supply issue to appease "the common people and so secure their election." Franklin then offered Hillsborough two plans for bringing the assembly to heel. Either the legislature should be suspended, "as was done in the case of New York on like occasion," or it should be allowed to strike money as legal tender at the treasury and loan offices "on condition that part of the interest should be annually applied to the support of the troops." He might have added, "as was also done in New York on like occasion." Franklin's plan was to prorogue the

---

ingenuous. Wheat production in the middle colonies as a whole soared in the late 1760s in response to favorable foreign markets, and there is no reason to believe that New Jersey did not share in these favorable conditions. On the other hand prices in the late 1750s and early 1760s were often a response to short crops in America. The debate seemed interminable. It ended only after Franklin prorogued the assembly, although not before he had the last word. See Apr. 29, 1777, N.J. Gen. Assembly. Franklin's claim about tax rates was essentially correct; see Shaw, *History of Essex and Sussex Counties*, I, 26.

19. June 1, 1771, *N.J. Archives*, X, 297–298.
20. May 31, 1771, N.J. Gen. Assembly.

house from time to time until the king made his pleasure known.[21]

Doubtless Franklin hoped to try his hand at a game Cadwallader Colden had played to a successful conclusion in New York a couple of years before. Like Colden, Franklin knew enough to ask for further revisions in the Currency Act of 1764. Unlike Colden he had testified earlier to the flourishing condition of the province and to the surplus of treasury funds. Consequently Hillsborough saw no emergency, and in his reply written late in the summer of 1771 he was careful to avoid committing himself to either scheme. From what Franklin had written, Hillsborough saw not the "least Colour" for refusing to supply the troops. The New Jersey action could only be viewed as a "wilfull Contempt for the Authority of Parliament."[22]

Hillsborough had lost any real influence with the North ministry by the end of 1771, so that there was no possibility of parliamentary intervention. Without committing himself on the public loan, therefore, the secretary suggested Franklin resubmit his request for supplies and see what happened. Seemingly the governor was left to make the most of a difficult situation. On the other hand Hillsborough's silence on the loan question may well have reflected the confusion at the Board of Trade over New Jersey's currency practices.

At about the same time Secretary Hillsborough had written to Franklin, the Board of Trade also inquired about a nebulous point in the last act for the support of government. Did the phrase, "Salaries to be paid out of such Money made current for His Majesty's Service in the late War that now is in the Treasury . . . ," mean that there were "quantities of Paper Bills remaining in the Treasury" whose redemption date had passed but that would be brought into circulation again by the particular bill's curious wording? In a long but illuminating reply Franklin outlined the system used in New Jersey to sink paper money. The wording of the bill, he noted, was faulty. The verb should have been "*granted*," not "paid out," since no money as such was to be found in the treasury. Under former currency acts all authorized bills of credit were either doled out to commissioners appointed to pay and clothe New Jersey troops or paid out for the support of government. Money "in the Treasury" simply referred to the amount of "several balances" due from the commissioners after they had performed "their duties." They sub-

---

21. June 1, 1771, *N.J. Archives*, X, 297–298.
22. Hillsborough to Franklin, July 19, 1771, *ibid.*, 304.

sequently settled these balances in gold, silver, and bills of credit of New Jersey and neighboring colonies. As for the old currency, the assembly regularly called it in and burned it. Still it sometimes happened that there was "but little among it of the particular Emission which ought to be sunk at that Time." Bills emitted in the year 1761, for instance, which by law might be current until 1774, when a portion was directed to be called in, "may be all sunk before that Period commences, and other bills of a former Emission, which ought to have been already sunk, may continue in Circulation until the Year 1783, the last Period allowed by Law for the Existence of Paper Currency." The practice "took its Rise from Necessity, the New Jersey Currency having such an extensive Circulation through the Neighbouring Provinces, that the Treasurers have never had it in their Power to collect a sufficient Quantity of the particular Emission directed to be sunk in any one Year."[23]

When the General Assembly reconvened in November 1771, Franklin let the supply question slide until a number of important bills had cleared the house. Only then did he ask that General Gage be reimbursed for purchases made between March and November for provisioning the king's troops presently stationed in Jersey. In his usual manner the governor advised that a refusal would have disagreeable consequences. On the other hand only a small appropriation was needed to tide the soldiers over until they permanently

23. B.T. to Franklin, June 21, 1771, Franklin to B.T., Oct. 21, 1771, *ibid.*, 300–301, 315–317. Because of this practice there was always the possibility of fraud on the part of the provincial treasurers. The classic example, of course, is the Robinson scandal. Fortunately New Jersey was spared that experience, although the record does reveal problems of a similar kind. For instance in one case the wife of a former treasurer returned to the province some £500 that she had "found" at home and that no one knew existed. Apparently the money was part of an issue of £10,000 that was slated to be exchanged for ragged and torn bills. More important was the Skinner affair. In the summer of 1768 the public money chest of Stephen Skinner, the treasurer of the eastern division, was rifled of some £6,000 to £7,000 in uncut paper bills and coin. The assembly subsequently found Skinner guilty of negligence and therefore accountable for the stolen money. But Governor Franklin refused to take action against Skinner, and the matter became a cause célèbre in the struggle between the legislature and the executive. Matters only worsened when in mid-1773 the Skinner question became entangled in the prosecution, in which Franklin took an active part, of a local counterfeiting ring that was supposedly responsible for the theft in the first place. The upshot was that in the early part of 1774 Skinner suddenly resigned his office and was immediately called to the Council. For its part the legislature then passed an act enabling the new treasurer to bring action against Skinner for the stolen money. But the Revolution terminated the contest, with Skinner joining the British. For a fuller discussion see Lundin, *Cockpit of the Revolution*, chap. 2, and Scott, "Counterfeiting in Colonial New Jersey," N.J. Hist. Soc., *Procs.*, LXXV (1957), 170–179.

quit New Jersey for the Floridas. The house refused. According to the members the treasury stood empty at a time when the rejection of the recent public loan deprived the province of every resource save additional taxes, an impossible alternative. Franklin became desperate. As before he caucused with the house leaders, and again he threatened to prorogue the assembly and put a stop to all business until Gage got his money. The strong-arm tactics seemed to work. A short while later, by a margin of one vote, the house granted £318 of the £418 requested. Franklin readily accepted, but not before a wider bargain was struck. By this time the New Jersey treasuries were short of ready cash to meet the current expenses of government for the coming year. Thus Franklin demanded a new tax levy to make up the expected deficits; the house agreed, if the governor would call an election with representation to be given to the newly created counties. He did.[24]

The General Assembly reconvened in August 1772, just weeks before the king's troops sailed south. As a result the house once more willingly supported the soldiery during the short while remaining.[25] With the final removal of the troops the connection between the supply question and paper money came to an end. Henceforth supply was a dead issue. The loan office scheme, however, awaited only an alteration in the Currency Act of 1764 before being resurrected. When other colonies, like North Carolina and Virginia, continued to issue paper money receivable for all public debts—in apparent violation of the Currency Act and with the approval of the Privy Council—some change in the law seemed necessary, if only to clarify its meaning.

NORTH CAROLINA, 1771–1772

In North Carolina the Regulator Movement ended in a spasm of violence in May 1771. Curiously the man most responsible for the bloodletting at Alamance Creek had sympathized with many of the Regulator grievances against local government. Governor Tryon had tried at different times to clean up the courthouse rings and to tighten control over the corrupt county sheriffs. But the assembly, with its close courthouse connections, had offered little more than token support. Tryon had also acted to meet backcountry demands

24. Dec. 16, 1771, N.J. Gen. Assembly; Franklin to Hillsborough, Dec. 27, 1771, *N.J. Archives*, X, 321.
25. Aug. 28, 1772, N.J. Gen. Assembly.

for more and better roads, ferries, and bridges, and for clearing rivers and streams by promoting a vast program of internal improvements. The plan had the additional goal of preventing backcountry trade from draining away to Charleston in the south and to Petersburg and Norfolk in the north. Ambitious and expensive, the project actually resulted in a strained local economy and increased the burdens on backcountry farmers already plagued by heavy wartime taxes, crooked tax collectors, a highly regressive tax structure, and a chronic stringency of cash. In consequence Regulator counties clamored incessantly for an ample currency supply for paying taxes and other public and private debts.

There was no issue on which Tryon exerted himself more than on the need for paper money. For the most part the lower house, and especially the representatives from the Cape Fear area, backed him all the way. Imperial authorities, however, blocked the path. Thus, facing mounting tax burdens, an obstructionist ministry, and empty promises of local reform, the Regulators grew more and more restive and aggressive in their demands. In the end, with law and order seemingly at stake, Tryon, as the governor and an old army man, met all the Regulator demands in the one effective way he knew—with a show of force.[26]

A few weeks after Alamance, Tryon left for a post in New York, where he found time to inform Hillsborough that the War of the Regulation would cost the Carolinians some £40,000. He also had a chance to meet and talk things over with Josiah Martin, his North Carolina replacement and a recent arrival from England. Shortly after, while Tryon remained in New York, Martin moved on to New Bern, only to find the unpaid bill for the Alamance campaign and an unrequited demand for paper money waiting for him. After a quick look at local problems and a hurried but sympathetic tour of the Regulator counties, Martin came up with a plan that largely reflected Tryon's influence. The new governor promptly wrote Secretary Hillsborough for permission for "a new Emission of such extent" as would settle the Regulator debt, provide an adequate medium of exchange "in this growing Country, the credit and commerce of which calls loudly for such aid and reformation," and replace the existing currency "peculiarly discredited by the great quantity of Counterfeit money" in circulation, a matter of some

26. For a more detailed discussion of these matters, see the sections on North Carolina in chap. 7 above.

concern to the Regulators. Whether he realized it or not, Martin was talking about an issue of approximately £120,000.[27]

It was not long before Governor Martin changed his views and revised his estimates. His first estimate, he informed Hillsborough in December shortly after convening the General Assembly, was far too high and was largely "formed upon the Judgment of Governor Tryon." On closer examination Martin thought that at most he might have to "satisfy the clamours of the people" who had recently stood forth at Alamance and agree to an issue sufficient to cover the Regulator costs, some £60,000 in debentures as it turned out. In general Martin's view was that paper money of any kind was "inducive of a fraudulent medium of circulation." Nonetheless he felt that the great deficiency of specie in North Carolina dictated the need for some paper currency. The only question was how much. Here Martin's guide seems to have been the current sterling exchange rate, which reportedly was "lower here than at New York." Accordingly the governor hoped to maintain currency at approximately existing levels. His plan was to press the assembly into passing "effectual measures" for calling in that part of the public debt presently lodged in the pockets of the tax collectors, an amount upwards of £66,000. Such action, he thought, might quickly bring into the treasury "at least £50,000," or just under the amount he expected to add to the currency supply.[28]

Before Hillsborough could respond to Martin's proposals, the lower house had taken the currency question into its own hands. It had little choice in the matter. If the Regulation was dead, Regulator grievances were very much alive. There was no end to the demand for a cut in taxes and an increase in the money supply. Even so the house split wide open over the question of the amount of new money to be issued. According to Governor Martin much of the legislative session "was consumed in the most disorderly speculations such as . . . are constantly the offspring of a necessity to raise money in this Country. A Majority from the Southern district in which the people are almost universally necessitous and in debt and whose policy it seems it has been to overflow the province with paper money would have availed themselves of this exigence and made

27. See Tryon to Hillsborough, Aug. 1, 1771, Martin to Hillsborough, Aug. 15, Dec. 12, 1771, *Col. Recs. N.C.*, VIII, 650–651, IX, 16–19, 67. See also *Pa. Jour.*, Apr. 25, July 18, 1771.

28. Martin to Hillsborough, Dec. 12, 1771, *Col. Recs. N.C.*, IX, 67–68.

it a pander to that pernicious design. The minority from the Northern districts as warmly opposed this system; the first plan was again
and again retrenched of extravagances."[29]

    While not very explicit about the specific interests involved,
Martin's meaning seems clear enough. In the counties in and around
the Albemarle, the connection with Virginia and indirectly with
Great Britain was especially strong. Caught in a web of credit
centered on Virginia, local farmers and planters paid their debts
as often in Virginia currency as in that of North Carolina. Judging
by the comments of Martin, and before him of Tryon, and by what
is known of the attitude of the Scottish in Virginia towards paper
money, it seems likely that the northern merchants favored a limited
emission of new paper, a short period of circulation, and prompt
redemption through adequate taxation. They wanted, that is, a
closely regulated currency that would maintain its value in relation to sterling. In the southern area around the lower Cape Fear
and Wilmington, the merchants had fewer ties to the great Scottish
and English houses. In addition the population and economy of the
area had grown rapidly after 1760, so that while British credit was
in shorter supply than in the north, the demand for it was greater.
And in competing with Charleston for backcountry trade, local merchants found themselves handicapped by the shortage of cash. It is
not surprising therefore that at the time of the Alamance campaign,
when "Mr. Tryon found only £500 in the Treasury," the treasurer
of the southern district readily agreed "to pay the Governor's War-
rants by promissory notes." The treasurer of the northern district,
on the other hand, refused to do anything of the sort.[30]

    Near the end of the fall session and after "long contention," the
lower house agreed on a debenture issue of £130,000. Receivable
for all public obligations, the money would theoretically suffice to
replace the existing currency supply and to settle the Regulator accounts. In addition the house again petitioned the crown for repeal
of the Currency Act. Scaled down from whatever horrendous figure
the Cape Fear interests had initially proposed, the debenture bill
should have proven somewhat attractive to the governor. On the
contrary Martin considered it "extravagant" and would have nothing to do with it. The most the governor would accept was a
£60,000 issue to defray the Alamance expenses, and that action

---

29. To Hillsborough, Dec. 26, 1771, *ibid.*, 76–77.
30. Martin to Hillsborough, Aug. 15, 1771, *ibid.*, 18. See also the discussion in
"The British Response: North Carolina, 1764–1768," in chap. 7 above.

could be successfully defended in Britain on the same grounds of expediency Tryon had used under similar circumstances nearly three years before.[31]

Nor would Martin countenance a related scheme to keep a large volume of paper currency afloat. Early in that same session the governor learned that out of a total of some £60,000 of full legal tender struck in 1748 and 1754 nearly £43,000 remained current. The money should have been sunk long before. Sinking funds had proven deficient, however, for several reasons. In the first place a large number of the tax collectors accountable for the public debt were insolvent. Second, as in Virginia, what funds had actually been set aside for the final redemption of the £60,000 had been tapped from time to time for other purposes but never replaced. Finally, a poll tax of three shillings appropriated to the fund had been discontinued by resolve of the General Assembly in 1768. At that time Governor Tryon had put a stop to the latter action by ordering the sheriffs to ignore the resolution, but for reasons largely political and not altogether clear, he later changed his mind and allowed collections to lapse.[32]

The lower house, of course, knew perfectly well of the existence of the £43,000 of overdue bills. Nonetheless on December 6 the house resolved that some £53,000 of the original £60,000 had already been burned and destroyed. The legislators also declared that another £13,000 accountable to the fund remained in the hands of "the Treasurers and Sheriffs and Receivers of duties." When paid it would provide a surplus of over £4,000. For this reason, and to satisfy Regulator demands for tax relief, the house passed a bill to repeal the taxes in question, including a one-shilling poll tax and a four-penny-per-gallon duty on all spirits. According to Martin, the measure was then "artfully carried through the Council when some Members who would have made a Majority against it were absent."[33]

Clearly something or somebody was wrong. Although nearly two-thirds of the original £60,000 continued in circulation, the house claimed that virtually all of the issue had already been burned and that only a small sum remained in the hands of the tax collectors

---

31. Martin to Hillsborough, Dec. 12, 26, 1771, *Col. Recs. N.C.*, IX, 68, 76; see also *ibid.*, 181, 213. In addition see the discussion in "North Carolina, 1768–1770" in chap. 7 above.

32. Martin to Hillsborough, Dec. 12, 1771, *Col. Recs. N.C.*, IX, 67–68.

33. *Ibid.*, 166–167, 233–234.

and the treasurers. In Martin's words the tax-relief bill did have an "air of fairness and Truth" about it—though in fact it was "only a species of fallacy." What had happened was that the lower house had chosen to ignore that in North Carolina, as in Virginia, taxes were never "specially applied to sinking the particular paper money for which they were imposed." The taxes in question had not gone towards redeeming the £60,000, but had been used from time to time for all sorts of purposes. Martin quickly perceived the error, if that is what it was, and on receiving the relief bill noted that the taxes and duties to be eliminated were all that remained to sink the £43,000 still in circulation—unless the house meant to lay new taxes or revive old ones. In summing up his view the governor declared that "having collected from the people more than the tax and the duty in question had been originally designed to raise signified nothing."

But the house members who had secretly approached Martin on the bill were not to be put off. To gain their point they tried the old carrot-and-stick routine: "It was insinuated," Martin revealed, that a veto of the tax-relief measure would "bring odium upon the dawn of my administration"; but if he went along with the scheme, the delegates promised that the house would apply as much of the arrears due the public as could be collected towards sinking the £43,000. The governor was not so easily persuaded. For one thing he had heard on good authority that of the £66,000 "arrearages not near one third will be paid into the Treasury" because of the insolvency of the tax collectors. In addition no member of the present legislature could legally or morally bind a future house to a private deal cooked up between the governor and some politicians. The result could only be the continued circulation of the overdue bills contrary to the express letter of the Currency Act of 1764. In the end the governor simply washed his hands of a measure he felt to be "teeming with fraud."[34]

Martin's instincts proved far more trustworthy than the delegates' promises. Rumor had it that if the tax bill failed the lower house would stop collection by simple resolution, as was tried under Tryon. And some observers even claimed that the treasurers already had instructions to drop the tax from the current list. Suspecting the whole business to be a tissue of lies, Martin vetoed both the tax and currency measures and then quickly dissolved the assembly in case

34. Martin to Hillsborough, Jan. 30, 1772, *ibid.*, 230–234.

there had indeed been "illegal intentions." However, at the last minute he did consent to an issue of £60,000, without a suspending clause, to cover the Regulator bill. Redeemable within ten years by an annual two-shilling poll tax payable in the notes of issue, the projected emission stuck Martin as unobjectionable under the terms of the Currency Act.[35]

For all his trouble, Martin had been gulled. After taking the drastic step of shutting down the legislature, the governor accidentally learned that by an order "clandestinely suggested through its Speaker" the treasurers had nevertheless stopped collection of the former taxes. To Martin such a "monstrous usurpation of authority," proved "irrefragably the propensity of this people to democracy." But he did what he could and promptly countermanded the order. Two years would pass before the matter came up again.[36]

Hillsborough's reply to Martin's original currency scheme arrived late in 1771, just after the legislature had disbanded. It revealed that the secretary hoped to tighten currency controls even further. As for Martin's plan, Hillsborough would only say that the crown could not approve any measure inconsistent with parliamentary law. He admonished the governor to pay careful attention to the act of 1764, noting, as already mentioned, that "some other Colonies have by framing their Acts for establishing a Paper Credit in such a manner as to make those Bills a Legal Tender at the Treasury of the Colony, laid the Privy Council under the necessity of advising the King to disallow them."[37]

When North Carolina's currency measure of December 1771 finally arrived in London, the crown gave it quick approval as an instrument founded upon both justice and policy. Busy with affairs at home, the North ministry showed no interest in becoming entangled in Hillsborough's schemes for a closer administration of the colonies. On the other hand North Carolina's call for a general repeal of the Currency Act, or at least the local right to issue legal tender paper, came to nothing. As for the illegal suspension of provincial taxes, Hillsborough instructed Martin to stop any attempt to reelect the Speaker responsible for the lower house's action. Ironically, at its next session the lower house did elect another man to the Speaker's

35. *Ibid.*, 232–233.
36. *Ibid.*, 233–235. Hillsborough supported the move; see Hillsborough to Martin, June 6, 1772, *ibid.*, 300–301.
37. See also Martin to Hillsborough, Aug. 15, 1771, Hillsborough to Martin, Dec. 4, 1771, *ibid.*, 18, 65.

chair, and the former occupant, Richard Caswell, turned out to be one of Martin's most reliable supporters in the troubled years ahead.[38]

The £60,000 quickly entered the local stream of circulation, where it did little to affect exchange rates—or to quiet the clamor for an additional currency issue.[39]

VIRGINIA, 1770–1773

Across the border in Virginia the demand for a circulating medium proved equally great. Although recent grain shipments to southern Europe and the West Indies had placed a small amount of specie back in circulation, they had done little to alleviate the demand for cash arising from the contraction of wartime paper supplies, the long-run expansion of the market economy, and short-run market fluctuations. Nor did the treasury-note emission of a scant £10,000 in 1769 do more than whet the appetites of the indebted planter class.

Even merchants spoke of the "want of currency," which to them meant the want of payments and want of sales. As merchant Thomas Adams reported in the spring of 1770, "The Scarcity of money is so great in this Country that it is impossible for ablest men to comply with their Engagements." Adams and others like him felt that the Burgesses should renew unsuccessful efforts made during the spring session of 1767 to establish local credit and currency through creation of a land bank backed by a British loan. If such a bank were "affected under prudent Regulations," Adams believed that it would be "of Singular service to the Merchants in Britain as well as America." It would, he told an English friend, "lessen the advancing of [credit] with you and enable your Correspondents here to be more punctual."[40]

Adams's proposal was a far cry from the nearly unanimous con-

38. Hillsborough to Martin, June 6, July 1, 1772, Martin to Hillsborough, Mar. 1, 1772, B.T. to Martin, Mar. 11, 1773, *Col. Recs. N.C.*, IX, 252–253, 301, 309, 597, and Schick, "Regionalism and the Revolutionary Movement in North Carolina," chap. 3.

39. Martin to Hillsborough, Mar. 6, 1772, *Col. Recs. N.C.*, IX, 260. See also *ibid.*, 579.

40. To Perkins, Buchanan, and Brown, Apr. 21, 1770, in "Letters of Thomas Adams (1) 1768–1775," *VMHB*, XXIII (1915), 56. See also Nathaniel Savage to John Norton, May 27, 1770, Norton, Savage, Dixon Papers, Brock Coll., Huntington Lib.

demnation of paper money by the merchant class a half-dozen years before. The action was consistent, however. Earlier, sterling exchange rates had rapidly advanced to new heights, cutting into merchants' profits. But present rates had slipped below par to a record low, as the supply of sterling bills outstripped the demand.[41] In general the situation early in 1771 was that, while cash remained short, the demand for a local trade medium had greatly increased in connection with heavy outlays for grain and tobacco by British buyers who were forced to exchange their sterling money into local purchasing power. In these conditions it was felt that a large, carefully regulated issue of bills of credit could now safely be made—that is, could be made without causing an upward spiral of exchange rates.[42]

The difficulty was that not all members of the mercantile community agreed with Adams. Many still blamed paper currency for the destructive jump in exchange a decade earlier, and they were understandably reluctant to risk a fresh emission now that sterling rates had fallen to par and below. Another obstacle proved to be the Virginia Council's unyielding opposition to paper money. But spring floods on the James, York, and Rappahannock rivers in 1771 swept away all doubts—along with thousands of hogsheads of tobacco, much tobacco land, and a number of public warehouses.[43]

In June the James River merchants petitioned the Council for relief from their disastrous flood losses. At first the Council president, William Nelson, a fellow trader and consistent foe of paper money, hesitated to do anything. But under the Council's prodding he finally agreed around the middle of July to convene the General Assembly and ask for help in saving the public credit. By the time the house actually met a month later, Nelson had undergone a change of mind and exhibited a positive willingness to plead the merchants' cause in the warmest manner. Recent news of a slump

41. See the discussion in "The Debate over Rising Exchange Rates, 1762," in chap. 3 and graph 4 in Appendix 2.
42. These generalizations are based on my reading of the letterbooks cited in this chapter and in chaps. 3, 6, and 7. See especially Richard Bland to Thomas Adams, Aug. 1, 1771, in "Letters," *WMQ*, 1st Ser., V (1896-1897), 152.
43. See Bland to Adams, Aug. 1, 1771, *WMQ*, 1st Ser., V (1896-1897), 152; William Aitchinson to Charles Steuart, Jan. 2, 1770, in Steuart Papers, Hist. Soc. Pa.; news item from Williamsburg dated June 6, 1771, *Pa. Jour.*, June 21, 1771; John C. Matthews, "Richard Henry Lee and the American Revolution" (Ph.D. diss., University of Virginia, 1939), 58-59.

in British tobacco prices together with the collapse of the local dry-goods market may have helped change his mind.[44] Or perhaps, as he himself explained it, he was simply moved by "sentiments of justice, honor, and humanity."[45] In any event the Burgesses wasted little time in agreeing to pay for all flood-damaged tobacco that had been stored in the public warehouses for not more than a year's time, or ultimately for more than three million pounds of tobacco, most of which belonged to the trading, not the planting, class.[46]

As might be expected, a few of the more "patriotic spirits" railed against any reimbursement of the hated merchants, that "plague of Egyptian locusts." Nevertheless the planter-burgesses declined to let feelings interfere with interest. The public credit was at stake, and, more to the point, the crisis offered an opportunity for striking an additional £30,000 of paper to cover the repayment. The proposal passed with ease, and this time the Council raised no objections to a currency issue. Not specifically declared a legal tender, the new notes were still receivable for all public obligations, including the imposts on carriages, licenses, writs, caveats, and exported tobacco that provided the fund to sink the additional currency. In addition the notes were exchangeable from time to time at the treasury for any available coin on hand, a provision giving the money a backing far beyond the mere demand for a circulating medium.[47]

The eagerness of the merchant-petitioners to accept the new treasury issue opened up some old wounds. Planters like Richard Bland reminded all who cared to listen that during the French and Indian War the response had been very different. As Bland remembered it, at that time the merchants had raised such a howl and "represented the House of Burgesses, by their Memorials to the Board of Trade and Plantations, in such dark and disadvantageous colours, that they drew very severe, and as time has demonstrated, very unjust censures from that Board upon the conduct of the Assembly." The merchants

---

44. Minutes of the Council, June 12, 13, 1771, C.O. 5/1330, P.R.O. See also John Norton to John Hatley Norton, Aug. 8, 1771, Mason, ed., *Norton and Sons*, 173. On the question of the heavy importation of dry goods during nonimportation see C.O. 16/1, P.R.O.

45. *Jours. of Burgesses, 1770–1772*, 119–120.

46. *Ibid.*, 127–128.

47. Hening, ed., *Statutes of Va.*, VIII, 493–503; Nicholas to Purdie and Dixon's *Va. Gaz.*, July 16, 1773, in "Paper Money in Virginia," *WMQ*, 1st Ser., XX (1911–1912), 236–237; Allason to Thomas Martin, July 25, 1771, Allason Letterbook, Va. State Lib.; Bland to Adams, Aug. 1, 1771, in "Letters," *WMQ*, 1st Ser., V (1896–1897), 152. The money passed at par with coin down to the beginning of the War of Independence.

had continued "till they procured an act of Parliament restraining the Governor from giving his assent to any act of our Legislature, for making Paper Bills of credit a Legal Tender. But now, when their private Interest is affected; when they are in danger of Bankruptcy, and their Credit is likely to be Injured, they are become the warmest the most Forward Solicitors with the Assembly for that very Species of Money they abused the Assembly for emitting to defend the Colony from a common enemy." Such was and forever would be the "conduct of men who prefer their own Interest to the Public good," Bland concluded.[48] As if to confirm Bland's harsh judgment, the merchants, having recouped their own losses, promptly resumed the dunning of the less fortunate, flood-devastated planters. More revealing was the "amazing struggle" over exchange. According to Robert Carter Nicholas, during the fall session of the Williamsburg court, "The Drawers" of sterling bills of exchange, or the big merchants, "endeavoured to raise [the exchange rate], upon the Emission of the Money to pay for the lost Tobacco." Nicholas viewed this action as "rather unhandsome considering the issuing of such a Sum of Money as an exertion of public faith to recompense some of these very Drawers," and he had the pleasure to find them mistaken and disappointed, "the Exchange remaining *Status Quo.*"[49]

By the time Virginia's latest currency measure reached London, Hillsborough had learned that the colony's treasury regularly accepted its paper notes for public debts. The secretary deemed the practice contrary to the Currency Act and hinted that the crown might veto the act on such grounds.[50] But the Privy Council thought otherwise. The crucial question was, not what the Virginia treasury did in practice, but what the Virginia statute provided, and the absence of any reference to legal tender seems to have satisfied any doubts in the matter. The Council quickly recommended the act for confirmation.[51]

48. To Thomas Adams, Aug. 1, 1771, in "Letters," *WMQ*, 1st Ser., V (1896–1897), 150–151.
49. See Thomson, "Merchant in Virginia," 341. The Nicholas quote is from Samuel M. Rosenblatt, "The House of John Norton and Sons: A Study of the Consignment Method of Marketing Tobacco from Virginia to England" (Ph.D. diss., Rutgers University, 1960), 117. The Madison quote is from Fairfax Harrison, *Landmarks of Old Prince William: A Study in the Origins of Northern Virginia* (Richmond, Va., 1924), 390.
50. To Dunmore, Dec. 4, 1771, C.O. 5/1375, P.R.O.
51. Nelson to Dartmouth, Mar. 31, 1773, *Jours. of Burgesses, 1770–1772*, ix–x; *Acts of Privy Council, Col.*, V, 586.

GEORGIA, 1770

One other indication at the time of a move by the Board of Trade and Secretary Hillsborough to tighten up enforcement of the Currency Act was their challenge to a small issue of less than £1,000 of tax certificates in Georgia during 1770. The money was specifically made lawful for all public debts. After discussion, however, with Governor Wright, who was in London at the time, the Board of Trade decided to follow precedent and let the matter pass—albeit with a stern warning against any future emissions of a similar kind. The discussion probably only occurred because two South Carolina laws had just been rejected on related grounds.[52]

On learning of the Board's action, acting Governor James Habersham wrote to Wright about the ruling's probable effect on an expected replacement of over £4,000 of previous issues. The money was overdue and was to be exchanged, instead of sunk, or redeemed, because of a "great deficiency" of taxes prior to 1770 and the complete lack of any tax act after that year. To preserve public credit and still keep the money in circulation, the assembly wished to consolidate its debts by replacing the old notes with new ones to be sunk within three years. The new money was to be lawful for all public obligations. Habersham remarked: "I do not see, how I can require all the outstanding Certificates to be called in without issuing others, and their being in some Manner a tender to the *Treasurer*, otherwise they will be no better, than blank Paper. The Case is plain, if the Treasurer issues them to the People for a valuable consideration, he must be *obliged* to take them again, and that must appear on the Face of them." He would do what he could to meet the Board's objection, but he thought that the ministry did not understand American conditions. "It is easy for People in England to speculate and refine," Habersham concluded, "but here we must act as *Necessity requires*, which is an infallible Rule."[53]

PENNSYLVANIA, 1770–1772

The one colony seemingly exempt from Hillsborough's threats of tighter controls over currency practices was Pennsylvania. The

52. June 27, Dec. 18, 1771, Jan. 30, Feb. 1, Nov. 2, 1772, *Jour. of Comm. Trade, 1768–1775*, 263, 274, 278, 280.
53. Dec. 4, 1772, *The Letters of Hon. James Habersham, 1756–1775* (Ga. Hist. Soc., *Colls.*, VI [Savannah, Ga., 1904]), 217. See also Habersham to Hillsborough, June 15, 1772, *ibid.*, 190.

secretary, it will be remembered, had already laid down a warning to Pennsylvania back in the spring of 1770—and failed to make it good. Henceforth Pennsylvania's handling of its currency went unchallenged.

By 1770 Pennsylvania had fairly well recovered from the acute stringency of a circulating medium that had plagued the economy in the late sixties. A ready supply of British credit and an infusion of £20,000 currency into the local stream of circulation had been of some help. So had the sharp decline in demand for sterling remittances accompanying nonimportation and the heavy shipments of flour and bread to southern Europe, the West Indies, and Britain. Together they had contributed to a relatively plentiful supply of money in local market places and a substantial drop in sterling exchange rates.[54] With conditions changed the popular demand for more paper money that had issued forth in a steady stream of newspaper articles and assembly petitions virtually disappeared. Nonetheless an additional appropriation of paper was made in March 1771. The occasion was the onset of rumors of an impending Spanish war and the consequent need to bolster the defenses of Philadelphia. The last allocation for the protection of the city, made some years before, had already been spent for other purposes, so that £15,000 in treasury notes was struck to cover the deficit. The new measure scrupulously avoided any mention of legal tender. As with similar legislation in the past, however, the treasury later did in fact accept the money in public payments and exchange it for lawful currency already on hand. That practice had won earlier approval in England, and as expected the Board of Trade found nothing wrong with the new law. Accordingly, when the Privy Council failed to report the measure out, it passed by lapse of time.[55]

A year later the House of Representatives revived the loan controversy, which was soon swallowed up in the larger struggle over public finance that had produced such bitter conflict during the war. The past was about to catch up with the assembly. Money and taxes again became a central issue in the fight over the power of the purse.

Shortly after the opening of the new legislative session in January 1772, the house launched a major investigation into the possibilities of increasing the public funds. The government had fallen three years behind in its debts payments, and the excise on imported and

54. *Pa. Jour.*, Oct. 4, 1770; *Pennsylvania Packet.; and the General Advertiser* (Philadelphia), Oct. 19, 1772.
55. Mitchell and Flanders, eds., *Statutes of Pa.*, VIII, 15–22, 570–587.

domestic spirits, the only source of revenue since the end of the war, was about to expire. Moreover returns from the excise were fully committed to the retirement of the currency issues of 1767 and 1769, issues made to cover similar government deficits in earlier years. The house resolved on January 24 that the best way to boost public revenues was to continue the excise and to strike £200,000 on loan for reestablishing the former loan office interest fund.

When finally presented, the excise bill increased the existing duty on all wine, rum, brandy, and other spirits sold and consumed in Pennsylvania from three to four pennies a gallon, extended the tax for ten years, and repealed the old law. Equally important, the bill authorized an extra £25,000 in treasury notes to pay off the current debt and pledged the excise as security. The tax returns were also pledged to the redemption of the remaining treasury notes of 1767 and 1769. As in the past, if any surplus materialized it would be at the disposal of the assembly.

Twenty years before, such proposals had drawn sharp protest as an encroachment on proprietary rights. But that battle was over. The Penns now accepted the excise as a necessary means to meet the ordinary expenses of government. Besides, no surplus was anticipated. Governor Richard Penn did insist on his right to offer amendments to all money bills, however, including this one. Specifically he objected to a provision giving local magistrates the right under oath to enter and search the premises of liquor importers for suspected evasions of the law. When the House of Representatives rejected the governor's amendments out of hand, it seemed as if another deadlock were in the making. In the end Penn surrendered his claim. With a £4,000 grant for the king's soldiers riding on his approval of the excise, he found himself, as one of his supporters put it, "under the necessity of SWALLOWING" the measure.[56] Only after the loan office came up for approval did Penn better than even the score.

The apparent reason for the revival of the plan for a public loan

56. The material for the preceding as well as the following two paragraphs dealing with the excise and loan office is from *Col. Recs. Pa.*, X, 24–39, 41, and *Pa. Archives*, VIII, 6768–6770, 6794, 6804, 6810, 6820–6826, 6838–6840, 6855. The quote is from Jasper Yeates to Colonel Burd, Mar. 28, 1772, in Balch, ed., *Letters and Papers Relating Chiefly to Pennsylvania*, 229. The excise tax gave rise to a number of excellent articles appearing in the local newspapers on the principles of taxation, a subject dear to the hearts of political economists in the period. See, for example, *Pa. Jour.*, Feb. 27, 1772, and *Pa. Packet*, Feb. 17, 1772. The entire subject needs careful study.

was the decline once more in economic fortunes throughout the northern colonies. The nonimportation movement accompanying the Townshend Acts had given the trading community a welcome chance to retrench, clear stock, and in general return to a sounder financial footing. But the collapse of nonimportation in the summer of 1770, the free flow of British credit, and eternal merchant optimism again led to excessive imports. As before, supplies of British goods outran demand. At the end of 1771 prices and profits, especially in the dry-goods trade, were down, while sales had slowed considerably, a situation that continued into 1772. By that summer Pennsylvania was in the full throes of an inventory depression with large quantities of goods dumped on the vendue houses. Trade had never been in such a situation, merchant William Pollard wrote from Philadelphia. "The city and country are glutted with every kind of goods and thousands of pounds worth are selling weekly at different vendues for much less than they cost." As was to be expected under such conditions, he reported "a very great Scarcity of circulating Cash and exceedingly dull times for Business."[57]

In most respects the 1772 bill for issuing £200,000 on loan was modeled after the old general loan office of 1723. An important difference was the planned decentralized administration of the new office. "Branch banks" would be established in the various counties and would be run by local trustees chosen by the county commissioners and three justices of the peace. The trustees, and indirectly the counties themselves, were to be responsible to the central loan office in Philadelphia for any losses growing out of defects in the local titles and mortgages. Nonetheless the real power would remain firmly in the hands of the city trustees and treasurers, whose duties were much the same as they had been under the earlier law. In plain fact the proprietary stood to lose its voice in the nomination of the county officials, and in the appointment of the central officers as well, should those persons named in the bill die or resign.

In effect the General Assembly was repeating an offer first made in 1770 that would give the executive a share in the disposal of the interest fund but not in the appointment of loan office officials. Predictably Penn saw no reason to create new offices of profit to be

57. This brief analysis of economic conditions in Pennsylvania during the years 1770 to 1772 grows out of my conversations with my colleague Mark Egnal of York University. The quotes are from the letters to Peter Holmes, June 22, 1772, and to John Woolmer, July 1, 1772, William Pollard Letterbook, Hist. Soc. Pa., Philadelphia. On the vendue question see esp. *Pa. Packet*, Feb. 17, Mar. 9, 1772.

filled by the assembly. He informed the house that if it would frame a bill that omitted the plan for county trustees, included the executive officer in the appointment of all central trustees and treasurers, and cut the loan to £150,000, he would gladly give his approval. The task of defending the innovation fell to Speaker Galloway. He pointed out that in 1723 at the time of the establishment of the first loan office, Pennsylvania consisted of only four eastern counties. A central office at Philadelphia therefore provided a satisfactory solution to the problem of administration. But the subsequent expansion of population and settlement, leading to the creation of five new counties, made the establishment of branch offices imperative. In addition the counties had sole responsibility for certain losses arising out of defective titles and mortgages. It was thus only simple justice that the people "on whose property those deficiencies were to be levied, should have a share in the appointment of the trustees who were to judge the validity of those titles and that value." Penn was not to be persuaded, and for the third time in as many years the house dropped the loan office with the recommendation that it be taken up by the new General Assembly at a later time.[58]

THE CURRENCY ACT OF 1773

By 1772 the colonial practice of having the treasurers regularly receive any and all paper money in the discharge of public debt had struck deep roots, and Secretary Hillsborough's belated attempt to question the practice had conspicuously failed. Nevertheless the secretary was able to hold the line against any revision of the Currency Act, despite repeated rumors that a number of the commissioners of trade and some of the ministers favored changes of one sort or another. Several of the colonies, meanwhile, continued to petition for repeal or revision and a return to former legal tender laws. Consequently when Hillsborough quit his government post in August 1772 after fellow ministers "tripped up his heels" over the question of the Grand Ohio Company, the way seemed clear for some serious alterations in British monetary policy.[59]

58. See n. 56 above. Delaware has not been included in this discussion because the colony took no action on the money question until the fall of 1775. Before then interest returns on a former public loan had sufficed to pay the current costs of government. The local medium of trade, on the other hand, had been largely provided by Pennsylvania.

59. Jensen, *Founding of a Nation*, 386–390.

First to take advantage of the new situation was Charles Garth, the South Carolina agent and a leader in the unsuccessful repeal movement in 1766 and 1767. Garth immediately pressed Lord Dartmouth, Hillsborough's successor in the American Department, for relief from the "many inconveniences arising from want of a proper medium on account of the scarcity of gold and silver" in America.[60] Unsuccessful at first, the agent persisted in his endeavors —with unexpected support for his position arising out of conditions connected with the deepening British financial crisis and the resulting increase in pressure on the American money supply.

The London banking house of Neal, James, Fordyce, and Down stopped payment on June 10, 1772, marking the end of prosperity and the onset of a great credit crisis, the second in a decade and one of the most severe in British history. The distress in London was said to be indescribable: the city was in "an uproar, the whole city was in tears." "Capital houses" were reportedly "breaking every day, and nobody knows whose turn will be next, so that all confidence between man and man, is at an end; and, when it will be restored, God only knows." To explain "this matter a little" to readers of the *Pennsylvania Journal*, a London correspondent noted "that the chief part of the trade of this city is carried on upon credit, and that paper of various denominations is employed to supply the place of money; this paper credit has been carried too far, both by persons of property, and those of none; and this circulation was got beyond all bounds, as the Bank was very free to discount to any amount, on what they called good paper; but when Fordyce, the Banker, blew up, it was then discovered what an immense chain of circulation was carried on, and a great part of it without any solid foundation."[61] The financial crisis toppled firms on both sides of the Atlantic and sent the American economy reeling.

Doubtless such events were of prime importance when in the early spring of 1773 Dartmouth prepared to sponsor an amendment to the Currency Act aimed at clarifying the meaning of that law, eliminating the many contradictions in its application, and easing the monetary stringency.[62] The secretary and his ministerial colleagues evinced no desire, however, to provoke a grand debate over

60. Garth to S.C. Comm. of Corres., Apr. 30, 1773, in Garth Letters, Force Transcripts, Lib. of Congress. See also Benjamin Franklin to William Franklin, Aug. 19, 1772, Smyth, ed., *Writings of Franklin*, V, 413–414.
61. Extract of a letter from London dated Aug. 27, 1772, *Pa. Jour.*, Oct. 28, 1772. See also *ibid.*, Aug. 19, Sept. 26, 1772.
62. Apr. 27, 1773, *Jour. of Comm. Trade, 1768–1775*, 353.

parliamentary control of the colonies by attempting an outright repeal of the act.

Word of the possible revision of the Currency Act had reached the ear of the great Charleston merchant, Henry Laurens, early in April. Laurens was in London at the time, and he learned from Garth that the government would soon bring in a bill to permit the colonies to issue a paper currency that was lawful for all public obligations. Amused by the news, Laurens wrote his brother James: "When I compare it with former proceedings under the same Head, I see how we sometimes gain and sometimes loose more by Chance or blunder than design of these people." In any event the measure would prove rather beneficial, and he "told Mr. Garth to let them go on their own way."[63] Shortly after, Bamber Gascoyne, a member of both the Board of Trade and of Parliament, quietly brought in a bill explaining and amending the Currency Act of 1764. It passed after only short debate, and two months later the king signed it into law.[64]

Assemblies in America could now do legally what most of them had been doing all along as best they could. They would hereafter be able to cover current and contingent costs by issuing "certificates, notes, bills, or debentures on the security of any taxes or duties given and granted to his majesty" and by making the "same a legal tender to the public treasurer in discharge of any taxes, duties or other debts due to or payable at or in" the public treasury.[65] The colonial system of "currency finance"—of paying government charges with paper money issued in anticipation of future taxes and made a lawful tender for all public debts enjoyed a parliamentary stamp of approval. Not that all the colonies were satisfied with the new arrangements, however. North Carolina, for instance, continued to petition for the right to make local currency "a legal Tender in all payments." So convinced were the Carolinians of the need for fiat money that in March 1774, after repeated failures to pass a suitable bill, the lower house unilaterally declared a stop in the collection of the taxes and duties levied against the lawful currency issues of 1748 and 1754. "The plain truth," Governor Martin noted,

63. To brother, Apr. 7, 1773, and to George Austin, Apr. 3, 1773, Laurens Letterbook, S.C. Hist. Soc.

64. Apr. 28, May 6, 21, 24, 27–29, June 7, 15, 21, 1773, *Jours. of Commons,* XXXIV, 302, 325, 332, 346, 348, 359, 373, 384; Pickering, ed., *Statutes of Great Britain,* XXX, 113–114.

65. Pickering, ed., *Statutes of Great Britain,* XXX, 113–114.

was that "the Assembly wishes to continue the legal tender Paper Bills in circulation forever."[66]

Nor did the Currency Act of 1773 address itself to the question of whether loan office bills could be lawful in the repayment of public loans and in the discharge of mortgages. The Privy Council ruling of 1770, declaring that any measure making bills of credit lawful tender at the loan office was in violation of the letter of the Currency Act of 1764, still carried weight. New York, of course, had later received a parliamentary dispensation from that ruling, but no other exceptions had been allowed. But if it did nothing to clarify this situation, the 1773 amendment could, and did, serve as a precedent for a further reconsideration of the Currency Act of 1764. With a supposed friend of the colonies in charge of the American Department, the time seemed opportune for pressing the ministry further.

66. See Weir, "North Carolina's Reaction to the Currency Act," *N.C. Hist.*, XL (1953), 196–197. The last time the house had adopted such a course it had done so surreptitiously. This time the challenge to Governor Martin was made openly, and Martin with the support of the Council acted as expected. He promptly dissolved the legislature and ordered the continued collection of the taxes in question.

Chapter 10
Toward Independence

The collapse of the short-lived British commercial boom that in 1771 had boosted colonial imports to new heights and the onset of the British credit crisis of 1772 had left the Americans hard pressed for an adequate supply of cash and credit.[1] As a result Pennsylvania, New Jersey, and Maryland all struck large amounts of money on loan in the fall of 1773.[2] To protect their new issues the colonies either omitted or, in the case of Maryland, obscured any reference to legal tender. Nonetheless the money was receivable for all loan office debts, a fact the North ministry simply chose to ignore. In consequence, barely nine months after passage of the Currency Act of 1773, currency controls in America had been further loosened, albeit this time without formal amendment of parliamentary regulations.

The new British concession proved to be too little and too late, and soon there were open violations of the Currency Acts. Starting in 1774 assembly after assembly, headed by South Carolina's Commons House, began striking notes in the name of the king but independent of the governor and Council. In the future the paper currency question turned less on the need for a circulating medium and source of public credit, or even on the demand for legal tender, than it did on the power of the purse. The logic of Revolutionary events, not the requirements of the marketplace, now led the popular houses to reject any parliamentary interference with their control over money—including the right to mint and to disburse paper dollars. From here it was but a short step to the claim of freedom from

1. See the discussion in chap. 9 above. For a general discussion of the impact of the crisis see Sachs, "Business Outlook," chap. 7.
2. Regarding the money on loan, or "land-bank emissions," see Thayer, "Land-Bank System," *Jour. Econ. Hist.*, XIII (1953), 145–159.

all imperial regulations over the colonial economy. And if the law of Great Britain did not bind the American economy, then, as Joseph Galloway asserted at the first Continental Congress, the empire was at an end; the colonies were so many independent states.[3]

MONEY AND POLITICS IN PENNSYLVANIA, 1773–1774

Before Pennsylvania's House of Representatives reconvened in January 1773, the province had slid into the trough of an economic slump. A major inventory depression had begun to affect business fortunes as early as the summer of 1772. But the worst was yet to come. The British credit crisis broke in June of that same year, drying up loan funds and diminishing the supply of good sterling bills of exchange while at the same time creating new and heavy pressures for colonial remittances.[4] A wave of bankruptcies swept over the merchant community. It was reliably reported from Philadelphia in October that "in many shops you may buy cheaper than in London, and the needy trader is constantly obliged for the sake of cash to send his goods (often bales unopened) to vendue."[5] Liquidity demand soared, and the merchants and traders again set up a clamor for an additional supply of paper currency and credit.

It was not only the commercial people who saw an advantage in a large emission of paper money on loan. On October 21 a committee of "Freemen" presented the newly elected representatives of the city and county of Philadelphia with a public address effectively outlining the popular party's program for the upcoming session of the legislature. The "Freemen" had recently gained control of a majority of the General Assembly seats in their area, and they selected five subjects as "matters either directly in themselves, or in their consequences, most likely to sap the liberties of our happy constitution." The last mentioned was the dire need for a loan office to provide an adequate medium of exchange and a supply of public credit. Local representatives received explicit instructions to strive to discover and support "every reasonable mode for an issue of money on loan."[6]

3. Worthington C. Ford *et al.*, eds., *Journals of the Continental Congress, 1774–1789*, I (Washington, D.C., 1904), 46–47.
4. See the discussion in "The Currency Act of 1773" in chap. 9 above.
5. Mrs. Reed to Mr. De Berdt, Oct. 20, 1772, in William B. Reed, *The Life of Esther De Berdt, Afterwards Esther Reed of Pennsylvania* (Philadelphia, 1853), 178.
6. *Pa. Jour.*, Oct. 21, 1772.

The first major bill brought into the new House of Representatives in January 1773 called for a public loan of £150,000 to run for a period of sixteen years—a cut of £50,000 from the same measure that had been offered during the previous session but had fallen through. The reduction was apparently intended as a concession to a demand already laid down by the governor. If this were the case, the compromise did no good. Penn persisted in seeking *all* the amendments he had requested the year before. And this time the assembly folded. It gave the government everything it had fought for since 1759: namely, a voice in the nomination of the tax officials and a share in the disposal of the loan office interest funds.[7] A need for cash and credit required political surrender. Then, too, the new lineup in the assembly gave added weight to proprietary interests. Representatives of the popular party had readily formed an alliance with the backcountry members, who were themselves already tied in with the proprietary faction.[8]

By 1773 the Penns had gained much lost ground in the fight over the power of the purse. And the vote on the loan office was an augur of things to come. The new allies would unseat Galloway as Speaker in the fall of the following year and in his place elect Edward Biddle, a staunch backcountry supporter of the proprietary cause. But in the long series of bitter fights over finance, the proprietary had won only the latest round, not the last. In 1775 the house would issue £115,000 currency on its own resolve—independently of the governor and the proprietor.[9]

All in all, according to one student of Pennsylvania currency, "the policies and business practices of the new Loan Office seem to have been very similar to those of the old."[10] There was an important departure, however. The act remained silent on the currency of the new bills, and on their value, "whether Sterling, or Proclamation, or any other." The omission was intentional, of course, for it offered a convenient way of evading the narrow interpretation of

7. *Col. Recs. Pa.*, X, 67–68.
8. See the concluding chapter in David Hawke, *In the Midst of a Revolution* (Philadelphia, 1961), on the backcountry question. See also Hutson, *Pennsylvania Politics*, chap. 4. Clearly a great deal more work needs to be done concerning the shifting political alignments in Pennsylvania after 1770 before the conflicting interpretations of politics in this period can be reconciled.
9. Mitchell and Flanders, eds., *Statutes of Pa.*, VIII, 488–489, 493–497.
10. Yoder, "Paper Currency in Colonial Pennsylvania," 318. Yoder's brief discussion of the practices of the new loan office is quite good.

the Currency Act of 1764 that banned any kind of lawful paper, including bills of credit, as a tender in the payment of government loans. But in practice the bills were receivable for all public debts both at the loan office and at the treasury.[11] Moreover they were quickly passed from hand to hand by the local merchants and traders, who expected their circulation to be of great advantage to trade.[12] Still business showed little signs of a quick recovery. Markets remained "gloomy and discouraging" throughout 1773, while commodity prices continued at moderate levels until the very end of that year. Not until early 1774 did the first signs of a business revival appear, but by then, as one historian has pointed out, "business was falling more and more under the sway of political influence."[13]

The loan office finally came up for consideration at the Board of Trade in January 1774. If it caused misgivings, the Pennsylvania agent heard none, and none were expected. As the day neared for carrying the loan office act into execution, agent Franklin informed the mayor of Philadelphia, Samuel Rhoads, that the law had not yet come before the Board of Trade. Franklin saw no difficulty "likely to arise . . . unless one should be started on the Uncertainty, there being no mention of the Value or kind of the Money to be struck," though he understood the money would be "of the Value of the present Currency of that Province" and therefore offer no problem.[14] Such was the understanding, and when the Board finally took up the measure, the commissioners found it to be a matter of "domestic economy and convenience." They quietly accepted the view of Richard Jackson, Board counsel and erstwhile agent for the province, that from the point of view of the law the measure was unobjectionable. The Privy Council subsequently failed to report the act out of committee, and it became law by lapse of time in accordance with the proprietary charter.[15] A scant six months later, in mid 1774, the Privy Council broke its silence and issued a clear statement on the desirability and legality of the colonial loan office. Behind that statement was the need to take some kind of action on the revival of the New Jersey loan office bill of 1770.

11. Mitchell and Flanders, eds., *Statutes of Pa.*, VIII, 284–300.
12. See William Pollard to Messrs. Benjamin and John Bower, Feb. 25, 1773, Pollard Letterbook, Hist. Soc. Pa.
13. Sachs, "Business Outlook," chap. 7, 223.
14. Jan. 5, 1774, "Unpublished Letters of Benjamin Franklin," *PMHB*, XV (1891), 40.
15. Mitchell and Flanders, ed., *Statutes of Pa.*, VIII, 610–615.

NEW JERSEY, 1774–1775

Following two years of bitter wrangling between the New Jersey General Assembly, Governor Franklin, and Secretary Hillsborough over the related issues of legal tender and of the supply of the king's troops under the terms of the Quartering Act, the question of a public loan was finally dropped in August 1772. Two summers later, on learning of Pennsylvania's recent success in issuing money on loan contrary to a strict interpretation of the Currency Act of 1764, Franklin advised the lower house to emulate the neighboring legislature. A loan office measure was to be drafted without mention of legal tender but with full knowledge that the emission would be acceptable for all public payments. In return for his support Franklin extracted from the assembly a promise, contingent upon royal approval of the currency scheme, of a long-awaited salary increase for himself and the other local crown officials—but not before he tried, and failed, to wheedle the increase out of the ministry. The house needed no prompting to adopt the plan as its own, though a couple of years earlier it had turned down a similar proposal. In the meantime, however, New Jersey, together with the other middle colonies, had fallen on evil times. In the wake of the British financial collapse and the overstocking of British imports, the pressure on the existing stock of paper money and coin had built up considerably. As for credit, it had reportedly sunk to a low ebb. In consequence the legislature showed no hesitation in authorizing a public loan for £100,000 currency to be allocated by county in amounts roughly proportional to population. Open to qualified property holders, the mortgage loans were payable at 5 percent annual interest in installments covering a period of twenty years. Loan officers were to be bonded and would hold office only at the pleasure of the local justices of the peace and of the freeholders, thus depriving Franklin of any patronage plums.

True to his word, Governor Franklin signed the measure and threw his full weight behind it. In a letter to Secretary Dartmouth he carefully outlined the manner in which the proposed emission would advance trade and agriculture, pay government expenses, and increase British exports. Franklin underscored the promise of a pay raise, a subject he had discussed with British officials a number of times during the past year.[16] Dartmouth and the Privy Council

16. Franklin to Dartmouth, June 13, 1774, *N.J. Archives*, X, 461. See also *ibid.*, X, 390–405.

proved sympathetic to Franklin's plea. In its report of February 1775 the Privy Council found that in the abstract a loan office admitted of some doubt. But the provision of the Currency Act of 1764 preventing bills of credit from being legal tender "removed the principal Ground of Objection." On the other hand, in what amounted to a rehash of Franklin's arguments, the Council noted that an issue of money on loan helped to extend agriculture, open new channels of commerce, and to "take off a greater Quantity of the Manufactures of Great Britain, and to pay for them with that Gold and Silver, which, was it not for the Advantage of this paper Medium must be retained in Order to answer the purposes of Circulation." Clearly the ministry was happy to concede that the loan provided a useful economic measure. Nor was there any question about its legality. It was well known that three years earlier the Privy Council had rejected a similar bill because the currency involved was specifically made a lawful tender at the loan office. Consequently this time the assembly dropped the troublesome phrase—though it might have been suspected that in practice the proposed issue would be receivable for all public debts. The Privy Council raised no objections, however, and the crown quickly confirmed the measure. The news arrived in the colony just before that of Lexington and Concord.[17]

In summary, by the time open fighting had begun between Britain and her American colonies, imperial authorities had conceded two points in the conflict over paper money. Under the terms of the Currency Act of 1773, colonial legislatures could issue treasury notes as legal tender at the local treasuries, but not the loan offices, for any and all public obligations. Further, ministerial interpretation allowed that the legislatures could also issue currency on loan that

---

17. *N.J. Archives*, X, 550. It is interesting to note that no effort was made to prevent Franklin's suggestion for evading the letter of the Currency Act of 1764 from being printed in the assembly journals at the time. On the other hand the Board of Trade records indicate that the journals for that year were not sent on to London. Still, it appears that the Board suspected the intent of the law. Certainly Franklin was called before the Board for consultation on the question of the loan office. See *Jour. of Comm. Trade, 1768–1775*, 404. For the law see 14 Geo. III, c. 5, N.J. Session Laws, in Jenkins, ed., *Microfilm Records of the States*. Under the terms of the loan the money was to be lent on a first mortgage on "lands, tenements, and herediments" of double the value of the loan. Interest was 5%; the loan period twenty years. Terms were repayment of one-twentieth of the total plus interest each year until the entire loan was repaid. Allocated by county, available funds were roughly proportionate to population. Monies paid into the loan office during the first ten years could be reloaned. Loan officers were bonded and held office at the pleasure of the local J.P.'s and freeholders.

for all intents and purposes was lawful at both the treasury *and* loan office. A bit of pettifoggery, the deletion of the words "legal tender" from any loan office bill, satisfied the letter of the Currency Act of 1764. In addition this loophole provided a means of extending to all the colonies outside New England the privileges accorded to New York under the parliamentary dispensation of 1770. But there were variations on the theme. Thus of the three colonies to issue currency on loan in 1773 and 1774, Maryland specifically made bills of credit lawful for any and all loan office debts. While Pennsylvania and New Jersey connived to make their paper emissions receivable at the loan office, Maryland, as usual, adopted her own approach. The Maryland General Assembly voted in November 1773 to strike £130,000 of currency. Providing, however, that the law in question was not to be "construed or taken to make any Tender of the said Bills of Credit in Discharge of any Contract whatsoever Lawful except such Contracts as shall or may be made expressly and Specifically for, or for the Delivery of such Bills of Credit."[18] In other words the proposed issue would not be a tender except for debts, like those to the loan office, that were payable—expressly and specifically—in the paper bills of 1773. It was an ingenious dodge, but probably unnecessary. In accordance with the charter of 1634, the crown had never reviewed Maryland laws. What mattered was that the measure receive the approval of the lord proprietor, and there was no trouble from that quarter. As it happened the importance of Maryland's currency act of 1773 lay elsewhere.

MARYLAND, 1770–1774

In Revolutionary Maryland the rhythms of political life often followed the ebbs and flows of the economy, a fact lost sight of because of the preoccupations of Maryland historians with constitutional questions. For nearly three years after 1764, for example, the General Assembly had remained deadlocked over the claims of the clerk of the Council and the payment of the journal of accounts until, in Charles Carroll's words, "the public necessity forced the house into a compromise." Then in 1766 a stringency of money and the resulting clamor for an additional issue of currency broke through the "resentment and spirit of party" and led to the passage

18. "An Act for emitting Bills of Credit and applying Part thereof," *Md. Archives*, LXIV, 242–253. The quote is from 251.

of the journal and a fresh emission of paper.[19] The enforced truce proved to be of only a few years duration.

It is a commonplace that the "quiet years" in Maryland produced a bitter contest for power between the two houses of the legislature over the "fee struggle" and the "vestry question," issues that gave as much impetus to the Revolutionary movement as any of the imperial grievances.[20] It is less familiar that in 1773, as in 1766, economic pressures brought about a shaky political peace. When the British financial crisis of 1772, followed by the sudden drop in tobacco prices a year later, threatened to topple Maryland's credit structure, the "spirit of party" had to give way once more to an insistent demand for a new issue of paper on loan; the assembly found it necessary to adopt a range of compromises covering problems involving far more than the regulation of official fees and clerical salaries.

In the fall of 1770 the tobacco inspection law, first passed in 1747 and thereafter extended from time to time, came up for renewal. A device essential for regulating the quality and the quantity of exported tobacco and for supplying a medium of exchange and short-term credit in the form of commodity-inspection notes, the law was nevertheless expected to "fall to the ground." The prediction had nothing to do with tobacco. As a result of an earlier political settlement between the two houses, the inspection law contained a provision giving the lower house control over the table of official fees and consequently over the incomes of the chief proprietary officers. The fee question had come up five years earlier in connection with the dispute over the allowance due to the clerk of the Council. The matter was shunted aside, however, as part of the compromise of 1766. With the approaching expiration of the inspection law, the matter of fees naturally arose all over again, together with the related problems of the clerk and of the need for a new journal of accounts.[21]

When the assembly convened in September 1770, the questions of excessive official fees and of possible extortion that had been aired briefly the year before came up for thorough discussion. Fees were high at the time, and common opinion held that several of the officers annually received thousands of pounds for their services, a sus-

19. See the discussion in "The Maryland Response to the Currency Act, 1764–1767," in chap. 5 above.

20. See Barker, *Revolution in Maryland*, chap. 10.

21. See the discussion in "Maryland Response to the Currency Act" in chap. 5 above.

picion the lower house confirmed when it published its finding on the matter a few weeks later. Rumors that the "patriots" of the lower house, Samuel Chase, William Paca, Matthew Tilghman, Thomas Johnson, and Matthias Hammond, would push for sharp cuts in the fee schedule—even at the risk of losing the tobacco-inspection law—received wide circulation. There were hints, too, that the allowance due Anglican clergymen, who were likewise regulated by the inspection law and whose popularity had recently sunk to a low ebb, would also be circumscribed.[22]

As predicted the Delegates did draft a lower fee schedule. Nevertheless, during the negotiations over extending the inspection law, the upper house tried to effect a compromise that directly concerned the fee question. As officials for whom fees constituted the chief source of income, they suggested maintaining the former schedule (and their dignity) while reducing revenues nearly a third —or far less than the lower house proposed. Under the old law those growing crops other than tobacco enjoyed the option of paying their fees in money at an exchange rate of twelve shillings sixpence per hundredweight of tobacco. Tobacco planters had to pay in kind. By contrast the new plan would extend commutation to planters and nonplanters alike at a time when tobacco prices far exceeded the legal exchange rate. In short the members of the upper house reacted as administrators always react: putting together solutions that went as far as they believed was politically possible while still being consistent with their vested interests. But the House of Delegates evinced no interest in compromise. The inspection law lapsed on October 22, 1770, leaving Maryland without an official fee table.[23]

Within days after the old law expired, Messrs. Chase, Paca, Johnson, Thomas Jennifer, and James Tilghman publicly announced that while attorneys' fees were now payable in tobacco only—which would prove burdensome—those indebted to Chase and the others could discharge their debts "in Tobacco, or in Common Money" at the rate of ten shillings per hundredweight, far less than the old rate of twelve shillings sixpence, until "other Provision" was made by the assembly.[24] Meanwhile the lower house revealed the depth of its opposition to Council interference in the matter by arresting and convicting a minor clerk of the Land Office for collecting official fees at the former rates. In order to release the victim, the new gov-

22. *Md. Archives*, LXII, 209–210, 212–219. See also *Md. Gaz.*, Nov. 15, 1770.
23. *Md. Archives*, LXII, 187–188, 234–251, 255, 271–272.
24. *Md. Gaz.*, Nov. 8, 1770.

ernor, Robert Eden, who had replaced Sharpe the year before, prorogued the assembly, and then hurriedly called it back into session with a request for a new inspection bill.[25] The ill-timed move only fanned the flames of discontent. The Delegates lost no time in rebuking the governor for his high-handedness and in passing another bill for the regulation of fees. Again the upper house rejected the measure, and on November 21 the Delegates ordered the publication of the act, together with a series of resolves. The resolutions asserted the exclusive and specific right of the lower house to regulate fees as well as the general power to control the public purse. In addition they charged that conflict of interest precluded upper house members, a number of whom had conducted their offices in an *"illegal* and *oppressive"* manner, from passing any fee bill of their own making.

The matter of the power of the purse had come up in another connection as well. The Delegates had sent to the senior house on November 16 a version of the journal of accounts carried over from the year before, together with a message insisting upon their sole right to fix money bills. In effect the upper house was invited simply to assent to the accounts, not to review them. The interpretation received no support, of course. Members of the senior house reserved to themselves the right to amend or reject the journal as they saw fit, and the bill was lost.[26]

By the end of November it was clear that Governor Eden had little choice except to dissolve the assembly in the vain hope of better treatment at the hands of the electorate. As one critic saw it, a cabal of lawyers was engaged in a "Warfare with the Upper House" and seemed willing to hazard all, even the "Total Overthrow of the Constitution."[27] But before any election could take place, the governor issued his well-known fee proclamation of November 26, 1770. Admittedly some interim provision seemed necessary if the wheels of administration were to be prevented from coming to a full stop. Eden, however, chose to adopt the face-saving solution first offered by the upper house—probably under the prodding of Daniel Dulaney—and ordered all officers to take fees according to the old table but to allow payment in either tobacco or money at the old rate of twelve shillings sixpence established back in 1763.[28]

25. *Md. Archives*, LXII, 304–305.
26. *Ibid.*, 362, 364–365, 407–408, 429–431.
27. Anonymous letter in *Md. Gaz.*, Mar. 7, 1771.
28. *Ibid.*, Nov. 29, 1770.

In the meantime the planters and merchants at the chief tobacco ports were busy at work to maintain a semblance of the old inspection system, as well as a supply of commodity notes, by substituting informal agreements for the public law.[29] Associations, as one observer dryly remarked, "continued to be the fashion of the Times": first it was nonimportation, then it was tobacco inspection. He concluded that soon there would be no laws except that of the "club."[30]

Elections the following fall centered on the fee question and Eden's ill-advised proclamation. The bold stand of the former lower house received enthusiastic support, and during the short two-month session that began in October 1771, the new house joined combat first with the governor over his declaration, which it declared to be robbery, and then with the upper house over the sale of offices.[31] The only other issue of any importance to come up that session was paper currency. Late in October the Delegates went into a committee of the whole to consider ways and means for striking bills of credit for the improvement of the colony and the advancement of trade.

The beginning years of the fee controversy were ones of general prosperity in Maryland. Though the prices of grain and grain products fell sharply in 1769 and 1770, they recovered again during the next two years when relatively moderate amounts of wheat, flour, and bread were sent to southern Europe and the West Indies. More favorable were the bullish markets for tobacco and lumber products. In 1770 and 1771 massive shipments of these commodities, together with a heavy influx of British credit, enabled the Marylanders to expand the value of both their imports and exports and to keep sterling exchange rates well below the par of exchange—despite the funneling of an additional $300,000 currency into the stream of local circulation in connection with the loan of 1769. In general then the desire for additional currency in the fall of 1771 had little to do with the state of the economy. Rather the new public loan was designed to plug the large gap in the local money supply occasioned by the absence of tobacco notes.[32]

29. See, for instance, *ibid.*, Dec. 6, 13, 1770, Feb. 21, Mar. 28, June 20, 1771.
30. *Ibid.*, June 20, 1771.
31. Jonathan G. Rossie, "The Revolutionary Movement in Maryland 1770–1776" (M.A. thesis, University of Wisconsin, 1959), 45–46.
32. See the discussion in "The Maryland Loan Office Act of 1769" in chap. 5 above. See also C.O. 16/1; Hoffman, "Economics, Politics, and Revolution in Maryland," chap. 5.

The loan proposed during that fall session of 1771 amounted to some £270,000. When the measure came before the upper house for approval, however, it was loaded down with amendments—all of which the Delegates rejected. Again they claimed as "their inherent, undoubted, and fundamental Right, the sole and exclusive formation of all Money Bills as well for the application and disposition as for the granting and raising all Public Money." The senior chamber argued in vain that precedent spoke otherwise. Once more the legislative mill ground to a halt, and the currency question was lost for the year. In the end Eden settled all arguments by proroguing the legislature, which, due to the death of Lord Baltimore, did not meet until mid-1773, nearly two years later.[33]

During the long intervening period the dispute between the popular house and the proprietary boiled over onto the pages of the *Maryland Gazette*—to the great profit of the publisher, who found that the resulting diatribes expanded circulation as well as political consciousness. And it was not long before the swirl of events swept other groups, such as the unwary Anglican clergy, into the gathering storm. After the inspection law lapsed, the salaries due the churchmen became an open question. The old law had cut by ten pounds of tobacco the head tax previously levied to support the established church, and some of the clergy therefore seized the opportunity at hand to insist that the original forty-pound levy was again in force. The popular reaction was violent. Although in this instance Governor Eden wisely remained above the fray, the assaults against the "rapacious" officers of government broadened out to include the Anglican clergy as well, so that the defenders of the proclamation and the dissenting churchmen came to join hands. Soon after, the attack on the proprietary and the church became even more vigorous—for reasons that were in large part economic.[34]

Governor Eden reported home in August 1772 that the inspection law was all but forgotten as the current high price of tobacco "prevented the Planters from being sensible of the Loss of it." With the economic pressure off, the governor discovered that the four great men and patriots of Anne Arundel County could begin to indulge to the full their political feelings about the "confederacy of the few to enslave the many" while they climbed into the notice and distinc-

33. Nov. 5–Nov. 18, 1771, *Md. Archives*, LXIII, 33–35; also see *ibid.*, 43–52, 74.
34. Barker, *Revolution in Maryland*, 358–365. See also Rossie, "Revolutionary Movement in Maryland," 35–36.

tion of the people, who seemed to be saying "down, down with them all: leave not an *officer*, or a *parson*, a *scholar*, or a *gentleman*."[35] To some the new popular voice rang with the sounds of liberty, but to Eden and others it had the sound of a hostile rabble.

Because of the recent succession of Henry Harford to the proprietorship in May 1773, Maryland was forced to hold its second General Assembly election in three years. As before, the major campaign issue was "The Proclamation, The Child of Folly and Oppression," and the result was the rout of the proprietary interest, or "court party." A coalition of popular leaders had begun to form around the question of official fees and Eden's proclamation in a move to seize political power from an entrenched proprietary faction. In a very short while the effort proved successful, and a new group of politicians emerged to guide Maryland through the gathering Revolutionary storm. Nonetheless for a brief moment in late 1773 the movement was arrested. Economic considerations came to overshadow all others, paving the way for a set of compromises that covered the more important political problems of the period: the fee and clergy questions, the payment due the clerk of the Council, the passage of the journal of accounts, and the jurisdiction of the county courts.

The Maryland economy retained its buoyancy throughout the first half of 1772. Even the arrival of news during that summer of a second great English credit crisis failed to dampen the economy. Effects of the collapse began to be felt by autumn, however, as British tobacco merchants trading to the area retrenched in the desperate struggle to remain solvent. The result was a slump in tobacco purchases and prices. There were also cutbacks in the supply of British credit. Never again, the British merchants swore, would credit be as high. Clearly history was repeating itself. As in 1762 and 1763 the collapse of the credit system, plus an unfavorable turn in the terms of trade, played havoc with the merchants and planters of Maryland. The excessive imports of prior years suddenly required payment. But at that very moment British creditors dunned for past debts, thereby rapidly boosting the demand for remittances and the price of exports, while supplies of good sterling bills sharply declined.[36]

---

35. Aug. 21, 1772, in "Correspondence of Governor Eden," *Md. Hist. Mag.*, II (1907), 297.

36. For a discussion of economic conditions in 1772–1773, see Hoffman, "Economics, Politics, and Revolution in Maryland," chap. 5.

For a brief moment at the start of 1773 the Maryland economy showed some signs of recovery. The first wave of panic had passed, and the healthy effects of consolidation and retrenchment were beginning to be felt. Sterling rates, which had reached a high of 170 late in 1772, slipped back below par to a low of 152 ½, or just about where they had been before the troubles began. Tobacco crops were reportedly "very abundant" and of "very good quality," so that prices for the best crops were expected to rise. Instead, by February exchange rates had jumped to 160 and were still advancing, while the upturn in tobacco prices proved to be wishful thinking. The demand for remittances was greater than ever as the bankruptcy rate in Britain continued to rise. As for tobacco markets, the spread of financial panic to Amsterdam led to the failure of a number of large firms in that city as well, "putting an end," as one merchant expressed it, "to the sale of tobacco to that part of the world for some time which you know takes much the greatest part from Maryland."[37]

The end was not in sight. News arrived from London in June of the collapse of the three largest tobacco houses in the Maryland trade. By autumn wheat prices had begun to sag, and local merchants were reporting that "there was no such thing as collecting debts in Maryland or drawing bills."[38] To make matters worse, business remained stagnant, leading to cut-rate sales of British wares in both Baltimore and Annapolis. Likewise dull sales and heavy demand for remittances also forced backcountry storekeepers to retrench and drastically reduce inventories. So severe were the cutbacks that at least one merchant predicted that in the future business in the country would be conducted on an entirely different basis.[39]

During the short summer session of 1773, the new Maryland General Assembly bogged down again over the same issues that had deadlocked the houses in 1770 and 1771.[40] By the end of the session, however, the straitened circumstances of the colony convinced

37. See graph 3 in Appendix 2. The quote is from Joshua Johnson to Matthew Ridley, Jan. 6, 1773, in Wallace, Davidson, Johnson Letterbooks, Md. Hall of Records, Annapolis.

38. See James Anderson to James Hollyday, received June 25, 1773, Corner Coll., Md. Hist. Soc. The quote is from Dick, James, and Stewart Co. to Duncan and Maury, Oct. 15, 1773, in Dick, James, and Stewart Co. Letterbook, 1773–1781, Md. Hall of Records.

39. See Dick, James, and Stewart Co. to Archibald Boyd, Sept. 4, 1773, in Dick, James, and Stewart Co. Letterbook.

40. See the discussion in Rossie, "Revolutionary Movement in Maryland," 49–51.

nearly everyone of the need for some sort of accommodation. Thus in August, Governor Eden, who together with his brother, Thomas, had recently turned his hand to tobacco trading in order to boost his income and reduce his indebtedness, wrote Secretary Dartmouth that tobacco had fallen "into great Disrepute at Home since dropping the Inspection Law" and that he anxiously looked forward to the speedy reestablishment of the former system of regulation.[41] Political compromise was in the offing.

Barely a week after the seating of the assembly early in October 1773, the lower house brought in a bill for the inspection of tobacco. The measure quickly passed, but when it came before the upper house, it was rejected out of hand for the simple but significant reason that it lacked any provision for the establishment and collection of officers' fees.[42] This was no accident. The attempt to divorce the fee question from the inspection law was a calculated move instigated by Charles Carroll of Carrollton, who a short time before as "First Citizen" had ably defended the stance of the lower house on the fee controversy in a series of windy polemical pieces that revealed at least as much about the author's private pique as they did his views on public policy.[43] In any event rejection of the new inspection bill failed to impress the Delegates. Within minutes of learning of the upper house's action, they took the unprecedented step of adjourning themselves for a couple of weeks in order, as they put it, to consult with their constituents on the question of the priority of the public business. Governor Eden was beside himself. He found the proceedings of the house "Extraordinary and extravagant" and was at a loss to know what to do. It was only on the advice of Council that he decided to look the other way and to prorogue the assembly for two weeks.[44]

When the legislature reconvened in the middle of November, the lower house promptly brought in and passed another inspection bill. Virtually identical to the measure previously rejected by the upper house, the new bill nevertheless readily passed into law with but minor changes.[45] Clearly, underlying economic conditions had dic-

41. Aug. 19, 1773, in "Correspondence of Governor Eden," *Md. Hist. Mag.*, II (1907), 304. See also Hoffman, "Economics, Politics, and Revolution in Maryland," chap. 6, 28–29.

42. *Md. Archives*, LXIV, 10, 12, 13, 18, 25, 29, 30.

43. On the political role of Carroll in this period see Hoffman, "Economics, Politics, and Revolution in Maryland," chap. 6.

44. *Md. Archives*, LXIV, 37–38, 434–437.

45. *Ibid.*, 42–43, 45–46, 48, 56, 83–86, 95–97, 107.

tated a change in attitude. For what seem to be obvious reasons, the senior house had sacrificed its demand for a new fee schedule to the need for tobacco inspection. A system of inspection had a broad appeal for all those directly or indirectly involved in the tobacco industry—including members of the upper house. It was after all expected to boost flagging tobacco prices and to provide a source of commodity notes and short-term credit. As for the fee question, having successfully divorced that matter from the business of inspection, the Delegates went on to pass a separate bill regulating fees at the same reduced rates suggested in earlier legislation. Under the circumstances the upper house had no choice but to reject the measure, and no further action was taken during the session.[46]

Defeat on the fee question was only a temporary setback. During that same session the lower house passed a bill fixing clergy salaries at thirty pounds of tobacco per poll, with a provision for commutation, to which the governor and Council consented. Admittedly the low market price for tobacco at the time took some of the sting out of the provision for payment in tobacco or money. Even so the measure does seem to have reduced clerical incomes as much as one-fifth.[47] A short while later the lower house chalked up yet another victory, when, during a conference between the two houses, the Delegates finally put the quietus on the old question of the allowance to be made to the clerk of the Council. After the upper house had made a written waiver of any future claims, the Delegates agreed to vote the clerk a last payment.[48] The way was now clear for the assembly to pass the long-overdue journal of accounts covering the major costs of provincial government. The necessary money would be raised through a fresh emission of paper bills of credit, a commodity much in demand. But that required yet another compromise. At the end of December 1773 the upper house surrendered its claims to any right to amend a money bill, and a measure to strike the enormous sum of $480,000 currency speedily passed into law.[49]

The new currency bill was a catchall. Slightly more than half the the issue, or $265,000, was to be lent out at 4 percent annual interest on a first mortgage of double the value of the loan. Principal and interest were payable in twelve years in any of the existing bills

46. *Ibid.*, 56–57, 58, 116.
47. *Ibid.*, 254–256. For a full discussion of the clergy question see Rossie, "Revolutionary Movement in Maryland," 35–37.
48. See the discussion in Kinnaman, "Internal Revenues of Colonial Maryland," 489–490.
49. *Md. Archives*, LXIV, 242–253.

of credit as well as in gold, silver, bills of exchange, and paper money of the proposed issue. About $134,000 was to be set aside as a fund to replace torn or worn-out bills. The remaining $80,000 was at the disposal of the assembly. The largest part of this money would go to pay the journal of accounts; a small amount, about $1,500, was to be used to sheathe the new "Stadt" House in Annapolis with copper roofing. Finally, some $40,000 of anticipated interest was allocated to public education and the building of a "seminary of learning." Another provision of the new law permitted surplus bank stock held by the London trustees to be lent out in the form of sterling exchange at the same interest rate as the bills of credit. The various funds and securities were to be lodged in the hands of the commissioners of the loan office.

No currency actually entered the stream of local circulation until the summer of 1774, but the mere promise of the money was enough to relieve some of the pressures on debtors. Wrote Alexander Hamilton, a Scottish factor, to his employers in May 1774, "The 6th day of next month the loan office will be opened for those who want to borrow money at four per Cent, the Sum to be lent is 266,666 ⅔ dollars. . . . I have received many promises of payment at that time with the money."[50]

The last of the concessions and compromises in the period involved the administration of justice. Near the end of the winter session the upper house submitted to the Delegates' long-standing desires for a law giving the county courts increased jurisdiction over debts; that is, to give local planter-aristocrats whose political power centered on the county courthouses far greater control over the adjudication of debts owed to local and English merchants.[51]

As with Pennsylvania and New Jersey, the latest Maryland loan caused no trouble in London. Thus we may infer that by 1774 imperial authorities had effectively brought their loan office policies into line, or nearly so, with the changes made governing treasury emissions under the Currency Act of 1773. Henceforth, the British government seemed to be saying, all paper issues, whether treasury or loan office, could be made lawful for public obligations of any

50. To James Brown and Co., May 18, 1774, in Richard K. MacMaster and David C. Skaggs, eds., "The Letterbooks of Alexander Hamilton, Piscataway Factor, Part I, 1774," *Md. Hist. Mag.*, LXI (1966), 156–157.

51. I am indebted to Sidney C. Colton for pointing this out to me. See his study, "The Anglican Church in Maryland Politics" (M.A. thesis, University of Wisconsin, 1968).

kind. In fact the government evinced a grudging willingness to go even further in the liberalizing of controls—in Virginia it permitted the legislature to extend a currency emission three years beyond its redemption date in strict violation of the Currency Act of 1764.

VIRGINIA, 1772–1773

The decade of the seventies began badly for the Virginians, for the economy seemed to go from bad to worse. The destructive flooding in the summer of 1771 was followed by the British financial crisis of 1772, which struck the province with devastating effect. It should be understood, however, that the hard-pressed citizenry had never fully recovered from the first and possibly greater shock of the crisis of 1762 to 1765. Though tobacco markets and prices had improved by the end of the sixties, crops remained generally short. In consequence the diversification of agriculture continued apace, as increasing numbers of planters and farmers strove to escape the strictures of a staple economy and their dependence on British merchant-creditors.

After the end of nonimportation associated with the Townshend Acts, British credit and trade goods had quickly flowed back into their accustomed Virginia channels. The tide of credit soon began to ebb again during the early summer of 1772, as Britain's largest mercantile firms faced a growing threat of bankruptcy. Among the first casualties of the credit crisis that year were a number of British merchants trading to America, including some of the larger Virginia houses. In order to remain solvent under such conditions, surviving firms had little choice but to retrench, thereby reducing the purchase and price of tobacco in Britain and the supply of credit in Virginia. As in Maryland the effect was to limit the local supply of sterling exchange at the very moment there was a spurt in demand for sterling bills and specie to satisfy dunning British creditors. The combined pressure of limited supply and increased demand quickly drove local exchange rates back to par in the summer of 1772. At that point Virginia's merchants, "hearing that Exchange was low to the Northward, and, in Hopes of giving a Check to it,"[52] shipped off whatever specie they could lay their hands on. The effort was in vain. By 1773 rates had climbed to 130. And only the heavy remittance of coin to Britain, the relatively large grain exports at the

52. Nicholas to Purdie and Dixon's *Va. Gaz.*, Sept. 22, 1773, in "Paper Money in Virginia," *WMQ*, 1st Ser., XX (1911–1912), 257.

time, and the drawing of sterling bills on Virginia wheat instead of the usual tobacco kept rates from going even higher that year. An additional factor in moderating rates was the heavy sale of tobacco in Virginia to cash buyers. Hard pressed to pay British creditors, the smaller traders with their limited capital resources found it necessary to liquidate their assets by selling off their tobacco as rapidly as possible and thus drive up the demand for currency.[53]

It was 1762 and 1763 all over again. The chain of credit had once more been broken with by now familiar results on both sides of the Atlantic. Not the least of the problems was the matter of the currency supply. Recalling the destructive rise in sterling exchange rates under similar conditions in 1762, a number of the merchants renewed the call for the reduction of the volume of paper money outstanding. "Our Exchange is so fluctuating," merchant William Reynolds noted in the summer of 1773, "that we are at a loss to know what Advance to sell at, for Goods that were sold when Exchange was at twenty percent, the money now collecting at thirty percent and am fearful Exchange will be still higher." "Would it not be wise," a scribbler in the *Virginia Gazette* wondered, "in the Merchants in Britain to endeavour at obtaining Instructions from the King to our Governour not to assent in future to any of our Acts for emitting Paper Money?"[54] Similarly, a short while before, Virginia's treasury notes had been preferred to either gold or silver "as being more convenient for transacting the internal Business of the Country." Now only the issues of 1769 and 1771 that were redeemable in specie continued to be accepted in private payment. And as rapidly as they were collected, they were exchanged for specie for remittance abroad.[55]

Nonetheless pleas for a cutback in the paper currency supply proved less popular in 1773 than they had been a decade earlier. For one thing, although sterling rates did climb above par, they did

53. The foregoing analysis is based on my reading of the mercantile correspondence for Virginia already cited. For a fuller analysis see Thomson, "Merchant in Virginia," 342–347, and Coakley, "Virginia Commerce during the Revolution," 82–92. On the matter of exchange rates see graph 4 in Appendix 2; on grain exports see C.O. 16/1, P.R.O.

54. The quotes are from William Reynolds to George Norton, July 1, 1773, as quoted in Keener, "Blair-Prentis-Cary Partnership," report to the Research Department, Col. Williamsburg, Apr. 1957; "Extract from a Letter of a Member of the Virginia Assembly, dated March 14, 1773," Purdie and Dixon's *Va. Gaz.*, July 15, 1773; Nicholas letters, "Paper Money," *WMQ*, 1st Ser., XX (1911–1912), 230.

55. Nicholas letters, "Paper Money," *WMQ*, 1st Ser., XX (1911–1912), 235–237, 256–257.

not skyrocket as in 1762. Furthermore the mercantile community complained repeatedly of the shortage of a local medium of exchange. With inventories overstocked and trade dull, many, perhaps most, merchants welcomed the possibility of a small increase in the currency supply in the common belief that plenty of money could not fail to increase sales.[56] Even the public treasurer supported the need for a reasonable addition to the local stream of circulation. True, some years before, Nicholas had argued publicly that the large amount of fiat money outstanding had driven exchange rates beyond reason. Presently he blamed the rising rates on the imbalanced trade with Britain. A moderate issue, he thought, would prove beneficial to the economy and have no significant effect on the course of exchange.[57]

Before Nicholas or anyone else could fully work out plans for a new currency issue, Virginia suffered a third catastrophe in as many years. In January and February 1773 the treasury published a series of lengthy notices concerning the "most ingenious" forgeries of local money—a problem by no means peculiar to Virginia.[58] The author was that "heavy gum head" Nicholas, which meant, according to James Parker, the notices were "not worth reading."[59] Stylistic deficiencies notwithstanding, the message was simple: a gang of forgers had heavily counterfeited the notes of 1769 and 1771 to the amount of some £37,000. They had also struck some bogus gold and silver coin. Operating out of Pittsylvania County, the gang included several men of "fortune and credit" whose handiwork proved capable of deceiving the "most penetrating geniuses." In any event it took two days for a select committee headed by Nicholas to separate the good from the bad bills. But it was only a short while before an informer betrayed the whereabouts of the forgers, who were quickly apprehended and on order of the governor were brought to Williamsburg for trial by the General Court. Nevertheless a sufficient number of bad bills had already entered the monetary stream to put almost a total stop to the circulation of paper money. "The united Voice of the whole Trade seemed to

56. See graph 6 in Appendix 2. The analysis is based on my reading of the mercantile correspondence already cited, but see esp. the Allason Letterbook, Va. State Lib., for the period.
57. See the discussion in "The Politics of Scandal, 1765–1766," in chap. 6 above, and Nicholas letters, "Paper Money," *WMQ*, 1st Ser., XX (1911–1912), 235, 255–256, 257.
58. See chap. 5, n. 7.
59. To Charles Steuart, Feb. 20, 1773, Steuart Papers, Hist. Soc. Pa.

be that all the Notes of both Emissions ought immediately to be called in."[60]

Within weeks Lord Dunmore, who had replaced acting Governor Nelson back in September 1771, convened the legislature and officially informed the Burgesses of the forgeries. He anxiously solicited their help in restoring the public credit, which, as he nicely put it, like morality had proven to be an extremely delicate bud. Notwithstanding a minor fracas over the governor's attempt to bypass the Pittsylvania county court in removing the counterfeiters to the capital, the house agreed to give the problem of the counterfeited bills serious consideration."[61]

As it turned out, it was the treasury, not the Burgesses, that saw in the turn of events a chance, however slim, to capitalize on conditions and to return Virginia to a hard money system. In effect Treasurer Nicholas proposed to borrow in the local marketplace enough specie to redeem the nearly £100,000 of paper still in circulation. Over £60,000 of this money, it will be recalled, had been scheduled for redemption in 1769 and was therefore overdue. As such it had no legal existence. This was currency that Robinson had misappropriated, that the tax collectors had failed to return, and that the planters and merchants until recently had contrived to keep out of treasury hands and in the monetary stream by using it largely for private transactions. By a stroke of financial wizardry Nicholas seemed prepared to turn this base money into gold. On the other hand he needed the full support of the Burgesses and of the local merchants to make his plan work.

In fact Nicholas lacked the support of either group. The most the house would agree to, for instance, was a move to raise sufficient specie to redeem or replace the £37,000 of counterfeited bills. Nothing more. And if Nicholas failed to find the necessary funds within a month's time, he was authorized to replace the counterfeited issues with a fresh emission of paper. Clearly the legislators intended to scale down the Nicholas proposal, if only because the

60. See Nicholas to Messrs. John Norton and Sons, Feb. 12, Mar. 17, 1773, Mason, ed., *Norton and Sons*, 302, 305–307; *Jours. of Burgesses, 1773–1776*, x–xi, 13, 22, 33; Feb. 6, 1773, Hillman, ed., *Exec. Jours. of Va. Council*, VI, 516–517; and Robert Beverley to Landon Carter, Mar. 18, 1773, Robert Beverley Letterbook, 1765–1776, Lib. of Congress. The quote is from Nicholas, "Paper Money," *WMQ*, 1st Ser., XX (1911–1912), 238; see also *ibid.*, 237, 242, 259.

61. *Jours. of Burgesses, 1773–1776*, 7; Nicholas to Messrs. John Norton and Sons, Mar. 17, 1773, Mason, ed., *Norton and Sons*, 305–306; Nicholas letters, "Paper Money," *WMQ*, 1st Ser., XX (1911–1912), 238.

drain on specie had been so severe that no one could say with certainty where so much as £1,000 in hard cash was to be had. Even then the modified scheme struck some observers as a dangerous precedent by which accommodation was being made for "false Bills." But perhaps the most significant difference between the treasury and the house views of the matter was the omission in the Burgesses' plan of any provision covering the Robinson money. There is good reason to believe that the Lee-Henry faction had no intention of allowing the house to levy additional taxes and to go into debt for money owed by the Robinson estate. There is equally good reason to think that the straitened planters in the legislature had little interest in favoring the merchants with a hard money system by eliminating the largest single source of paper outstanding and a source for which there was no definite sinking fund. If the Robinson money were replaced by coin, as Nicholas evidently hoped, common opinion held and experience had taught that the hard cash would be quickly swept off to England, leaving the local currency system in worse shape than ever. Barring any such move, however, the existing paper supply would continue in circulation until sunk —and there was no guarantee of that ever happening.[62]

Governor Dunmore signed the house bill to replace the counterfeit money late in March 1773. Yet even in its truncated form, the monetization scheme still failed for the same reason as had a similar plan some twenty years before. The authorized interest rate of 5 percent proved far too low to whet merchant appetites, and the treasury could raise no more than £4,000 specie. At market interest, current sterling exchange rates were high enough so that coin had more value either as a cash loan or, more likely, as a sterling remittance or a means of purchasing sterling bills in Philadelphia. In the end the treasury had no choice but to replace the forgeries with some £29,000 of new notes. That spring the Virginia government effectively created good money out of bad. More to the point, in doing so it shortened the emission of 1771 one year while extending that of 1769 three years, in direct violation of a provision in the Currency Act of 1764. No new taxes were levied. The law provided, however, that if existing tax funds proved deficient the public would make up the deficits. In addition elaborate preparations were taken to prevent future forgeries, including the printing of the new

62. See the discussion in chap. 6 above. See also Nicholas letters, "Paper Money," *WMQ*, 1st Ser., XX (1911–1912), 241–243; Hening, ed., *Statutes of Va.*, VIII, 647–651; and Laurens to Oswald, May 31, 1773, Laurens Letterbook, S.C. Hist. Soc.

bills on quality paper "imported some Years ago by one of our Considerable Merchants, who, with several others, had a Design of establishing a private Bank."[63]

Dunmore had violated his instructions in signing the bill, and he defended his action to the home authorities by telling a half-truth: the new measure, he claimed, served as a mere replacement for two earlier measures already approved by the crown. Hinting at the real reason behind his action, he then added that it was in any event impolitic to let the assembly "feel the weight of government too severely" when to do so would have wrecked the local economy. The act produced no objections in London. It arrived after Parliament had passed the Currency Act of 1773 and after the ministry had eased up on the strict enforcement of former policies.[64]

SOUTH CAROLINA, 1770–1775

By 1774 outright repeal of the Currency Act of 1764 appeared to be only a matter of time. A series of parliamentary laws and ministerial decisions had already undermined the more important provisions of the original law. But the course of Revolutionary events moved too quickly for any final settlement. As early as the spring of 1774, South Carolina's Commons House took the unprecedented step of rejecting all royal and parliamentary interference with its control over money—including the minting and disbursing of paper notes. The house simply assumed the right to issue, in anticipation of future taxes and under its own authority, some £200,000 of promissory notes as a medium of local trade and as lawful tender for all public obligations. Likewise at the same time the lower house also rejected the claim of the Council, sitting as the senior house of the assembly, to limit in any way the demands of the Commons House for absolute power of the purse. Underlying the house action was the "Wilkes Fund Controversy."[65]

On December 8, 1769, the Commons House resolved that the

63. The quote is from the Nicholas letters in "Paper Money," *WMQ*, 1st Ser., XX (1911–1912), 238. See also *ibid.*, 242; Nicholas to John Norton and Sons, Sept. 10, 1773, Mason, ed., *Norton and Sons*, 349; Hening, ed., *Statutes of Va.*, VIII, 647–651. In addition the General Assembly made it a felony to counterfeit the money of other colonies in Virginia; see Hening, ed., *Statutes of Va.*, VII, 651–652.

64. Mar. 31, 1773, *Jours. of Burgesses, 1773–1776*, ix–x.

65. The standard account is Jack P. Greene, "Bridge to Revolution: The Wilkes Fund Controversy in South Carolina, 1769–1775," *Jour. So. Hist.*, XXIX (1963), 19–52.

public treasury pay into assembly hands £105,000 currency to be remitted to England for the support of the just and constitutional rights and liberties of the people of Great Britain and America. Beneficiary of the gift, which amounted to £15,000 sterling, was the notorious John Wilkes. While a member of the House of Commons, Wilkes had published gibes about the honor of the crown that had landed him in jail, where he promptly became a symbol of the rights of Parliament, a rallying point for the Whigs, and—though actually no friend to America—a popular hero on both sides of the Atlantic.[66]

News of the South Carolina gift traveled rapidly. Consequently Lieutenant Governor Bull lost no time in officially informing imperial authorities of the move and of his reasons for failing to dissolve the assembly. Bull wrote a hasty account to Hillsborough on December 12 explaining that in emergencies, on joint resolve of the governor and the senior house, the lower house had often authorized an issue of money from the treasury and later replaced it. More recently "a mode of an order in the Commons House to the treasurers to advance money" had been adopted that had left the other branches of government little control in the matter. The governor and Council did retain the option of vetoing any tax bills designed to replace the money. But that meant withholding payment from all public creditors. In addition, Bull continued, the local support for Wilkes and for the assembly's contribution suggested that any move to dissolve the legislature would produce no change in men or measures.[67]

In London meanwhile the affair had come to the attention of the city newspapers, which gave it considerable play. Some kind of ministerial action seemed in order, and shortly after receiving Bull's letter Hillsborough directed the king's attorney general, William de Grey, to scrutinize the provincial records to determine whether or not the position taken by the Commons House was justified. He charged Bull with the same task. De Grey submitted a strictly legal gloss in February 1770 based on the premise that the crown's instructions and commissions to the governor of South Carolina formed a fundamental part of the colonial constitution and consequently gave the Council equal jurisdiction with the Commons

---

66. The following account is based largely on Ernst, "Growth of the Commons House of Assembly," chaps. 6–7, and Greene, "Bridge to Revolution: The Wilkes Fund Controversy," *Jour. So. Hist.*, XXIX (1963), 19–52.

67. Sept. 8, 1770, C.O. 5/379, P.R.O.

House over money bills. These findings conformed to a well-established imperial view of such matters, and in his analysis de Grey ignored any organic developments that might have been dictated by local traditions, practices, laws, and precedents. By contrast Bull's report, arriving a short while later, avoided easy assumptions about the ultimate nature of the constitution. Instead it carefully traced the various changes that had gradually taken place in the methods of advancing money from the treasury.[68]

Hillsborough and his fellow ministers had no time to wait for a reply from the lieutenant governor—and little interest in doing so. After only a cursory review of the available evidence, on April 14 the king in Council sent an additional instruction to South Carolina covering de Grey's objections and prohibiting the governor and Council, under pain of being promptly removed from office, from assenting to any money bills except for strictly local services or upon the express request of the crown. The instruction also limited the use of public money to the purpose originally intended. Furthermore it directed that future tax laws stipulate that any treasurer issuing money on the order of the Commons House alone would be declared unfit for office and be sued for an amount three times the sum involved.[69]

While the crown was preparing the additional instruction, the South Carolina assembly busily schemed to replace the Wilkes money. As presented by the Commons House during the spring session of 1770, the tax bill for 1769 contained a charge in favor of the treasurer, Jacob Motte, for £10,500 currency. The Council, however, viewed the inclusion of the item as repugnant to the king. It pointedly denied that the lower house had any right to disburse public funds for other than provincial purposes. Disclaiming any intention of entering upon such a sensitive subject, the Council members nonetheless explained that they felt it necessary to reject the bill because the governor might interpret their silence as tacit advice to give his approval. The Commons House found the message insulting, said so, and then returned the bill for "calm" reconsideration. When as expected the Council again disapproved the measure,

68. *Ibid*. A summary of de Grey's opinions may be found in *Acts of Privy Council, Col.*, V, 234–235.

69. The most convenient reference is John Drayton, *Memoirs of the American Revolution...as Relating to The State of South-Carolina...* (Charleston, S.C., 1821), I, 92–94. See also Aug. 15, 1770, in Journals of His Majesty's Honourable Council of South Carolina, in Jenkins, ed., *Microfilm Records of the States*.

the lower house handed the matter over to a special committee made up of the very men responsible for remitting the Wilkes gift in the first place. The original resolution authorizing the gift had badly divided the delegates to the Commons House. But there was no division over the need and obligation to reimburse the treasurer, who had made the money available. Consequently the Council action had the unintended effect of diverting attention away from the matter of the gift as such and elevating the debate to a new, more important, and ultimately more dangerous level. It took no time for the house committee to determine that any grant for the protection of the rights and liberties of the people of Great Britain and America could not possibly affront the king, that great patron of liberty and the rights of all his subjects. As to the more important question of the lower house borrowing from the public treasury, the committee stressed that no governor had ever interfered with this right in the past and that such monies had always been "faithfully and punctually" returned. Finally, reflecting the antagonism engendered by the latest in a long series of objectionable Council actions, the committee suggested that the king be asked to provide the province with an upper house "distinct from the Privy Council" and composed of men of independent mind and property.[70]

The question of the Council's right to function as a legislature dated back to the 1740s, and after 1754 the Commons House simply had struck the title "Upper House" from all communiqués to the Council. Some years later the crown had begun filling the Council with English placemen, an action that had further aggravated relations between the two bodies. In 1763 and again the following year, the lower house had gone even further and had rejected all messages from the Council signed by the "Speaker," a title appropriate for a member of a legislature, not a privy councillor. The upshot was that in 1765 the Council had retaliated in kind by resolving that it would have no intercourse with the Commons House and that it was sitting "as an Upper House and as such ready to receive" all bills. Weeks had passed before the press of public business had forced the Council to give up the boycott together with the demand to be addressed as an upper house. Thus when in the spring of 1770 the Commons House resolved that the self-styled upper house was

70. See Apr. 5, 1770, Jours. of S.C. Council, and Apr. 7, 10, 1770, Jours. of S.C. Assembly, Jenkins, ed., *Microfilm Records of the States.*

a mere body of councillors serving in the executive branch of government and that there was no senior house of assembly as such in South Carolina, it was stepping up an on-going attack.

The Commons House unanimously adopted the committee recommendations on April 10, 1770, adding only an address to the lieutenant governor acquainting him with indignities suffered at the hands of the Council. Bull remained unruffled. He simply prorogued the house from time to time in an effort to cool tempers while awaiting official word from London concerning the Wilkes contribution.[71] Passions, it seems, only rose higher, as South Carolina's newspapers took up the cry for "Wilkes and Liberty." Ever the realist, Bull harbored no illusions about the situation, and he finally and quietly reconvened the Commons House in mid-August to present the newly arrived royal instructions. If the Council's earlier objections had already transformed the Wilkes question into a potentially dangerous issue, then royal interference in the affair only guaranteed that it would remain a constitutional sore spot. Politics were threatening to become confused with principles, leaving no room for compromise.

A few days later the Commons adopted a series of resolutions reaffirming its earlier position and the charge of improper conduct by the Council. For its part the Council also reiterated its former accusations and pointedly added that now the king himself had joined in the condemnation of the house's action. In the meantime the instruction came under the scrutiny of a special house committee, which on August 22 requested copies of any messages sent to the crown in connection with the affair. Bull demurred. The Council had sent none, he declared. As for himself he could not honor the request without the king's permission.[72] The Commons House was not so easily put off. The committee found Bull's answer unsatisfactory and recommended five resolutions, which the house subsequently adopted: that it was the exclusive right of the lower house to grant money to the king for any purpose; that the order of December 8, 1769, was based upon accepted precedent and was therefore constitutional; that the king's new instruction was founded upon "false, partial, and insidious" representations; that the ministerial attempt to dictate how money bills should be framed constituted an infringement of the sacred rights and privileges of

71. See Ernst, "Growth of the Commons House of Assembly," 152–153; Apr. 10–11, 1770, Jours. of S.C. Assembly.
72. Aug. 16, 17, 21, 22, 23, 29, 1770, Jours. of S.C. Assembly.

the Commons House, "to whom it alone belongs," to originate and prepare money bills for the consent of the governor and Council without any alteration or amendment; and finally that the resolutions should be sent to the London agent for the purpose of edifying the king and obtaining the withdrawal of the instructions.[73]

In the event that anybody had missed the point, a short while later the Commons House once more tried, and failed, to get past the Council a tax bill in defiance of the recent instruction. Within a week Bull adjourned the house at its own request until January 1771. Just before closing their doors, the delegates again badgered Bull for letters in connection with the instruction. In addition they took time to remind the Council that the good people of South Carolina had sole and absolute disposal of their own money, that they, the people's representatives, were the only guardians of the public treasury, and that the Council by styling itself an upper house was becoming absurd and ridiculous. In sum by the late summer of 1770 the Commons House claimed exclusive authority to appropriate and disburse public money for any purpose it considered legitimate.[74]

Bull amicably greeted the return of the house in January 1771 with a warm request for a badly needed tax measure. He cautioned the delegates, however, that he would have to veto any bill not in accord with the king's recent instruction, a directive calculated, as he put it, not to restrain the acknowledged right of the Commons House to grant money to His Majesty for the service of the province, but rather to set guard on the treasury by preventing the governor, Council, and lower house independently of each other from diverting public money from those uses for which it was originally granted. Though not expressly stated, Bull continued, this principle was implied in every bill granting money for particular purposes in the past. The instruction therefore could be considered as "now positively enjoining what was before tacitly intended."[75] The tact was Bull's, the sentiment Hillsborough's. As early as August 1770 the lieutenant governor saw and discussed the need to compromise the differences between the Commons House claim to an exclusive right to order money from the treasury for any purpose and the king's directive. Unfortunately Hillsborough remained unconvinced. Then as later he insisted that Bull follow

73. Aug. 29, 1770, *ibid.*
74. For a fuller discussion of this point see the explanatory footnote in Ernst, "Growth of the Commons House of Assembly," 146, n. 29.
75. Jan. 16, 1771, Jours. of S.C. Assembly.

the royal instructions to the letter in dealing with the lower house.[76] The Commons House made its rejoinder a week after receiving Bull's request for a tax bill. It had indeed wanted to do its duty on the tax bill, but the Council barred every move. And the delegates did not want to be told that monies raised by law were to be expressly limited to the purposes for which they were raised; common sense was sufficient to inform them of that. As for Bull, the house members declared that he could not be more devoted to ministerial will than they were to their duty to the king. Such remarks struck home. Bull found the delay in answering his request for a tax bill disrespectful, and the comment about his devotion to the ministry "invidious." The delegates showed no interest in bandying words. Bad weather had caused the delay, and there was nothing more to be said about the ministers and the rest.[77]

At the end of January the Commons House hit upon yet another device for asserting its control over the purse strings and for circumventing the recent instruction: it ordered the public treasurer to pay into Bull's hands a specified sum of money, twenty shillings for each poor Irish Protestant newly arrived in the province. But Bull easily saw through this scheme to nullify the royal instructions by circumventing the requirement that money be voted out of the treasury only with the consent of all three branches of the legislature, not the Commons House alone. He was thus outraged at this insult to his understanding and to his integrity in the discharge of his duty.[78] Thwarted in their plan by Bull, the members of the Commons House presently divined the strategy that Secretary Hillsborough would adopt in his dealings with the house during the next couple of years. Neither Bull nor anyone else, the Commons House asserted, could in any way advance the royal interest by putting a stop to public business and injuring public credit in order to enforce an instruction that the lieutenant governor had not shown to be either just, constitutional, necessary, or more binding than any other instruction to which Bull and his predecessor had ever paid obedience. Hillsborough thought otherwise. The Commons House, he believed, would soon tire out.[79]

76. Bull to Hillsborough, Aug. 23, Sept. 8, 1770, Hillsborough to Bull, Oct. 19, Nov. 15, 1770, Records in the British Public Record Office Relating to South Carolina, 1663–1782 (microfilm), South Carolina Archives Department, Columbia.

77. Jan. 24–25, 1771, Jours. of S.C. Assembly.

78. Jan. 31, 1771, *ibid*. For a fuller discussion of this point see the explanatory footnote in Ernst, "Growth of the Commons House of Assembly," 147, n. 34.

79. Feb. 13, 1771, Jours. of S.C. Assembly.

A short time after, the house presented Bull with a full defense of the assembly's action together with some interesting casuistry. The members argued that in England surpluses from the king's funds were expressly given to the crown for immediate use, "or as it is called the civil list," while the surpluses of all other funds were applied to the sinking fund by parliamentary acts so that the Treasury could not at any time contain unappropriated money. In South Carolina, on the other hand, revenue from annual tax returns ordinarily exceeded the amounts appropriated for the king's use. This balance could be used as the Commons House saw fit. By contrast money in special funds could not be, and never had been, appropriated without the consent of the Council and governor. The house went on to explain that the king apparently believed that in the Wilkes case special funds had been tapped and that he was therefore falsely led to issue his additional instruction. As for the Irish money, it had been borrowed with a safe conscience from the general surplus, and in any event appropriations to the king "ought to flow" merely from the motion of the people. They were absolutely free gifts. Consequently the matter, manner, time, and every other circumstance relative to money bills "are and ought to be judged by their Representatives only."[80]

By this time the positions of the various participants in the fight over the Wilkes fund had been made abundantly clear. And with the loss of the tax bill Bull saw no reason to prolong the session. The Commons House adjourned on March 20, 1771, and did not reassemble until six months later. By then Bull had handed over the reins of government to Governor Lord Charles Greville Montagu, who had just returned from a two-year stay in England.

As administrators, Bull and Montagu differed completely in their approach to the problem of working with the legislature. Lieutenant Governor Bull had been the epitome of tact in his relations with the Commons House. Even so he failed miserably to reconcile the house to the king's directive. Governor Montagu's instincts were the opposite. Like Hillsborough, his idea was to bulldoze, not cajole, the house into submission. The results were the same. Abetted by rumors of an imminent withdrawal of the instruction following Hillsborough's ouster early in 1772 and by highly favorable markets for rice, political will in South Carolina noticeably stiffened. Two years after his return to South Carolina, the defeated and disgusted gov-

---

80. Feb. 26, 1771, *ibid.*; Garth to S.C. Comm. of Corres., June 3, 1772, Theodore Jervey, ed., "Garth Correspondence," *S.C. Hist. Gen. Mag.*, XXXIII (1932), 239.

ernor sailed over the bar for England. For a fifth time executive responsibilities of the colony fell upon the experienced shoulders of William Bull II.[81]

Lieutenant Governor Bull opened a new assembly session in March 1773 with a strong request for a tax bill, now four years in arrears, as well as a general duty law. As a result, from this point forward the right of Council to sit as an upper house and of the Commons House to exercise exclusive control over public finance became hopelessly entangled.

The annual tax and duty laws as requested by Bull provided the two principal ways in which South Carolina met its public expenses. The customary method for covering the contingent costs of government was for the Commons House to solicit all claims on the treasury in the fall of each succeeding year to be reviewed by a special committee on public accounts. Next a committee of the whole went over the separate charges for final approval, following which a balance was struck, the treasury surplus subtracted from the debits, and the tax levy determined. If the tax bill became law, the authorized creditors received treasury or credit certificates that were lawful for public obligations and were redeemable at some later date in specie or in fiat money. The general duty law, on the other hand, provided revenues for specific and recurrent funds, such as the salaries of judges, ministers, schoolmasters, the attorney general, sextons, and clerks. First levied in 1751, the import-export duties were renewed in 1767 for five years. If after the five years, the legislature remained in session, the law would be continued until the end of the session.[82]

This last technicality gave rise to an interesting situation. A session was defined as any sitting of the General Assembly during which at least one act was passed. But the bitter struggle over the Wilkes fund and the king's additional instruction had prevented the passage of any legislation since 1770. In 1773 the duty law was still in force. Bull therefore was understandably anxious to approve a new law before any other act was passed and the old law automatically lapsed.

In his request for new tax legislation the lieutenant governor had

81. See the discussion in Ernst, "Growth of the Commons House of Assembly," 137–142. For a contemporary view of the governor see Peter Manigault to [?], Dec. 24, 1772, Manigault Letterbook. It is "not impossible," Manigault declared, "for a Man to be too great a Fool to make a good Governor." See also Manigault to Ralph Izard, Feb. 28, 1772, *ibid*.

82. Ernst, "Growth of the Commons House of Assembly," 152–154.

tactfully avoided any reference to the additional instruction and focused instead on the plight of the treasury. The Commons House, however, was in no mood to make any concessions to economic necessity. The duty act was ignored, and the house turned to the job of preparing the public accounts for the years 1769 and 1770. Included was an item to replace the Wilkes money. When as expected the Council rejected the proposed tax measure, the representatives asked to be adjourned until summer. Upon reconvening the assembly in August 1773, Bull repeated his plea for legislation to pay off the public debt. The Commons House responded by merely reviving the former tax bill, which the Council again rejected. As a consequence the house explored the possibility of finding other ways to cancel the Wilkes debt and enforce its claim to the right to disburse surplus monies on its own authority. It first ordered Attorney General Sir Egerton Leigh to sue the estate of the former treasurer, Jacob Motte, for some £50,000 currency due the colony—or £10,500 less than the estate actually owed. Bull again penetrated its scheme and ordered Leigh to sue for the full amount. The Commons House then ordered £1,500 from the treasury, ostensibly to help some recent Irish immigrants to get located and settled. The public treasurers nevertheless stood by the king's additional instruction and refused to comply.[83]

Doubtless in time the maneuverings of the lower house would have provoked another bitter dispute had not the Council been busily engaged in a political scheme of its own in an effort to assert its power over treasury affairs. Concerned with such matters and knowing of the province's shaky financial condition, the Council had called in the provincial treasurers to inquire into the state of the public funds. It soon became apparent that nearly £128,000 currency was due for public duties to June 1, 1773, and that there was not more than £10,000 actually on hand in the treasury—though not less than £50,000 would be needed to pay current debts before October, just weeks away. Under the circumstances the Council promptly asked Bull to compel those persons longest indebted for public duties "forthwith" to pay into the public treasury a total of £50,000 and after three months to direct Attorney General Leigh to sue for the remaining debt. Diplomatic as always, Bull thanked the Council for its advice, adding that he needed time to consider the matter so that no one be hurt in the process. The Council refused

83. Greene, "Bridge to Revolution: The Wilkes Fund Controversy," *Jour. So. Hist.*, XXIX (1963), 42.

to be put off. It immediately published its findings, presumably in an effort to rally public support.[84]

In reality Bull thought the Council's advice stupid and dangerous. He carefully outlined what he took to be the real situation in a letter to Lord Dartmouth, Hillsborough's replacement as secretary of the American Department. In general the reason for the treasury deficit, asserted Bull, was the scarcity of any adequate medium of exchange.[85]

As Bull and others recognized, the dearth of cash in South Carolina in mid-1773 grew out of conditions rooted in the events of the immediate past as well as in certain long-term changes taking place. Of first importance was the British financial crisis of the past summer that had rocked the entire American economy. At the time it seemed as though the collapse of credit would have much the same effect on South Carolina as on the colonies to the north. As a direct result of the shock to credit, British rice prices tumbled in late 1772. Merchants in the trade warned American suppliers against overtrading in the commodity, especially since prices and markets were expected to suffer even sharper declines. As it happened, however, wheat harvests in Britain and on the Continent that year turned out so poorly that unusually large demands were once again made on American granaries. Grain exports to Britain reached peak levels, while rice shipments fell just short of that mark. Despite the heavy rice shipments, prices early in the period remained generally favorable. The upshot was that the boom trade in rice did much to dampen the effects of the financial panic. As one South Carolina writer put it, "Many and great losses are sustained in this province, in consequence of the late failures in Europe; but happily the sufferers are most able to bear them."[86]

Nevertheless the boom produced problems of its own. One was the creation of a heavy demand for a means of local trade. "Our whole circulating Currency including a large computed Sum for Gold and Silver which are indeed become very scare Commodities did not exceed one-fifth part of the value of the crop of rice and indigo in the present year," Laurens reported in late 1770. It was for

84. Aug. 13, 1773, Journals of the Upper House of Assembly of South Carolina, in Jenkins, ed., *Microfilm Records of the States*.
85. Aug. 14, 1773, Jours. of S.C. Upper House; Bull to Hillsborough, Aug. 26, 1773, C.O. 5/380, P.R.O.
86. The preceding analysis is drawn from my reading of the Laurens Letterbook, S.C. Hist. Soc., for the period and from the figures in C.O. 16/1, P.R.O. The quote is from *Pa. Jour.*, Oct. 28, 1772.

this reason that in the following spring, "by Agreement between the principal Inhabitants and Merchants," gold and silver coin were revalued upwards. The advance, according to Peter Manigault, quickly "brought many a Piece of Gold and Silver abroad which had not seen the Light for many Years." Unfortunately the ameliorative effects of an increased circulation were short-lived. The credit crisis of the next year and the dunning for local debts quickly led to renewed complaints about the shortage of ready cash.[87] More serious, the favorable rice markets prompted the well-heeled planters to purchase upwards of ten thousand newly imported Negroes at an estimated cost of £350,000 sterling, a staggering sum that seriously tipped the balance of trade against the province. This imbalance, as Henry Laurens warned early in 1773, threatened to "drive Guarantors and Creditors" in England "to push Debtors on the other side," to boost sterling exchange rates, to delay payments, and in general to produce failures where least expected.[88] That is, while the purchase of Negroes was normally expected to channel into the stream of local circulation monies otherwise held by the rice planters—and thereby to ease the currency shortage—the imbalance of trade, on top of the credit crisis in Britain, would only aggravate the monetary stringency. Collect all the money you can, Laurens advised his brother, and remit it in sterling bills to London.[89] The imbalance of trade also meant, as another merchant pointed out a short while later, that the planters would henceforth "make a point of paying their Negroe Merchants before their dry Goods Merchants."[90]

The willingness of the planters to pay their debts was one issue, but their ability to do so was another. The great importation of Negroes meant in effect a siphoning off of the coin and sterling bills already available. In addition a decline in rice prices, such as the one that occurred in early 1773 largely because of overstocked European markets, meant a further imbalance of trade and a cutback in the new supply of sterling bills and specie.[91] In any event the com-

87. Laurens to Reynolds, Getley, and Co., Sept. 7, 1770, Laurens Letterbook, and Manigault Letterbook. On the shortage of cash see, for instance, Laurens to Garden, Apr. 8, 1773, Laurens Letterbook.

88. Laurens to his brother, Mar. 11, 1773, Laurens Letterbook. See also Laurens to John Wright, Liverpool, Mar. 17, 1773, *ibid.*, and Peter Manigault to William Blake, Dec. 17, 1772, Manigault Letterbook.

89. See Laurens to his brother, Mar. 11, 1773, Laurens Letterbook. See also the discussion in "South Carolina, 1767–1770," in chap. 7 above.

90. Pollard to B. V. J. Bower, Feb. 1, 1774, Pollard Letterbook, Hist. Soc. Pa.

91. See, for instance, Laurens to Wright, Mar. 17, 1773, Laurens Letterbook.

bined effect was to build up the pressure on the local money supply. A long-term consideration aggravating the shortage of cash was the additional increase in demand generated by a growing population and economy. Thus in the summer of 1773 Bull reiterated a point he had made to the ministry a couple of years earlier, namely that the insufficiency of money had already forced the merchant class to conduct a substantial part of their business with the backcountry, where both trade and population boomed, by a system of barter exchange. Nor was such trade confined to South Carolina alone. As the most profitable market in the region, Charleston also received considerable amounts of produce from the western parts of North Carolina. Another long-range problem mentioned by Bull was the annual loss of £7,000 to £8,000 sterling spent by the local planters and merchants on pleasure trips to the northern colonies.[92]

Given such conditions, the trick, as Bull explained it to Lord Dartmouth, was to keep as much money in circulation as possible at all times. For this reason the public treasurers, each of whom was in bond for £40,000 proclamation money, typically extended credit to the merchants for public duties. This was good for the community, because there was no "dead money" about, and it was good for the treasury, because of the interest paid on such credits by the hundred or so merchants involved. Legally, Bull noted, the treasurers were personally responsible for the outstanding debt. If, as the Council insisted, the merchant-debtors were sued, he continued, it would only do more harm than good. Merchants, together with their creditors, would be forced into bankruptcy until the entire credit structure of Carolina came down like a house of cards. On the other hand if nothing was done, according to Bull, the merchants would be able to redeem their promissory notes in gold by November, when the rice and indigo crops were sold for export. Payment in specie as opposed to paper was imperative. Any fiat money returning to the treasury, except the £100,000 or so that bore no redemption date, had to be burned, which meant a serious dent in the money supply.[93]

By this time the Commons House had conducted its own investigation into the treasurers' accounts. Late in August the house revealed that it, too, had found on hand nearly £10,000 in gold, silver,

92. Aug. 26, 1773, C.O. 5/380, P.R.O. On trade ties with North Carolina see Merrens, *Colonial North Carolina*, 127, 165.
93. Aug. 26, 1773, C.O. 5/380, P.R.O.

and a "trifle of negotiable bills." With respect to the critical question of the merchants' debts, however, the delegates resolved that the £128,000 owed for duties through June 1, 1773, was to be looked upon as "actually in the treasury"—because the treasurers had testified that the money could be raised whenever necessary. The action of the Council appeared "not only hasty and unprecedented, but disrespectful to William Bull, contemptuous to the representatives of the people, and tending to endanger the public credit."[94] The Council refused to budge. The money, it declared, was *not* in the treasury, and to say otherwise was clearly an affront to reason. As for the custom of permitting public duties to remain in private hands for private gain, it could only be considered a gross perversion. Had the Commons House passed regular tax bills in the years after 1769, concluded the Council, there would be some £300,000 to £400,000 in paper in circulation by 1773 and consequently no need to take up merchants' promissory notes in lieu of cash.[95]

At this point the Commons House dropped the question concerning the state of the treasury in order to take up a bill to prevent the counterfeiting of paper money in neighboring colonies. The measure grew out of a request from Virginia where, as already noted, bogus money threatened to undermine the entire currency system.[96] This was ostensibly not a partisan issue, for the propriety of passing the counterfeiting bill could hardly be denied. In reality, however, if the Council gave it its stamp of approval, the current session of the General Assembly would come to an end. In consequence the general duty law would lapse, and the chief source of public revenue since 1769 would dry up, depriving the royal officers—including the councillors—of their salaries. It was therefore expected that in a very short time self-interest would lead the Council to call for a new duty law. The Commons House had only to submit a bill, without regard to the king's additional instruction, in order to nullify that directive and force the Council into submission.[97]

The Council was still considering the matter of the public funds when on August 25 the counterfeiting bill arrived. It was promptly read and returned to the house, where it received the customary

94. Aug. 21, 1773, Jours. of S.C. Upper House.
95. Aug. 24, 1773, *ibid.*
96. Aug. 25, 1773, *ibid.*
97. See p. 342 above.

third reading before being returned to the Council for final approval. Aware of the implications of the measure, yet reluctant to
reject the admittedly important proposal, and even more reluctant
to trigger a move in violation of the royal instruction, the Council
deferred the third reading *sine die* and resolved to pass no further
bills until a "satisfactory" general duty law was enacted.[98] The
maneuver backfired. Council members John Drayton and his son,
William Henry Drayton, entered into the Council journal a formal
protest demanding an explanation for the decision to postpone the
counterfeiting bill. That measure was "highly expedient." A resolve
not to consider any bills until a general duty law was on the books
might appear therefore as "pressure" upon the lower house—or as a
desire on the Council's part to usurp the exclusive right of the Commons House to originate money bills. On August 30 the dissenters
had their protests published in the *South-Carolina Gazette*, an action
that led to the eventual arrest of publisher Colonel Thomas Powell
on charges of "a high breach of the privilege and a contempt" of
the upper house and a drawn-out judicial dispute over whether or
not the Council was, as it claimed to be, a legislative body. The assault against the legislative power of the Council seemed to be reaching near-crisis proportions, when the Commons House returned to
the practical question of control over the public revenues.[99]

Bull had prorogued the legislature in September 1733 to cool
down the dispute over the counterfeiting bill and the Powell arrest.
Nevertheless the delegates were as hot as ever when the Commons
House reassembled the following March and made another of its
many moves to pass a money bill without including the clauses required by the additional instruction. The occasion was the need for
militia to defend the southern frontier against Indian marauders.
The Council, on the other hand, proved to be as ready as before to
reject any violation of the royal instruction. Obviously the house
had not yet found the political leverage necessary to effect its end.
It had, however, already set in motion a far more ambitious plan to
nullify the directive, to pay the public creditors, and to inject some
£200,000 of much-needed promissory notes into the monetary
stream. A stagnation in the sale of rice, a slump in local trade, an
excessive importation of slaves into South Carolina, a jump in the
sterling exchange rate, and the dearth of a circulating medium, all

98. Aug. 25, 1773, Jours. of S.C. Upper House. See also Bull to Dartmouth, Aug.
23, 1773, S.C. Archives, and *S.-C. Gaz.*, Aug. 18, 20, 1773.
99. See Ernst, "Growth of the Commons House of Assembly," 159–166.

operated to bolster the demand for an increased money supply as one way of reviving a flagging economy.[100] The Commons House began an audit of all the unpaid public accounts on March 3, 1774. A week later it informed Bull that, because of the captious opposition of the ministerial hacks who ran the Council, the ruin of the public creditors was at hand. In order to "alleviate the distresses of their unfortunate fellow subjects," the delegates found it necessary to grant certificates of indebtedness, or promissory notes, to all creditors who desired them. The clerk, the Speaker, and four of the most influential leaders of the house would personally sign the notes, which were to be redeemed by the next tax law. In the meantime interest was to be paid on all accounts through January 1, 1773. The representatives, together with those merchants belonging to the Chamber of Commerce, many of whom had already suffered at the hands of the Council over the payment of the former general duty law, pledged in advance to receive the certificates in common payment.[101] The Council publicly protested the move, though like everyone else in South Carolina the individual councillors readily accepted the new addition to the currency supply and their back salaries. The only holdout in fact was William Bull. He preferred "the satisfaction arising in my own mind, from the consciousness of performing my duty to the King, and of my attachment to the true interest of this province which this expedient appears to me to have a tendency to undermine."[102]

No doubt the Commons House had violated the Currency Acts of 1764 and 1773. It had issued under its own authority promissory notes as a legal tender for all public obligations. But in doing so, it had temporarily settled the question of the public debt in South Carolina. The one remaining problem concerned the Council's right to sit as an upper house of the assembly and the enforcibility of the king's additional instruction. When the next full session of the legislature took place early in 1775, the Commons House revived the counterfeiting bill on February 2 and sent it up to the Council for final approval. In all probability Council action on the bill would have been postponed—on grounds that all Council members were

100. *Ibid.*, 166. The discussion of economic conditions at the time is drawn from my general reading of the mercantile correspondence cited in this chapter. But see in particular Laurens to Jean Laurens, Apr. 8, 1774, in Laurens Letterbook. See also graph 5 in Appendix 2.

101. Mar. 3, 10, 24, 1773, Jours. of S.C. Assembly.

102. Quoted in W. Roy Smith, *South Carolina as a Royal Province, 1719–1776* (New York, 1903), 394.

not present—had not William Henry Drayton again publicly challenged the wisdom of holding up important legislation under any pretext. Recognizing that its position was untenable and that the public was genuinely apprehensive about the fate of the bill, the Council quietly passed the measure into law. Three weeks later the General Assembly enacted a new general duty law for a period of twelve months—with *no* mention of the objectionable clauses required by the additional instruction.[103]

The procedure was to have been repeated the next year. With the Council wholly dependent upon the law, and therefore upon the lower house, for the salaries of the royal officers, "a complete surrender to the Commons would be unavoidable," as John Drayton correctly pointed out.[104] The Council had, of course, surrendered its potential claim to any power over money bills. The right of the Council to sit as an upper house was never fully resolved, however. The General Assembly was destined never to meet again in full session.

103. Feb. 2, Mar. 3, 4, 1775, *Jours. of S.C. Assembly.* See also *S.-C. Gaz.*, Feb. 8, 13, 1775.
104. Quoted in David D. Wallace, *The History of South Carolina*, II (New York, 1934), 100–101.

Part Four
Coda

Chapter 11

The Political Economy of Revolution

Historians of colonial currency have been preoccupied with the *visible* money supply. How much coin there was in circulation, how much paper was struck, how much issued, how much sunk, how much was outstanding, and the extent to which all of this affected the larger economy are characteristic questions. And it must be conceded that these concerns fairly reflect the views of the colonists. The amount and kind of money in the monetary stream and its impact on economic activity was an overriding interest of the people of the time.

Undoubtedly the many and serious problems associated with the visible money supply help to explain this preoccupation. A lack of any gold and silver mines in British America, the failure of imperial authorities to provide the colonists either with a local coinage or with the sort of continental currency Benjamin Franklin and others from time to time had advocated, the inability of the Americans to accumulate coin in the normal course of trade, and the inconvenience and inefficiency of commodity money comprised one set of difficulties. An increase in the overall demand for money following a business upsurge, population expansion, and military activities, especially after Queen Anne's War, constituted another. The greater specialization of the marketplace that seems to have taken place after mid-century also contributed to a growing demand for monetary expansion.

Ironically the "solution" to these problems, the colonial currency system, had little to do either with British neglect of monetary requirements or with rapid economic growth in America. Instead, the colonial currency system developed mainly in response to urgent financial and credit demands. The need to cover rising costs of administration and of war and to provide a public source of agricultural and business credit were the principal reasons for the creation of a system of "currency finance" and of land banks. As a result colonial currency practices were governed by financial as well as purely monetary considerations.

Historians have been quick to recognize this mixed character of the colonial currency system. And several good institutional studies of the complex origins and operation of "currency finance" and of the loan offices already exist. But monetary historians have been primarily interested in the question of the relationship between the currency supply and economic fluctuations in the period. Here again one sees a tendency to conceptualize colonial currency problems in present-day terms. It is well known, for instance, that some colonists believed that the only "sound" money was specie, that any system of fiat money was fundamentally unsound. Certain nineteenth-century monetary historians who shared this view of the evils of paper currency condemned colonial monetary practices on precisely these grounds. Recent scholars, however, have rarely been so crude in their assumptions. And in any event they have been more concerned with another colonial view: that plenty of money made trade easy.

That plenty of money made trade easy was a widely held though not unqualified belief. For most colonists it meant that there had to be enough currency in the monetary stream to cover the exchange of goods, ease the payment of domestic debts, and provide a normal amount of elasticity in periods of ordinary and predictable market and seasonal strains on existing money stocks. The belief conveyed, too, the idea that the visible money supply should at least match the rise in business activity at the time. In short local governments were responsible for providing for the usual transaction and liquidity demand for money.

For other colonists a policy of monetary expansion under government auspices signified a temporary program of "easy" money for the remedy of business slumps. This is not to say that contemporaries believed in a system of cheap money. They did not, at least not in the sense that we associate that term today with conditions of low interest rates. Rather, whenever local markets were badly glutted or sales were down, the conventional wisdom taught that moderate injections of paper money into the economy stimulated short-run changes in the pattern of spending.

Present-day monetary historians have accepted that some kind of colonial fiat money system was indeed necessary. The ordinary marketplace demands for money in a rapidly developing economy had to be met. But these historians have divided in their views of the wisdom and success of colonial attempts to use paper issues to affect economic behavior in the other sectors of the economy. Some have postulated the simplest kind of quantity theory of money to be found in textbooks on money and banking. Ignoring everything except the expansion of the paper money supply, they have discovered what their classical economic model had prepared them for: that the only effect of increasing the currency supply was inflation in the general price level (especially as reflected in rising sterling exchange rates) and that the effect of contraction was deflation. By contrast other historians of colonial currency, echoing a point of view prevalent in the 1930s and 1940s among self-styled Keynesians, have found instead that the Americans were remarkably successful in using paper emissions in a conscious Keynesian-like effort to overcome economic depression.

The conclusions of this study differ sharply from these traditional views of the colonial currency system. It is true that there were problems associated with the visible money supply. And they were recognized as such by contemporaries. But there were other monetary questions that the people of the time either failed to identify or misjudged. Recent scholars have often missed this point. "Replicating" the past is not the same as understanding it, even when monetary historians have been ready to use advanced models of explanation.

SOURCES OF MONETARY BEHAVIOR

The fact remains that students of colonial currency have shown a surprising reluctance to extend their discussions beyond the traditional question of the visible money supply—to include questions of credit and capital flow. Yet, as the present work has tried to show, it is impossible to understand monetary behavior in the period without coming to grips with the close links between visible money, debt, and credit. Furthermore, in their concern with the impact of the visible money supply on the larger economy, modern writers have also demonstrated a remarkable lack of interest in the other side of the question—the effects of the larger economy on money. According to the view expressed here, it was this effect rather than the traditional problems of the currency supply that explains mone- tary "crises" and developments in eighteenth-century America.

An example is the question of money as liquidity. While changing liquidity demands were a normal outgrowth of colonial economic activity, the liquidity problems that plagued the Revolutionary gen- eration arose out of the disruptions in the colonial business structure. These disruptions in turn were caused by the rapid expansion of the Atlantic marketplace in the half-century before Independence. After 1750 dynamic developments within the British economy gave rise to a growing spread between colonial exports to Britain and British exports to the colonies, and as American businessmen availed themselves of increased English and Scottish credit to expand their British purchases, there was a quantum jump in American debt. In addition these new "loans" were quickly passed on to the colonial consumer in the form of book credit to become a major part of the colonial money supply.

Inevitably, when British houses cut back their credit and repatri- ated their colonial assets, as they did during the financial crises fol- lowing 1763 and 1772, much of this new credit-money was wiped out. The drain on hard money proved equally severe when coin was swept away to Britain in the form of remittances. Likewise the amount of sterling bills available, at least in the staple colonies, would be sharply reduced at the very time the demand for such bills rap- idly increased. An abrupt and general contraction of money, a vast increase in the demand for remittances, and a consequent hike in sterling exchange rates was the result. As merchants on both sides of the Atlantic dunned for debts, a rush for liquidity and a cry for monetary relief invariably occurred. This was a predictable, if in- effectual, response to the problem. Increasingly dependent after mid-century on British "loans" for closing the gap in the balance of payments, and increasingly sensitive therefore to fluctuations in British credit and capital markets, colonial merchants and planters were attempting to use local currency systems in an effort to pro- vide liquidity and to protect their interests.

This widening spread between imports and exports and the grow- ing reliance on British credit placed other strains on the monetary system. The spiraling of exchange rates in Virginia after 1763, which members of the trading and planting community falsely attributed to an oversupply of paper currency, was one of these. The collapse of real estate values in the mid-1760s was another. When demand for liquidity significantly increased in the period, realty prices tumbled, threatening all economic classes. Real estate provided the basic security for American debts, and as John Dickinson pointed out, in the rush for liquidity "reputable freeholders" found it "impossible to pay debts which are trifling in comparison to their estates. If creditors sue, and take out executions, the lands and personal estate, as the sale must be for ready money, are sold for a small part of what they were worth when the debts were contracted. The debtors are ruined. The creditors get but part of their debts, and that ruins them. Thus the consumers break the shopkeepers; they break the merchants; and the shock must be felt as far as *London*."[1] The cry went up for more money.

A final example is the dumping of dry goods on the American market. After 1750, taking advantage of favorable trade and market conditions at home, British suppliers increasingly unloaded their wares on the colonies. This was accomplished not only through liberal offers of credit to established merchants in colonial ports but also through auction sales and the setting up of new outlets in the form of many new and marginal importers. Consequent depressions in dry goods and related sectors threatened the very existence of the older and larger merchants and gave rise to continued complaints about the scarcity of money.

That these relationships between money and credit, as well as between the long- and short-run changes in the Atlantic economy and monetary behavior, were not fully comprehended by the Revolutionary generation is not surprising. The merchants, planters, artisans, or farmers who probed the workings of the colonial economy were rarely theorists. For the most part they functioned as businessmen who seldom rose above short-term considerations. Whatever their theoretical shortcomings, however, contemporaries were able to reduce the movements of the economy to a recognizable pattern. Their response to the Currency Act of 1764 suggests that their understanding of the linkages between money and the economy rested upon a relatively few practical assumptions and concerns growing out of daily business experience.

The failure of monetary historians to identify and to analyze these relationships is less easy to understand. Probably, as we have seen,

1. Paul Leicester Ford, ed., *The Writings of John Dickinson* (Philadelphia, 1895), 227–228.

this failure has to do with a ready acceptance of traditional monetary theories and of contemporary definitions of the problems concerning the visible money supply. But it may also reflect the paucity
of realistic or adequate studies of the eighteenth-century economy.
This point is fundamental. It lies at the heart of the failure of scholars to recognize the economic situation in the Revolution.

Students of the colonial economy have generally focused on the
organization of business in the great ports of colonial America, on
the economic functions or power relations of the merchant class,
on the production and distribution of at least one staple export,
tobacco, and on "mercantilism" and its putative effects on the well-
being of the colonists. In addition a few earlier works have centered
on the economy of a particular colony, but always while viewing
it in a static way and from inside that colony's political boundaries.
Money, trade, agriculture, and manufacturing have usually been
handled as if they were separate and distinct and had only a passing
relationship to one another.

More recently the rage has been for the study of economic
growth, for "cliometrics," and for the formal, conceptual approach
of the economist. All authors in the past have employed some statistics in their work. But only recently have some been systematic
in their use. And only recently have very large claims been made
for statistics. The truth is that neither the old economic history nor
the new has told us very much about the shape, the feel, or the functioning of economic life in colonial America. As a result, until we
have studies describing, detailing, and analyzing that economy in
all its complexities, our conclusions about the role of money, or about
any vital and interesting economic problem, must be crudely put
and taken only as tentative and suggestive. In particular we need
a host of regional and dynamic studies of both the long- and short-
run fluctuations in the various sectors of the colonial and Revolutionary economy and of the interconnections between these sectors.
In this regard a wealth of material, both quantitative and nonquanti-
tative, is to be found in business correspondence and business records, sources that only a handful of historians have as yet exploited.
Legal records, official documents, private diaries, newspaper reports,
and travel accounts are only slightly less valuable.[2]

2. The preceeding paragraph is drawn from a paper, "Southern 'Worlds' in the
Atlantic Economy," that H. Roy Merrens and I presented at the South Carolina
Tricentennial Celebration, Mar. 1970, Columbia, S. C.

While based upon such materials, this study cannot claim to have exhausted them. They are too voluminous. My concern here has been with the broad tendencies and the characteristic features of the regional economies of the time. The somewhat more detailed economic discussions take up the specific phenomena of supply, demand, and price; they deal, that is, with the network of exchange and credit transactions in the eighteenth-century Atlantic marketplace wherein the colonies functioned as both a supplier of foodstuffs and raw materials and a consumer of European, and especially British, manufactures. But what is needed is further research and a more highly refined analysis of colonial economic behavior and of the interrelationships between money and the economy.

MONEY AND THE POLITICAL ECONOMY OF REVOLUTION

It is against the background of these monetary conditions and objective economic circumstances, as well as of the contemporary perceptions of the situation, that the problem of currency and the political economy of the Revolution is to be approached and understood. Thus the parliamentary enactments and royal policies after the end of the French and Indian War for the regulation of currency did not operate in some economic void or in a mythical state of economic equilibrium to be contemplated by minds steeped solely in the literature of eighteenth-century history and political theory. Instead these regulations were interventions in the Atlantic economy at a time of profound internal structural change and crisis. Their impact is to be seen in the light of their effect on the fortunes and formulations of the economic and political elites that ruled the colonial political sphere and played a major role in the colonial marketplace. In broad terms these elites included the merchants and planters. Their farmer and artisan constituents, lacking power, played a far less conspicuous role.

The impact of these interventions on the British suppliers and creditors is equally important. It may be safely assumed that British merchants were no less fully aware of their economic interests and no less determined to have control over their economic destinies than their American counterparts. Viewed in this light, the Currency Act of 1764 appears as a move to safeguard British investments in America, a move dictated by metropolitan, not colonial, needs. Similarly the seesaw battle for revision and repeal of the Currency

Act in the decade after 1764 may be seen as a reflection of the shifting interests of the elite classes in America and of their understanding of the patterns of economic change.

Ultimately these colonial elites turned to politics. Whether inside
or outside the existing institutional and governmental arrangements,
politics seemed to offer a remedy for their economic ills. And given
their position of economic dependency, there was little else colonial
interests could do. The purposes of the British merchants and creditors, on the other hand, could often be more easily achieved through
normal economic processes over which these classes exercised a
substantial amount of control. If at times they felt a need to ask for
parliamentary interference in these processes, it was only to extend
the scope of their control or to mediate between the claims of rival
British interests.

In any event, once it is accepted that much of the important political activity in the Revolution represented an attempt to deal with
economic crises and conditions, it must also be admitted that the
greatest part of this activity—whether it took the form of assembly
protest, lobbying activities in England, or nonimportation—provided only weak and partial solutions to problems at hand. Moreover, seen as a whole the structural changes in the Atlantic economy
and the parliamentary restrictions on currency and trade all seemed
to point to fundamental weaknesses in the British imperial system
and also to reveal the extent of the British attempt at total domination
of the American economy, even if the result was the extinction of
established colonial interests. American economic and political leaders began therefore to adjust their views and to feel that there was
another course of action open to them. As they came to feel more
and more the need to rearrange their world, they came also to believe with increasing conviction that this could not be achieved
within the empire.

Ideology and the Political Economy of Revolution

Whatever else it may achieve, the predictable outpouring of books
and articles in honor of the bicentennial celebration of American
Independence will offer a more complex view of the Revolution
than has yet appeared. It seems certain, however, that any new system of explanation must take into account the realities of colonial
political economy. A new generation of historians should come to
recognize that the Revolutionary years were a time of repeated

economic crises. While the precise dimensions and the causes of these crises are open to debate, the affected classes in America ultimately turned to the political sphere for a solution to their problems. The outcome was an integration of economic and political concerns firmly rooted in a system of elitist politics that was essential to the Revolutionary movement. Such at any rate is the leading argument in this book.

But additional studies in the political economy of the American Revolution will not by themselves explain the causes and the nature of that singular event in American history. Any complete account of Revolutionary developments, any grand synthesis of views about the Revolution, will have to be ideological, that is, will have to deal with thought on all levels of life and with the interconnections and accommodations between these ideas and the concrete economic and sociopolitical circumstances of the period.

Discussions of the central role of ideology in the American Revolution have taken place largely within the ranks of the so-called "neo-whigs." But it may be argued that they have been ambiguous in their definition and use of the term "ideology." Generally they have taken it to be synonymous with what is conventionally meant by idealism. They have written of Americans united to defend traditional ideals and liberties against British encroachments. Their ideology is reducible to a question of principle. The considerations of interest and conflict that informed the writings of earlier historians are not an issue.[3]

But "the nature of the ideas expressed," as one historian has recently reminded us, "is determined as much by the character of the world being confronted as by the internal development of inherited and borrowed conceptions."[4] There is simply no substitute for a

3. See the discussion and bibliography in Gordon S. Wood, "Rhetoric and Reality in the American Revolution," *WMQ*, 3d Ser., XXIII (1966), 3–32. For additional references, see Jack P. Greene, ed., *The Reinterpretation of the American Revolution, 1763–1789* (New York, 1968), 2–59.

4. Wood, "Rhetoric and Reality," *WMQ*, 3d Ser., XXIII (1966), 24. In his discussion of the role of ideas in the Revolution, Wood understands ideology generally to mean a body of ideas seen in their political and social context. Opposed to his view is the more simplistic notion of ideas as rationalization or propaganda, which Wood ascribes to the Progressives, or as idealism, which he ascribes to the neo-whigs. Curiously, in his own formulation Wood omits the economic side of ideology, although he clearly feels that ideology properly defined involves the interaction of thought and the empirical circumstances of an age. On the other hand it is also apparent that the omission of the economic realities of the Revolution permits him to discover an irrationality in the conduct of the patriots, to discover, that is, patterns of behavior dictated by insecurity and anxiety as opposed to rational con-

continued analysis of the subtle dialectic between the perceptions of men and the conditions of life, between thought and action. Nor will it do to insist in the face of the mounting evidence of severe economic crises during the Revolutionary period that the strains in colonial society were minimal.

And we shall have to know more about the ideas of other groups than simply the commonwealthmen.[5] The categories of thought they passed on to American political leaders were inadequate to any understanding of the problems of political economy. More to the point are the ideas of Adam Smith's and Max Weber's "economic man," of the merchants, mechanics, farmers, and planters. These were ideas that achieved their expression on a lower level of historical abstraction. Nonetheless it was these marketplace views that served to illuminate the weaknesses in the British imperial system and the risks to established colonial interests inherent in the changes taking place in the Atlantic economy after mid-century.

If ideology is to be seen as the interplay between historical awareness and the thoughts and theorizing of the Revolutionaries, on one hand, and the events and conditions of the concrete reality of the period, on the other, then historians of the American Revolution will have to return for their models of explanation to the traditions of Marx, Weber, and, closer to home, of C. Wright Mills.

---

siderations of concrete economic events and conditions. Consequently Wood ends up advocating not an ideological but a "psychologizing" approach to the period. It is interesting to note that John Higham in his discussion of historiography advocates this same approach; see *History* (Englewood Cliffs, N.J., 1965), 87-232.

5. See the introduction in Bernard Bailyn, ed., *Pamphlets of the American Revolution, 1750-1776*, I (Cambridge, Mass., 1965).

Appendixes
A Select List of Sources
Index

Appendix 1: Tables

Year	Authorized	Canceled	Total Outstanding at End of Year
1755, June	£63,000	£6,000[a]	
Nov.		4,000	
1756, June	62,000	5,000	
Nov.		5,000	
1757, June		6,000	
Nov.		5,000	
1758, June	100,000	6,000	
Nov.		6,000	
1759, June	250,000	18,000	
Nov.		58,000	
1760, June	60,000	52,000	
Nov.		79,000	495,000[b]
1761, June		25,000	
Nov.		20,000	365,000
1762, June		23,000	
Nov.		12,000	330,000
1763, June		20,000	
Nov.		23,000	285,000
1764, June		19,000	
Nov.		24,000	240,000
1765, June		54,000	
Nov.		23,000	165,000
1766, June		20,000	
Nov.		12,000	130,000
1767, June		15,000	
Nov.		10,000[c]	110,000
1768, June		16,000	
Nov.		7,000	85,000
1769, June		2,000	
Nov.		3,000	
1770, June & Nov.		1,000	80,000

Year	Authorized	Canceled	Total Outstanding at End of Year
1771, June & Nov.	120,000^d	3,000	195,000
1772, June & Nov.		4,000	190,000
1773, June & Nov.		4,000	190,000
1774, June & Nov.		3,000	185,000

SOURCES: Lott, ed., *Jour. of N.Y. Assembly*, II, 281, 325, 336, 350, 362, 422–423, 457, 489, 518–519, 554, 570, 602, 606, 634, 644, 668, 672, 707, 728, 750, 785; June 28, Dec. 13, 1766, June 6, 1767, Nov. 23, Dec. 29, 1768, Dec. 12, 1769, Jan. 11, 1771, Jan. 14, 1772, Jan. 12, 1773, Jan. 22, 1774, Jan. 25, 1775, Jour. of N.Y. Assembly in Jenkins, ed., *Microfilm Records of the States; Col. Laws N.Y.*, III, 688–692, IV, 57, 60, 215, 317, 350, 398.

NOTES: In Lott, ed., *Jour. of N.Y. Assembly*, for Mar. 11, 1762, is a report of the "State of the Paper Currency" from 1714 to 1760, which gives the amount of bills of credit outstanding as of Nov. 1761. This figure provides the base line for the foregoing calculations.

^{a} This figure and the following figures are rounded off to the nearest 1,000.

^{b} This figure and the following figures are rounded off to the nearest 5,000.

^{c} This figure is taken from a table in Brock, "Currency of the American Colonies," 345–346.

^{d} This was a public loan that was lawful at the loan offices only.

TABLE 2. CURRENCY EMISSIONS OF NEW JERSEY

Year	Treasury Notes Full Legal Tender Authorized	Scheduled to Be Canceled	Actually Western Treasury	Canceled Eastern Treasury	Total Outstanding at End of Year
1755	£40,000	£1,530			
1756	17,500	1,530			
1757	45,000	6,530			
1758	60,000	11,530			
1759	50,000	11,530			
1760	45,000	16,530			
1761	25,000	14,030	10,000[a]		
1762	30,000	16,530	10,000		
1763	10,000	16,530	12,000		
1764	25,000	12,500	6,000		
1765		12,500	7,000		
1766		12,500	5,000		
1767		12,500	7,000	— 6,000	
1768		12,500	5,000	— 5,000	
1769		12,500	5,000	— 7,000	190,000[b]
1770		12,500	6,000	— 0	
1771		12,500	7,000	— 0	
1772		12,500	7,000	— 3,000	
1773		12,500	8,000	— 4,000	
1774	100,000[c]	15,000	4,000	— unknown	
1775		15,000	8,000	— unknown	

SOURCES: *N.J. Archives*, IX, 144, X, 249, XVII, 399–403, XVIII, 57–62, 78–82, 208, 223–225, 320–321, 409–411, 494–496, 554–557; Letters of Joseph Sherwood to Samuel Smith, Treasurer of New Jersey, and "An Account of Bills of Credit created and Issued in the Colony of New Jersey since January 1749 . . . ," N.J. Hist. Soc., *Procs.*, 1st Ser., V (1851), 144–147; 10 Geo. III, c. 8, N.J. Session Laws.

NOTES:
[a] This figure and the following figures are rounded off to the nearest 1,000.
[b] This is an approximate figure.
[c] This was a public loan that was lawful at the loan office only.

TABLE 3. CURRENCY EMISSIONS OF PENNSYLVANIA

Treasury Notes—Legal Tender at Treasury

Year	Authorized	Total Outstanding at End of Year
1756	£ 30,000	
1757	100,000	
1758	100,000	
1759	100,000	
1760	100,000	
1761		
1762		
1763		
1764	55,000	330,000[a]
1765		
1766		295,000[b]
1767	20,000	
1768		
1769	30,000	
1770		205,000[a]
1771	15,000	
1772	25,000	
1773	11,000	
1774	150,000[c]	

SOURCES: Mitchell and Flanders, eds., *Statutes of Pa.*, V, 201, 243, 294, 303, 337, 379, 427, VI, 7, 344, VII, 100, 197, 204, VIII, 15, 204, 264, 284, 417, 423, 447; *Pa. Archives*, V, 3877, VII, 5824, VIII, 7247, 7359.

NOTES:

[a] These figures, taken from a table in Brock, "Currency of the American Colonies," 382–387, are rounded off to the nearest 5,000. Those interested in estimates of the amount of paper currency outstanding for the years 1750 to 1775 should refer to the tables, *ibid.*, cited above. But compare his figure for 1766 with the figure to be found in *Pa. Archives*, VII, 5824.

[b] *Pa. Archives*, VII, 5824.

[c] This was a public loan that was lawful at the loan offices only.

TABLE 4. CURRENCY EMISSIONS OF MARYLAND

Year	Treasury Notes Authorized	Bills of Credit Authorized	Total Outstanding at End of Year
1756	£34,000		
1757			
1758			
1759			
1760			
1761			
1762			
1763			
1764			40,000[a]
1765			5,000
1766	$173,000[b]		
1767			$145,000[c]
1768			
1769		$300,000[b]	
1770			
1771			
1772			
1773		$347,000[b]	
1774			

SOURCES: *Md. Archives*, III, 169–170, LIX, 66–70, 264–275, LXI, ci, 264–275, LXII, 131–151, LXIV, 242–253.
NOTES:
[a] This figure is rounded off to the nearest 5,000.
[b] These figures are rounded off to the nearest 1,000. They represent paper money that was legal tender at the treasury and loan offices.
[c] This figure is for dollars; the other two figures in the column are for pounds. A dollar in current money of Maryland equals seven shillings and sixpence.

TABLE 5. CURRENCY EMISSIONS OF VIRGINIA

Year	Treasury Notes—Full Legal Tender Authorized		Total Outstanding
1755, June	£20,000	(pay 5 percent)	
Oct.	40,000	"	35,000[a]
1756, Apr.	25,000	"	
Apr.	30,000	"	
Apr.	12,000	"	110,000
1757, Apr.	179,963		
1758, Apr.	32,000		
Sept.	57,000		
1759, Feb.	52,000		
Nov.	10,000		
1760, Mar.	20,000		
May	32,000		
1761			
1762	30,000		
1763			
1764			230,000[b]
1765			
1766			
1767			205,000
1768			170,000
1769	10,000[c]		130,000
1770			
1771	30,000[c]		105,000
1772			90,000
1773	36,834[c]		55,000
1774			
1775			75,000

SOURCES: Hening, ed., *Statutes of Va.*, VI, 461, 522, VII, 9, 26, 46, 69, 163, 171, 255, 331, 347, 357, 495, VIII, 346, 501, 648; *Jours. of Burgesses, 1766–1769*, 69, 120, 155, XII, 218. Correspondence of the Board of Trade, XXI, 97ff, transcriptions in Hist. Soc. Pa., Philadelphia; *WMQ*, 1st Ser., XX (1911–1912), 152, 228; Harriet Talmage, "Financial History of Virginia during the Revolutionary War" (M.A. thesis, University of Wisconsin, 1947), 17–18.

NOTES:
[a] This figure and the following figures are rounded off to the nearest 5,000.
[b] This is a minimum figure.
[c] These issues were legal tender for public obligations only.

TABLE 6. CURRENCY EMISSIONS OF NORTH CAROLINA

Year	Treasury Notes Authorized	Bills of Credit Authorized	Debentures Authorized	Total Out-standing
1748		£21,350[a]		21,000[b]
1749				21,000
1750				21,000
1751				20,000
1752				19,000
1753				18,000
1754		40,000		58,000
1755				56,000
1756	£3,600[c]			58,000
1757	14,806			68,000
1758	11,000			70,000
1759				70,000
1760		12,000		76,000
1761		20,000		95,000
1762				85,000
1763				85,000
1764				75,000[d]
1765				75,000
1766				68,000
1767				68,000
1768			20,000	98,000[e]
1769				
1770				
1771			60,000	
1772				
1773				
1774				

SOURCES: *Col. Recs. N.C.*, VI, 1308–1311, VII, 213–215, VIII, 9, 215, IX, 166, 231; Clark, ed., *State Recs. of N.C.*, XXIII, 781–782, 850.

NOTES:

[a] Bills of credit were full legal tender.

[b] This figure and the following figures are rounded off to the nearest 1,000. The figures for the total amount of paper money outstanding for the several years are based on the figures for the treasury notes and bills of credit outstanding. These figures may be found in the sources cited above.

[c] Treasury notes were legal tender for public obligations only.

[d] Compare the estimate to be found in the Report of Gov. Arthur Dobbs to the Board of Trade, Jan. 1, 1765, in Corres. of Board of Trade (transcripts), XXI, 105ff.

[e] This is the last estimate of the total amount of paper money outstanding. Estimates of the amount of bills of credit and of treasury notes for the years 1770 and 1771 are available, however.

Appendix 1: Tables

TABLE 7. CURRENCY EMISSIONS OF SOUTH CAROLINA

Year	Public Orders Authorized	Bills of Credit Authorized	Tax Certificates Authorized	Total Out-standing
1755	£ 33,600[a]		42,322	
1756	50,000		85,159	
1757	229,300		96,628	
1758				
1759			74,167	
1760	371,693		77,650	
1761			180,571	
1762	15,000		88,692	
1763				
1764			93,834	585,000[c]
1765			48,045	
1766			37,742	
1767	60,000		86,420	
1768			105,000	
1769		£ 24,959[b]	70,000	
1770	70,000[d]			
1771				
1772				
1773				390,000
1774			200,000	

SOURCES: Aug. 6, 1764, Mar. 3, 1774, Mar. 1, 1775, Jours. of S.C. Commons House; Corres. of Board of Trade (transcripts), XXI, 125ff.

NOTES:

[a] Public orders were legal tender at the treasury only.

[b] Bills of credit were full legal tender.

[c] This figure and the following figure are rounded off to the nearest 5,000.

[d] This issue was disallowed. Nonetheless, as of Mar. 1, 1775, some £ 35,000 continued in circulation.

TABLE 8. CURRENCY EMISSIONS OF GEORGIA

Year	Government Certificates Authorized	Bills of Credit Authorized	Total Out- standing
1755		£2,987[c]	
1756			
1757		636	
1758			
1759		799	
1760	1,100[a]		
1761	720[b]		4,000[d]
1762		7,410	
1763			
1764			8,000
1765	650		
1766	1,815		
1767			
1768	2,200		
1769			
1770	106[e]		
1771	3,355[f]		
1772			
1773	4,299[g]		11,000
1774	800		

SOURCES: Candler, ed., *Col. Recs. Ga.*, XVIII, 422, 478, 645, 745, XIX, pt. 1, 86, 150, 198, 423, XIX, pt. 2, 3; Corres. of Board of Trade (transcripts), 130ff.

NOTES:

[a] Government certificates were ordinarily full legal tender, but see the exceptions as noted below.

[b] At least £540 of this amount was full legal tender. Probably all of it was.

[c] Loan office bills were full legal tender.

[d] This figure and the following figures are rounded off to the nearest 1,000.

[e] The legal tender of this issue was unspecified.

[f] These were tax certificates, not government certificates, and were legal tender at the treasury.

[g] This issue was legal tender for all public obligations. In addition it was exchangeable at the treasury at any time for money that was full legal tender. It should be noted that the £4,299 amounted to a monetization of the deficit in the tax collections of previous years. In other words, the £4,299 was money that should have been redeemed by 1773 but was still outstanding. In order to insure the redemption of the existing paper currency supply, the old notes were replaced with new notes and a new redemption fund was created.

Appendix 2: Graphs

GRAPH I

Average Rate of Exchange: New York Paper Money on Sterling, 1762–1768

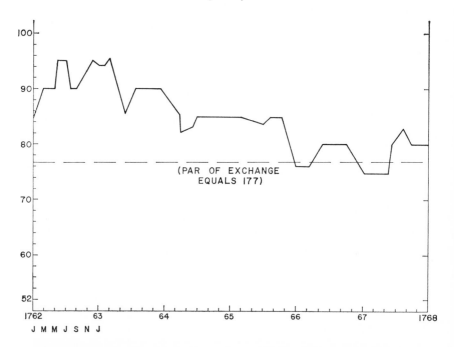

NOTE: Figures on rates of exchange were gathered from the various collections cited in this study. Exchange rates are for sterling bills drawn on London at sixty days sight.

374

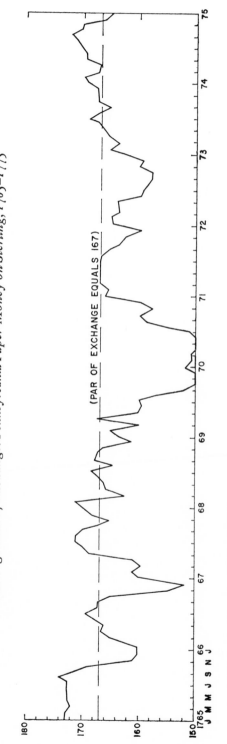

GRAPH 2

Average Rate of Exchange: Pennsylvania Paper Money on Sterling, 1765–1775

(PAR OF EXCHANGE EQUALS 167)

NOTE: These figures were collated with similar figures to be found in Anne Bezanson, Robert D. Gray, and Miriam Hussey, *Prices in Colonial Pennsylvania* (Philadelphia, 1935), and in Marc Egnal's forthcoming dissertation at the University of Wisconsin.

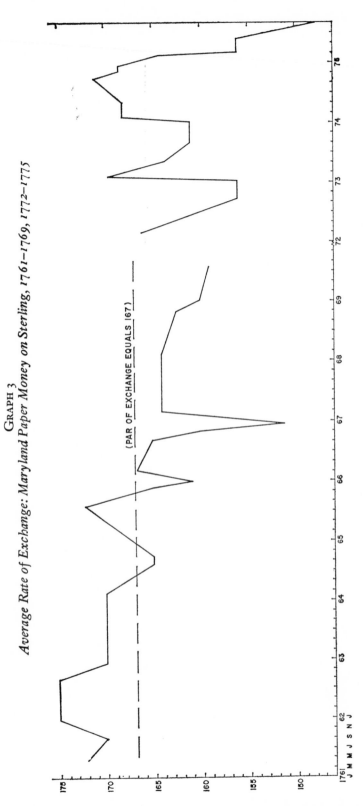

GRAPH 3

Average Rate of Exchange: Maryland Paper Money on Sterling, 1761–1769, 1772–1775

NOTE: Figures on rates of exchange were gathered from the various collections cited in this study.

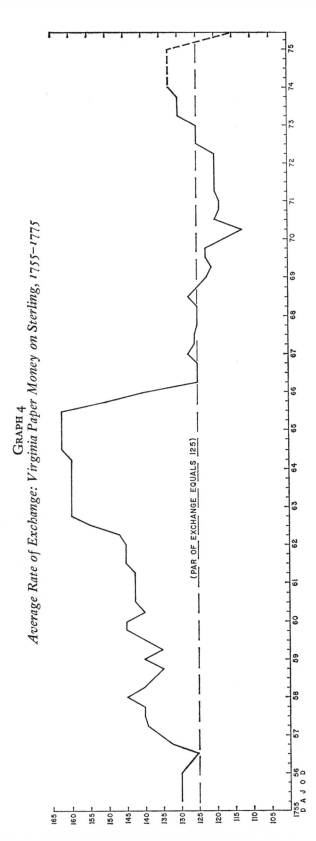

GRAPH 4

Average Rate of Exchange: Virginia Paper Money on Sterling, 1755–1775

NOTE: Figures on rates of exchange were gathered from the various collections cited in this study. Exchange rates were generally settled at the General Court, which met in Williamsburg in April and October, and at the court of oyer and terminer, which met in June and December.

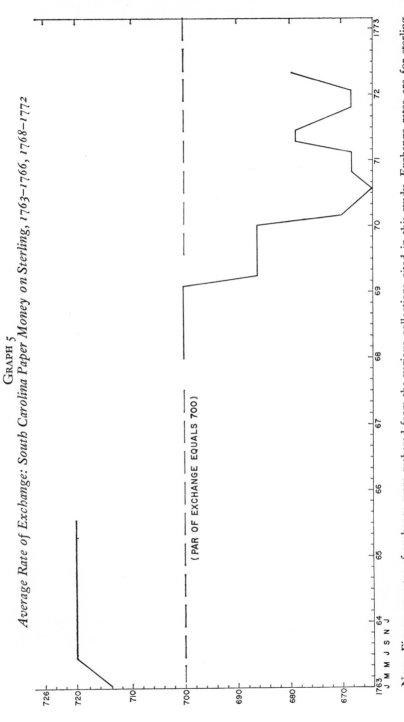

GRAPH 5

Average Rate of Exchange: South Carolina Paper Money on Sterling, 1763–1766, 1768–1772

(PAR OF EXCHANGE EQUALS 700)

NOTE: Figures on rates of exchange were gathered from the various collections cited in this study. Exchange rates are for sterling bills drawn on London at sixty days sight.

A Select List of Sources

Manuscripts

*Indicates that microfilm is available at the Colonial Williamsburg Foundation Research Department Library, Williamsburg, Virginia.

Alderman Library, University of Virginia, Charlottesville
  Landon Carter Papers
William L. Clements Library, University of Michigan, Ann Arbor
  Benjamin Franklin: Original Letters to Joseph Galloway, 1766–1775
  Shelburne Papers
Colonial Williamsburg Foundation Research Library, Williamsburg, Va.
  British Public Record Office, Customs Office Series (microfilm)
  Robert Carter of Nomini Hall Letterbook, 1764–1768
  Richard Corbin Letterbook, 1764–1768
  Parker Family Papers, Liverpool Record Office, Liverpool, Eng. (microfilm)
Charles Townshend Papers at Dalkeith: Material Relating to America from the Charles Townshend Papers in Possession of the Duke of Buccleuch at Dalkeith House, Midlothian, Eng. (microfilm)
Duke University Library, Durham, N.C.
  Hogg and Clayton Letterbook and Accounts, 1767–1771
  Nathaniel Williams Letterbook and Accounts, 1758–1768
Historical Society of Pennsylvania, Philadelphia
  Correspondence of the Board of Trade in the Public Record Office (transcripts)
  Clifford Correspondence
  Gratz Collection
  Hollingsworth Correspondence
  William Pollard Letterbook
  William Smith Letterbook
  Charles Steuart Letterbook, 1754–1763*
  Richard Waln, Jr., Letterbook
Huntington Library, San Marino, Calif.
  Papers of Neil Jamieson*
Maryland Archives, Annapolis
  Black Books

Maryland Hall of Records, Annapolis
  Wallace, Davidson, and Johnson Letterbooks*
Maryland Historical Society, Baltimore
  Alexander Hamilton Papers*
New Jersey Historical Society, Newark
  Joseph Sherwood Letters
New-York Historical Society, New York City
  Alexander Papers
  James Beekman Letterbook
  James Duane Papers
  William Lux Letterbook, 1763–1768
  Rutherfurd Collection
New York Public Library, New York City
  Bancroft Collection
  Chalmers Papers Relating to New York
  Galloway Correspondence
  Philip Schuyler Papers
  Stirling Manuscripts
  John Van Cortlandt Letterbook, 1762–1769
Peabody Institute Library, Baltimore
  Callister Papers
Franklin Delano Roosevelt Library, Hyde Park, N.Y.
  Livingston-Redmond Papers (used on microfilm)
Earl Gregg Swem Library, College of William and Mary, Williams-
burg, Va.
  Francis Jerdone Letterbook, 1756–1763
South Carolina Historical Society, Charleston
  Papers of Henry Laurens
University of North Carolina Library, Chapel Hill
  John Snelson Letterbook, 1757–1775*
Virginia Historical Society, Richmond
  Jenings Family Mementos and Papers
Virginia State Library, Richmond
  James Abercromby Letterbook*
  William Allason Letterbook, 1757–1770*
  Caroline County, Virginia, Appeals and Land Cases, 1771–1807*
  U.S. Circuit Court, Virginia District, Ended Cases, 1791–1824
  Tazewell Family Papers*
Wisconsin State Historical Society, Madison
  Draper Collection*

NEWSPAPERS

Cape-Fear Mercury (Wilmington, N.C.)
Maryland Gazette (Annapolis)

New-York Journal, or General Advertiser
North-Carolina Gazette (New Bern)
North-Carolina Gazette (Wilmington)
Pennsylvania Chronicle, and Universal Advertiser (Philadelphia)
Pennsylvania Gazette (Philadelphia)
Pennsylvania Journal; and the Weekly Advertiser (Philadelphia)
Pennsylvania Packet; and the General Advertiser (Philadelphia)
South-Carolina Gazette (Charleston)
South-Carolina Gazette; And Country Journal (Charleston)
Purdie and Dixon's *Virginia Gazette* (Williamsburg)
Rind's *Virginia Gazette* (Williamsburg)

OFFICIAL RECORDS AND DOCUMENTS

Browne, William Hand, et al., eds. *Archives of Maryland.* 65 vols. Baltimore, 1883–1952.
Candler, Allen D., and Knight, Lucian Lamar, eds. *The Colonial Records of the State of Georgia.* 26 vols. Atlanta, 1904–1916.
Clark, Walter, ed. *The State Records of North Carolina, 1777–1790.* 16 vols. Winston and Goldsboro, N.C., 1895–1907.
The Colonial Laws of New York from the Year 1664 to the Revolution. 5 vols. Albany, N.Y., 1894–1896.
The Colonial Records of Pennsylvania. 16 vols. Philadelphia, 1852–1853.
Cooper, Thomas, and McCord, David J., eds. *The Statutes at Large of South Carolina.* 10 vols. Columbia, S.C., 1836–1841.
Grant, W. L., and Munro, James, eds. *Acts of the Privy Council of England, Colonial Series.* 6 vols. London, 1908–1912.
Hening, William Waller, ed. *The Statutes at Large; Being a Collection of All the Laws of Virginia, from the First Session of the Legislature, in the Year 1619.* 13 vols. Richmond, Va., 1819–1823.
Hoban, Charles F., ed. *Pennsylvania Archives.* 8th Ser., VII. Harrisburg, Pa., 1935.
Jenkins, William Sumner, ed. *Records of the States of the United States of America: A Microfilm Compilation.* Washington, D.C., 1949.
Journal of the Commissioners for Trade and Plantations . . . Preserved in the Public Record Office. . . . 14 vols. London, 1920–1938.
Labaree, Leonard Woods, ed. *Royal Instructions to the British Colonial Governors, 1670–1776.* 2 vols. New York, 1935.
Lott, Abraham, ed. *Journal of the Votes and Proceedings of the General Assembly of the Colony of New York. . . .* 2 vols. New York, 1764–1766.
McIlwaine, H. R., ed. *Legislative Journals of the Council of Colonial Virginia.* 3 vols. Richmond, Va., 1918–1919.
McIlwaine, H. R., and Kennedy, John Pendleton, eds. *Journals of the*

House of Burgesses of Virginia, 1619–1776. 13 vols. Richmond, Va., 1905–1915.
Mitchell, James T., and Flanders, Henry, eds. *Statutes at Large of Pennsylvania from 1682 to 1801.* 16 vols. Harrisburg, Pa., 1896–1911.
O'Callaghan, E. B., ed. *The Documentary History of the State of New York.* 4 vols. Albany, N.Y., 1849–1851.
O'Callaghan, E. B., and Fernow, B., eds. *Documents Relative to the Colonial History of the State of New York.* 15 vols. Albany, N.Y., 1853–1887.
Pickering, Danby, ed. *Statutes at Large . . . of Great Britain. Anno 1761, continued to 1806.* 20 vols. Cambridge, 1762–1807.
"Proceedings of the Virginia Committee of Correspondence, 1759–1767." *Virginia Magazine of History and Biography,* X (1902–1903), 337–356; XI (1903–1904), 1–25, 131–143, 345–357; XII (1904–1905), 1–14.
Sainsbury, W. Noel, *et al.*, eds. *Calendar of State Papers, Colonial Series, America and West Indies.* 42 vols. London, 1860–1953.
Saunders, William L., ed., *The Colonial Records of North Carolina.* 10 vols. Raleigh, N.C., 1886–1890.
Stevens, John Austin, Jr., ed. *Colonial Records of the New York Chamber of Commerce, 1768–1784.* New York, 1867.
United States Bureau of the Census. *Historical Statistics of the United States, Colonial Times to 1957.* Washington, D.C., 1960.
Whitehead, William A., *et al.*, eds. *Documents Relating to the Colonial History of the State of New Jersey. Archives of the State of New Jersey,* 1st Ser., I–XXXIII. Newark, Paterson, Trenton, etc., 1880–1928.

CORRESPONDENCE, COMMENTARIES, AND
PERSONAL AND PUBLIC PAPERS

Allen, William. *Extracts from Chief Justice William Allen's Letter Book,* ed. Lewis B. Walker. Pottsville, Pa., 1897.
———. "William Allen-Benjamin Chew Correspondence, 1763–1764," ed. Donald A. Kimball and Miriam Quinn. *Pennsylvania Magazine of History and Biography,* XC (1966), 202–226.
Balch, Thomas, ed. *Letters and Papers Relating Chiefly to the Provincial History of Pennsylvania. . . .* Philadelphia, 1855.
Beekman family. *The Beekman Mercantile Papers, 1764–1799,* ed. Philip L. White. 2 vols. New York, 1956.
Burnaby, Andrew. *Travels Through the Middle Settlements in North-America. In the Years 1759 and 1760. With Observations upon the State of the Colonies.* Ithaca, N.Y., 1960; orig. publ. London, 1775.

Calvert, Cecil, Lord Baltimore. "The Calvert Papers, Number Two." Maryland Historical Society, *Fund-Publications*, X. Baltimore, 1894.

Carroll, Charles, Jr. "Extracts from the Carroll Papers." *Maryland Historical Magazine*, XI (1916), 66–73, 175–189, 261–278, 322–348.

———. *Unpublished Letters of Charles Carroll of Carrollton, and His Father, Charles Carroll of Doughoregan*, ed. Thomas Meagher Field. New York, 1902.

Colden, Cadwallader. *The Colden Letter Books, 1760–1755*. New-York Historical Society, *Collections*, IX–X. New York, 1877–1878.

———. *The Letters and Papers of Cadwallader Colden*. New-York Historical Society, *Collections*, L–LVI, LXVII–LXVIII. New York, 1918–1937.

Dickinson, John. *The Writings of John Dickinson*, ed. Paul L. Ford. Historical Society of Pennsylvania, *Memoirs*, XIV. Philadelphia, 1895.

Dinwiddie, Robert. *Robert Dinwiddie Correspondence . . .*, ed. Louis K. Koontz (microfilm). Berkeley and Los Angeles, 1951.

———. *The Official Records of Robert Dinwiddie, Lieutenant-Governor of the Colony of Virginia, 1751–1758 . . .*, ed. R. A. Brock. Virginia Historical Society, *Collections*, N.S., III–IV. Richmond, Va., 1883–1884.

Eden, Sir Robert. "Correspondence of Governor Eden." *Maryland Historical Magazine*, II (1907), 227–244.

Franklin, Benjamin. *Letters and Papers of Benjamin Franklin and Richard Jackson, 1753–1785*, ed. Carl Van Doren. Philadelphia, 1947.

———. *Benjamin Franklin's Letters to the Press, 1758–1775*, ed. Verner W. Crane. Chapel Hill, N.C., 1950.

———. *The Writings of Benjamin Franklin*, ed. Albert Henry Smyth. 10 vols. New York, 1905–1907.

Gage, Thomas. *The Correspondence of General Thomas Gage with the Secretaries of State, 1763–1775*, ed. Clarence E. Carter. 2 vols. New Haven, Conn., 1931.

Garth, Charles. "Hon. Charles Garth, M.P., the Last Colonial Agent of South Carolina in England, and Some of his Work," ed. Joseph W. Barnwell. *South Carolina Historical and Genealogical Magazine*, XXVI (1925), 67–92. Continued as "Garth Correspondence," ed. Joseph W. Barnwell and Theodore D. Jervey, XXVIII (1927), 79–93, 227–235; XXIX (1928), 41–48, 115–132, 212–230, 295–305; XXX (1929), 27–49, 105–116, 168–184, 215–235; XXXI (1930), 46–62, 124–153, 228–255, 283–291; XXXIII (1932), 117–139, 228–244, 262–280.

Gibbes, Robert W., ed. *Documentary History of the American Revolution: Consisting of Letters and Papers. . . .* 3 vols. New York, 1853–1857.

Habersham, James. *The Letters of Hon. James Habersham, 1756–1775*. Georgia Historical Society, *Collections*, VI. Savannah, Ga., 1904.

Lee, Richard Henry. "Selections and Excerpts from the Lee Papers." *Southern Literary Messenger*, XXVII (1858); XXX (1860).

————. *The Letters of Richard Henry Lee*, ed. James C. Ballagh. 2 vols. New York, 1911–1914.

"New York Broadsides, 1762–1779." *New York Public Library Bulletin*, III (1899), 25–28.

New York City during the American Revolution; Being a Collection of Original Papers (now first published) from the Manuscripts in the Possession of the Mercantile Library Association of New York City. New York, 1861.

Nicholas, Robert Carter. Letters to Purdie and Dixon's *Virginia Gazette* (Williamsburg), printed as "Paper Money in Colonial Virginia." *William and Mary Quarterly*, 1st Ser., XX (1911–1912), 244–256.

Norton, John. *John Norton and Sons, Merchants of London and Virginia: Being the Papers from their Counting House for the Years 1750 to 1795*, ed. Frances Norton Mason. Richmond, Va., 1937.

Pownall, Thomas. *The Administration of the Colonies*. 2d ed. London, 1765; 4th ed. London, 1768.

Smith, William. *Historical Memoirs . . . of William Smith . . .*, ed. William H. W. Sabine. 2 vols. New York, 1956.

Stokes, I. N. Phelps, comp. *The Iconography of Manhattan Island, 1498–1909*. 6 vols. New York, 1915–1928.

Watts, John. *Letter Book of John Watts, Merchant and Councillor of New York.* . . . New-York Historical Society, *Collections*, LXI. New York, 1928.

Wayles, John. "John Wayles Rates His Neighbours," by John M. Hemphill II. *Virginia Magazine of History and Biography*, LXVI (1958), 302–306.

Books, Articles, and Dissertations

Abbot, William W. *The Royal Governors of Georgia, 1754–1775*. Chapel Hill, N.C., 1959.

Ashton, T. S. *An Economic History of England: The Eighteenth Century*. London, 1964.

Ashton, T. S., and Sayers, Richard, eds. *Papers in English Monetary History*. Oxford, 1953.

Bailyn, Bernard. *The Ideological Origins of the American Revolution*. Cambridge, Mass., 1967.

Barker, Charles A. *The Background of the Revolution in Maryland*. New Haven, Conn., 1940.

Becker, Carl L. *The History of Political Parties in the Province of New York, 1760–1776*. Madison, Wis., 1909.

Behrens, Kathryn L. *Paper Money in Maryland, 1727–1789.* Baltimore, 1923.

Berg, Harry D. "Economic Consequences of the French and Indian War for the Philadelphia Merchants." *Pennsylvania History*, XIII (1946), 185–193.

Bezanson, Anne; Gray, Robert D.; and Hussey, Miriam. *Prices in Colonial Pennsylvania.* Philadelphia, 1935.

Billias, George A. *The Massachusetts Land Bankers of 1740.* University of Maine Studies, 2d Ser., no. 74. Orono, Me., 1959.

Bonomi, Patricia U. *A Factious People: Politics and Society in Colonial New York.* New York, 1971.

Bridenbaugh, Carl. "Virtue and Violence in Virginia, 1766: Or, the Importance of the Trivial." Massachusetts Historical Society, *Proceedings*, LXXVI (1964), 3–29.

Brock, Leslie Van Horn. "The Currency of the American Colonies, 1700–1764: A Study in Colonial Finance and Imperial Relations." Ph.D. dissertation, University of Michigan, 1941.

Brown, Lawrence H. "The Grafton and North Cabinets, 1766–1775." Ph.D. dissertation, University of Toronto, 1963.

Brown, Richard Maxwell. *The South Carolina Regulators.* Cambridge, Mass., 1963.

Brown, Robert E. and B. Kathryn. *Virginia, 1705–1786: Democracy or Aristocracy?* East Lansing, Mich., 1964.

Bullock, Charles J. *Essays on the Monetary History of the United States.* New York, 1900.

Cannon, John. "Henry McCulloch and Henry McCulloh." *William and Mary Quarterly*, 3d Ser., XV (1958), 71–73.

Castles, William Henry, Jr. "*The Virginia Gazette,* 1736–1766: Its Editors, Editorial Policies, and Literary Content." Ph.D. dissertation, University of Tennessee, 1962.

Chalmers, George. *An Introduction to the History of the Revolt of the American Colonies.* ... II. Boston, 1845.

———. *Opinions of Eminent Lawyers.* ... Burlington, N.J., 1858.

Champagne, Roger. "Family Politics versus Constitutional Principles: The New York Assembly Elections of 1768 and 1769." *William and Mary Quarterly*, 3d Ser., XX (1963), 57–79.

———. "Liberty Boys and Mechanics of New York City, 1764–1774." *Labor History*, VIII (1967), 115–135.

———. "The Sons of Liberty and the Aristocracy in New York Politics, 1765–1790." Ph.D. dissertation, University of Wisconsin, 1960.

Coakley, Robert W. "Virginia Commerce during the American Revolution." Ph.D. dissertation, University of Virginia, 1949.

Coulter, Calvin B., Jr. "The Virginia Merchant." Ph.D. dissertation, Princeton University, 1944.

Crane, Verner W. "Benjamin Franklin and the Stamp Act." Colonial Society of Massachusetts, *Transactions*, XXXII (1937), 56–77.

Currie, Harold W. "Massachusetts Politics and the Colonial Agency, 1762–1770." Ph.D. dissertation, University of Michigan, 1960.

Deane, Phyllis, and Cole, W. A. *British Economic Growth, 1688–1959: Trends and Structure.* Cambridge, 1962.

Dickson, P. G. M. *The Financial Revolution in England: A Study in the Development of Public Credit, 1688–1756.* New York, 1967.

Dillon, Dorothy R. *The New York Triumvirate: A Study of the Legal and Political Careers of William Livingston, John Morin Scott, and William Smith, Jr.* New York, 1949.

Duer, W. A. *The Life of William Alexander, Earl of Stirling.* . . . New York, 1847.

East, Robert. "The Business Entrepreneur in a Changing Economy, 1763–1795." *Journal of Economic History*, Supplement, VI (1946), 16–27.

Elmer, Lucius Q. C. *History of the Early Settlement and Progress of Cumberland County, New Jersey and of the Currency of This and Adjoining Colonies.* Bridgeton, N.J., 1869.

Ernst, Joseph A. "Growth of the Commons House of Assembly of South Carolina, 1761–1775." M.A. thesis, University of Wisconsin, 1958.

Ernst, Joseph A., and Merrens, H. Roy. "Southern 'Worlds' in the Atlantic Economy." Paper presented at the South Carolina Tricentennial Commission Meeting, March 1970, Columbia, S.C.

———. "The View from Philadelphia: An Interdisciplinary Approach to the South Carolina Economy of the Middle of the Eighteenth Century." Paper presented at the Southern Historical Association Meeting, October 31, 1969, Washington, D.C.

Evans, Emory G. "Planter Indebtedness and the Coming of the Revolution in Virginia." *William and Mary Quarterly*, 3d Ser., XIX (1962), 511–533.

Farnie, D. A. "The Commercial Empire of the Atlantic, 1607–1783." *Economic History Review*, 2d Ser., XV (1962), 205–218.

Ferguson, E. James. "Currency Finance: An Interpretation of Colonial Monetary Practices." *William and Mary Quarterly*, 3d Ser., X (1953), 153–180.

Field, Richard S. *The Provincial Courts of New Jersey.* New York, 1849.

Fitzmaurice, Edmund. *Life of William, Earl of Shelburne.* . . . 2 vols. London, 1875–1876.

Freiberg, Malcolm. "Thomas Hutchinson and the Province Currency." *New England Quarterly*, XXX (1957), 190–208.

Friedman, Bernard. "The New York Assembly Elections of 1768 and

1769: The Disruption of Family Politics." *New York History*, XLVI (1965), 3–24.

Fuhlbruegge, Edward A. "New Jersey Finances during the American Revolution." New Jersey Historical Society, *Proceedings*, LV (1948), 167–190.

Giddens, Paul H. "Trade and Industry in Colonial Maryland, 1753–1769." *Journal of Economic and Business History*, IV (1932), 512–538.

Gipson, Lawrence H. *The Triumphant Empire: Thunder-Clouds Gather in the West, 1763–1766*. New York, 1961.

————. "Virginia Planter Debts before the American Revolution." *Virginia Magazine of History and Biography*, LXIX (1961), 259–277.

Gould, Clarence P. "The Economic Causes of the Rise of Baltimore." In *Essays in Colonial History Presented to Charles McLean Andrews* . . . , pp. 225–251. New Haven, Conn., 1931.

————. *Money and Transportation in Maryland, 1720–1765*. Baltimore, 1915.

Greene, Jack P. "Bridge to Revolution: The Wilkes Fund Controversy in South Carolina, 1769–1775." *Journal of Southern History*, XXIX (1963), 19–52.

————. *The Quest for Power: The Lower Houses of Assembly in the Southern Royal Colonies, 1689–1776*. Chapel Hill, N.C., 1963.

Greene, Jack P., and Jellison, Richard M. "The Currency Act of 1764 in Imperial-Colonial Relations, 1764–1766." *William and Mary Quarterly*, 3d Ser., XVIII (1961), 485–518.

Griffith, Lucille B. *The Virginia House of Burgesses, 1750–1774*. Northport, Ala., 1963.

Hamilton, Henry. *An Economic History of Scotland in the Eighteenth Century*. Oxford, 1963.

Hanna, William S. *Benjamin Franklin and Pennsylvania Politics*. Stanford, Calif., 1964.

Harrington, Virginia D. *The New York Merchant on the Eve of the Revolution*. New York, 1935.

Harrison, Fairfax. *Landmarks of Old Prince William: A Study in the Origins of Northern Virginia*. 2 vols. Richmond, Va., 1924.

Harrold, Frances Long. "Governor William Tryon of North Carolina 1765–1771." M.A. thesis, University of Wisconsin, 1954.

Hawke, David. *In the Midst of a Revolution*. Philadelphia, 1961.

Heath, Milton B. *Constructive Liberalism: The Role of the State in Economic Development in Georgia to 1860*. Cambridge, Mass., 1964.

Hemphill, John M. II. "Virginia and the English Commercial System, 1689–1733: Studies in the Development and Fluctuations of a Colonial Economy under Imperial Control." Ph.D. dissertation, Princeton University, 1964.

Hemphill, W. Edwin. "George Wythe and the Colonial Briton: A Background Study of the Pre-Revolutionary Era in Virginia." Ph.D. dissertation, University of Virginia, 1937.

Herndon, George M. "The Story of Hemp in Colonial Virginia." Ph.D. dissertation, University of Virginia, 1959.

Hewatt, Reverend Alexander. *Historical Account of the Rise and Progress of the Colonies of South Carolina and Georgia*. South Carolina Historical Society, *Collections*, I. New York, 1836.

High, John. "Henry McCulloh, Progenitor of the Stamp Act." *North Carolina Historical Review*, XXIX (1952), 24–38.

Hinkhouse, Fred J. *The Preliminaries of the American Revolution as Seen in the English Press, 1763–1775*. New York, 1926.

Hoffman, Ronald. "Economics, Politics, and Revolution in Maryland." Ph.D. dissertation, University of Wisconsin, 1969.

Horsefield, J. Keith. *British Monetary Experiments, 1650–1710*. Cambridge, Mass., 1960.

Hughes, J. R. T. "Fact and Theory in Economic History." *Explorations in Entrepreneurial History*, 2d Ser., II (1966), 75–100.

Hutson, James H. "Benjamin Franklin and the Parliamentary Grant for 1758." *William and Mary Quarterly*, 3d Ser., XXIII (1966), 575–595.

————. *Pennsylvania Politics, 1746–1770: The Movement for Royal Government and Its Consequences*. Princeton, N.J., 1972.

Jellison, Richard M. "Paper Currency in Colonial South Carolina, 1703–1764." Ph.D. dissertation, Indiana University, 1952.

Jensen, Arthur L. *The Maritime Commerce of Colonial Philadelphia*. Madison, Wis., 1963.

Jensen, Merrill. *The Founding of a Nation: A History of the American Revolution, 1763–1776*. Oxford, 1968.

Johnson, Allen S. "The Political Career of George Grenville, 1712–1770." Ph.D. dissertation, Duke University, 1955.

Kammen, Michael G., "The Colonial Agents, English Politics, and the American Revolution." *William and Mary Quarterly*, 3d Ser., XXII (1965), 244–263.

Kay, Marvin L. Michael. "The Institutional Background of the Regulation in Colonial North Carolina." Ph.D. dissertation, University of Minnesota, 1962.

————. "The Payment of Provincial and Local Taxes in North Carolina, 1748–1771." *William and Mary Quarterly*, 3d Ser., XXVI (1969), 218–240.

————. "Provincial Taxes in North Carolina during the Administrations of Dobbs and Tryon." *North Carolina Historical Review*, XLII (1965), 440–453.

Keener, William G. "Blair-Prentis-Cary Partnership: The Store and Its Operation." Report to the Research Department, Colonial Williamsburg Foundation, April, 1957.

Kemmerer, Donald L. "A History of Paper Money in Colonial New Jersey, 1668–1775." New Jersey Historical Society, *Proceedings*, LXXIV (1956), 106–130.

Keyes, Annis J. "New Jersey Paper Currency." M.A. thesis, Yale University, 1927.

Kinnaman, John A. "The Internal Revenues of Colonial Maryland." Ph.D. dissertation, University of Indiana, 1954.

Klein, Milton M. "The American Whig: William Livingston of New York." Ph.D. dissertation, Columbia University, 1954.

Knollenberg, Bernhard. *Origin of the American Revolution: 1759–1766.* New York, 1960.

Land, Aubrey C. "Economic Behavior in a Planting Society: The Eighteenth-Century Chesapeake." *Journal of Southern History*, XXXIII (1967), 469–485.

Leder, Lawrence H. "The New York Elections of 1769: An Assault on Privilege." *Mississippi Valley Historical Review*, XLIX (1963), 675–682.

————. *Robert Livingston, 1654–1728, and the Politics of Colonial New York.* Chapel Hill, N.C., 1961.

Lescure, William J. "The Early Political Career of Robert Carter Nicholas, 1728–1769." M.A. thesis, College of William and Mary, 1961.

Lester, Richard. *Monetary Experiments, Early American and Recent Scandinavian.* Princeton, N.J., 1939.

Lundin, Leonard. *Cockpit of the Revolution: The War for Independence in New Jersey.* Princeton, N.J., 1940.

Mark, Irving. *Agrarian Conflicts in Colonial New York, 1711–1775.* New York, 1940.

Matthews, John C. "Richard Henry Lee and the American Revolution." Ph.D. dissertation, University of Virginia, 1939.

Mays, David J. *Edmund Pendleton, 1721–1803: A Biography.* 2 vols. Cambridge, Mass., 1952.

Mereness, Newton D. *Maryland as a Proprietary Province.* New York, 1901.

Merrens, H. Roy. *Colonial North Carolina in the Eighteenth Century: A Study in Historical Geography.* Chapel Hill, N.C., 1964.

Metz, William D. "Politics and Finance in Massachusetts 1713–1741." Ph.D. dissertation, University of Wisconsin, 1945.

Morton, Richard L. *Colonial Virginia.* 2 vols. Chapel Hill, N.C., 1960.

Namier, L[ewis] B. "Charles Garth, Agent for South Carolina, Part II." *English Historical Review*, LIV (1939), 632–652.

Namier, Sir Lewis, and Brooke, John. *Charles Townshend.* London, 1964.
———. *The House of Commons, 1754–1790.* 3 vols. New York, 1964.
Nettels, Curtis P. *The Money Supply of the American Colonies before 1720.* Madison, Wis., 1934.
Norkus, Nellie. "Francis Fauquier, Lieutenant Governor of Virginia, 1758–1768: A Study in Colonial Problems." Ph.D. dissertation, University of Pittsburgh, 1954.
Norris, John M. *Shelburne and Reform.* London, 1963.
Olm, Elmer. "The Chatham Ministry and the American Colonies, 1766–1768." Ph.D. dissertation, University of Michigan, 1960.
Owen, James K. "The Virginia Vestry: A Study in the Decline of a Ruling Class." Ph.D. dissertation, Princeton University, 1947.
Plummer, Wilbur C. "Consumer Credit in Colonial Philadelphia." *Pennsylvania Magazine of History and Biography,* LXVI (1942), 385–409.
Price, Jacob M. "The Rise of Glascow in the Chesapeake Tobacco Trade, 1707–1775." *William and Mary Quarterly,* 3d Ser., XI (1954), 179–199.
Reed, William B. *The Life of Esther De Berdt, Afterwards Esther Reed of Pennsylvania.* Philadelphia, 1853.
Reich, Jerome R. *Leisler's Rebellion: A Study of Democracy in New York, 1664–1720.* Chicago, 1953.
Ritcheson, Charles R. "The Preparation of the Stamp Act." *William and Mary Quarterly,* 3d Ser., X (1953), 543–559.
Rolland, Siegfried B. "Cadwallader Colden, Colonial Politician and Imperial Statesman, 1718–1760." Ph.D. dissertation, University of Wisconsin, 1952.
Rosenblatt, Samuel M. "The House of John Norton and Sons: A Study of the Consignment Method of Marketing Tobacco from Virginia to England." Ph.D. dissertation, Rutgers University, 1960.
Rossie, Jonathan G. "The Revolutionary Movement in Maryland, 1770–1776." M.A. thesis, University of Wisconsin, 1959.
Sachs, William S. "Agricultural Conditions in the Northern Colonies before the Revolution." *Journal of Economic History,* XIII (1953), 274–290.
———. "Business Depression in the Northern Colonies, 1763–1770." M.A. thesis, University of Wisconsin, 1950.
———. "The Business Outlook in the Northern Colonies, 1750–1775." Ph.D. dissertation, Columbia University, 1957.
———. "Interurban Correspondents and the Development of a National Economy before the Revolution: New York as a Case Study." *New York History,* XXXVI (1955), 320–335.
Sachs, William S., and Hoogenboom, Ari. *The Enterprising Colonials: Society on the Eve of the Revolution.* Chicago, 1965.

Saladino, Gaspare J. "The Maryland and Virginia Wheat Trade from Its Beginnings to the American Revolution." M.A. thesis, University of Wisconsin, 1960.

Scheick, Donald B. "The Regulation of Commodity Currency in Colonial Virginia." Ph.D. dissertation, Indiana University, 1954.

Schick, James B. "Regionalism and the Revolutionary Movement in North Carolina, 1765–1776: The Administrations of Governor William Tryon and Governor Josiah Martin." M.S. thesis, University of Wisconsin, 1963.

Schumacher, Max. "The Northern Farmer and His Markets during the Late Colonial Period." Ph.D. dissertation, University of California, Berkeley, 1948.

Scott, Kenneth. *Counterfeiting in Colonial America.* New York, 1957.

———. "Counterfeiting in Colonial Maryland." *Maryland Historical Magazine,* LI (1956), 81–100.

———. "Counterfeiting in Colonial New Jersey." New Jersey Historical Society, *Proceedings,* LXXV (1957), 170–179.

———. *Counterfeiting in Colonial New York.* New York, 1953.

———. *Counterfeiting in Colonial Pennsylvania.* New York, 1955.

———. "Counterfeiting in Colonial Virginia." *Virginia Magazine of History and Biography,* LXI (1953), 3–33.

Sellers, Charles G., Jr. "Private Profits and British Colonial Policy: The Speculations of Henry McCulloh." *William and Mary Quarterly,* 3d Ser., VIII (1951), 535–551.

Sellers, Leila. *Charleston Business on the Eve of the Revolution.* Chapel Hill, N.C., 1934.

Sheridan, Richard B. "The British Credit Crisis of 1772 and the American Colonies." *Journal of Economic History,* XX (1960), 161–186.

Shy, John. *Toward Lexington: The Role of the British Army in the Coming of the American Revolution.* Princeton, N.J., 1965.

Sirmans, M. Eugene. *Colonial South Carolina: A Political History, 1663–1763.* Chapel Hill, N.C., 1966.

Smith, B. R. "The Committee of the Whole House to Consider the American Papers (January and February 1766)." M.A. thesis, University of Sheffield, 1956.

Soltow, James H. *The Economic Role of Williamsburg.* Charlottesville, Va., 1965.

———. "The Role of Williamsburg in the Virginia Economy, 1750–1775." *William and Mary Quarterly,* 3d Ser., XV (1958), 467–482.

———. "Scottish Traders in Virginia, 1750–1775." *Economic History Review,* 2d Ser., XII (1959), 83–99.

Sosin, Jack M. *Agents and Merchants: British Colonial Policy, 1763–1775.* Lincoln, Neb., 1965.

———. "Imperial Regulation of Colonial Paper Money, 1764–1773."

Pennsylvania Magazine of History and Biography, LXXXVIII (1964), 174–198.

———. "A Postscript to the Stamp Act. George Grenville's Revenue Measures: A Drain on Colonial Specie?" *American Historical Review*, LXIII (1958), 918–923.

Stetson, Kenneth W. "A Quantitative Approach to Britain's American Slave Trade, 1770–1773." M.S. thesis, University of Wisconsin, 1967.

Sutherland, Lucy S. "The City of London in Eighteenth-Century Politics." In *Essays Presented to Sir Lewis Namier*, ed. Richard Pares and A. J. P. Taylor, 49–75. New York, 1956.

Thayer, Theodore. "The Land-Bank System in the American Colonies." *Journal of Economic History*, XIII (1953), 145–155.

Thomas, Leslie J. "The Non Consumption and Non Importation Movements, 1767–1770." M.S. thesis, University of Wisconsin, 1949.

Thomas, P. D. G. "Charles Townshend and American Taxation in 1767." *English Historical Review*, LXXXIII (1968), 33–51.

Thompson, Robert Polk. "The Merchant in Virginia, 1700–1775." Ph.D. dissertation, University of Wisconsin, 1955.

Van Schaack, Henry Cruger. *Memoirs of the Life of Henry Van Schaack....* Chicago, 1892.

Varga, Nicholas. "The New York Restraining Act: Its Passage and Some Effects, 1766–1768." *New York History*, XXXVII (1956), 233–258.

Vickers, Douglas. *Studies in the Theory of Money, 1690–1776*. Philadelphia, 1959.

Viner, Jacob. "Power versus Plenty as Objectives of Foreign Policy in the Seventeenth and Eighteenth Centuries." *World Politics*, I (1948), 1–29.

———. *Studies in the Theory of International Trade*. New York, 1937.

Wallace, David Duncan. *The History of South Carolina*. 4 vols. New York, 1934.

Watson, D. H. "Barlow Trecothick and Other Associates of Lord Rockingham during the Stamp Act Crisis, 1765–1766." M.A. thesis, University of Sheffield, 1957.

Waxberg, Miriam R. "Money in Morris County, 1763–1782." New Jersey Historical Society, *Proceedings*, LIII (1935), 20–26.

Weir, Robert M. "North Carolina's Reaction to the Currency Act of 1764." *North Carolina Historical Review*, XL (1963), 183–199.

Weiss, Roger W. "The Issue of Paper Money in the American Colonies, 1720–1774." *Journal of Economic History*, XXX (1970), 770–784.

White, Philip L. *The Beekmans of New York in Politics and Commerce, 1647–1877*. New York, 1956.

Yoder, Paton S. "Paper Currency in Colonial Pennsylvania." Ph.D. dissertation, Indiana University, 1941.

Zimmerman, John J. "Benjamin Franklin: A Study of Pennsylvania Politics and the Colonial Agency, 1755–1775." Ph.D. dissertation, University of Michigan, 1956.

Index

DATE DUE

OCT 13

ret 12/1/8%

DEC 1 4 1994

MAY 0 7 2001

PRINTED IN U.S.A.

GAYLORD